An Immigration History
of Britain

An Immigration History of Britain

Multicultural Racism Since 1800

Panikos Panayi

Longman
is an imprint of

Harlow, England • London • New York • Boston • San Francisco • Toronto
Sydney • Tokyo • Singapore • Hong Kong • Seoul • Taipei • New Delhi
Cape Town • Madrid • Mexico City • Amsterdam • Munich • Paris • Milan

PEARSON EDUCATION LIMITED

Edinburgh Gate
Harlow CM20 2JE
United Kingdom
Tel: +44 (0)1279 623623
Fax: +44 (0)1279 431059
Website: www.pearsoned.co.uk

First edition published in Great Britain in 2010

© Pearson Education Limited 2010

The right of Panikos Panayi to be identified as author
of this work has been asserted by him in accordance
with the Copyright, Designs and Patents Act 1988.

ISBN: 978-1-4058-5917-2

British Library Cataloguing in Publication Data
A CIP catalogue record for this book can be obtained from the British Library

Library of Congress Cataloging in Publication Data
A CIP catalog record for this book can be obtained from the Library of Congress

10 9 8 7 6 5 4 3 2 1
14 13 12 11 10

Set in 9/13.5pt Stone Serif by 35
Printed and bound in Malaysia (CTP-VP)

Contents

Preface

Since the middle of the nineteenth century immigration has become a central issue in political and social discourse in Britain. Attention reached a peak following the Irish famine migration of the late 1840s and would increase again after the arrival of East European Jews from the 1880s. Although newcomers and their offspring have not constantly made the headlines since then, they have periodically surfaced as a media issue, especially when sections of the press develop fears about a new influx of migrants and their potentially deleterious consequences for British society. While the groups of migrants who have moved to the country may have changed over the past two hundred years, the negative views towards them have remained fairly constant.

In view of the attention which migrants have attracted in public discourse, scholars have also studied them. During the course of the nineteenth and early twentieth centuries the Irish, Jewish and German communities already had their own histories written, which would develop further before the end of the Second World War especially through the efforts of pioneer scholars such as J. E. Handley in the case of the Irish and Cecil Roth in the case of Jews. These two particular minorities have solid historiographical foundations, which developed further after 1945. The arrival of newcomers in significant numbers from beyond Europe in the early decades after the end of the Second World War quickly attracted the attention of anthropologists and sociologists. By the 1970s and 1980s professional historians also began to examine immigration so that, by the end of the twentieth century, some could make their names by concentrating almost entirely upon migration. Despite this, mainstream historians in Britain still tend to turn a blind eye to the subject.

A vast amount of literature has now become available for anyone attempting to write a history of immigration to Britain over the last two hundred years. Colin Holmes previously took a long term perspective in his seminal *John Bull's Island: Immigration and British Society, 1871–1971*. Published in 1988 and covering a period of a century, this work could rightly claim to have used the extant research on the subject. In 2004 there appeared Robert Winder's *Bloody Foreigners: The Story of Immigration to Britain*, which covers the history of all new arrivals to Britain, including invaders. While Winder used much of the existing literature, his study did not have the depth of coverage of *John Bull's Island*.

The approach of *An Immigration History of Britain* lies somewhere in between these two works, although, as it is written by an academic, it would claim more in common with *John Bull's Island* than with *Bloody Foreigners*. However, in view of the enormous amount of literature which has emerged from historians and, more especially, social scientists since the end of the 1980s, as well as the broader time scale, it does not claim to have the thoroughness of coverage evident in *John Bull's Island*. Nevertheless, it has used a good deal of the central literature produced by historians and social scientists, especially the former, as a glance at the footnotes and bibliography indicates.

Although the volume examines the experiences of a wide range of groups, it tends to focus upon a smaller number of the larger communities, which have attracted the most attention. These include the Irish and Jews in particular, but also African-Caribbeans, South Asians, Poles, Italians and Germans. It does not claim to have used the whole range of social science literature published on Commonwealth migrants and their descendants, although it cites many of the key texts.

The volume takes a thematic rather than a chronological approach, divided into six main chapters followed by a conclusion. The first chapter, 'A country of immigration?' remains introductory in nature and attempts to examine the importance of immigration in British history. It covers three main themes, beginning with a survey of the existing literature and wider memory of immigration and then examining migration to Britain before 1800, before concluding with a section outlining the main developments over the last two centuries. Chapter 2, 'Migration to Britain', begins with an overview of the main groups who have moved to the country and also attempts to measure the scale of immigration, suggesting that it has totalled around nine million people. The rest of the chapter then examines the reasons for the scale of migration, tackling 'Underlying factors', 'The role and attractions of Britain', and 'Local and personal factors', before concluding with a section on 'The complexity of migration motivations'. The third chapter then moves on to the key issue of integration, by examining 'Geography, demography and economics'. Using the work of Leo Lucassen, it argues that these three aspects of immigrant lives offer three possible indications of the integration process, although it also suggests that integration remains a complex issue and a far from smooth path. The chapter also provides background information on the changes in geographical concentration amongst migrant groups in the last two centuries. 'Ethnicity, identity and Britishness' begins with an introduction to ideas of ethnicity and identity, especially within a British context. It points out that while 'block ethnicities' may have represented a traditional approach to this topic, scholars have increasingly dealt with this theme upon an individual basis, which has allowed a greater understanding of the transition from immigrant to Briton and an analysis of the complexity of ethnic identifications. The chapter focuses upon the key themes of religion, politics and 'cultural identities'. The fifth chapter, dealing with 'Xenophobia and racism' might be described as taking a more traditional approach, as it outlines the main manifestations of British exclusionism over the past two centuries involving the state and public opinion. The chapter on 'The evolution of multiculturalism' takes a new and long-term historical approach to this subject. After suggesting various definitions for this concept, it suggests that we can identify the history of multicultural Britain in three main ways. First by examining the incorporation of migrants and their descendants into the mainstream of British society by legislation, beginning with the Catholic Relief Act of 1829. Secondly, by focusing upon popular positive attitudes, especially towards refugees. And thirdly, by examining the impact of immigration upon British life, looking at high culture, popular music, dress and, particularly, food. The conclusion outlines the contradictions and continuities in the history of immigrants in Britain over the last two centuries.

Despite this thematic approach, this is a history book written by a historian who has worked on the key themes of this volume for over two decades. Not only does it summarize the work of other scholars, it brings together much of my own research which has covered, in particular, the history of Germans in Britain, the history of racism, especially racial violence, the historiography and memory of immigration and, most recently, the relationship between food and immigration. Nevertheless, this is a new book written largely from scratch.

As a volume produced by a historian it takes a historical approach, which means, above all, that it deals with long-term trends, rather than focusing upon a particular moment, which much social science research tends to do. Consequently, this book does not simply deal with the migrants themselves, but also their descendants and thus tackles ethnicity and ethnic communities. This long-term approach, following Leo Lucassen, also demonstrates the different experiences through generations and therefore examines issues such as integration, especially in the chapters dealing with identity, racism and multiculturalism. While the migrants themselves may remain distinct from British society, their descendants increasingly move closer to the norms of the mainstream. This also means that hostility towards subsequent generations tends to decrease, although it certainly does not disappear and can reach new heights at times of heightened tension such as war.

This volume does not therefore dismiss the dominant paradigms which have guided both historical and social science approaches to immigration, which consist of race relations and identities. The former, which emerged from the 1960s, has focused specifically upon the problems faced by migrants arriving after 1945 and also increasingly came to influence the approach of historians dealing with the century until that time. More recently, identities have come to the fore in the study of the experiences of migrants in Britain. As Chapter 5 demonstrates, this book certainly accepts the centrality of racism in the lives of both migrants and their offspring, while Chapter 4 tackles collective and personal identities, which change through genera-tions. Nevertheless, Chapter 3 demonstrates that while racism may blight the social and economic lives of many communities and individuals, a com-plete picture of their experiences also needs to accept long term integrative processes. At the same time, Chapter 6 outlines the ways in which British society has become increasingly multicultural, a process which began at the start of the nineteenth century, instead of the 1960s as is commonly assumed. This long term historical approach allows us to tackle change over a period of two centuries. It also demonstrates the complexity of migrant experiences. While racism may represent the norm, so does integration, changing identity and multiculturalism. *An Immigration History of Britain* therefore points to the diverse, complex and contradictory experiences of migrants and their descendants in Britain over the last two centuries.

As the volume demonstrates, there is no single pattern which applies to all migrant groups who have moved to Britain. Some have experienced rela-tively straightforward integration, usually over a long time period. Others have faced more extreme racism and xenophobia than others. But following the patterns established by recent students of identity, the volume argues that experiences need examination not simply at a community level but also on an individual basis, a process easier to carry out in twentieth century communities with the use of interviewing. The book therefore aims to pro-vide a synthesis of the main trends in the immigration history of Britain over the past two centuries by taking a thematic approach.

This volume has evolved over many years of researching issues of migra-tion, ethnicity and racism. During that time, I have benefited from working with or discussing my findings with a wide range of scholars including:

Klaus Bade, John Belchem, Kathy Burrell, David Cesarani, Lorna Chessum, Frank Caestecker, Dave Dee, Andreas Demuth, Andreas Fahrmeier, Colin Holmes, Anne Kershen, Tony Kushner, Jan Lucassen, Kenneth Lunn, Donald MacRaild, Stefan Manz, Peter Marschalck, Euphemia Mupinga, Jochen Oltmer, Alex Peach, Bernard Porter, Gavin Schaffer, Gurharpal Singh, John Solomos, Lucio Sponza, Johannes-Dieter Steinert, John Stevenson, Matthew Taylor, Pippa Virdee and Wendy Ugolini. I would also like to thank my wife Mundeep, with whom I constantly discuss issues of immigration, racism and ethnicity and who has been extremely supportive during the period when I have been writing this book.

Publisher's acknowledgements

The publisher would like to thank the following for their kind permission to reproduce photographs:

Alamy Images: p. 105; City of London, London Metropolitan Archives: p. 147, **Corbis:** p. 57, E.O. Hoppé p. 120, Hulton-Deutsch Collection p. 69, p. 112, p. 154, Gideon Mendel p. 275, Reuters p. 272, Selwyn Tait/SYGMA p. 234, Inge Yspeert p. 289; **Mary Evans Picture Library:** Illustrated London News Ltd p. 5; **Getty Images:** Popperfoto p. 52, Terrence Spencer/Time Life Pictures p. 311; **Manx National Heritage:** p. 220; Panikos Panayi: p. 15, p. 157, p. 159; **Punch Cartoon Library:** p. 225.

Every effort has been made to trace the copyright holders and we apologise in advance for any unintentional omissions. We would be pleased to insert the appropriate acknowledgement in any subsequent edition of this publication.

List of illustrations

CHAPTER 1

A country of immigration?

Migrant histories

In his groundbreaking study of the history and memory of refugees in Britain, Tony Kushner contrasted the way in which society, more especially sections of the press, fondly remembered past exiles (above all Huguenots and refugees from Nazism) with the hostility which 'asylum seekers' faced. Kushner argued that the contemporary British society which he studied used the apparently harmonious integration of past refugees as a stick with which to beat the problematic and scavenging 'asylum seekers'. But he also revealed the way in which, in fact, previous refugees who had fled to Britain had received the same hostile reception as 'asylum seekers'. While Kushner primarily wished to show how the history and memory of migrations to Britain change over time and do not reflect the initial realities, difficulties, complexities and negative reactions,[1] his volume can also act as a starting point to demonstrate the continuities in migration processes over the past two centuries.

One of the reasons for the increasingly fond remembrance of past migration to Britain lies in the fact that the descendants of those who initially made their way to the country and who increasingly become assimilated into society, forget the trauma of initial arrival and concentrate upon the more positive aspects of the history of their community in Britain. Kushner has demonstrated this process by focusing particularly upon the way in which Jewish memory and historiography has emerged since the late nineteenth century, led by the Jewish Historical Society of England. The emergence of Jewish museums in Britain has also helped to perpetuate this positive memory.[2]

At the beginning of the twenty-first century the reality of multicultural Britain seems to exist in every British high street, whether in terms of the physical appearance of populations or through the existence of the ubiquitous Chinese or Indian restaurant. The extent to which the history of migration to Britain is remembered and recorded by both professional historians and wider society does not prove so obvious.

Since the emergence of history as an academic discipline during the nineteenth century, the most important identified 'groups' have been national, and history has been largely written, understood and recognized through the prism of the nation.[3] British historians have written mostly about their own country, partly due to the implicit influence of nationalism[4] and partly due to a lack of linguistic training which limits the possibility of a wider geographical focus. Standard histories of Britain have tended, until recently, to exclude minorities, whether based on class, gender or ethnicity.

The combined influence of academic Marxism and the more recent 'turn' towards postmodernism has ensured that this situation has altered. Academic writing demonstrates a greater interest in 'alternative' histories which now stress those previously neglected areas of class, gender and ethnicity – in short a focus on multiple histories rather than one overarching history. Concentrating specifically upon the study of ethnicity, the evolution of a multicultural society and, more especially, the ubiquity of Black and Asian people in British urban settlements, has facilitated this process.

Attempts to uncover and commemorate the past are not only restricted to an academic process of producing scholarly publications. Historical recovery also involves public heritage initiatives designed to record local histories, often in collaboration with migrants who actively contribute to the collective remembering of their own communities. In addition to this, immigrants nurture their own individual memories, passing stories down to future generations and making histories which are ultimately destined to never reach any sort of academic or public arena. Academic and heritage projects, combined with a growing recognition of the evolution of a multi-cultural Britain, have worked together to give the experiences of immigrants a heightened presence in everyday media discourse.

The history of immigration in Britain is therefore 'remembered' (researched, recorded, selected and presented for current and future consumption) in three different ways. First, the development of 'professional' immigration history, a process which dates back to the nineteenth century largely led by historians with immigrant roots themselves. Second, the more recent popularization of the experiences of immigrants and their memories. Third, the individual perpetuation of memories.

The academic study of immigrants has only recently begun to con-cern 'mainstream' historians. Nineteenth-century historical writing was characterized by the production of glorified histories of England in the Whig tradition, whose central argument focused upon a progression away from the arbitrary power of medieval monarchy towards liberal democratic freedom. Such writing believed in progress and tended to ignore the position of the working classes, whose fate improved gradually as a result of the democratization process consequent upon industrialization.[5]

In opposition to such writing, a distinct working-class historiography began to develop during the first half of the twentieth century, especially under the influence of scholars such as G. D. H. Cole,[6] J. L. and L. B. Hammond,[7] and E. P. Thompson.[8] The expansion of higher education during the 1960s brought into emerging economic and social history departments men with working class origins, who had made their way up the educational ladder through the grammar school system implemented by the 1944 Education Act. Essentially, by writing about the working classes, they were reconstructing the history of their parents and grandparents.[9]

Few of the historians appointed during the 1960s and 1970s ventured into the field of immigration history. But this could not remain the situation for long, primarily because of the visibility of post-war immigrants from the Empire and Commonwealth. Social scientists such as Michael Banton[10] and Ruth Glass[11] immediately focused upon them, ensuring that the contemporary concern with race would eventually seep through to historians, whose methodology and areas of interest change less quickly than those of social scientists. The small number of historians with immigrant origins, who often write about the group from which they originate, has helped the growth of the history of migrants.

As the different historiographies of immigrant groups illustrate, the study of migrants in British history did not begin with the post-war influxes. The two largest groups in Britain at the end of the nineteenth century, the Irish and the Jews, had already begun to produce their own historiographies. Beginning with the Irish, an important starting point was John Denvir's informative 1892 *The Irish in Britain*, which provided an account of contemporary Irish settlements, as well as much detail about their history. The next major contribution appeared in the 1940s in the form of J. E. Handley's meticulously researched two-volume social history of the Irish in Scotland.[12] In 1963 there followed J. A. Jackson's *The Irish in Britain*. The influx of over a million Irish into Britain after 1945 has led to an explosion of interest in the mass migration of the Victorian period. The leading scholars who have worked in this area have included Patrick O'Sullivan,[13] Roger Swift and Sheridan Gilley,[14] Mary Hickman[15] and Donald MacRaild,[16] most of whom have some Irish antecedents. Furthermore, an Irish Studies Institute has been established at the University of Liverpool[17] together with an Irish Studies Centre at London Metropolitan University,[18] each of which heavily focus upon Britain. Nevertheless, the immigration of the second half of the twentieth century has remained largely ignored, with the exception of Enda Delaney's recent account.[19]

The historiography of Anglo-Jewry dates back to at least 1738 with the publication of *Anglia Judaica* by D'Blossiers Tovey. The year 1851 offers a better starting point because it witnessed the publication of Moses Margoliouth's monumental three-volume history of Jewish settlement in Britain from pre-Roman times to the Victorian era. The period leading up to the First World War also saw further scholarly studies.[20] The Jewish Historical Society of England came into existence in 1893, one of the first immigrant history organizations in Britain, which has also published its own scholarly journal in the form of its *Transactions*.[21] Consequently, the groundwork was laid for Cecil Roth, the father of twentieth-century Anglo-Jewish history, who began his productive career in the inter-war years and continued to write on numerous general and specific aspects of the Jews in England after 1945.[22] The only other figure who could really compare with Roth was V. D. Lipman, producing a series of books, most notably his *Social History of the Jews in England* in 1954.

The 1960s and 1970s witnessed a breakthrough in the historiography of the Jews in Britain, with the publication of three major social histories on the late nineteenth-century influx from Eastern Europe.[23] Since then, Jewish history has witnessed the production of numerous studies, focusing especially upon antisemitism, ethnicity and relations between different groups within Anglo-Jewry. The leading figures in the field have consisted of British Jews, most notably Geoffrey Alderman, David Cesarani, David Feldman, David S. Katz and Tony Kushner, together with two American Jews, Todd M. Endelman and W. D. Rubinstein. Also included here should be the non-Jewish Colin Holmes and Bill Williams.[24] Most importantly for the future development of Anglo-Jewish academic history is the Parkes Centre for Jewish Non-Jewish Relations, established by Tony Kushner at the University of Southampton.[25]

Few other minorities in Britain have a historiography as long and detailed as the Jews. The one exception consists of the Huguenots, as the Huguenot Society of Great Britain and Ireland, as well as the *Proceedings* published by this group, date back to 1885, preserving the memory of this now assimilated group. Although it is a scholarly body, much of its work is genealogical, used by people trying to trace their Huguenot ancestors.[26] This minority also has a detailed historiography.[27]

FIGURE 1 Engraving showing a dark, cramped tailor's sweat shop with Jewish immigrants sewing at a bench or asleep in beds in same room, London, 1904. This engraving was part of an article in the *Illustrated London News* entitled 'The Alien in England: Scenes of the Foreign Invasion of the East End of London'. (© Illustrated London News Ltd/Mary Evans)

The study of Germans, like the Irish and Jews, dates back to the nineteenth century, beginning with Karl Heinrich Schaible's *Geschichte der Deutschen in England* from 1885. The works of the next two authors on the subject, Ian Colvin and C. R. Hennings, however, can be considered to be unreliable because in both cases the First World War coloured the perspectives of the authors.[28] Only from the 1970s has the history of Germans in Britain begun to attract close attention, with a focus upon refugees from Nazism, but also, in more recent years, on the nineteenth century and the immediate post-Second World War period. Although a couple of the early authorities who founded this subject consisted of non-Germans,[29] the history of this group is increasingly written by German scholars.[30] Furthermore, the history of German refugees from the Third Reich has taken on a life of its own,[31] most notably through the establishment of a Centre for German and Austrian Exile Studies at the University of London's Institute of German and Romance Studies, which now publishes a *Yearbook*.[32]

Italians have attracted serious academic attention since the end of the 1980s. The two leading scholars consisted of Lucio Sponza and Terri Colpi, both of whom proudly displayed their Italian origins: the former was an immigrant himself (now returned to Venice)[33] and the latter described herself as a 'third generation Italian Scot'.[34] In addition, several smaller scale studies, usually written by people with Italian origins or connections, have also recently appeared.[35] People of Eastern European origin have also received attention from scholars who often originate from these communities, as the example of the Poles illustrates.[36]

When the focus is turned to the major migrant groups originating beyond Europe, it might appear that their historiography is in its infancy, but this statement applies to some ethnic communities more than others. Certainly, the study of Black people in Britain is not a recent development, although most of the older volumes on this group had been written by white males,[37] a situation which is now changing.[38] The history of Indian groups, meanwhile, is a more recent phenomenon, beginning with Rosina Visram's volume originally published in 1986.[39] The best of the other volumes include Shompa Lahiri's, *Indians in Britain: Anglo-Indian Encounters, Race and Identity, 1880–1930* from 2000 and Katy Gardner's *Age, Narrative and Migration: The Life Course and Life Histories of Bengali Elders in London* from 2002. More recently, Lahiri has jointly written *A South Asian History of Britain*.[40] It is important, again, to acknowledge the role of social scientists in producing early accounts of Black and Asian people who settled in Britain after the Second World War. In fact, most work on these groups has been concerned with the wider issues of diaspora and postcolonialism.[41]

Migrant historiography has made significant strides forward. A large percentage of books have been produced by individuals working on their own community, indicating the importance of history in creating group identity. But how have mainstream historians dealt with the history of immigrants in Britain? Despite the transformative impact of post-war migration[42] and the fact that ethnic minorities now make up nearly eight per cent of the population,[43] as well as the centrality of immigration in the evolution of Britain,[44] mainstream historians continue to pay scant attention to them, a fact which experts on immigration have previously highlighted.[45] For the leading historian of Britain, Professor Sir David Cannadine, immigrants simply do not exist, even though he deals with core social history issues such as class.[46] Similarly, for scholars such as Robert Colls the 'identity of England' excludes immigrants as his lavishly praised book on the subject devotes just 20 from 409 pages to this issue.[47] With regard to mainstream British history it still proves difficult to argue against Paul Gilroy's assertion that *There Ain't No Black in the Union Jack*.[48] The explanation for this state of affairs largely lies in the ethnic make up of British historians, who generally encounter members of ethnic minorities as restaurant owners or cleaners of their offices, rather than as their academic colleagues.[49]

But a series of general studies have attempted to explain immigration as a phenomenon in British history. The first example of such a book was published as long ago as 1897.[50] In recent decades a series of historians have produced such general volumes, focusing mostly on the last two centuries.[51] These books ensure that scholars, students and the general reader have a good awareness of the importance of immigration in the country's recent history, even if mainstream historians regard it as marginal.

This certainly contrasts with the situation in the social sciences where the study of immigration, ethnicity and racism in Britain has become central, building upon the work of pioneer scholars such as Banton and Glass and reflecting the situation elsewhere in Europe and the USA. Edited books comparing the situation throughout Europe have become the norm.[52] A series of journals edited from Britain and focusing upon ethnicity have also emerged, most notably *Ethnic and Racial Studies* and the *Journal of Ethnic and Migration Studies*. Furthermore, research centres and institutes with a focus upon diasporas have also emerged, perhaps most notably the Centre for Research in Ethnic Relations at Warwick University.[53] In addition, many social scientists have made their careers by focusing upon the study of diasporas in Britain.[54]

While the academic focus upon migration represents one aspect of its emergence into collective memory, personal experiences have also been remembered in a more popular manner, encapsulated in publicly manu-factured histories. Not only have migrants themselves reconstructed their life experiences for these projects, but mainstream organizations have also become engaged in these activities, using immigrant memories to illustrate Britain's increasingly multiracialized character. This effort to remember migrant experiences is not purely a post-war development. Contributions to a book edited by Tony Kushner have previously demonstrated that Jewish heritage emerged before 1945.[55] Yet recent decades have really seen the beginning of the construction of migrant identities, a process which has worked at all levels and in which oral history has played a particular role. It is now possible to identify several examples of this remembrance of migrant experiences, involving both members of ethnic minorities and their representatives, as well as local government bodies, especially in areas which have significant ethnic concentrations.

One key development in the memorialization of immigrants can be found in the field of genealogy. While an interest in family history has gathered momentum amongst the ethnic majority,[56] it has also attracted attention amongst minorities, although this interest has largely arisen from members of the ethnic majority tracing their foreign roots. This is apparent in the evolution of two organizations in particular. First, the Anglo-German Family History Society, which has existed since 1987, has held annual meetings, produced publications about the history of Germans in Britain, and has, most importantly, offered genealogical information for Britons wishing to trace their German ancestry.[57] In addition, the much larger Jewish Genealogical Society of Great Britain, which has an international membership, 'encourages genealogical research and promotes the preservation of Jewish genealogical records and resources'.[58] As yet, probably because of the recent arrival of such groups to Britain, there do not seem to be any formally registered genealogical societies developed specifically by post-war Imperial and Commonwealth migrants.[59]

The initiatives for organizations such as these clearly come from people who have awareness of their foreign ancestry essentially working as a group. In addition, local authorities, above all libraries and archives, have also played a key role in the process of constructing migrant histories. A project from the late 1980s and early 1990s organized by Hammersmith and Fulham Council, produced a series of introductory leaflets by an organization called the Ethnic Communities Oral History Project on a variety of immigrant communities in London. These leaflets essentially consisted of members of particular groups recalling their experiences of migration and settlement in Britain.[60] Since then other libraries in areas with significant ethnic minority communities have also participated in the popularisation of the history of specific ethnic minorities. Leicestershire's Multicultural Oral and Pictorial Archive Project, a joint venture between Leicestershire Libraries and De Montfort University, resulted in the Highfields Remembered Project, a collection of interviews with a variety of ethnic groups who have lived in this inner city area of Leicester. All of these have been transcribed for the website of the project.[61]

Archives, some of which possess a range of sources on immigration,[62] have also increasingly recognized the multiethnic past of the areas which they serve.[63] One of the most notable indications of the memorialization of migrant experiences is the development of the Moving Here website, supported by the National Archives and financed by the New Opportunities Fund of the National Lottery. It is a virtual archive of hundreds of thousands of items from collections throughout the country on a variety of groups (although concentrating upon African-Caribbeans, Irish, Jews and South Asians) who have made their way to Britain over the past 200 years.[64] The Black Cultural Archives, meanwhile, was 'established in 1981 . . . to collect, document, preserve and disseminate materials concerning the history and culture of Black people in Britain, and to make these resources available and accessible nationally and internationally.' It 'ultimately hopes to establish the first national museum of Black history in Britain'.[65]

Museums have also played a role in the popularization of migrant experiences. Perhaps the most important exhibition in this context consisted of the 'Peopling of London' which took place at the Museum of London in 1993.[66] In fact, while the UK does not yet have a Museum of Immigration, the Jewish community has developed small Jewish Museums in Manchester and London, which hold exhibitions and act as a resource for those interested in aspects of Jewish life in Britain.[67] However, perhaps the most spectacular indication of the popularization of immigrant experiences can be found in the development of Black History Month (inspired by a similar event in the USA), begun in 1987 and now a truly national celebration of the history of the Black presence in Britain, with much focus on contemporary experiences, held in October every year. In 2004 it hosted 1,400 events.[68]

A variety of developments are therefore increasingly commemorating the immigrant experience in Britain, mostly initiated from people with migrant origins. This can be understood against the background of the economic and social success of post-war migrants, as well as those who arrived before that time, and can be seen to correspond with a growth in the media presence of people with immigrant origins. In fact, it could be argued that this coincides with a more general acceptance of 'alternative' experiences and histories in fiction, film and television, with Zadie Smith's *White Teeth*, Monica Ali's *Brick Lane* and Andrea Levy's *Small Island* as acclaimed examples.

This popularization of ethnic history within the UK, however, is not without its problems. If community leaders are involved, they may not represent the entire group and may select interviewees. These issues are important because this type of project does not always acknowledge issues of gender and class, or experiences of hardship and racism. Following Kushner, there is a tendency to focus on the positive stories of integration and economic success, sidelining the less comfortable experiences of destitution and hostility. Above all, any signs of internal conflict along class, religious, gender or generational lines can be silenced completely, allowing a more harmonious image to be conveyed. When minority histories are constructed to try to create a sense of community there is a danger that they are not accurate histories at all.[69]

Although there is strong evidence to suggest that some degree of progress has taken place, immigrant history has remained largely absent from the ultimate form of mass media, the television screen, despite the increasing popularity of history in general.[70] Even away from the forum of television, public histories have not managed to counteract the sense that immigrant history is a separate history. Black History Month, for example, is allocated a short period for the commemoration of ethnic minorities, but what about the rest of the year? Black History Month reflects trends towards a segregated national memory.[71] Therefore, 'mainstream' memorialization tends to ignore the role of Black people and migration generally, despite their role in British history.[72]

While much commemoration of immigration has found a national or community scope, an increased academic interest in the use of oral history and in-depth interviewing for migration studies has aided a better under-standing of the relationship between memory, ethnicity and migration on an individual basis.[73] The use of interviewing has allowed the migrants themselves to take centre stage.[74] Migration movements are no longer name-less masses, homogenous and predictable, but are instead revealed as divided, complex, intensely human phenomena. For immigrants, questions of memory and history are particularly pertinent: migration compels a confrontation with the past that non-migrants might never have to face. Immigrant memory is as concerned with life before arrival in Britain as it is with life since. While histories of community development in Britain are important, for many immigrants, and refugees especially, they can only provide, at best, half of the context of what it means to migrate. This focus upon individual life stories has partly been pioneered by scholars who can use such experiences to break down 'block' approaches to the study of migration and ethnicity.[75]

The history and memory of immigration in Britain has therefore developed in three different ways: professionally through the growth of academic historiography; popularly through community and heritage history initiatives; and finally by individuals themselves. Immigration has been, and remains, neglected in national history and in public memory. While some progress has occurred, immigration is still largely viewed as a peripheral area of academic concern within the discipline of history itself. This contrasts significantly with the social sciences. In society at large, immigration history is still perceived as something separate and different, outside of the accepted scope of popular historical memory. When it is embraced, there is some-times a danger that in the rush to create positive, attractive histories the complexities of immigrant experiences are lost.

But there is no doubt that the histories and memories of immigration in Britain are strong, and are probably growing stronger. Technological develop-ments have helped migrants preserve their own ethnic memories through closer connections with their homelands, and have simultaneously given impetus to community history projects which work with these memories. Immigration history may in some respects still remain marginalized, but it is undeniably dynamic and will continue to grow.

Despite the fact that the mainstream historical profession may still tend to ignore the importance of immigration in the evolution of the British nation state, migrants themselves have increasingly attempted to bring their experiences to the attention of wider British society, albeit with limited success. It is more comfortable for those of migrant origins themselves to accept Britain as a country of immigration than it is for those who are not, whether this assertion refers to the historical profession or wider society.

Immigration before 1800

Another way of addressing the issue of Britain as a country of immigration lies in examining population movement towards the country throughout its history. Referring to the USA Oscar Handlin, in his now classic study on the subject, began his book by asserting: 'Once I thought to write a history of immigration in the USA. Then I discovered that the immigrants *were* American history'.[76] It may prove more difficult to apply such a bold phrase to the development of Britain over the last two centuries, but an analysis of the whole course of British history would indicate the way in which migration to the British Isles helped to create the peoples who would eventually describe themselves as British or English by the eighteenth and nineteenth centuries. Robert Winder has recognized this fact in his *Bloody Foreigners: The Story of Immigration to Britain*, which precisely takes this long-term approach. William Cunningham took a similar view, although his volume began with the Norman Invasion.[77] Colin Holmes, meanwhile, briefly examined invasions until 1066[78] and also tackled streams of people who moved into the country between the middle of the eleventh and the middle of the nineteenth centuries.[79]

However, a central reason for regarding Britain as a country of immigration lies precisely in the fact that the populations which would eventually become the ethnic majority, originated in movements from continental Europe and perhaps beyond. These consisted of Celts, Romans, Angles and Saxons, the central elements used by nineteenth century historians and myth makers to construct the people of England.[80] In this sense, Britain, like most other European nation states has majority populations which originate in the 'Age of Migrations' which took place from the collapse of the Roman Empire until the early medieval period.[81]

The concept of migration as used in contemporary political and academic discourse generally refers to the arrival of populations after the construction of nation states, especially during the nineteenth and twentieth centuries. The idea of migrants, especially in political circles, works upon the idea that the populations and governments already resident in a particular nation state have long established rights in contrast to newcomers from other parts of the world. The former, who, by circumstances of history, have evolved in that particular geographical area, can therefore choose whether or not to allow entry and rights to 'outsiders' usually (in the West) based upon the needs of the economy. Nevertheless, any historian who has traced the history of a nation state back far enough would discover that the population which now considers itself as the majority originated in a previous migration. Population movements created all 'nations' throughout Europe. Klaus J. Bade, referring to Germany, has written about 'Homo Migrans',[82] as well as constructing 'humans across borders' and 'borders across humans',[83] the latter idea working upon the fact that people often predate borders.[84]

A focus upon Britain would demonstrate these processes in action. We can divide population movements towards Britain before 1800 into four periods: first, the age of invasions, which lasts until the eleventh century; second continental tradesmen, bankers and craftsmen during the high and late middle ages; religious refugees, economic migrants and slaves, c.1500–1650; and a growth in economically based migration from the middle of the seventeenth until the beginning of the nineteenth century. The first period, which encompasses a series of groups, differs significantly from the last three. The age of invasions provided the basic ingredients which would subsequently form the majority population which emerged in Britain. Just as importantly, by the early medieval period, state structures had emerged. These could not only repel future invasions, but could also create the concept of immigrants, controlled by a primitive but often draconian system of regulation.[85] The year 1066 proves symbolic for the migration history of Britain: after that year population movements into the country change from invasions to migrations and it is from the Normans that immigration control and the concept of migrants evolves. Nevertheless, a survey of the population movements which occurred until the early nineteenth century will demonstrate two things: first, the importance of migratory movements in the origins of the majority population of Britain; and secondly, the continued and constant migration of people, especially from Ireland and continental Europe, due to a combination of political and economic factors, from the eleventh century. The movements of the centuries following the Norman invasion established patterns replicated since c.1800.

Even those arguing that the Celts formed the original inhabitants of Great Britain could trace their history back far enough to see that they originated from further afield. This group spoke dialects of a common language with similar religious patterns and settled throughout the British Isles, although much debate exists about the reality of such assertions and the subsequent construction.[86]

The Roman invasion had a profound impact upon the evolution of Britain and brought into the country thousands of settlers who Romanized the British Isles.[87] The newcomers brought with them people from throughout the Empire including areas covered by contemporary Germany,[88] Gaul, the Iberian peninsula[89] and Africa, pointing to the complex ethnic composition of the Empire, which integrated people from throughout its domains.[90] Peter Fryer opened his history of Black people in Britain with the statement: 'There were Africans in Britain before the English came here'.[91]

Fryer bases his assertion upon the fact that the Angles and Saxons, from whom the concept of Englishness evolves, did not arrive in the British Isles until the second half of the fifth century. These invaders, settlers or migrants came from north Germany, counting as many as 100,000 people and making up ten per cent of the population. More importantly, this group laid the foundations of the English state.[92]

There then followed the Viking invasions, viewed as a marauding horde in British myth making, but playing a significant role in the development of the country and in the populations which subsequently evolved. While people from Scandinavia initially arrived as invaders and fought with 'Anglo-Saxon' rulers and peoples, they also settled in Britain, focused upon particular areas, especially in the north.[93]

The final and perhaps most important invasion occurred in the eleventh century with the arrival of the Normans. They focused upon the south of England, centred upon London, to which the populations of Norman towns moved, but also colonized much of the rest of the country. William the Conqueror and his successors also imported soldiers from the continent. The Normans consolidated the foundation English statehood.[94]

The settlement of people from the continent in Britain changed after the eleventh century, as they never again consisted of invaders. 'Immigration from now on was a matter of peaceful entry, and had to fit into a more or less orderly society under unified control',[95] which also meant the development of concepts of aliens and primitive restrictions upon entry. From now on migrants, especially Jews, developed their own distinct communities and faced sometimes brutal and endemic hostility.

The twelfth to the sixteenth centuries witnessed the arrival of a series of groups distinct from wider British society in terms of their ethnicity based upon a combination of language, religion and area of origin. The most distinct group in medieval European, including British, society consisted of the Jews, who had numerous legal restrictions imposed upon them and faced everyday hostility, which could erupt into murderous pogroms, often leading to expulsion, as happened in Britain in 1290. In fact the survival of the Jewish community in both Britain and other areas of Europe largely depended upon the strength of antisemitism at any one time from one part of the continent to another.[96]

The Jewish community of England witnessed expansion at the end of the eleventh century because of an influx of refugees from the continent fleeing pogroms at the time of the First Crusade. Further streams followed from Spain, Italy and even Russia. Estimates of the size of the Jewish community in the thirteenth century range from 5,000 to 16,500, making up to one per cent of the urban population.[97] The Jewish population initially focused upon London but by the early thirteenth century Jews resided in twenty other locations including Bristol, Cambridge, Exeter, Gloucester, Lincoln, Oxford and York.[98]

The best known occupation of Jews in the Middle Ages consisted of money lending as gentiles could not involve themselves in usury under canonical law. But they also worked as clerks, doctors, merchants, goldsmiths, soldiers, vintners, fishmongers and cheesemongers.[99] However, the 'great majority' lived 'either in a state of abject poverty or bordering on that condition', depending heavily upon service to their co-religionists.[100]

Jews developed a sense of community, forced upon them, whether they liked it or not, by the endemic antisemitism which existed, especially the requirement to live within specific geographical concentrations or 'Jewries'.[101] Marriages usually took place to other Jews. Most communities counted at least one synagogue while Jewish learning flourished in medieval England.[102]

Antisemitism fundamentally influenced every aspect of the Jewish communities, to the extent of their very survival. In the first place, they faced all manner of legal restrictions, particularly upon where they could reside. Other measures limited their ability to work as money lenders.[103] Ethnic cleansing became a feature of medieval and early modern England, culminating in the expulsion of the Jews from England in 1290,[104] a measure which remained in force until the middle of the seventeenth century, indicating a longstanding tradition of extreme intolerance, repeated many times in British history.

The attitudes of the medieval state legitimized popular antisemitism, which manifested itself in a variety of ways. These included the development of ritual murder accusations, whereby myths circulated in particular locations that Jews killed Christian children in order to use their blood for medical purposes as part of the Passover ritual. The most famous of such accusations occurred in Norwich in 1144 and Lincoln in 1255.[105] Just as seriously, antisemitic attacks became endemic in medieval society. Indeed, for some Christians, their 'first introduction' to a Jew 'was often a riot'.[106] One of the worst pogroms occurred in 1190 in York resulting in 150 deaths by suicide.[107] However, anti-Jewish riots broke out elsewhere at the same time including Dunstable, Lynn, Stamford and Bury St Edmunds. In the last of these 57 Jews perished. Between 1262 and 1266 further murders occurred in Worcester, Northampton, Canterbury, Lincoln and Ely.[108]

Another significant group in medieval England consisted of the north German Hanseatic merchants focused upon the 'Kontor' in the city of London from 1281. During the fourteenth century 'branches' of this medieval trading group ventured to other east coast ports including Ipswich, Yarmouth, Hull, York, Newcastle, Lynn and Boston. Hanseatic merchants also ventured to sell their goods at fairs in Norwich, Stamford, Lincoln, Westminster, Canterbury and Winchester. Furthermore, they also traded and settled with Scottish towns such as Dunbar, Glasgow and Aberdeen. The main commodities which they imported included wool, cloth, herrings, wine, grain,

FIGURE 2 A contemporary British landscape: Leicester 2009, author's own photograph

furs and wax. From the late fourteenth until the end of the sixteenth century the history of the Hansa in Britain involved the gaining and losing of privileges depending on the prevailing political and economic conditions. They played a significant role as money lenders. The group faced increasing hostility during the reign of Queen Elizabeth, especially from a rival group of English traders, the Merchant Adventurers. The Hansa eventually faced the same fate as several other medieval and early modern communities, when, in 1598, Queen Elizabeth ordered their expulsion from England.[109]

In her study of Italians in more recent British history Terri Colpi ventured back to the Middle Ages in order to trace the evolution of the modern community. While the links between medieval settlers and modern migrant communities prove tenuous, from the end of the thirteenth century, colonies of merchants from Genoa and Venice developed on the Thames and in Southampton. After the expulsion of the Jews, Lombards became especially important in banking. Furthermore, as in the case of people from areas now covered by Germany, temporary migrants made their way to Britain from the Italian peninsula including artists, writers, musicians, scholars and churchmen.[110] Craftsmen also came from Flanders, while London acted as home to merchants from the Iberian peninsula and Gascony.[111]

One group always present in Britain, largely because of geographical proximity, consists of the Irish. An influx occurred during the twelfth century, some of whom worked as street vendors and labourers. Others fell into the medieval underclass, which meant that they also became victims of an act of expulsion in 1243 following the passage of a statute to expel Irish beggars.[112]

Several distinct migratory movements to Britain occurred during the sixteenth and early seventeenth centuries. Those fleeing the Counter-Reformation, especially in France, Germany and the Low Countries, represent the first identifiable refugee group in Britain. The second stream makes up a more economically based migration continuing some of the movements of merchants which had occurred in previous centuries but also including craftsmen working in specific occupations involved in a skills transfer. Another identifiable group after 1500, falling into the category of forced migrants, consists of the first Black slaves. The sixteenth century also witnessed the arrival of the first Romanies in Britain. Irish migration also continued.

Protestant refugees began to arrive from the 1540s. Calvinist services occurred in Canterbury in 1548 while foreign congregations existed in London and other parts of southern England by 1550. The largest and most important centred on the Austin Friars' church in the capital where Germans, French, Walloons and Flemings worshipped separately. The accession of the Catholic Queen Mary to the throne in 1553 forced them to leave the country but they would return in larger numbers following Elizabeth's accession in 1558. Three groups in particular moved to England during the reign of Elizabeth. The first two fled the suppression of the Dutch revolt by the Duke of Alba, the Habsburg ruler of the Low Countries. They divided into the French dialect speaking Walloons from the southern Netherlands covering present day Belgium and Dutch speaking Flemings from the north. The third group consisted of the initial French Protestant Huguenots who moved to Britain following the massacre of St Bartholomew's Day in 1572.

The newcomers settled throughout south east England, including London, Norwich, Colchester, Sandwich, Harwich, Dover, Yarmouth and Kings Lynn. The largest concentration outside the capital consisted of Norwich, which housed 3,000 'strangers'. Economic activities outside London revolved especially around textiles while, in the capital, the newcomers worked in a variety of trades including jewellery and leather production.

The refugees continued to practise their religion. In Norwich, for instance, both the Walloon and Flemish communities had their own churches, while Colchester had a Flemish minister from 1571. The greatest and most varied activity took place in London. The French church had a membership of over 1,500 from the late 1560s to the 1580s, while the Austin Friars church, which had become Dutch, counted 1,850 members in 1583 and still carried out 42 baptisms as late as 1680.

The refugees, despite their initial welcome, would face the same hostility endured by the twentieth century successors. In Sandwich, for instance, local legislation limited the range of economic activities of the newcomers, a pattern repeated elsewhere, including London. Popular xenophobia accompanied the legislation. In Colchester the refugees faced accusations of remaining aloof from English society and taking the jobs of natives. Riots occurred quite regularly, including disturbances in London in 1586, 1593, 1595 and 1599. The most serious attacks occurred in Norwich in 1570.[113]

The sixteenth and seventeenth centuries also witnessed an economically based migration resulting in the arrival of merchants and craftsmen working in specific occupations not staffed by natives, who facilitated a skills transfer as recognized by Lien Bich Luu, who, in fact, tackles the entire period from 1400–1700.[114] She has demonstrated, for instance, how beer brewing in England during these centuries spread as a result of the arrival of experts from Germany and Holland.[115] Raingard Esser has also pointed to this development and has further demonstrated the importance of Germans in the evolution of mining and smelting technology during the sixteenth century.[116] Italian craftsmen, scholars, miners, artists and industrialists also moved to Britain during this era so that the Italian church in London had a membership of about 150 in 1568. A variety of foreign merchants, in addition to the Hansa, also retained a presence in Britain during the sixteenth and seventeenth centuries, trading in a range of products. Hostility towards such groups never remained far below the surface and exploded most famously in xenophobic riots in 1517 known as 'Evil May Day'.[117]

Another group which made a significant appearance in Britain during the sixteenth century consisted of Africans, most of whom made their way to the country as slaves. In fact, as early as the beginning of the fifteenth century James IV of Scotland had a series of Africans attached to his court. The first five slaves arrived in England in 1555. Their numbers grew as the century progressed, but by the 1590s hostility began to arise towards them so that in 1601 Queen Elizabeth, in yet another act of ethnic cleansing, authorized the deportation of all 'Blackamoores' from her realm. Only a few survived this action.[118]

The early sixteenth century also witnessed the arrival of the first Romanies in Britain, originating in an exodus out of the Punjab in the fifth century and gradually moving westwards to the Middle East and the Balkans, progressing into western Europe and finally arriving in England and Scotland between 1505 and 1515.[119] The history of the Romanies in all of the states where they have settled has involved both official and unofficial persecution. In England a series of Acts passed between the sixteenth and eighteenth centuries forbade them from travelling. In fact, until 1783 they could face imprisonment and expulsion simply for being Romanies.[120]

The Irish also continued to move to Britain during the fifteenth and sixteenth centuries, partly to escape relentless warfare in their country. 'Speaking a different language and coming from a less regimented if besieged tribal society', most migrants 'again sought solace in the lower echelons of the host society'.[121] Once again they faced hostility ranging from negative stereotyping in serious literature to the passage of yet another measure facilitating ethnic cleansing in the form of an Act to expel Irish vagrants in 1629.[122]

Taking the period from the Norman invasion until the middle of the sixteenth century as a whole, a series of patterns reveal themselves. Firstly, migration occurred on a fairly small scale. Secondly, a combination of economic and political reasons caused population movement. While Britain acted as an attraction for craftsmen and merchants, the upheavals of the Reformation served as the driving force sending Protestant refugees to Britain. Intermarriage and assimilation clearly occurred between the eleventh and seventeenth centuries.[123] But so did the most extreme forms of marginalization and persecution.[124] Ethnic cleansing represents normality in medieval, Tudor and Stuart Britain.

The 150 years after the end of the English Civil War represent a new phase in the history of migration to Britain. This may not seem so obvious because some of the previous migration flows continue including Protestant refugees, Black slaves and the Irish. Nevertheless, the period holds together and looks forward to the nineteenth century for three reasons in particular. First, while exclusion and persecution from both the state and the population continue, ethnic cleansing disappears. Secondly, these years witnessed a take off in the migration history of Britain and Europe of streams which would come to characterize the nineteenth century, above all German, Jewish and Irish migration. Finally, precisely because of this increase in migration, the foundations of these nineteenth-century communities established themselves by 1800.

Some of the growth which would occur after 1650 had links with movement before then. This applies, for instance, to the Huguenots, continuing victims of the fallout from the Reformation, despite the revocation of the Edict of Nantes by Louis XIV in 1685, which granted religious toleration in France. Of the 150,000 to 180,000 refugees who left France both before and after this measure, about 50,000 may have made their way to Britain,[125] focused originally upon London but subsequently moving to other settlements in southern England from Ipswich to Plymouth. Like their sixteenth-century predecessors the Protestant Refugees of the seventeenth century became heavily involved in textiles, especially silk weaving, a particularly important activity in east London. Other trades included watch and clock making, jewellery and even the professions. The Huguenots developed a rich religious life in the areas where they settled. They initially faced a positive response from British society, manifesting itself especially in the establishment of funds to assist them upon their arrival.[126] However, 'the popular picture of a uniform welcome for the Huguenots is naïve',[127] as they endured hostility both because of their perceived economic threat and cultural distinctiveness, facing identification with the French King Louis XIV and his foreign policy, from which they actually fled.[128] Kushner has stressed the hostility which Huguenots endured in his analysis of the dichotomy between the experiences and myths about refugees in British history.[129]

Black slaves also increased, linked with the development of transatlantic trading in this 'commodity', which would transport millions of people from Africa to the Americas.[130] Black people found their way to Britain when brought to the country by returning sugar planters or slave ship captains. Other Asian and African slaves had previously worked for government officials abroad and made their way to the country when their masters returned home. A few Africans arrived as free sailors who had served on ships.

Between 10,000 and 15,000 Black people may have lived in Britain during the course of the eighteenth century. They were concentrated particularly in London and the other major slave ports of Bristol and Liverpool. Most remained slaves who worked as servants, valets and butlers for the upper classes. Free Black people, meanwhile, worked in a variety of occupations including road sweeping, fruit vending and street entertainment, while some tried to survive through begging. Males predominated amongst the Black population. Enslaved women usually acted as maids, while freed ones found employment in laundry work, sewing and prostitution.

By the end of the eighteenth century a sufficient number of free Black people allowed the development of a community in London, which held informal meetings. But, in an example of complete assimilation of what might appear (by physical appearance) a group vastly different from the majority population, this early Black community had disappeared by the early nineteenth century. Part of the reason for this lies in the ceasing of further migration of this group to the country, an important factor determining the survival of any diaspora. Partly as a result of this, together with the prevalence of males, marriage with Englishwomen became the norm.

As in the case of many of the groups who would arrive during the nineteenth and twentieth century, intermarriage and assimilation went together with racism. The hostility directed towards Black people during the eighteenth century had state backing because of the position of Black slaves as property, which meant that they did not even have a status as human beings. Popular racism, reflecting attitudes towards Africa, reinforced their position. Stereotypes viewed them as lazy and promiscuous.[131]

The increase in the Irish population of Britain during the eighteenth century had links with earlier migratory movements as well as forming a basis for subsequent growth after 1800. Expansion took place especially in London as well as in Liverpool and Bristol.[132] Significant numbers of Irish worked as summer harvesters in the countryside. Demographic growth and the economic changes caused by proto-industrialization helped to push people towards England. The Irish worked in occupations at the bottom end of the social scale, as they would do during the Victorian years, ranging from begging and stealing to street selling and bricklaying. Like much of the urban population, the Irish lived in unsanitary conditions, concentrated on particular parts of the capital especially St Giles. Roman Catholic Churches had emerged by the end of the eighteenth century especially in London and Liverpool. While such developments might suggest increasing toleration following the anti-Catholic hatred released by the Reformation in Britain from the early sixteenth century, hostility towards Irish Catholics never remained far below the surface. It surfaced most notably in the murderous Gordon Riots of 1780, although violence also occurred in 1736, 1740 and 1763.[133]

Two new groups, which would become major communities in the nineteenth century, also emerged in the second half of the seventeenth. The first of these, the Jews, represented a rebirth, while the second, Germans, consisted of a whole variety of streams, which would develop a sense of community revolving around religion. Although some Jews had lived in England after the expulsion of 1290, the Readmission of 1656[134] represents the starting point of the modern history of Anglo-Jewry. Those who made their way to the country in the second half of the seventeenth century from both the Iberian Peninsula and central and western Europe included merchants and physicians, who came together with 'persons with little capital or training' including 'peddlers, servants, vagabonds, and the like'.[135] Until the early eighteenth century Iberian Sephardic Jews escaping the Inquisition made up the majority of migrants but this changed from about the 1720s, when Ashkenazi Jews from Holland, Germany and Poland, escaping a combination of deteriorating economic conditions and antisemitism, moved in increasing numbers. Endelman has pointed to the fact that many of those who entered Britain had very few material resources and found themselves employed in a variety of activities including street trading and begging. But, as would happen during the nineteenth and early twentieth centuries, the Jewish community became extremely diverse before 1800 encompassing a range of religious practices and social classes in which the more wealthy established groups remained highly distinct from new arrivals eking out a living on the streets of London or other urban locations.[136] Between 20,000 and 30,000 Jews may have lived in England by 1800. Although centred upon London, they had moved, during the course of the eighteenth century, to numerous other locations, reaching as far as Exeter, Plymouth, Leeds, Manchester, Liverpool and Edinburgh.[137] The Sephardic and Ashkenazi groups maintained their separate sense of Jewishness largely through the opening of synagogues. The major London places of worship included the Bevis Marks in the case of the former and the Great and Hambro in the case of the latter, all established during the seventeenth century. In addition, smaller congregations also evolved in the capital, as well as in the locations beyond where Jews would settle. Benevolent organizations and schools had also developed, meaning that, by the beginning of the nineteenth century, the foundation stones of the established Ashkenazi and Sephardic communities were firmly in place.[138]

Todd Endelman stressed the tolerance which Jews experienced in eighteenth century Britain,[139] especially compared with the situation on the continent and has viewed this as a facilitating factor in, what he views as, a process of radical assimilation.[140] Nevertheless, antisemitism remained embedded in British society. The revocation of the legal restrictions which existed against Jews, especially political rights (in which sense they resembled the mass of the population), and consequent full emancipation, would not occur until the nineteenth century.[141] On some occasions endemic but dormant antisemitism could explode into overt hostility, most notably in 1753 following the passage of the Jewish Naturalization Act, which consequently faced repeal.[142]

Before 1914 those residents of Great Britain who originated in German states would not experience such hostility, although they also did not have full civil rights between 1650 and 1800. A variety of migratory streams moved to the country from parts of Germany during this period. In the first place a group of about 15,000 migrants from the Palatine made their way to London in 1709 due to a combination of political and economic reasons. They received a generally hostile reception which meant that the government decided to disperse them to North America. New streams which would continue into the nineteenth century also evolved. Many Germans found themselves in Britain during a transatlantic crossing which necessitated that they spend time in the country changing ships, during which time some decided to remain. The beginnings of industrialization in Britain attracted businessmen and merchants. The latter also proceeded to the country as a result of the decline of the continental fair, which meant that they wished to make direct contact with their customers. The accession of the House of Hanover to the throne in 1714 acted as a further magnet for Germans.

Settlement focused overwhelmingly upon London but encompassed a wide range of social classes and occupations ranging from the aforementioned merchants at the top through musicians to sugar bakers who worked in wretched conditions in the East End throughout the eighteenth and much of the nineteenth century. Religion acted as a glue which held German migrants together during the eighteenth century. The first Church opened in London during the 1670s followed by six others (one of them Roman Catholic) by the beginning of the nineteenth century. Two of these, St Mary's Lutheran Church in the Savoy and St George's in Whitechapel developed schools. Germans experienced some hostility on a variety of occasions, most notably during the Palatine refugee crisis when the press sparked attacks upon them.[143]

By the beginning of the nineteenth century many of the communities which would expand over the following two hundred years, above all the Jews and the Irish as well as the Germans, had therefore developed solid roots.

Other eighteenth century migrant populations, above all the Black communities, had disappeared largely as a result of intermarriage and consequent assimilation. While many of the communities outlined above remained small in number, the constant migratory flows point to the importance of the history of immigration into Britain.

Immigration since 1800

The patterns which had developed from as early as the eleventh century, encompassing migration, the development of ethnic groups and identities and the disappearance of such identities either as a result of intermarriage or xenophobia, would continue during the course of the nineteenth and twentieth centuries. While we can argue that migration to Britain had formed a constant stream before 1800, suggesting a country of immigration, after this time, and, in particular, since 1945, the reality, regularity and scale of immigration makes it a central factor in the evolution of the country.

In the first place, the volume of immigration increases significantly, connected especially with the global population explosion and the transport revolution. While the scale may develop significantly after 1945, it begins to take off during the nineteenth century. Between 1800 and 1914 about a million people crossed the Irish Sea to settle in Britain. Since the First World War movement of this group has increased even further so that since 1945 alone a further million Irish have moved to Britain pointing to the fact that they always make up the largest migrant population in the country. While they may have become increasingly invisible since the Second World War as a result of the arrival of groups from beyond, during much of the nineteenth century they remained the major group of outsiders in Britain.[144] Although the migration of Jews may have taken place on a smaller scale, they formed a major visible community by the end of the nineteenth century, reaching around half a million by 1945 having built upon the foundations of the eighteenth century. The migrants of the second half of the nineteenth century arrived mostly from eastern Europe, followed by exiles from the Nazis during the 1930s.[145] Apart from these two major groups the other significant minorities before 1945 consisted of the Germans, counting around 60,000 by 1914 but destroyed by the Germanophobia of the Great War,[146] together with smaller French and Italian communities reaching between 20,000 and 30,000 by the 1930s.[147]

Despite the historiographical focus upon the longevity of Black and Asian settlement in Britain,[148] non-European groups only counted a few thousand people in the period 1800–1945. The new communities of Chinese, South

Asian and Black peoples, especially the third of these, had little connection with any pre-Second World War migrant groups. While some Asian
and Chinese settlement in a small number of areas may have built upon
previous settlement, the migration history of Britain after 1945 takes a new
turn because of the origins of many newcomers, as well as the scale and
diversity. For the first time, movement on a significant level occurs from
beyond the European continent, notwithstanding the importation of slaves
during the eighteenth century. Millions of people have migrated to Britain
from the Caribbean, South Asia, Hong Kong and Africa, while smaller
numbers have moved from the Americas. By the census of 2001, eight per
cent of the population of Britain identified themselves as belonging to a
particular ethnic minority. While migration from beyond Europe may have
taken off since 1945, it has also remained constant from the continent.
Apart from the movement of a million Irish to Britain, hundreds of thousands
of people have moved to the country from Poland and Italy, while tens of
thousands have made their way from a variety of European states including
Cyprus and Malta.[149] But these simply represent some of the most prominent
ethnic groups. A focus upon London would reveal an extraordinary variety
of ethnic origins.[150]

Migration to Britain, however, has increasingly moved out of the
London heartland to reach the country as a whole. Before 1945 a large
percentage (up to half in the case of Italians and Germans)[151] of all ethnic
groups focused upon the capital. This did not apply so much to the larger
Irish population, which had not only developed concentrations in the
south and east of London, but also became visible in most of the larger
northern cities, especially Liverpool, Glasgow and Manchester, as well as
locations such as Newcastle, Leeds and York.[152] The Jewish migration of
the late nineteenth century concentrated heavily upon the East End of
London but, by 1914, new concentrations had also emerged in large cities
outside the capital, including Manchester, Leeds and Glasgow.[153] The smaller
migrant groups, on the other hand, while they may have lived outside the
capital, rarely counted over a few thousand people. This situation changes
dramatically after 1945. Not only do the new migrants of the early post-war
years move into places barely touched by foreigners before 1945, they
also move out of the traditional areas of settlement in London, above all the
East End, to locate themselves throughout the capital. Post-war London
developed hand in hand with immigration. At the same time vast swathes
of the Midlands experienced significant numbers of foreigners for the first
time, including Coventry and Leicester, as did smaller northern cities, such
as Bradford and Blackburn.[154]

Migrants have also changed the demography of Britain. This does not only apply to the presence of people from different ethnic groups as measured from the 1991 census. In addition, at least initially, newcomers often have higher birth rates than more established populations, although, in the longer term, the descendants of migrants increasingly develop the same fertility patterns as the population as a whole.[155]

Migrants have also played an important role in the economic development of Britain during the nineteenth and twentieth centuries. This would appear to apply especially to those involved in industry, such as the Irish throughout the entire period, or the post-war newcomers from Pakistan and the Caribbean. But migration often mirrors the economic demand of the economy at a particular point in time. While the Irish who settled in Britain during the nineteenth century and the early post-war years may have moved towards heavy industry, more recent Eastern European newcomers have increasingly worked in the service sector. However, it would be erroneous to suggest that all migrants have simply moved to Britain as fodder for the economy. Throughout the past two hundred years entrepreneurs and skilled and professional foreigners have worked in the country. Migrants make their presence felt in all sections of British economy and society, from top to bottom.[156]

The movement of millions of people to Britain since 1800 has had profound implications for identity and concepts of Britishness, especially in recent decades. All migrant groups of any size have developed their own communities from the few hundred German refugees living in London in the middle of the nineteenth century to the millions of South Asians in the post-war period who have constructed their own identities encompassing a variety of South Asian groups. In fact, all ethnic identities in Britain remain constructs which bring together elements from the homeland and reconstitute them in the new environment. While, in the case of South Asian Muslim migrants, for instance, religious practice may offer a fairly good representation of reality in India, Bangladesh or Pakistan,[157] other elements of South Asian lives in Britain, such as dress or food, combine elements of both the original and new homeland.[158] In fact, as more recent research has demonstrated, individuals increasingly choose their own identity, combining elements from a variety of geographical locations.[159] In the longer term a process of assimilation may take place, although deep rooted aspects of the lives of the original migrants, such as religion, will often remain in subsequent generations.[160]

Migrants have clearly played a central role in the evolution of the concept of multiculturalism, especially in the post-war period. Governments, especially Labour regimes, have established the legislative basis of this concept, which, however, has roots dating back to the early nineteenth century. But multiculturalism appears more visible in the transformations which have taken place in everyday life since the end of the Second World War. This would appear to apply especially to popular culture, dress and food.[161] Nevertheless, a perspective which went back into the nineteenth century would indicate immigrants playing a role in the transformation of food and high and popular culture.[162]

As this volume will show, Britain has been a country of immigration over the past two hundred years in a variety of ways. But at the same time as 'positive' developments have taken place, an iron girder of racism and xenophobia has remained. The nature of racism may appear to have changed over time, in the sense that the violent peaks, especially against the Irish for much of the nineteenth century and, above all, Germans during the First World War appear to have subsided. But some elements have remained constant such as the development of immigration laws since the end of the nineteenth century and the hostility of the press towards all new groups. The victims of xenophobia may change, from the Victorian Irish to the early twentieth century Jews, First World War Germans, West Indians during the 1950s, Asians from the 1960s to the 1980s, asylum seekers during the 1990s and, most recently, Muslims. But the hostility towards outsiders, which usually focuses upon one particular group at one particular time, remains constant. While Britain has certainly evolved as a country of immigration over the past two centuries, a strand of hostility has always existed to oppose this development,[163] resulting essentially in a situation of multicultural racism.

Notes and references

1   Tony Kushner, *Remembering Refugees: Then and Now* (Manchester, 2006).

2   Tony Kushner, ed., *The Jewish Heritage in British History: Englishness and Jewishness* (London, 1992).

3   Stefan Berger, Mark Donovan and Kevin Passmore, eds, *Writing National Histories: Western Europe Since 1800* (London, 1999).

4   Discussed in Michael Billig, *Banal Nationalism* (London, 1995).

5   Herbert Butterfield, *The Whig Interpretation of History* (London, 1965).

6   His most important work, written with Raymond Postgate, is, perhaps, *The Common People* (London, 1938).

7   See, for instance, *The Skilled Labourer, 1760–1832* (London, 1919).

8   E. P. Thompson, *The Making of the English Working Classes* (London, 1963).

9 A good starting point for working class history is the *Labour History Review*, which reached its seventieth year of publication in 2005, having previously appeared as the *Bulletin of the Society for the Study of Labour History*.

10 Michael Banton, *The Coloured Quarter: Negro Immigrants in a British City* (London, 1955).

11 Ruth Glass, *Newcomers: The West Indians in London* (London, 1960).

12 The titles of the books are: *The Irish in Scotland, 1798–1945* (Cork, 1943); and *The Irish in Modern Scotland* (Cork, 1947).

13 Patrick O'Sullivan, ed., *The Irish World Wide: History, Heritage, Identity*, 6 Volumes (Leicester and London, 1992–7).

14 Roger Swift and Sheridan Gilley have edited three important books in the form of: *The Irish in the Victorian City* (London, 1985); *The Irish in Britain, 1815–1939* (London, 1989); and *The Irish in Victorian Britain: The Local Dimension* (Dublin, 1999).

15 Mary Hickman, *Religion, Class and Identity: The State, the Catholic Church and the Education of the Irish in Britain* (Aldershot, 1994).

16 Donald M. MacRaild: *Culture, Conflict and Migration: The Irish in Victorian Cumbria* (Liverpool, 1998); *Irish Migrants in Modern Britain, 1750–1922* (Basingstoke, 1999); ed., *The Great Famine and Beyond: Irish Migrants in Britain in the Nineteenth and Twentieth Centuries* (Dublin, 2000).

17 http://www.liv.ac.uk/irish/

18 http://www.londonmet.ac.uk/pg-prospectus-2004/research/centres/isc.cfm

19 Enda Delaney, *The Irish in Post-war Britain* (Oxford, 2007).

20 Moses Margoliouth, *The History of the Jews in Great Britain*, 3 Volumes (London, 1851); John Mills, *The British Jews* (London, 1863); A. M. Hyamson, *The History of the Jews in England* (London, 1908).

21 http://www.jhse.dircon.co.uk/html/about_us.html

22 *A History of the Jews in England* (Oxford, 1941) summarizes much of his work.

23 Lloyd P. Gartner, *The Jewish Immigrant in England, 1870–1914* (London, 1960); John A. Garrard, *The English and Immigration, 1880–1910* (London, 1971); Bernard Gainer, *The Alien Invasion: The Origins of the Aliens Act of 1905* (London, 1972).

24 The most important books include: Geoffrey Alderman, *Modern British Jewry* (Oxford, 1992); David Cesarani, ed., *The Making of Modern Anglo-Jewry* (Oxford, 1990); Todd M. Endelman, *The Jews of Britain, 1656–2000* (London, 2002); David Feldman, *Englishmen and Jews: Social Relations and Political Culture, 1840–1914* (London, 1994); Tony Kushner, *The Persistence of Prejudice: Anti-Semitism in British Society during the Second World War* (Manchester, 1989); W. D. Rubinstein, *A History of the Jews in the English Speaking World: Great Britain* (Basingstoke, 1996); Colin Holmes, *Anti-Semitism in British Society,*

1876–1939 (London, 1979); Bill Williams, *The Making of Manchester Jewry, 1740–1875* (Manchester, 1976); and David S. Katz, *The Jews in the History of England, 1485–1850* (Oxford, 1994).

25 http://www.parkes.soton.ac.uk/

26 http://www.huguenotsociety.org.uk/

27 See, for instance: Robin D. Gwynn, *Huguenot Heritage: The History and Contribution of the Huguenots in Britain* (London, 1988); and B. J. Cottrett, *The Huguenots in England: Immigration and Settlement, c.1550–1700* (Cambridge, 1992).

28 Ian Colvin, *The Germans in England, 1066–1598* (London, 1915); C. R. Hennings, *Deutsche in England* (Stuttgart, 1923).

29 Rosemary Ashton, *Little Germany: Exile and Asylum in Victorian England* (Oxford, 1986); Panikos Panayi, *The Enemy in Our Midst: Germans in Britain during the First World War* (Oxford, 1991); Panikos Panayi, *German Immigrants in Britain during the Nineteenth Century, 1815–1914* (Oxford, 1995); Panikos Panayi, ed., *Germans in Britain Since 1500* (London, 1996).

30 See, for instance, Ulrike Kirchberger, *Aspekte deutsch-britischer Expansion: Die Überseeinteressen der deutschen Migranten in Großbritannien in der Mitte des 19. Jahrhunderts* (Stuttgart, 1999); Johannes-Dieter Steinert and Inge Weber-Newth, *Labour & Love: Deutsche in Grossbritannien nach dem Zweiten Weltkrieg* (Osnabrück, 2000); Stefan Manz, *Migranten und Internierte: Deutsche in Glasgow, 1864–1918* (Stuttgart, 2003); Stefan Manz, Margrit Schulte Beerbühl and John R. Davis, eds, *Migration and Transfer from Germany to Britain, 1660–1914* (Munich, 2007).

31 The seminal work on this subject consists of W. E. Mosse, et al., eds, *Second Chance: Two Centuries of German-Speaking Jews in the United Kingdom* (Tübingen, 1991).

32 http://www.sas.ac.uk/igs/HPEXILECENTRE.htm

33 Lucio Sponza: *Italian Immigrants in Nineteenth Century Britain* (Leicester, 1988); *Divided Loyalties: Italians in Britain during the Second World War* (Frankfurt, 2000).

34 Terri Colpi, *The Italian Factor: The Italian Community in Great Britain* (Edinburgh, 1991), p. 5.

35 The most recent include: Azadeh Medaglia, *Patriarchal Structures and Ethnicity in the Italian Community in Britain* (Aldershot, 2001); Claudia Baldoli, *Exporting Fascism: Italian Fascists and Britain's Italians in the 1930s* (Oxford, 2003); Anne Marie Fortier, *Migrant Belongings: Memory, Space, Identity* (Oxford, 2000); Wendy Ugolini, 'Communal Myths and Silenced Memories: The Unremembered Experience of Italians in Scotland During World War Two' (University of Edinburgh Ph.D thesis, 2006).

36 See, for instance: Jerszy Zubrzycki, *Polish Immigrants in Britain: A Study of Adjustment* (The Hague, 1956); Keith Sword with Norman Davies and Jan

Ciechanowski, *The Formation of the Polish Community in Great Britain, 1939–1950* (London, 1989); Peter D. Stachura, ed., *The Poles in Britain, 1940–2000: From Betrayal to Assimilation* (London, 2004).

37   These include Peter Fyer, *Staying Power: The History of Black People in Britain* (London, 1984); David Killingray, ed., *Africans in Britain* (London, 1993); Kenneth Little, *Negroes in Britain* (London, 1972); James Walvin, *Black and White: The Negro and English Society, 1555–1945* (London, 1973).

38   See, for instance, Jagdish S. Gundara, and Ian Duffield, eds, *Essays on the History of Blacks in Britain* (Aldershot, 1992); Ron Ramdin, *The Making of the Black Working Class in Britain* (Aldershot, 1987); Hakim Adi, *West Africans in Britain, 1900–1960: Nationalism, Pan-Africanism and Communism* (London, 1998); Mike and Trevor Phillips, *Windrush: The Irresistible Rise of Multi-Racial Britain* (London, 1998).

39   Rosina Visram, *Asians in Britain: 400 Years of History* (London, 2002).

40   Michael H. Fisher, Shompa Lahiri and Shinder Thandi, *A South Asian History of Britain* (Oxford, 2007).

41   See, for instance: N. Ali, V. S. Kalra and S. Sayyid, eds, *A Postcolonial People: South Asians in Britain* (London, 2006); and Roger Ballard, ed., *Desh Pradesh: The South Asian Presence in Britain* (London, 1994).

42   Panikos Panayi, *The Impact of Immigration: A Documentary History of the Effects and Experiences of Immigrants and Refugees in Britain Since 1945* (Manchester, 1999).

43   http://www.statistics.gov.uk/cci/nugget.asp?id=273, accessed 15 November 2004. This figure only refers to non-white groups. European immigrants and their offspring, particularly the Irish, would probably bring the percentage to around 12 per cent.

44   One of the key themes of Robert Winder, *Bloody Foreigners: The Story of Immigration to Britain* (London, 2004).

45   Tony Kushner and Kenneth Lunn, 'Introduction', in Kushner and Lunn, eds, *The Politics of Marginality: Race, The Radical Right and Minorities in Twentieth Century Britain* (London, 1990); Panayi, *Impact*, p. 29.

46   Immigrants are absent from David Cannadine, *Class in Britain* (London, 1998).

47   Robert Colls, *Identity of England* (Oxford, 2002).

48   Paul Gilroy, *There Ain't No Black in the Union Jack: The Cultural Politics of Race and Nation* (London, 1987).

49   Unlike the American Historical Association, which has, for decades, kept figures on the ethnic make up of the profession, groups such as the Royal Historical Society and History UK have not addressed such issues, again reflecting the ethnic make up of those who run such organizations. For the situation in the USA see, for instance, Robert D. Townsend, 'The Status of Women and Minorities in the History Profession', *Perspectives*, April 2002.

50 William Cunningham, *Alien Immigrants in Britain* (London, 1897).

51 See, most importantly: Jim Walvin, *Passage to Britain: Immigration in British History and Politics* (Harmondsworth, 1984); Colin Holmes, *John Bull's Island: Immigration and British Society, 1871–1971* (Basingstoke, 1988); Panikos Panayi, *Immigration, Ethnicity and Racism in Britain, 1815–1945* (Manchester, 1994); Panayi, *Impact*; Tony Kushner and Katherine Knox, *Refugees in an Age of Genocide: Global, National and Local Perspectives During the Twentieth Century* (London, 1999); Winder, *Bloody Foreigners*.

52 For two of numerous examples see: John Wrench and John Solomos, eds, *Racism and Migration in Western Europe* (Oxford, 1993); Alice Bloch and Carl Levy, eds, *Refugees, Citizenship and Social Policy in Europe* (Basingstoke, 1999).

53 http://www.warwick.ac.uk/CRER/index.html

54 Prominent examples include Michael Banton, Paul Gilroy and John Solomos.

55 Kushner, *Jewish Heritage*.

56 As a starting point see the following websites: Federation of Family History Societies at http://www.ffhs.org.uk; and a BBC website, http://www.bbc.co.uk/history/familyhistory. The existing family history magazines include the following: *Genealogy Magazine*; *Ancestors*; *Family History Monthly*; *Who Do You Think You Are?*; *Your Family Tree*; *Family History*; and *Family Tree Magazine*.

57 http://www.art-science.com/agfhs/events.html

58 http://www.jgsgb.org.uk

59 See the list of societies in http://www.genuki.org.uk/Societies/index.html, GENUKI, Family History and Genealogy Societies.

60 The titles include: *Asian Voices: Life-Stories from the Indian Sub-Continent* (London, 1993); *The Motherland Calls: African Caribbean Experiences* (London, 1992); *Xeni: Greek Cypriots in London* (London, 1990); and *Passport to Exile: The Polish Way to London* (London, 1988).

61 http://westworld.dmu.ac.uk/fmp/web/highfields/mainmenu.html

62 Imtiaz Habib, *Black Lives in the English Archives, 1500–1677: Imprints of the Invisible* (Aldershot, 2008).

63 See CASBAH, 'a pilot web site for research resources relating to Caribbean Studies and the history of Black and Asian Peoples in the UK', at http://www.casbah.ac.uk

64 http://www.movinghere.org.uk/default.htm

65 http://www.movinghere.org.uk/about/ambh.htm

66 See Nick Merriman, ed., *The Peopling of London: 15,000 Years of Settlement from Overseas* (London, 1993).

67 http://www.jewishmuseum.org.uk; http://www.manchesterjewishmuseum.com

68 http://www.Black-history-month.co.uk/home.html. See Darcus Howe's view of this event in *New Statesman*, 25 October 2004.

69 Kevin Myers, 'Historical Practice in the Age of Pluralism: Educating and Celebrating Identities', in Kathy Burrell and Panikos Panayi, eds, *Histories and Memories: Migrants and their History in Britain* (London, 2006), pp. 35–53.

70 Sarita Malik, *Representing Black Britons: A History of Black and Asian Images on British Television* (London, 2002).

71 Tony Kushner, 'Great Britons: Immigration, History and Memory', in Burrell and Panayi, *Histories and Memories*, p. 24.

72 See Jo Littler and Roshi Naidoo, eds, *The Politics of Heritage: The Legacies of Race* (London, 2005).

73 Mary Chamberlain, *Narratives of Exile and Return* (London, 1997); Paul Thompson, 'Moving Stories: Oral History and Migration Studies', *Oral History*, vol. 27 (1999), pp. 24–37.

74 Caroline B. Brettell and James F. Hollifield, 'Introduction: Migration Theory – Talking Across Disciplines' in Caroline B. Brettell and James F. Hollifield, eds, *Migration Theory: Talking Across Disciplines* (London, 2000), pp. 1–26.

75 See Chapters 2 and 4.

76 Oscar Handlin, *The Uprooted: The Epic Story of the Great Migration that Made the American Peoples*, 2nd edn (Boston, MA, 1973), p. 3.

77 Cunningham, *Alien Immigrants*.

78 Holmes, *John Bull's Island*, p. 5.

79 Ibid., pp. 5–12.

80 Panayi, *German Immigrants*, pp. 209–14.

81 Panikos Panayi, *Outsiders: A History of European Minorities* (London, 1999).

82 Klaus J. Bade, *Homo Migrans: Wanderungen aus und nach Deutschland: Erfahrungen und Fragen* (Essen, 1994).

83 Klaus J. Bade, ed., *Menschen über Grenzen: Grenzen über Menschen: Die Multikulturelle Herausforderung* (Herne, 1995).

84 Panayi, *Outsiders*.

85 T. W. E. Roche, *The Key in the Lock: Immigration Control in England from 1066 to the Present Day* (London, 1969), pp. 13–46.

86 See Simon James, *The Atlantic Celts: Ancient People or Modern Invention?* (London, 1999).

87 Edward James, *Britain in the First Millenium* (London, 2001), pp. 39–64; Nicholas J. Higham, *Rome, Britain and the Anglo-Saxons* (London, 1992), pp. 17–68.

88 Karl Heinrich Schaible, *Geschichte der Deutschen in England* (Strasbourg, 1885), pp. 1–19.

89 V. G. Kiernan, 'Britons Old and New', in Colin Holmes, ed., *Immigrants and Minorities in British Society* (London, 1978), p. 24.

90 Alexander Demandt, 'Patria Gentium: Das Imperium Romanum als Vielvölkerstaat', in Bade, *Menschen über Grenzen*, pp. 22–37.

91 Fryer, *Staying Power*, p. 1.

92 Catherine Hills, *Origins of the English* (London, 2003); C. J. Arnold, *Roman Britain to Saxon England* (Bloomington, IN, 1984).

93 James, *Britain*, pp. 214–70; P. H. Sawyer, *From Roman to Norman England*, 2nd Edn (London, 1998), pp. 114–20; Julian D. Richards, *Viking Age England* (London, 1991).

94 Brian Goulding, *Conquest and Colonization: The Normans in Britain, 1066–1100* (London, 1994); Nicholas J. Higham, *The Norman Conquest* (Stroud, 1998).

95 Kiernan, 'Britons', p. 25.

96 Mark R. Cohen, *Under Crescent and Cross: The Jews in the Middle Ages* (Princeton, 1994).

97 Paul Hyams, 'The Jewish Minority in Medieval England, 1066–1290', *Journal of Jewish Studies*, vol. 25 (1974), p. 271; Hyamson, *History of the Jews in England*, p. 107.

98 H. G. Richardson, *The English Jewry under Angevin Kings* (London, 1960), pp. 6–14.

99 Ibid., pp. 25–6.

100 Hyamson, *History of the Jews*, p. 108.

101 Ibid., p. 277.

102 Hyams, 'Jewish Minority', pp. 284–7.

103 Robin R. Mundill, *England's Jewish Solution: Experiment and Expulsion* (Cambridge, 1998).

104 Ibid.

105 Hyamson, 'Jewish Minority'.

106 Ibid., p. 277.

107 R. B. Dobson, *The Jews of Medieval York and the Massacre of March 1190* (York, 1974).

108 Hyamson, *History of the Jews*, pp. 39, 48, 88.

109 T. H. Lloyd, *Alien Merchants in England in the High Middle Ages* (Brighton, 1982), pp. 82–94; T. H. Lloyd, *England and the German Hanse, 1157–1611: A Study of their Trade and Commercial Diplomacy* (Cambridge, 1991); Friedrich Schulz, *Die Hanse und England: Von Edwards III bis auf Heinrichs VIII Zeit* (Stuttgart, 1978), pp. 11, 13; Inge-Maren Peters, *Hansekaufleute als Gläubiger der Englischen Krone (1294–1350)* (Cologne, 1978), pp. 99–104; Elenora M. Carus-Wilson, 'Die Hanse in England', in Kölnisches Stadtmuseum, ed., *Hanse in Europa: Brücke zwischen den Märkten 12.–17. Jahrhundert* (Cologne, 1973), pp. 91–101; J. W. Archer, 'The Steelyard', *Once a Week*, vol. 5 (1861), p. 54; Georg Syamken,

'Englandfahrer und Merchant Adventurers', *Hamburger-Wirtschafts-Chronik*, vol. 5 (1975), pp. 17–28; W. E. Lingelbach, *The Merchant Adventurers of England: Their Laws and Ordinances* (Philadelphia, 1902), pp. xv–xxxi.

110 Colpi, *Italian Factor*, pp. 25–6. For other medieval German groups see Panayi, *German Immigrants*, pp. 6–7.

111 Nick Merriman, 'From Prehistoric Times to the Huguenots', in Merriman, ed., *The Peopling of London: 15,000 Years of Settlement from Overseas* (London, 1993), pp. 36–8; Kiernan, 'Britons', p. 28.

112 Kevin O'Connor, *The Irish in Britain* (Dublin, 1974), p. 13.

113 The above account of Protestant refugees has used the following sources: C. W. Chitty, 'Aliens in England in the Sixteenth Century', *Race*, vol. 8 (1966), pp. 129–45; Nigel Goose, 'The "Dutch" in Colchester', *Immigrants and Minorities*, vol. 1 (1982), pp. 261–80; Marcel Backhouse, 'The Strangers at Work in Sandwich', *Immigrants and Minorities*, vol. 10 (1991), pp. 70–99; David Ormond, *The Dutch in London: The Influence of an Immigrant Community* (London, 1973); Panayi, *German Immigrants*, pp. 7–8; Andrew Pettegree, *Foreign Protestant Communities in Sixteenth Century London* (Oxford, 1986); Randolph Vigne and Charles Littleton, eds, *From Strangers to Citizens: The Integration of Immigrant Communities in Britain, Ireland and Colonial America, 1550–1750* (Brighton, 2001), pp. 7–105.

114 Lien Bich Luu, *Immigrants and the Industries of London* (Aldershot, 2005).

115 Lien Bich Luu, 'Dutch and their Beer Brewing in England, 1400–1700', in Anne J. Kershen, ed., *Food in the Migrant Experience* (Aldershot, 2002), pp. 101–33.

116 Raingard Esser, 'Germans in Early Modern Britain', in Panayi, *Germans in Britain*, pp. 21–7.

117 Martin Holmes, 'Evil May-Day 1517: The Story of a Riot', *History Today*, vol. 15 (September 1965), pp. 642–50; Irene Scouloudi, 'Alien Immigration in London, 1558–1640', *Proceedings of the Huguenot Society of London*, vol. 16 (1938), pp. 27–49; Michael Wyatt, *The Italian Encounter with Tudor England: A Cultural Politics of Translation* (Cambridge, 2005).

118 Fryer, *Staying Power*, pp. 4–12; Florian Shyllon, *Black People in Britain, 1555–1833* (London, 1977), p. 3; Paul Edwards, 'The Early African Presence in the British Isles' in Gundara and Duffield, *Essays*, pp. 15–24.

119 Angus Fraser, *The Gypsies* (Oxford, 1992), pp. 10–44; Jean-Paul Clebert, *The Gypsies* (London, 1964), pp. 15–29; Brian Vesey-Fitzgerald, *Gypsies of Britain: An Introduction to their History*, 2nd edn. (Newton Abbot, 1973), pp. 20–32.

120 David Mayall, *English Gypsies and State Politics* (Hatfield, 1995), pp. 18–26.

121 O'Connor, *Irish in Britain*, p. 13.

122 Jackson, *Irish in Britain*, p. 73.

123 Mark Greengrass, 'Protestant Exiles and their Assimilation in Early Modern England', *Immigrants and Minorities*, vol. 4 (1985), pp. 76–8; Vigne and Littleton, *Strangers to Citizens*; Lien Luu, 'Alien Communities in Transition', in Nigel Goose and Lien Luu, eds, *Immigrants in Tudor and Early Stuart England* (Brighton, 2005), pp. 192–210.

124 For contextualization see: R. I. Moore, *The Formation of a Persecuting Society: Power and Deviance in Western Europe, 950–1250* (Oxford, 1987); and David Nirenberg, *Communities of Violence: Persecution of Minorities in the Middle Ages* (Princeton, NJ, 1996).

125 Greengrass, 'Protestant Exiles', pp. 67, 71.

126 Anne J. Kershen, *Strangers, Aliens and Asians: Huguenots, Jews and Bangladeshis in Spitalfields, 1660–2000* (London, 2005), pp. 76–83, 109–14, 168–72; Gwynne, *Huguenot Heritage*, pp. 32–7, 67–9.

127 Gwynn, ibid., p. 124.

128 Ibid., pp. 110–28.

129 Kushner, *Remembering Refugees*, p. 30.

130 James Walvin, *Black Ivory: Slavery in the British Empire*, 2nd Edn (Oxford, 2001).

131 The above account is based upon: Fryer, *Staying Power*, pp. 67–236; Little, *Negroes in Britain*, pp. 187–229; Walvin, *Black and White*; Scobie, *Black Britannia;* and Norma Myers, *Reconstructing the Black Past: Blacks in Britain, 1780–1830* (London, 1996).

132 O'Connor, *Irish in Britain*, p. 18.

133 Brenda Collins, 'Proto-Industrialization and pre-Famine Emigration', *Social History*, vol. 7 (1982), pp. 127–46; O'Connor, *Irish in Britain*, pp. 14–15; John Denvir, *The Irish in Britain* (London, 1892), pp. 76–7, 102; D. Bogan, 'History of Irish Immigration to England', *Christus Rex*, vol. 12 (1958), pp. 38–48; Dorothy M. George, *London Life in the Eighteenth Century* (London, 1979 reprint), pp. 16–31.

134 Endelman, *Jews of Britain*, pp. 15–27; Katz, *Jews in the History of England*, pp. 15–144.

135 Endelman, ibid., p. 29.

136 Ibid., pp. 41–77.

137 Cecil Roth, *The Rise of Provincial Jewry: The Early History of the Jewish Communities in the English Countryside* (London, 1950). See also, for Portsmouth during the eighteenth century, Tony Kushner, *Anglo-Jewry Since 1066: Place, Locality and Memory* (Manchester, 2009), pp. 121–49.

138 Todd Endelman, *The Jews of Georgian England: Tradition and Change in a Liberal Society* (Philadephia, PA, 1979); Roth, ibid.

139 Endelman, ibid., pp. 13–85.

140 Todd M. Endelman, *Radical Assimilation in English Jewish History, 1656–1945* (Bloomington and Indianapolis, 1990).

141 See Chapter 6.

142 Endelman, *Jews of Georgian England*, pp. 86–117; Thomas W. Perry, *Public Opinion, Propaganda and Politics in Eighteenth Century England: A Study of the Jew Bill of 1753* (Cambridge, MA, 1962).

143 Panikos Panayi, 'Germans in Eighteenth Century Britain', in Panayi, *Germans in Britain*, pp. 29–48; Manz, Schulte Beerbühl and Davis, *Migration and Transfer*.

144 MacRaild, *Irish Migrants*, p. 43; Delaney, *Irish in Post-war Britain*.

145 Endelman, *Jews of Britain*.

146 Panayi, *German Immigrants*; Panayi, *Enemy*.

147 Nicolas Atkin, *The Forgotten French: Exiles in the British Isles, 1940–44* (Manchester, 2003), p. 188; Colpi, *Italian Factor*, p. 72.

148 See, especially: Fryer, *Staying Power*; Visram, *Asians in Britain*; and Fisher, Lahiri and Thandi, *South Asian History of Britain*.

149 Colpi, *Italian Factor*, Kathy Burrell, *Moving Lives: Narratives of Nation and Migration among Europeans in Post-war Britain* (Aldershot, 2006); Floya Anthias, *Ethnicity, Class, Gender and Migration: Greek Cypriots in Britain* (Aldershot, 1992); Geoff Dench, *Maltese in London: A Case Study in the Erosion of Ethnic Consciousness* (London, 1975).

150 Panikos Panayi, 'Cosmopolis: London's Ethnic Minorities', in Andrew Gibson and Joe Kerr, eds, *London from Punk to Blair* (London, 2003), pp. 67–71; Anne J. Kershen, ed., *The Promised Land: The Migrant Experience in a Capital City* (Aldershot, 1997).

151 Panayi, *German Immigrants*, p. 93; Colpi, *Italian Factor*, p. 74.

152 See contributions to the three Swift and Gilley volumes: *Irish in the Victorian City*; *Irish in Britain*; and *Irish in Victorian Britain*.

153 Williams, *Making of Manchester Jewry*; Joseph Buckman, *Immigrants and the Class Struggle: The Jewish Immigrant in Leeds, 1880–1914* (Manchester, 1983); Kenneth E. Collins, *Second City Jewry: The Jews of Glasgow in the Age of Enterprise, 1790–1919* (Glasgow, 1990); Ben Braber, *Jews in Glasgow 1879–1939: Immigration and Integration* (London, 2007).

154 Pippa Virdee, *Coming to Coventry: Stories from the South Asian Pioneers* (Coventry, 2006); John Martin and Gurharpal Singh, *Asian Leicester* (Stroud, 2002); Vaughan Robinson, *Transients, Settlers and Refugees: Asians in Britain* (Oxford, 1986); Sodhi Ram, *Indian Immigrants in Great Britain* (New Delhi, 1986).

155 See, for instance, Barry Kosmin, 'Nuptuality and Fertility Patterns of British Jewry, 1850–1980', in D. A. Coleman, ed., *Demography of Immigrant and Minority Groups* (London, 1982), pp. 246–61.

156 See, for instance: John Wrench, Andrea Rea and Nouria Ouali, eds, *Migrants, Ethnic Minorites and the Labour Market* (Brighton, 1999); Jan Rath, ed., *Unravelling the Rag Trade: Immigrant Entrepreneurship in Six World Cities* (Oxford, 2002); and Mosse, *Second Chance.*

157 Danièle Joly, *Britannia's Crescent: Making a Place for Muslims in British Society* (Aldershot, 1995).

158 Panikos Panayi, 'Immigration and Food in Twentieth-Century Britain: Exchange and Ethnicity', *Journal for the Study of British Cultures*, vol. 13 (2006), pp. 15–16; Parminder Bhachu, *Dangerous Designs: Asian Women Fashion the Diaspora Economies* (London, 2004).

159 See, for instance, Anne J. Kershen, ed., *A Question of Identity* (Aldershot, 1998).

160 Leo Lucassen, *The Immigrant Threat: The Integration of Old and New Migrants in Western Europe since 1850* (Chicago, 2005).

161 Panikos Panayi, *Spicing Up Britain: The Multicultural History of British Food* (London, 2008); Bhachu, *Dangerous Designs*; Paul Oliver, *Black Music in Britain: Essays on the Afro-Asian Contribution to Popular Music* (Milton Keynes, 1990).

162 See, for instance, Manz, Schulte Beerbühl and Davis, *Migration and Transfer.*

163 Colin Holmes, *A Tolerant Country? Immigrants, Refugees and Minorities in Britain* (London, 1991).

Migration to Britain

The scale of migration

Although migrants played an important role in the evolution of Britain throughout its history, from about the middle of the eighteenth century and, more especially, the nineteenth, the scale of migration to Britain changed. The Irish Famine migration, totalling over a quarter of a million people in a decade, provided an indication of the magnitude of movement which would occur over the following 150 years.

In terms of the geographical origins of migrants, it proves instructive to divide movement to Britain since 1800 into two phases covering the years before and after 1945. Between 1800 and 1945, while a few people originated from beyond the European continent, the overwhelming majority of newcomers came either from Ireland, which has remained the largest supplier of migrants to Britain throughout the past 200 years, or from the near continent. As Tony Kushner has demonstrated, using the files of the public opinion organization Mass Observation, Black and Asian people represented a rarity in the early twentieth century, with whom the majority of the population had little or no contact.[1] While writers such as Peter Fryer, Rozina Visram and Ron Ramdin[2] may rightly point to the longevity of the Black presence in Britain, such groups remained small in the 150 years before the middle of the twentieth century, never counting more then a few thousand people originating in Africa, the West Indies, India or China.[3] Large scale migration to Britain from beyond the European continent takes off from the 1950s. By the beginning of the twenty-first century, the whole world has a representation in the unique global capital of London.[4]

In the period between c.1800 and 1945 the overwhelming majority of migrants to Britain therefore originated in Europe. In fact, most of them came from Ireland. While the crisis caused by the Great Irish Famine of the 1840s may have sent over two million people abroad between 1847 and 1855, 300,000 of whom moved to Britain,[5] this phase simply represents the tip of the iceberg in terms of both migration out of Ireland and towards Britain. Between 1815 and 1930 around 7.3 million people left Ireland.[6] Although the majority ventured to North America, a significant percentage moved to Britain. The global figure probably excludes the seasonal agricultural labourers in Britain throughout the nineteenth century,[7] but it would include the regular flows of migrant labour, which moved to and settled in British cities before, during and after the Great Famine. If we use the research of Donald Macraild, Cormac Ó Gráda and Enda Delaney, it would seem that about 1.5 million people made their way from Ireland to Britain in the years 1815–1945.[8]

This meant that throughout the century and a half between 1800 and 1945 Ireland remained the most important source of migrants to Britain in purely numerical terms. Before 1945 a series of other migratory movements from the European continent also occurred, but on a significantly smaller scale. The largest consisted of Jews. For much of the nineteenth century a slow trickle originated predominantly from two areas. First, a maximum of about ten thousand mostly middle class German Jews. In addition, a steady stream of perhaps 15,000 migrants of more humble social origins moved from the Pale of Settlement established by the Russian monarchy in the eighteenth century to ghettoize its Jewish population in the western half of its territories.[9] If an equivalent of the Great Irish Famine occurs in Jewish migration history before 1945 then it actually happens twice, as a result of two explosions in antisemitism. The first wave out of the Pale of Settlement takes place between c.1880 and 1914 when 3 million people may have left 'oppression and poverty in Tsarist Russia'. As many as 2.5 million may have made their way to the USA during these years, with 150,000 settling in Britain.[10] Only a few thousand Jews moved to Britain between 1914 and the early 1930s due to the First World War and the introduction of tight immigration controls.[11] However, Nazi antisemitism during the 1930s led to a second Jewish refugee crisis which may have caused as many as 300,000 people to emigrate.[12] Despite the fact that the British government and public opinion displayed considerable hostility to the idea of an influx of refugees, 78,000 lived in Britain by the time the War broke out.[13] Few Jews made it to Britain during the conflict, as the government made no concrete efforts to save Holocaust victims.[14] Even at the end of the War, antisemitism, which had always played a large role in determining immigration policy towards foreign Jews, meant that only a few hundred survivors of Nazi polices entered Britain.[15] In fact, little Jewish immigration has occurred in the years after 1945 as the Israeli state has attracted the vast majority of Jews leaving the European continent. About 2,000 moved to Britain from the Hungarian Revolution of 1956, together with a similar number fleeing Egypt during the Suez crisis and a few others moving from Aden after 1967. However, as many as 75,000 Israelis may have recently settled in Britain.[16] Over thirty thousand Jews have left Britain for Israel since 1948, although some of these have returned.[17] Taking the last two hundred years as whole, we can estimate that around 220,000 Jews moved to Britain from a variety of predominantly European destinations, a figure which places them far behind the movement of the Irish, even considering just the pre-war period for that group.

A series of other movements also occurred from a variety of European states to Britain before 1945, all of which would also continue in the post-war period, usually on a larger scale. Significant German migration occurred before 1945, away from a country that lost millions of people mostly to the USA. While a peak figure of around 60,000 Germans lived in Britain by the outbreak of the First World War,[18] others had also spent shorter periods of time in the country earlier in the nineteenth century, sometimes passing through Britain as transmigrants on their way to the USA, which might account for hundreds of thousands of people in total.[19] But it seems unlikely that more than 100,000 permanent German migrants would have settled in Britain during the nineteenth century.[20] Movement from Germany to Britain declined in the aftermath of the xenophobia of the First World War, but some had occurred to allow a limited recovery of the German communities destroyed during the conflict. We can estimate a maximum of 20,000 between 1918 and 1939,[21] although this would have to increase by a further 60,000 if it included German Jewish refugees, most of whom felt themselves just as German as they did Jewish.[22] This means that a maximum of 180,000 people moved from Germany to Britain before 1945, although this falls to around 120,000 excluding the German Jews.

The three groups of Irish, Germans and Jews far outnumber any other migratory movement which took place to Britain before 1945. Italy and France may have sent a maximum total figure of 40,000 each.[23] Interestingly, 44,592 Americans lived in Britain by the time of the 1931 census,[24] suggesting that at least 70,000 must have moved to Britain before 1945. Adding the millions of GIs in World War Two would seriously exaggerate this position.[25] Below such figures would come the small numbers of Indians, Chinese, Africans and West Indians, who made little impact on the census. We can suggest that a maximum of 20,000 each of Indians, Chinese and Black people moved to Britain between 1800 and 1945.[26] To these we would need to add miscellaneous other groups, including a few thousand European refugees fleeing from repression on the continent in the middle of the nineteenth century,[27] about 100,000 exiles from Hitler's Europe during the Second World War[28] and 240,000 Belgians during the First World War, although the overwhelming majority of the last two groups returned home.[29] While we have not used a full proof scientific methodology to come to firm conclusions about the numbers of people who migrated to Britain before 1945, but have referred to the standard sources upon individual migrant groups, we can suggest a figure of 2.5 million. This would increase significantly if it included sailors who spent a limited amount of time in British ports,[30] transmigrants passing through during the nineteenth century and, more especially, American GIs during the Second World War.

An acceptance of a pre-1945 figure of approximately 2.5 million people moving to Britain, clearly points to the fact that it had become a significant country of immigration before the Second World War, even though 11.4 million people left the country between 1815–1930.[31] While scholars such as Charlotte Erickson have established the fact that Britain had become a country of mass emigration before 1945,[32] it had also become one of large scale immigration.

The latter situation becomes even clearer after 1945. More people have moved to Britain in the 65 years since the end of the Second World War than had done so in the previous 145 years. Just as significantly, migration to Britain has become increasingly international. This partly resulted from the settlement of citizens from former imperial possessions in the 'mother country', together, by the end of the twentieth century, with the attractions of London as a global city. However, this internationalization of migration to Britain should not hide the fact that many of the streams established before 1945 have continued to operate since that time. Three in particular stand out in the form of the Irish, Italians and Germans, with clear pre-War origins. A significant European new group also emerges in the form of Poles. Nevertheless, a variety of other continental groups, who would probably surpass the entire number of Chinese or Indian migrants who moved to the country before 1945, have also entered Britain.

Once again, despite increasing Europeanization and internationalization, one of the most significant migratory movements to Britain after the Second World War continued to come from Ireland. As Enda Delaney has correctly asserted, 'contrary to popular perception, the Irish were by far the largest ethnic minority in Britain in 1971', totalling 709,235 people according to the census of that year.[33] About half may have moved after 1945, although the 1931 figure stood as high as 505,385.[34] Delaney has pointed to temporary migration, a pattern which has continued in recent decades.[35] By the end of the twentieth century the number of Irish born people in Britain still stood at about half a million.[36]

Together with the Irish, a series of continental European groups have also moved to Britain since 1945. East Europeans, above all Poles, may now represent the most significant migratory movement to post-war Britain. An initial influx of approximately 145,000 settled in 1945 consisting of members of the Polish army and government in exile who chose to remain in Britain at the end of the War rather than return to a country which had fallen under Stalin's influence.[37] In the aftermath of the War the British state also recruited the labour power of 91,151 'displaced persons' who did not want to return home for the same reason as the exiled Poles. This group included Latvians, Lithuanians, Estonians, Ukrainians and Sudeten Germans.[38]

From the late 1940s until the end of the Cold War migration from eastern Europe to Britain changed from a steady stream to a trickle, although some increase occurred in the form of two refugee movements, as a reaction against Soviet backed repression. The first occurred following the crushing of the Hungarian uprising of 1956, which sent as many as 22,000 people to Britain.[39] Similarly, following the failure of the Prague Spring of 1968 about 600 Czechs may have entered the country.[40] Nevertheless, as Kathy Burrell has demonstrated with regard to Poland, migration from the Eastern Bloc to Britain, for both political and economic reasons, did not cease completely during the Cold War. 'Estimates put the figures at a minimum of several thousands, peaking in the 1980s'.[41]

The end of the Cold War sent new groups of Eastern Europeans to Britain, some of whom had not previously counted as a significant presence in the country. One of the earliest consisted of refugees from the Yugoslav Wars, although hostility towards 'asylum seekers' helped to keep the numbers down to just 12,000.[42] During the course of the 1990s economic migration had also taken place from Eastern Europe. This would increase to hundreds of thousands of people, above all Poles, following entry into the EU of a series of eastern European states in 2004. Since 1945 perhaps 750,000 Eastern Europeans may have made their way to Britain, especially Poles, who may count 500,000, although some of these, especially those arriving after 2004, would only remain temporarily.[43]

Another group of Europeans to make their way to Britain, in significantly smaller numbers, consist of those whose countries had imperial connections with Britain in the form of Cyprus and Malta. Migration from the former took place in two distinct phases. The first economically motivated movement during the 1950s and early 1960s brought in over 70,000, about 80 per cent of whom probably consisted of Greeks, with Turks making up the rest, reflecting the ethnic composition of the island. In 1974, following the Turkish invasion of Cyprus, a further 10,000 Greek Cypriots fled to Britain.[44] Similarly, around 35,000 Maltese seem to have settled in Britain.[45]

Italian settlement in Britain has also occurred on a significant scale since 1945 in a series of phases. In the first place, about 1,500 prisoners of war remained in 1945.[46] According to Terri Colpi a further 148,140 Italians arrived between 1948 and 1968 although about twenty per cent returned home,[47] a pattern which would continue during the 1970s and 1980s.[48] By 2001 the number of Italians in Britain stood at 107,244.[49] Another significant, but less visible, European migration which has occurred since 1945 has consisted of Germans, who have entered the country in a series of waves. During the second half of the 1940s various groups settled in Britain as a result of the fallout from the Second World War including about 24,000 former prisoners of war, about 11,000 labour recruits, and 10,000 German women who married members of the occupying British army and subsequently migrated with their husbands, giving a total of about 45,000 by the early 1950s.[50] Nevertheless, a significant increase has occurred since that time consisting mostly of middle class and professional migrants, facilitated by the free movement of labour under the Treaty of Rome. By the beginning of the twenty-first century 266,136 Germans lived in Britain. This figure suggests that at least that many had moved to Britain since 1945, although Ceri Peach believes that 'this number includes a significant number of children born to British forces stationed in Germany'.[51] Poles, Germans and Italians represent the largest post-war migrant groups who have moved to Britain with the assistance of the Treaty of Rome clause allowing free movement of labour in the EU. In 2001 there were 729,967 EU nationals living in the UK.[52] Migration from the European continent to Britain since 1945 has surpassed that which took place in the century and a half before then.

Only after outlining the millions of Europeans who have moved to Britain, can we turn to those who have migrated to the country from outside the continent. These divide in various ways. One obvious categorization consists of those who made their way to Britain because of imperial connections compared with those who did not even have this link. Clearly, those in the former would include West Indians, Hong Kong Chinese and South Asians. Most migration from the West Indies took place in the first couple of decades after the end of World War Two, while movement from South Asia occurred more gradually, especially as a result of families joining the initial male pioneers. From the 1980s, especially as the Cold War thaw resulted in the emergence of ethnically exclusive nationalistic states, migration to Britain began to increase from new areas.

Attempting to establish numbers proves particularly problematic. We can begin with the Imperial and Commonwealth migration. West Indians already had an increased presence in Britain during the Second World War either as a result of service in the armed forces or because of the increasing labour demands of the War economy.[53] By 1951 the number of West Indians in Britain stood at 17,218 and would increase dramatically over following decades, reaching 173,659 in 1961 and a peak of 304,070 by 1971, declining since that time to less than 250,000 by 2001.[54] It proves extremely difficult to reach conclusions about the total number of people who would have moved from the West Indies (the majority from Jamaica) to Britain. Margaret Byron has suggested that 221,676 migrated in the years 1955–61 alone, pointing to a significant rate of return migration, which would continue after 1971. She suggests, for instance, that 27,000 went back during the 1980s.[55] Her figures actually imply that as many as 400,000 West Indians may have moved to Britain, a significant percentage of whom returned.[56]

The movement of Chinese people to Britain, especially from Hong Kong, has a close link with the development of the catering trade. Chinese restaurants began to take off during the 1950s and have continued to recruit workers from Hong Kong since that time. About 30,000 Chinese made their way to Britain between 1946 and 1962, rising to about 60,000 by the middle of the 1970s.[57] A further increase has occurred since that time, bringing the total number of people in Britain of Chinese ethnic origin to about 150,000, meaning that perhaps 250,000 Chinese people have moved to Britain since World War Two.

The most substantial non-European migration to Britain since 1945 consists of 'South Asians', who, however, divide into three main groups consisting of Bangladeshis, Indians and Pakistanis, who originate from distinct locations in their countries of origin. Some South Asians also moved to Britain via East Africa. While migration began during the 1950s, it peaked in the 1960s and early 1970s largely due to family reunification. The selection of marriage partners from South Asia, as well as the entry of professionals, has ensured that some movement has continued since then. By 2001 the census pointed to the presence of 2,027,000 people of Asian ethnicity, about half of whom had migrated themselves. The former figure divided into 1 million Indians, 747,000 Pakistanis and 280,000 Bangladeshis. At least 1 million South Asians have made their way to Britain over the past six decades, a figure which would increase further if it included demographic change due to mortality and return migration.[58]

Ceri Peach has pointed to a variety of other groups who have found themselves in Britain as a result of the imperial connection. In the first place, he identifies 340,000 'Whites born in the New Commonwealth', consisting of 'returning administrators and settlers from the colonies with their white but colonial-born families'. In addition, hundreds of thousands of 'settlers, students, and transients' moved from South Africa, New Zealand, Australia and Canada. The 2001 census also identified 834,107 Africans originating from a variety of countries including Ghana and Zimbabwe and incorporating a range of refugee groups.[59]

Refugees from beyond Britain migrated as localized political crises impacted upon the nation states in which they lived from the 1970s. These have included over 30,000 exiles from the Iranian revolution of 1979, 3,000 Chileans fleeing the Pinochet dictatorship, 15,000 Vietnamese (mostly of Chinese ethnicity) escaping the consequences of the Civil War in their country, 15,000 Kurds fleeing persecution in their homeland, especially in Turkey, and 15,000 Zaireans escaping repression during the 1980s and 1990s. Others who have moved to Britain in recent decades have included about 28,000 Sri Lankans, 7,500 Ghanaians, and over 26,000 Somalis.[60] More recently, several hundred thousand Zimbabweans may have moved to Britain.[61]

TABLE 2.1 Estimated numbers of migrants to Britain since *c.* 1800

Migrant Group	Migration before 1945	Migration since 1945	Total migration
Africans	10,000	1,000,000	1,010,000
Americans	70,000	250,000	320,000
Arabs	10,000	290,000	300,000
Belgians	240,000	40,000	280,000
Chinese	20,000	320,000	340,000
Cypriots	2,000	80,000	82,000
French People	40,000	100,000	140,000
Germans	100,000	300,000	400,000
Hungarians	2,000	38,000	40,000
Irish	1,500,000	700,000	2,200,000
Italians	40,000	160,000	200,000
Jews	220,000	80,000	300,000
Poles	5,000	500,000	505,000
South Asians	20,000	1,000,000	1,020,000
West Indians	10,000	400,000	410,000
Others	50,000	1,000,000	1,000,000
Total	2,339,000	6,231,000	8,570,000

To these we also need to finally add wealthier professional migrants in recent decades. Two which stand out consist of US citizens and 'Arabs', who would have included Lebanese, Yemenis and Palestinians.[62] Ceri Peach has estimated that 290,000 of the latter lived in Britain by 1991, while 158,439 US citizens resided in the UK in 2001.[63] An attempt to establish the number of migrants to Britain over the last two centuries can only provide an estimate. Only a self-standing long-running statistical project would reveal accurate answers. Table 2.1 only allows us to guess at the numbers of people involved, but it emphasizes the centrality of immigration in the evolving history of Britain over the last two centuries. While the country primarily attracted migrants from Europe before 1945, it increasingly became a magnet for those from beyond the continent after 1945 and, as the twentieth century progressed, the origins of newcomers became increasingly diverse. Table 2.1 gives an indication of the variety of migrants to Britain, but does not take into account either return migration or the children of migrants born in Britain. It is an estimate based upon the extant literature on migration, rather than a conclusive total based upon a thorough examination of thousands of pages of primary sources.

The causes of migration to Britain

Actually attempting to establish the reasons for the migration of millions of people from a variety of locations throughout the world towards Britain over the course of two centuries proves a task which does not easily lend itself to generalizations. It is tempting to return to Ravenstein's approach to migration,[64] which examined push and pull factors, but this approach has become increasingly unfashionable amongst those examining the motivations which have sent people to Britain.

Most scholars increasingly take one of two approaches. The first of these sees migration to Britain as a result of the implementation of British immigration and nationality controls, especially since 1945.[65] It would certainly prove impossible to understand the migration of millions of people to Britain since World War Two without a full understanding of the whole range of measures introduced by the British state, beginning with the 1948 British Nationality Act, progressing through the Commonwealth Immigrants Acts of the 1960s to the passage of legislation to deal with refugees from the 1980s. Yet such approaches have three weaknesses. First, they do not have enough historical perspective and therefore do not stress the origins of British immigration policy. The works of scholars such as Bernard Gainer, Bernard Porter, Andreas Fahrmeier, Louise London and Vaughan

Bevan point to the fact that immigration policy, while not as developed as it may have become in the second half of the twentieth century, played an important role in the movement and exclusion of people to Britain throughout the period 1800–1945.[66] Second, they simply do not pay enough attention to the areas from which migrants originate. A reading of Spencer, Paul, Hansen does not tell us why people left former British colonies. Finally, and inevitably, given their British state centred approaches, such scholars pay virtually no attention to individual motivation or why one human being decided to move from, say, the Punjab to London.

The other increasingly popular approach would certainly seem to solve this last problem. By interviewing individual migrants who moved to Britain in recent decades scholars such as Mary Chamberlain, Katy Gardner and Kathy Burrell allow themselves to get inside the minds of people leaving the West Indies, Bangladesh or specific parts of Europe respectively.[67] These scholars view their interviewees as active. Burrell has written that 'accepting migrants as agents opens up research into the complexity of decision making that surrounds migration'.[68] Both Chamberlain and Burrell take objection to the work of scholars who have focused upon 'economic and structural models' which 'assumed that all migrants were motivated by economic necessity, the result of economic deprivation (unemployment, overpopulation) at home and the promise of abundant employment elsewhere.'[69] They view structural factors as the background to individual migration choices. This approach links with the development of the concept of transnationalism, which has come to play a large role in understanding migration in recent years. Transnationalism stresses the connection between the migrant diaspora and the homeland, giving rise to networks which facilitate further migration.[70] This seems an adaptation of the more traditional 'chain-migration' approach, used by scholars of nineteenth-century movements, especially towards the USA. Kathleen Neils Conzen, for instance, recognized the connection between migrant groups and their homelands in the development of nineteenth-century Milwaukee.[71]

Despite the attractiveness and apparent totality as an explanation for migration of the life narrative and transnational approaches, we need to apply some caution, especially when attempting to use them for a variety of population movements towards Britain involving millions of people over 200 years. In the first place, it clearly proves impossible to interview dead people. While we can come to conclusions about the individual motivations of migrants moving to Britain after 1945, we are at the mercy of incomplete sources when trying to investigate the reasons why an individual may have moved from the German states of Hanover or Hesse to London during the course of the 1840s. Circumstantial evidence certainly points to the fact that migrant networks existed,[72] but a life narrative approach would now prove difficult for any German, if not any migrant, who moved to Britain before 1939. Just as importantly, the transnational approach proves difficult to apply to the concept of forced migration, which has affected tens of millions of people since the First World War. In situations of invasion, extreme racial persecution or even the onset of famine, reaching the nearest place which will accept a particular population often proves the most important factor.

While the life narrative approach may accept the importance of structural or global factors, it does not fully engage with such issues. Our attempt to account for the millions of people who have moved to Britain since 1800 must examine the changes in world demography and economy which have occurred over the past 200 years. Scholars such as Klaus J. Bade, tackling European migration since 1800,[73] Dirk Hoerder, who has focused upon transatlantic movements during the nineteenth century,[74] Stephen Castles and Mark J. Miller, dealing with migration movements in the contemporary world,[75] or Michael Marrus, looking at twentieth century refugee movements,[76] have to take a structural approach, because their work deals with tens of millions of people moving in a variety of directions and from a range of geographical and ethnic origins. The volume which comes closest to tackling all levels of causation when dealing with migration to Britain consists of Tony Kushner and Katherine Knox's, *Refugees in an Age of Genocide: Global, National and Local Perspectives During the Twentieth Century*.

Structural factors need examination in their own right, because only with an appreciation of the underlying global changes which have taken place over the past two centuries can we appreciate personal motivations. These structural changes act as the soil out of which personal motivations emerge. While migration may always have characterized British, European and global history, population movements over the past two centuries have surpassed all of those which have taken place in previous human history.[77] The deepest rooted causation of all, consists of the increase in population, which inevitably means that more people move. Economic transformation, more specifically the rise of industrialization and capitalism, has created an insatiable demand for labour. Just as importantly, the introduction of the steam engine and then the motor engine has made population movement easier, because of their application to railways, ships, cars and aeroplanes. All of these changes have played a central role in creating the conditions which make migration easier. Political change also proves fundamental.

Since the First World War forced migration has increasingly become normal, affecting tens of millions of people, whether we examine the European continent in the first half of the twentieth century or broaden this further in more recent decades.

A full understanding of the reasons which have sent millions of people to Britain since 1800 therefore needs to appreciate a variety of issues and levels of causation. First of all, the underlying demographic, economic, political and transportation factors, which have made migration more likely. Second, the attractions of Britain, more specifically the role of immigration policy (positive as well as negative) and the wealth of Britain compared with most of the rest of the world. Finally, the personal and transnational factors, which have determined distinct migratory movements from specific areas of the world towards Britain. The connections between Britain and the origins of migrants, whether as a result of geographical proximity or imperial connections, have played a large role.

Underlying factors

Since the middle of the eighteenth century the number of people in the world has increased from about 79 million to over six billion. The population explosion which initially impacted upon Europe and caused pressure upon land, increasingly spread to the rest of the world during the twentieth century.[78] While increasing population does not in itself lead to migration, it often provides a prerequisite which makes such movement possible. The growth of population in South Asia and China may have made migration more likely, but movement has only taken place from specific areas.

We can examine the underlying role of population change by firstly focusing upon nineteenth-century Europe. The stable demographic structure which had characterized the early modern period progressed through sudden growth, caused mainly by a decline in mortality, to the larger and more stable population which characterizes twentieth century Europe, although some states reached this situation earlier than others. Ireland and Italy, for example, would not achieve stable populations until the second half of the twentieth century. The nineteenth century in Europe partly represents a period of readjustment, when sudden population growth created pressure on resources.[79] The increase began in western Europe and moved southwards and eastwards. The Irish population, for instance, grew 'from about 6 million in 1801, to 8 million in 1841', although it subsequently fell,[80] while Germany showed a steady increase from 24,831,000 in 1816 to 64,568,000 by 1910.[81] Similar patterns reveal themselves in Italy and Russia.

In the former, the population went from 21,776,824 in 1861 to 34,671,377 in 1911,[82] while in the latter the Jewish population rose from 2.4 million in 1851 to 5.6 million in 1910.[83]

Population growth resulted in smaller plots, which could no longer sustain the same number of people as previously. Therefore, an area which had previously sufficed for one family might have to support more as population continued to grow. In the German case demographic change worked in the same way in areas where inheritance took place equally among sons (especially in south-west Germany), and areas such as East Prussia, where the eldest inherited everything, as the remaining sons would often have to find alternative employment, which often meant emigration.[84] In the German case a clear link exists between the population growth of the nineteenth century, internal migration and emigration. German industrialization could not have taken place without the supply of mobile domestic labour. For much of the nineteenth century the latter exceeded the number of jobs available, leading to emigration to the USA. Only from the end of the 1880s did jobs match labour supply, and, in fact, exceed them, leading to immigration.[85]

Many of the patterns described above in nineteenth century western Europe also became apparent in parts of the world from which migrants would move to Britain after 1945. Cyprus, for instance, experienced significant population growth from the 1920s due to a sharp decline in death rates, which caused unemployment on the land and a consequent migratory pressure towards towns and, during the 1950s and 1960s, towards Britain.[86] Similarly, a crisis also affected the West Indies during the early post-war period, in which rapid population growth acted as the background factor, but against which short-term economic crises intervened.[87]

Population growth may not in itself cause emigration, but it often results in internal movement from rural to urban areas.[88] Modern industrializing processes could not have occurred without internal migration.[89] Similarly, nineteenth century US industrialization or post-war economic growth in the West could not have taken place without a ready supply of international labour.[90]

Some spurts of migration to Britain have occurred as a result of short term economic crises. Walter D. Kampfhoefner and Brenda Collins, referring to south-western Germany and Ireland respectively, have written about the consequences of the collapse of proto-industrialization during the early nineteenth century, whereby labour intensive cottage industries were destroyed by the threat of more cheaply produced British industrial goods, leading to emigration because of consequent unemployment.[91]

A series of short-term agricultural crises have also made movement towards Britain more likely, and, in at least one case, almost inevitable. This case consists of the Irish potato famine of 1845–9, which resulted in a large short-term influx, leading Frank Neal to speak of a famine refugee crisis.[92] Many of the 300,000 people who moved to Britain between 1847 and 1855 landed in Liverpool, which experienced the brunt of the 'refugee crisis'.[93] Irishmen and women simply moved to 'the nearest place that wasn't Ireland'. As well as the emigration of perhaps 1.75 million people,[94] as many as 1.5 million people may have died. MacRaild has argued that those areas most heavily dependent upon the potato crop, especially in the west, witnessed the highest rates of emigration,[95] while Lynn Hollen Lees asserted that those with the lowest and highest rates of pauperism suffered the lowest incidence of emigration: 'In the former case, people lacked an incentive to leave; in the latter they lacked the means'.[96]

In fact, the Irish famine formed part of the last great agricultural crisis to affect western Europe,[97] which would also form one of the background factors to the outbreak of the 1848 Revolutions across the continent. In some areas, such as Germany, this malaise led to both revolution and emigration. The year 1845 had resulted in a below average crop yield in many areas and, in the following year, there followed potato, rye, wheat, and fruit failures. During the early 1850s similar agricultural failures took place, affecting a wide variety of crops. Inevitably, widespread poverty followed. Against this background, which built upon increasing population and the failures of protoindustrialization, nearly 1.5 million people left Germany, the vast majority of whom went towards the USA, although many travelled via English ports.[98]

We can also detect similar short-term economic crises, which acted as background factors for migration to Britain during the twentieth century. Returning to movement out of the West Indies, and, more especially, Jamaica, immediately after the Second World War economic conditions had deteriorated due to agricultural problems. Simon Taylor has asserted that 'the sugar industry suffered from serious over-production between 1946 and 1950', leading many smallholders to sell their land to larger estates and face subsequent unemployment. By the end of the 1940s about one quarter of Jamaica's population was jobless.[99] A Colonial Office memorandum from 1948, focusing upon a long-term crisis in the sugar trade, made the link between unemployment and population growth, if not migration, in the West Indies, asserting that 'the inflow into the labour market greatly exceeds the wastage. The birth rate remains high while the death rate has fallen and is still falling'.[100] Similarly, most of the Chinese migrants who moved to Britain to work in the restaurant trade during the early 1960s originated in Hong Kong, which experienced a series of economic problems, partly caused by a transition from rice to vegetable farming, as well as increasing pressure on land caused by an influx of refugees from the Chinese revolution into Hong Kong.[101]

Underlying demographic and economic factors play a role in creating the conditions for migration to take place. In some cases, such as the failure of the Irish potato crop, we do not need to impose many other developments to understand the reasons for the influx to Britain. But this remains exceptional. In most other instances intervening factors prove important, if only at the basic level of a political connection between Britain and the land of origin, as the example of the West Indies illustrates.

A further factor consists of improvements in transportation during the course of the nineteenth and twentieth centuries. Migration does not require the steam engine or the motor or jet engine to occur. Movement of peoples before the nineteenth century, often involving hundreds of thousands of people, took place on foot or with carts, but these could take centuries to reach a specific destination. The Romanies may have left northern India in the fifth century, but they did not reach Britain until the beginning of the sixteenth.[102] Similarly, the first Age of Migrations, which saw mass population movement throughout Europe, especially in the aftermath of the fall of the Roman Empire, took place on foot and with carts.[103]

The end of the period of relatively small amounts of migration into and out of Britain, mirroring the European situation, comes to an end in the early nineteenth century with the development of the steam engine, coinciding with the British and European population explosion. These two factors increase the likelihood, volume and speed of migration throughout the world, playing an especially important role in transporting people from Europe to the USA to help with American industrialization.[104]

Britain played a key role in transatlantic migration, facilitating the settlement of Irish people, Germans and Jews within the country, because, for much of the nineteenth century, emigrants sailed into a British port before changing ships to travel to America. From the 1860s, ships increasingly proceeded directly from continental ports to the USA. A small minority of transmigrants chose to remain in Britain rather than travel further.[105]

Improvements in transportation also facilitated the journey across the Irish Sea. The development of the steamship during the second decade of the nineteenth century 'brought a regularity of crossings that sail could not because of the dependence on weather conditions'.[106] By the time of the Famine dozens of routes existed from Ireland to Britain.[107] The availability of shipping therefore played a role in the influx of the Irish to Britain during the 1840s.[108] Many Irish people hoped to subsequently proceed to the USA. David Fitzpatrick used the term 'stepwise' to describe this migratory process. 'Impecunious emigrants could walk and beg their way to a sea port, rough it across the Irish Sea, save a few pounds from casual labour in Scotland and northern England, and ultimately invest their savings in a transatlantic passage'.[109]

The development of the steam engine played a central role in the mass emigration out of Germany during the nineteenth century, which involved over 4 million people. While the steamship speeded up the journey, railways helped to transport emigrants to the newly improved German ports of

FIGURE 3 Immigrants from the Caribbean island of Jamaica arrive at Tilbury, London, on board the 'Empire Windrush'. This party are 5 young boxers and their manager, 22 June 1948 (Photo by Popperfoto/Getty Images)

departure in Bremen and Hamburg. By the 1860s railway lines had developed to bring emigrants towards them from all over Germany. For much of the nineteenth century many of the routes across the Atlantic, with the USA as the ultimate destination of most Germans, involved sailing to an east coast port, especially Hull or London, but also Hartlepool and Grimsby, and then travelling by train to a point of departure, usually Liverpool. While the vast majority did make it to the USA, a minority remained in Britain, helping to build up the German communities.[110]

Transmigration also played a role in the development of the European Jewish communities during the nineteenth century. Harold Pollins has written that: 'One sometimes gets the impression that the Anglo-Jewish community was built up of those who did not get to America'. Progressing on similar routes to those used by Germans, they travelled by 'train westwards to Liverpool from Hull, alighted at Leeds or Sheffield, or Manchester, and stayed in the Jewish quarter near the railway station'.[111] Similarly, Bill Williams has described the east European Jewish settlements which emerged in northern cities from the 1840s as 'the local residue of a movement destined chiefly for the United States'.[112]

The development of shipping and, more especially, the British merchant fleet during the nineteenth century and beyond, also played a role in the settlement of Asians in Britain. As Rozina Visram pointed out, one of the earliest groups of Asians to settle in Britain consisted of 'Lascars', arriving before 1800.[113] Many consisted of Sylhettis, who would continue to spend time in Britain and form the basis for the evolution of the Bangladeshi community after 1945.[114]

Most of those arriving in the early decades after the Second World War travelled through a combination of rail and steamship. While the landing of the *Empire Windrush* in Tilbury docks in June 1948 has become the iconic image of the beginning of West Indian and, more generally, Commonwealth immigration to post-war Britain,[115] it also symbolizes, in this discussion, the importance and dominance of shipping in international travel and migration.[116]

Since the 1960s long distance travel has tended to involve aeroplanes. The main effect of this, like the advent of the steam engine before it, has been to make journeys quicker and easier rather than to necessarily facilitate migration. But air travel has probably increased the likelihood of migration.[117] Stephen Castles and Mark J. Miller have acknowledged this.[118] As has British immigration policy. In 1988 the Immigration (Carriers Liability) Act imposed a fine of £1,000 (increased to £2,000 in 2000) on airlines for each passenger brought to the UK without valid documents.[119]

Despite the relative lack of attention which scholars of migration have paid to the evolution of transport in international migration and movement towards Britain, it would prove impossible to conceive of the history of population movement over the past two centuries without considering the role of ships, trains, planes and cars. The transport revolution has played a fundamental role at a structural level.

For much of the twentieth century a factor over which people on the move had limited control has consisted of persecution, although even here, a level of choice, no matter how limited, often presents itself. Although some scholars examining the flight from the Irish potato famine may imply forced migration,[120] this concept has usually focused upon those who have fallen foul of political change in the twentieth century, when the idea of the refugee has developed. As Marrus has written, while 'people obliged by war or persecution to leave their dwellings and seek refuge abroad have tramped across the European continent since time immemorial . . . only in the twentieth century have European refugees become an important problem of international politics'.[121] Most definitions of refugees go back to the 1951 UN Convention, which recognized individuals fleeing their homeland due to 'a well founded fear of persecution'. Yet the line between political refugees and economic migrants remains far more complicated than late twentieth-century immigration policy makers believe, most classically demonstrated by Diana Kay and Robert Miles examining the arrival of 'European Volunteer Workers' in Britain in the late 1940s.[122] But even the concept of the refugee remains unsatisfactory when dealing with forced migration to Britain because it would not account for the transfer of German and Italian prisoners of war to Britain during the Second World War, many of whom would subsequently remain.

Including these two groups in an examination of forced migration to Britain since 1800 does not change the fact that most refugees have moved to the country as a result of political intolerance on the European continent. More specifically, most forced migration occurred as a result of two intolerant states in particular in the form of Germany, in its various guises until 1945, and Russia or the Soviet Union. Refugee movements towards Britain from beyond Europe only begin in the early 1970s, as a result of the persecuting policies of Idi Amin against Ugandan Asians. Since that time most forced migration, which has become increasingly tightly policed by asylum legislation, has occurred from a variety of areas, with a significant increase caused by the end of the certainties of the Cold War and the consequent rise of persecuting nationalisms.

Between 1800 and 1945 Germany sent most forced migrants to Britain. Until 1914 the vast majority of these few thousand people consisted of political activists opposing the existing order and fearing jail sentences as a result of their activities. The exiles came in three stages. First, those fleeing a clamp-down on the liberal Young Germany movement by the German Confederation during the 1830s, who eventually made it to Britain via Switzerland. A second grouping arrived after the failure of the 1848 revolutions counting around 1,150 people, including Karl Marx. A final influx occurred after the passage of the Anti-Socialist Laws in October 1878, following two assassination attempts upon the Kaiser.[123]

During the 'age of catastrophe' in Europe as German armies marched across Europe between 1914 and 1945[124] the few thousand refugees who had fled to Britain during the Victorian period became hundreds of thousands of forced migrants. The first group, resembling the Irish potato famine migrants in terms of the volume of people involved over a short period of time, consisted of the 240,000 Belgians who fled the German invasion of their country in 1914, virtually all of whom would return home at the end of the First World War.[125] Although, as Louise London in particular has demonstrated,[126] the influx of refugees, especially Jews, from the Nazis during the 1930s depended to a large extent upon British government policy towards them, the underlying factor in the desire to flee from the Third Reich consisted of persecution.[127] The outbreak of the Second World War and the German invasion of much of Europe sent a series of new groups to Britain, counting hundreds of thousands of people. In the first place, about 75,000 people fled from a variety of countries taken over by the Nazis including Belgium, France, Norway, Holland and Czechoslovakia.[128] At the same time, a maximum of 362,000 German prisoners of war, out of the total of 3.7 million held by the British military forces, found themselves interned in Britain in August 1946, of whom 15,000 would remain.[129] Similarly, about 75,000 Italian prisoners found themselves in Britain in 1943, of whom 1,500 did not return home.[130]

A combination of the fallout from the Second World War and Soviet policy in the immediate aftermath of the conflict would lead to further flows of refugees in the late 1940s. However, Tsarist and Soviet autocracy before 1939 had led to influxes before 1917 consisting of Poles, political exiles and Jews. Polish refugees fleeing from phases of persecution which affected their homeland, made their way to Britain after the failed revolutionary outbreaks of 1830–1, 1848, 1863–4 and 1905.[131] Russian political exiles also fled their country at the start of the twentieth century as a result of Tsarist repression including Lenin, who moved to London.[132] Over one million refugees escaped the Russian Revolution, mostly destined for France and Germany, although 15,000 entered Britain.[133] In the decades leading up to the First World War antisemitism, combined with a deterioration in living conditions, sent about 2.5 million Jews westwards out of the Pale of Settlement, mostly destined for America. Jews faced restrictions upon residence and quotas upon employment in the professions while murderous pogroms broke out in 1881, 1903 and 1905. This persecution combined with population growth and the emancipation of the serfs who moved to the towns where Jews concentrated, resulting in a pressure upon urban resources, created the desire to move to already established Jewish communities further west.[134] The westward movement of Jews before the First World War illustrates the complexity of refugee movements.

Smaller groups also fled more obvious political persecution before 1945. For instance, several hundred Italians arrived following the failure of the 1821–2 and 1831 revolutions on the peninsula, while others fled the suppression of the 1848 revolutions, together with French and Hungarians. As many as 7,000 refugees may have lived in Britain in the early 1850s.[135] French refugees also arrived after the suppression of the Paris Commune in 1871.[136] Although several hundred thousand Spaniards fled the Civil War in their country, only about 4,000 Basque refugee children made it to Britain.[137]

Many of the major refugee movements of the post-war period have taken place against the background of the onset and thawing of the Cold War, although the limited movement towards Britain indicates the role played by connections with the destination. In 1945 'Europe choked with refugees'[138] as the Nazi Empire unravelled itself. From 1944 to the early 1950s, a series of migratory streams fled across Europe in different directions counting as many as 25 million people between 1945 and 1947,[139] with Germany as the focus. Under such circumstances it seems almost inevitable that some of these refugees would make their way towards Britain. In fact the 250,000 who arrived in the country partly did so as a result of a government decision to recruit people from the continent to help in the rebuilding of war torn Britain. One group consisted of the Polish Army and Government in Exile. They found themselves stationed in Britain during the War, but had no desire to return to a Poland taken over by the Soviet Union. The Polish Resettlement Act allowed them and their families to remain.[140] The arrival of around 90,000 'displaced persons' in Britain at the end of the 1940s took place as a result of direct recruitment of foreign labour from the camps of Europe, against the background fear of expansion of Soviet rule.[141]

The Cold War freeze actually meant that global refugee movements remained fairly small from the end of the 1940s until the 1970s. Soviet repression against Hungary in 1956 and Czechoslovakia in 1968 sent smaller numbers to Britain.[142] Until the 1980s the other refugees who progressed to Britain did so against the background of the unravelling of the European

FIGURE 4 Hungarians in Britain, 1956 (Corbis)

colonial empires and the ethnic unmixing which occurred. Interestingly, the partition of India in 1947 and the thirteen million refugees which it created[143] did not result in direct migration towards Britain. However, the legacy of Empire played a role in the movement of Ugandan Asians to Britain, as Idi Amin tried to eliminate people who had moved from India to the part of Africa which he controlled, from the nineteenth century.[144] The flight of about 12,000 Greek Cypriots to Britain in 1974 took place against the background of an ethnic cleansing which would see the Greek population of the north of the island moving south while the Turks moved north, part of the unravelling of both the Ottoman and British administrations which had controlled the island since the sixteenth century.[145] Cold War and imperial legacy (French, US and Soviet) came together to send hundreds of thousands of 'boat people' away from Vietnam during the 1970s, of whom about 15,000 moved to Britain.[146] The only other significant, but unrelated, group to progress to Britain before the 1980s consisted of Chileans fleeing repression by the Pinochet government.[147] New streams arriving during the 1980s included Iranians escaping the fallout from the revolution and Sri Lankan Tamils, fleeing ethnic conflict in their homeland.[148]

The Cold War thaw played a large role in the emergence of a global refugee crisis during the 1990s. The so-called 'End of History' did not result in a liberal paradise[149] but in reborn nationalisms intent on ethnic purification. The number of 'people of concern' to the UNHCR had risen from about two million in 1975 to 27 million by 1995.[150] Much of the movement towards Britain came from Eastern Europe following the collapse of the Soviet Union, but other flows have come from Africa and the Middle East. Despite the global figures and the mass hysteria which greeted their arrival, only 70,405 people applied for asylum in Britain between 1990 and 2000. A total of 48,855 had their cases turned down.[151]

The role and attractions of Britain

The discrepancy between the global number of refugees and those entering Britain during the 1990s points not only to the existence of a profoundly xenophobic strand in British media and society[152] but also to the need of a direct connection with Britain for significant movement to take place. Despite the underlying changes which have occurred globally over the past two centuries, only a small percentage of migrants have moved towards Britain. The specific attractions and role of the country therefore need consideration under two specific headings: the strength of the British economy; and the role of immigration policy.

As the 'first industrial nation',[153] Britain always had the potential to attract migrants to man the economy which has emerged and sustained the country since the beginning of the nineteenth century. The need to rebuild after the Second World War created a greater demand for foreign labour. By the beginning of the twenty-first century, despite the decline of British industry and the change to a service economy, the country still had a need for foreign labour.[154]

Economic strength has meant that Britain has remained one of the wealthiest countries in the world over the past two hundred years particularly when examined in relation to many of the areas from which migrants have originated. To give just one example from the post-war period, in 1967 per capita GNP stood at $125 in Pakistan, $250 in Jamaica and $1,977 in the UK.[155] In his pioneering study of the Pakistani community in Britain Muhamad Anwar asked 103 people why they migrated, of whom 81 gave economic reasons, whether 'to get work and earn money' or 'to have a better future for the children and the family'.[156] A focus on the middle of the nineteenth century displays similar motivation. An account of the German community of London from 1881 claimed that many migrants held a perception of a 'rich England, where money lies on the street'. Newcomers would spend several days in hotels upon arrival while orientating themselves and then begin their search for permanent employment and accommodation.[157]

A series of scholars have addressed the relationship between the British economy and the migration of Irish people to Britain during the nineteenth century. This community could move from economic insecurity in their homeland to at least the opportunity of employment in London, Lancashire, Yorkshire, the north-east or Scotland, even though they often found themselves living and working in difficult conditions.[158] J. A. Jackson wrote that 'The existence of a large pool of cheap labour at a time of national expansion abroad proved an essential ingredient to the rapid industrial advance'.[159] Similarly, Robert Miles believed that 'Irish labour was a crucial component of capitalist development' focusing especially upon the west of Scotland where he asserts that 'it is difficult to see how capitalist industrialization could have happened at the scale and speed that it did without Irish labour'.[160] On the other hand, Jeffrey Williamson claims that between the 1820s and the 1860s 'The Irish were too small to matter much'.[161] But Irish migrants also played a significant role as agricultural labourers during the nineteenth century.[162]

Until the twentieth century no direct connection appears to exist between big business, government and the migration of workers towards Britain, a situation which would change, as immigration policy increasingly evolved according to the needs of the British economy. This becomes clear during the First World War, when military conscription left gaps in the labour market.[163] Peter Cahalan wrote, 'But for self-interest the British record on Belgian refugees might have been less generous. The shipment of refugees from Holland was essentially part of British economic policy rather than an exercise in philanthropy'.[164] The Black population also grew during the course of the First World War, especially in the area of shipping and munitions work.[165] The labour needs of the Second World War economy resulted in increasingly direct labour recruitment, including that of Irish people and West Indians. Although the British government initially imposed restrictions on travel between Britain and Ireland after the outbreak of the conflict, the development of manpower shortages in Britain and increased unemployment in Ireland meant that the Ministry of Labour and the Irish Department of Industry and Commerce signed an agreement to facilitate the movement of Irish workers to Britain.[166] Meanwhile, the Colonial Office and the Ministry of Labour made efforts to recruit West Indian workers, many of whom worked in munitions.[167]

The actions of the Ministry of Labour during the Second World War acted as a precedent, followed during the late 1940s and beyond and indicating co-operation between industry and the state. This becomes most obvious in the immediate post-war period with the recruitment of so-called European Volunteer Workers. Interviewers from the Ministry of Labour visited European Displaced Persons camps in order to recruit potential employees in good working health for a restricted range of industries with shortages including the National Health Service, farming, coal mining and textile production.[168]

The continuing strength of the British economy played a role in the development of immigration. The 1962 Commonwealth Immigrants Act, despite its exclusion of immigrants from beyond Europe, still introduced a work permit (or voucher) system allowing the entry of people in shortage areas.[169] Entry into the country would decline during the 1970s and 1980s at a time of high unemployment, but at the beginning of the twenty-first century, immigration had become a tenet of government policy, reflecting the health of the British economy, labour shortages and, perhaps, an increasing acceptance of migration.[170]

While the British state has assisted industry, big business did not play the sort of role in direct recruitment that it did on the continent. In the German case, for instance, firms who needed labour would apply to the Federal Labour Office, which set up offices in countries from where recruitment would take place and interviewed potential employees.[171] However, some active recruitment did take place in the British case. For instance, in the second half of 1946 the Ministry of Labour persuaded 2,200 Irishmen to move to Britain to work in coalmining. The following year 29,000 received assistance to migrate for work in agriculture, mining, and nursing. Active assistance declined as migration took on a life of its own because of the job opportunities available in an expanding economy.[172] But the Ministry of Labour also initiated schemes to recruit Italians to work in specific occupations including the Welsh metal working industries and coalmining and brick making in Bedford and Peterborough, which played a large role in the development of the Italian communities in these towns. Altogether, around 15,000 Italians moved into the brick industry in this way, joined by their families.[173] Taking the period 1946–53 collectively 228,000 Europeans and their families with work permits entered Britain from the European continent.[174]

While migration from the Caribbean does not appear to have directly involved the Ministry of Labour, its representatives, together with others from the Colonial Office met the 417 people who travelled on the *Empire Windrush* in June 1948 in order 'to do everything in their power to help the men find employment as quickly as possible'.[175] Some direct recruitment took place in the West Indies involving large companies such as British Rail, London Transport, the National Health Service and the British Hotels and Restaurants Association, although it proves difficult to establish the number of people who migrated because of such efforts.[176] Interestingly, despite the focus of many scholars upon the importance of personal contacts, 'there is a consistent correlation between migration from the Caribbean and labour shortage in Britain during the 1950s and early 1960s' increasing in the boom years of 1951, 1955, 1960 and 1965 and bottoming out in the 'recession' years of 1953, 1958, 1962 and 1967. In addition, movement from South Asia to Britain showed 'similar but weaker correlations with British conditions'.[177]

Moving to the beginning of the twenty-first century, the migration of Poles and, in fact, other Europeans to Britain reveals a similar link with the British economy. Travelling to a country with liberal employment policies and a steady rate of economic growth hundreds of thousands of Polish people left a country with lower standards of living because of the higher pay available, even though they often took on employment below their educational standards.[178]

The economic causation of migration to Britain during both the nineteenth and twentieth centuries fits into theorizing carried out by scholars (often with Marxist roots), which evolved during the 1970s. Although such ideas revolved around the concept of movement from undeveloped regions to the wealthier economies of the USA and Europe, most of them recognized the subtlety of factors involved in the evolution of mass migration during the nineteenth and twentieth centuries.[179]

The wealth of Britain and the strength of the British economy has clearly acted as a central factor in attracting people over the past two centuries, a fact recognized by British governments who have largely attempted to control the flow of newcomers by the use of immigration policy. A summary of the role of the state since the late eighteenth century would suggest a generally *laissez-faire* approach from the end of the French Revolutionary period until the late Victorian period. Since that time, the British state, influenced by a combination of a xenophobic and racist public opinion, whipped up by right-wing newspapers and populist politicians, together with a desire to meet the labour needs of the British economy, has, beginning with the Aliens Act of 1905, passed a series of nationality and immigration laws to placate the racists and meet the needs of the British economy.

Contemporary immigration control in Britain therefore essentially begins in 1905. As Bernard Porter pointed out, 'from 1826 until 1848 and again from 1850 to 1905, there was nothing on the statute book to enable the executive to prevent aliens from coming and staying in Britain as they liked . . . This freedom of entry applied to all foreigners, whether refugees or not, and for whatever reason they desired entry'.[180] Although immigration and aliens control may have become particularly tight and obsessive by the beginning of the twenty-first century, the Victorian *laissez-faire* period remains somewhat unusual. As scholars such as T. W. E. Roche, Vaughan Bevan and Thomas Perry have demonstrated, aliens control remained important in the evolution of the British state from the Middle Ages.[181] The explanations for the free movement of people into and out of Britain for much of the nineteenth century include the relative prosperity of the mid-Victorian period, which would come under threat with the Great Depression of the late nineteenth century,[182] coinciding with the campaign for the Aliens Act of 1905. Just as importantly, the Edwardian years and, more especially, the First World War, signified the end of state *laissez-faire* attitudes, after which would follow the increasing intrusion of government in all aspects of the lives of its citizens, perhaps most symbolically indicated by the introduction of conscription in 1916.[183]

The relatively relaxed attitudes of the mid-Victorian years partly resulted from the political security of the period. Unlike its continental neighbours, which intervened to a far greater extent in the lives of their citizens,[184] Britain remained free from serious fears of invasion or domestic revolution. The introduction of immigration legislation occurred when this peace and security came under threat. The Alien Act of 1793 and a series of measures which followed it controlling the entry and residence of foreigners, as well as giving power of deportation, came into operation with Britain at war.[185] Similarly, the Act passed in 1848 to control entry of aliens came at a time of revolutionary upheaval on the continent.[186] While it may seem tempting to suggest the small scale of immigration into Britain as a reason for the lack of control, this ignores one of the biggest 'refugee' crises of modern Britain following the Irish famine, when local councils, especially in Liverpool, came under intense pressure, but when movement from Ireland to the mainland remained free, despite complaints from local authorities.[187]

The template for the history of British immigration control arrives with the Aliens Act of 1905. Like similar pieces of legislation which would follow, a campaign proceeded it, on this occasion essentially focusing upon the immigration of poor eastern European Jews into the East End of London.[188] Although its terms remained quite limited, it acted as a deterrent for further prospective immigrants.[189] But it was a 'watershed for aliens entry' as it had breached the 'liberal tradition of most of the nineteenth century'.[190]

The obsessive Germanophobia and more general rise in anti-alienism of the First World War resulted in the passage of new measures, most importantly the Aliens Restriction Act of 1914 and the Aliens Act of 1919. The former focused upon the German community in Britain and did not prevent the entry of the Belgian refugees. The 1919 Act, passed in the anti-alien hysteria at the end of the First World War, gave the Home Secretary power to introduce Orders in Council to control any aspect of immigration. The Order of 1920 required all immigrants to obtain work permits and forbade anyone who could not support themselves from entering the country.

The 1919 Act largely helps to explain the absence of refugees during the 1920s, despite the millions created by the Russian Revolution and Armenian genocide.[191] The situation changed during the 1930s, especially with regard to Jewish refugees, whose numbers increased as the Second World War approached, owing to an easing of government policy. While only 11,000 had entered by 1938, the *Kristallnacht* pogrom meant the arrival of another 55,000. Older interpretations, such as that of A. J. Sherman stressed the generosity of Britain in relation to other European nation states. Louise London and Tony Kushner have pointed to the fact that specific schemes operated to allow refugees into the country, including 20,000 who entered as domestic servants and almost ten thousand children who would never see their parents again.[192]

The British Nationality Act of 1948 created a single British citizenship for Britain and the Empire, allowing both to reside and work in Britain. The Act represents the legislative basis of the creation of 'multicultural Britain', even though it did not have this as its aim. It acted as a facilitator for Commonwealth migration to Britain, which a series of local and personal factors turned into reality. However, by the 1950s a campaign against the arrival of West Indians in Britain emerged, culminating in the 1958 Nottingham and Notting Hill riots and leading to the passage of the 1962 Commonwealth Immigrants Act. This withdrew the right of those with Imperial or Commonwealth citizenship to reside in Britain unless they could obtain a work permit, therefore essentially subjecting such people to the same restrictions on entry as foreigners under the 1919 Aliens Act. However, loopholes remained, exposed by the fact that East African Asians holding British passports moved to Britain during the 1960s against the background of Africanization policies. Once again, the British government surrendered to racism by passing the Commonwealth Immigrants Act of 1968 and the Immigration Act of 1971, which restricted the right to reside in Britain to those who had at least one grandparent born in the country, which therefore excluded non-whites while including the offspring of those who had recently emigrated. There followed the British Nationality Act of 1981, which effectively repealed that of 1948.[193]

The legislation introduced from the early 1960s until the 1980s did not deal with another form of uncontrolled migration in an era in which the state spread its tentacles into more and more aspects of life.[194] This consisted of refugees. During the course of the 1990s, as their numbers increased, they became 'asylum seekers' because the state, egged on by the press, increasingly decided that they should prove their refugee status under the 1951 UN Convention. Consequently, a series of measures followed during the 1990s to control their numbers and their lives in Britain, crowned with a Blair Government White Paper in 2002 entitled *Secure Borders, Safe Haven*. The legislation of these years, reacting to pressure from local government and the local and national press, attempted to disperse refugees away from London and the South East to the rest of the country.

Bizarrely, it also prevented asylum seekers from working, which caused most resentment, as they became stereotyped as 'scroungers'.[195] This bizarreness becomes apparent against the background of the acknowledgement of the British government in 2000 that the economy depended upon migrant labour.[196] But, since the Second World War, and in common with the rest of Europe, successive regimes wanted immigrants with the right racial stock and economic productivity.[197] While the state increasingly blocked arrivals from beyond Europe, the entry of Britain into the European Union in 1974 meant that it accepted the free movement of labour. This became most apparent in 2004, when, unlike most other EU members, Britain allowed the entry of nationals from the new accession states, above all Poland.[198] Just as importantly, immigration controls in Britain since the 1960s have failed to exclude illegal immigrants,[199] whose numbers may now stand at hundreds of thousands.[200]

Local and personal factors

Stephen Castles has used the rise of illegal immigration globally to demonstrate the ineffectiveness of migration policies, especially against the background of inequalities between the north and south of the globe.[201] In the British case, especially in the post-war period, we cannot dismiss controls as they have played a significant role in determining the countries and regions of origins of newcomers. Castles, in his volume with Mark J. Miller, has also pointed to migration systems theory to explain flows throughout the world. This approach recognizes 'the existence of prior links between sending and receiving countries based on colonization, political influence, trade, investment or cultural ties'. Castles and Miller argue that, upon these 'macro-structures', we need to impose micro or personal factors.[202]

This approach certainly helps us to better understand movement to Britain over the past two centuries. Our narrative has so far considered many of the macro-factors in the form of demographic change, availability of transportation, economic growth and the influence of immigration laws. An examination of the main streams of migration to Britain over the past 200 years demonstrates the importance of the existence of prior links, especially in terms of colonialism. Imperial connections played a role in sending millions of people and a wide range of groups to Britain not only from the obvious origins of South Asia and the West Indies since 1945, but also Ireland throughout our period and a whole series of smaller British colonies after 1945. In addition, 'political influence' also helps to explain EU migration. Just as importantly, connections with Britain would also serve as the basis for the vast numbers of foreign soldiers stationed upon British soil or fighting with Britain since the French Revolutionary and Napoleonic Wars, whether they originate in Ireland, Africa, the West Indies, China, India or the USA.[203] Another important, but obvious, factor here consists of geographical proximity, which largely helps to explain the fact that most movement to Britain before 1945 originated from Europe.

But whatever structural, macro and geopolitical factors may exist, scholars have increasingly recognized that migration has personal motivations. These include family reunification (traditionally viewed as chain migration), movements from specific regions, as well as distinct forms of labour recruitment. If placed under the microscope all groups and individuals demonstrate personal motivation.

The recently developed historiography of the nineteenth-century German community in Britain has recognized the importance of personal influences in the evolution of this community or, more accurately, communities. Rosemary Ashton's *Little Germany* examined refugee groups which emerged in London from the 1830s until the 1850s. The people involved fled from a politically repressive Germany to an England which allowed much greater personal and political freedom. While some individuals had already moved to Britain from the 1830s, others followed after the failure of the 1848 Revolutions. As had happened in Germany, the revolutionaries divided according to their political beliefs, ranging from communists to liberals.[204]

These revolutionaries had a politically motivated reason for moving to Britain. In addition, migrants originated from specific parts of Germany, especially, in the middle of the nineteenth century, Hanover or Hesse.

The former appears to have sent people since the unification of Hanover with Britain during the eighteenth century. The second probably evolved as a result of the settlement of transmigrants on their way to the USA in specific locations. However, much German migration to Britain during the nineteenth century had close connections with the recruitment practices of particular occupations, based especially upon London. Thus, sugar-baking in the East End of London from the late eighteenth until the middle of the nineteenth century involved the migration of males especially from Hanover to work in this particularly difficult employment. In this case we can identify an area of origin, a point of settlement and a specific occupation. Other German occupations reveal similar, if not such precise, patterns. For instance, fifty per cent of foreign correspondence clerks in Britain between 1900 and 1914 consisted of Germans filling a skills gap because of the lack of language training of Britons. Similarly, a stream of German waiters moved to Britain during the late Victorian and Edwardian years and even after the First World War. Like foreign correspondence clerks, they carried out a sort of apprenticeship, partly to increase their experience but also to improve their English in the hope that they would secure a better position when they returned to employment in Germany or another part of the continent. The growing numbers of German bakers by the outbreak of the First World War also depended upon a process of direct recruitment. Already established shopkeepers would import agricultural labourers and provide them with food and lodging for two years after which they would find another position, save money and then bring in more of their countrymen. As well as these regional and occupational groups from Germany, Ulrike Kirchberger and Stefan Manz have identified further pieces in the jigsaw of the German community in Britain. Manz, for instance, pays particular attention to businessmen and teachers at all levels from private tutors to University Professors. Kirchberger focuses upon specific German interest groups who saw business and other opportunities in the British Empire and therefore based themselves on British soil. They included missionaries and others interested in colonizing parts of the British Empire.[205]

The evolution of the nineteenth-century German population in Britain reveals the importance of networks, whether political, regional or occupational, which would mean that a series of separate German communities would develop in the land of settlement. Those scholars who have examined the movement of Italians to Britain before 1914, led by Lucio Sponza, have also revealed distinct regional origins, as well as demonstrating specific occupational importations. Placing his explanation against changing agricultural patterns, fears of military service and taxation, Sponza has nailed down the origins of most Italian immigrants in Victorian and Edwardian Britain to four areas in the Como, Parma, Lucca and Liri Valleys in central and northern Italy. He focuses especially upon the second of these, 'the Appenine region south of Parma, at the juncture of Emilia, Liguria and Tuscany', within which 'it was from the twin valleys of the rivers Taro (Valtaro, or Valditaro) and Ceno (Valceno) that the largest number of people came, especially from the former'. Those who originated in this area formed part of an occupational chain migration who worked as plaster figure makers in London.[206] Those from Parma, meanwhile, often worked as street musicians, forming part of a cycle of exploitation, as they included boys sent to London with the knowledge of their parents, who worked under a system of *padrones*, who looked after them. They would return home with some of the money they had earnt. This process would last for much of the nineteenth century.[207] The South Wales Italian community, meanwhile, originating in the late nineteenth and early twentieth centuries, also came from a similar area, particularly the town of Bardi between Parma and Genoa. Resembling the German bakers, Italian café owners recruited from this town, offering the newcomers 'a fixed contract, with food, clothes, accommodation and the price of a return fare to Italy at the end of a stipulated period of two or three years'.[208] Similarly, an examination of Italian settlement in Scotland from 1877 to 1939 reveals that the vast majority of the migrants came from four distinct provinces: one town in Lucca (Barga) actually provided 13.6 per cent of all Italians in Scotland during this period.[209]

Despite the growing Jewish historiography, we do not have the sort of detailed information on the origins of the Jewish community and their patterns of migration that exist for the evolution of the Germans and Italians before 1914. Even the micro-study of Spitalfields by Anne Kershen does not say much about the mechanics of Jewish migration to this area before the First World War.[210] Primary sources indicate the importance of networks. Adam Francoise, questioned by the Select Committee on Emigration and Immigration in 1888, stated that he originated 'three Russian miles from Memel'. Asked why he moved to England, he replied: 'I was very anxious to marry a daughter of mine, but I had no dowry for her, and someone wrote and said that if she came over and learnt some trade, she might be able to save sufficient to have a dowry'.[211]

Migration after the Second World War reveals transnationalism in operation as we can see by focusing on the Chinese, West Indians and South Asians, all of whom reveal distinct migration patterns. In fact, even before 1945 Chinese people already moved as distinct groups. These included students, and sailors serving on British ships which led to the formation of Chinese settlements in the coastal areas of Liverpool, South Wales and the East End of London.[212] The post-war community largely developed as a result of the movement of people from Hong Kong to work in the emerging restaurant trade from the 1950s onwards, replicating the patterns of Italian caterers in South Wales and German bakers before 1914. Migration from Hong Kong to Britain increased during the early 1960s due to the impending introduction of the Commonwealth Immigrants Act of 1962. A type of recruitment had developed during the 1950s, formalized in the establishment of the Association of Chinese Restaurants in 1961. Even after 1962 movement for the purpose of staffing the restaurant trade continued, as owners were allowed to import people from Hong Kong as long as they could prove both the need for them and the absence of native workers who could do the same job.[213] James L. Watson stressed the importance of kinship and lineage in the selection of immigrants, pointing to the fact that specific villages have sent people abroad in this way.[214]

Research on Caribbean migration to Britain has revealed the operation of personal motivations. Mary Chamberlain has focused upon Barbados. Recognizing the background factors involved in the migration to Britain, such as direct recruitment by British firms and the positive attitude towards emigration of the island government, she also stresses individual family histories, pointing out that the migration patterns of relatives helped to determine the decision to move.[215] Stuart Philpott, meanwhile, in his study of migration from the tiny island of Montserrat, with a population of just 14,333 in 1946, falling to 12,167 by 1960, examines in great detail the background economic factors, but also stresses family ties and the importance of a tradition of migration.[216] Similarly, Margaret Byron, in her study of movement from another small island, Nevis, to Leicester, has also stressed the importance of family ties in this specific journey.[217]

The region of the world with the greatest migration potential, especially towards Britain, because of its former colonial connections, consists of South Asia. Yet, despite a population of over one billion, which lived in the successor states to British India by the end of the twentieth century only between one and two million people have actually made the move to Britain. The various pieces of legislation passed from the 1960s clearly had a significant role to play in this small number. However, as a series of scholars have revealed, the movement of South Asians to Britain had quite distinct areas of origin. Some South Asians did not even come from India or Pakistan, but moved from Africa or the West Indies, as a result of a previous migration under the British Empire.[218] Those who came directly from South

FIGURE 5 One of 37 Indian nationals allowed to enter Britain after being detained on board a ship at Dover, 21 November 1959. Image by © Hulton-Deutsch Collection/Corbis

Asia originated from four areas in particular: the Mirpur district of Pakistan; Sylhett in Bangladesh; and Gujurat and the Punjab in India. In fact, most migrants came from specific areas within these regions. As Ceri Peach has pointed out: 'The Mirpur District of Pakistan-administered Kashmir and the nearby Chach area of Campbellpur District are thought to account for 80 per cent of the British Pakistani population. The Sylhett District accounts for over 80 per cent of the British Bangladeshi population. Jullundur District in Indian Punjab accounts for 80 per cent of British Sikhs. Gujurat state accounts for probably 70 per cent of Indian Hindus.'[219]

Gujuratis and Punjabis often came via East Africa, pointing to long term traditions of migration. Gurharpal Singh and Darshan Singh Tatla, referring specifically to the migration of the Sikh community to Britain, have even written of the development of a 'culture of migration', which they date back as far as the eighteenth century.[220] Kinship networks determined specific patterns of migration from small sub-districts of Jalandhar, which would form the basis of the Sikh community in Britain.[221]

Pakistani migration to Britain, specifically from Mirpur, evolved in a similar way. Kinship ties from particular villages determined the movement, initially of males, but increasingly, from the 1960s and especially into the 1970s, of wives and children. The initial migration of men (a pattern which applied to the other South Asian groups) who lived together, increasingly changed to family units as dependents followed their men folk.[222]

Sylhetti migration to Britain, especially East London, also has deep roots. It originated in the fact that many Sylhettis served on board British ships and would eventually find themselves in British ports by the end of the eighteenth century, a tradition which continued into the middle of the twentieth. During the 1950s and 1960s, especially before the passage of the Commonwealth Immigrants Act of 1962, increasing numbers of male Sylhettis moved to Britain, mirroring the Mirpuri pattern, subsequently followed by their families during the 1970s.[223]

The complexity of migration motivations

When Ravenstein produced his laws of migration in the 1880s[224] he attempted to simplify a complex process with a variety of causes and motivations. The movement of millions of people to Britain over two hundred years does not (as recent research, which has examined individual life journeys, has demonstrated) lend itself easily to generalizations, and certainly not to rules. Nevertheless, the above narrative has attempted to offer an explanation operating on three levels.

While underlying factors may not directly cause migration in themselves, it would prove difficult to offer a full explanation of the scale and origins of movement to Britain without taking into account some of the fundamental developments in the evolution of the modern world. Population pressure does not mean that a person born in Hesse in 1825 automatically moves to Britain twenty-five years later, but it provides a background factor, which means that he may migrate somewhere if other factors operate. One of the consequences of rapid population growth in a pre-industrial economy often consists of unemployment and poverty, which becomes an issue when knowledge of richer pastures, whether in the same country or further away, emerges. While some German migration in the nineteenth century moved to the USA, as well as to other parts of Europe, most German migrants simply moved from one part of Germany to another.[225] Similarly, the various transport revolutions over the last two centuries may not have caused migration but they have made it easier. In the case of Britain during the nineteenth century, transatlantic shipping brought transmigrants to the country, some of whom decided to stay. Finally, the most direct background factor which has caused emigration, of a forced variety, has consisted of political persecution, especially during the twentieth century.

Most of the above developments essentially constitute traditional push factors. The attractions and role of Britain mirror more traditional pull factors. The wealth of the country compared to most of the rest of the world since the industrial revolution has played a major role, whether knowledge of this feeds through as a result of networks or because of direct recruitment. British immigration policy, determined by the labour needs of the economy and pressure from a racist media and extreme right, has determined the volume and origins of migration to the country.

However, distinct specific factors, often with long historical traditions and often of a local or personal nature, have also determined why distinct groups moved to Britain. The geographical proximity of Ireland, combined with a less developed economy than England, Scotland and Wales, made migration to the these countries almost inevitable, yet, as scholars such as Collins and Delaney have demonstrated for the nineteenth and twentieth centuries respectively, networks determined areas of origin and settlement. Similarly, the imperial connection, especially after the passage of the British Nationality Act of 1948, against the background of the relative poverty of most parts of the Empire and Commonwealth, made migration possible. But scholars working on South Asian movement to Britain have demonstrated the regional, local, kinship, family and personal motivations which sent individuals to the heart of the Empire and Commonwealth.

Movement to Britain therefore needs to be understood on a variety of levels. The regional and local origins of migrants play a large role in determining the lives and identities of the newcomers once in Britain, as well as that of their children. Origins also play a significant role in residence patterns and employment. As subsequent chapters will demonstrate, the distinctiveness of migrants' origins remain with individual communities in the new environment.

Notes and references

1   Tony Kushner, *We Europeans? Mass Observation, 'Race' and British Identity in the Twentieth century* (Aldershot, 2004), pp. 111–12.

2   Rosina Visram, *Asians in Britain: 400 Years of History* (London, 2002); Peter Fryer, *Staying Power: The History of Black People in Britain* (London, 1984); Ron Ramdin, *Reimagining Britain: 500 Years of Black and Asian History* (London, 1999).

3   Michael H. Fisher, *Counterflows to Colonialism: Indian Travellers and Settlers in Britain, 1600–1857* (Delhi, 2004), p. 384; J. P. May, 'The Chinese in Britain', in Colin Holmes, ed., *Immigrants and Minorities in British Society* (London, 1978), pp. 111–24; Fryer, ibid., pp. 237–97.

4   Panikos Panayi, 'Cosmopolis: London's Ethnic Minorities', in Andrew Gibson and Joe Kerr, eds, *London from Punk to Blair* (London, 2003), pp. 67–71.

5   Donald M. MacRaild, *Irish Migrants in Modern Britain, 1750–1922* (Basingstoke, 1999), p. 33.

6   Dudley Baines, *Emigration from Europe 1815–1930* (London, 1991), p. 9.

7   See, for instance, D. Morgan, *Harvesters and Harvesting, 1840–1900* (London, 1982), pp. 76–87; Sarah Barber, 'Irish Migrant Agricultural Labourers in Nineteenth Century Lincolnshire', *Saothar*, vol. 8 (1982), pp. 10–23; B. M. Kerr, 'Irish Seasonal Migration to Great Britain, 1800–38', *Irish Historical Studies*, vol. 3 (1942–3), pp. 365–80.

8   MacRaild, *Irish Migrants*, pp. 10, 33; C. Ó Gráda, 'A Note on Nineteenth Century Irish Emigration Statistics', *Population Studies*, vol. 29 (1975), pp. 143–9; Enda Delaney, *Demography, State and Society* (Liverpool, 2000), pp. 45, 130.

9   Panikos Panayi, *German Immigrants in Britain during the Nineteenth Century, 1815–914* (Oxford, 1995), pp. 83–7; Leonard Schapiro, 'The Russian Background of the Anglo-American Jewish Immigration', *Transactions of the Jewish Historical Society of England*, vol. 20 (1959–60), pp. 215–22; V. D. Lipman, *A History of the Jews in Britain Since 1858* (Leicester, 1990), pp. 12–13; Todd M. Endelman, *The Jews of Britain, 1656–2000* (London, 2002), 79–81.

10   W. D. Rubinstein, *A History of the Jews in the English Speaking World: Great Britain* (Basingstoke, 1996), p. 95.

11   Tony Kushner and Katherine Knox, *Refugees in an Age of Genocide: Global, National and Local Perspectives During the Twentieth Century* (London, 1999), pp. 44–7, 64–100.

12   Herbert A. Strauss, 'Jewish Emigration in the Nazi Period: Some Aspects of Acculturation', in Werner E. Mosse, et al., eds, *Second Chance: Two Centuries of German-Speaking Jews in the United Kingdom* (Tübingen, 1991), p. 83.

13   Louise London, *Whitehall and the Jews, 1933–1948: British Immigration Policy and the Holocaust* (Cambridge, 2000), pp. 11–12.

14   Ibid.

15   David Cesarani, *Justice Delayed: How Britain Became a Refuge for Nazi War Criminals* (London, 1992), pp. 77–80.

16   Bernard Wasserstein, *Vanishing Diaspora: The Jews of Europe Since 1945* (London, 1996), p. 73; *Jewish Chronicle*, 18 May 2007.

17   Wasserstein, ibid., pp. 91–2.

18   Panikos Panayi, *The Enemy in Our Midst: Germans in Britain during the First World War* (Oxford, 1991), p. 1.

19   Ulrike Kirchberger, *Aspekte deutsch-britischer Expansion: Die Überseeinteressen der deutschen Migranten in Großbritannien in der Mitte des 19. Jahrhunderts* (Stuttgart, 1999), pp. 32–41.

20   But see the discussion on numbers in Stefan Manz, *Migranten und Internierte: Deutsche in Glasgow, 1864–1918* (Stuttgart, 2003), pp. 13–44.

21   See James J. and Patience P. Barnes, 'London's German Community in the Early 1930's', in Panikos Panayi, ed., *Germans in Britain Since 1500* (London, 1996), pp. 131–46.

22   Marion Berghahn, *German-Jewish Refugees from Nazi Germany* (Oxford, 1988).

23   Nicholas Atkin, *The Forgotten French: Exiles in the British Isles* (Manchester, 2003), pp. 187–94; Terri Colpi, *The Italian Factor: The Italian Community in Great Britain* (Edinburgh, 1991), pp. 48, 72.

24   *Census of England and Wales 1931: General Tables* (London, 1935), p. 221; *Census of Scotland 1931: Report of the Fourteenth Census of Scotland*, vol. 2 (Edinburgh, 1993), p. 112.

25   David Reynolds, *Rich Relations: The American Occupation of Britain 1942–45* (London, 1995).

26   Fisher, Lahiri and Thandi, *South Asian History of Britain*, pp. 47–157; May, 'Chinese in Britain', pp. 111–24; Fryer, *Staying Power*, pp. 237–67; K. C. Ng, *The Chinese in London* (London, 1968), pp. 5–7.

27   Sabine Freitag, ed., *Exiles from European Revolutions: Refugees in Mid-Victorian England* (Oxford, 2003).

28   M. J. Proudfoot, *European Refugees, 1939–52* (London, 1957), pp. 71–2.

29   Kushner and Knox, *Refugees*, p. 48; Peter Cahalan, *Belgian Refugee Relief in England during the Great War* (New York, 1982), pp. 1, 448.

30   See, for instance, Visram, *Asians in Britain*, pp. 54–63.

31   Baines, *Emigration from Europe*, p. 9.

32   Charlotte Erickson, *Leaving England: Essays on British Emigration in the Nineteenth Century* (London, 1994).

33   Delaney, *Demography*, p. 264.

34   *Census of England and Wales 1931: General Tables*, p. 221; *Census of Scotland 1931*, p. 112.

35   Enda Delaney, *The Irish in Post-war Britain* (Oxford, 2007), pp. 63–70.

36 Brendan Halpern, 'Who are the Irish in Britain? Evidence from Large-Scale Surveys', in Andy Bielenberg, ed., *The Irish Diaspora* (London, 2000), p. 89.

37 Keith Sword, Norman Davies and Jan Ciechanowski, *The Formation of the Polish Community in Great Britain* (London, 1989).

38 Diana Kay and Robert Miles, *Refugees or Migrant Workers? European Volunteer Workers in Britain* (London, 1992).

39 Kushner and Knox, *Refugees*, pp. 241–61.

40 Panikos Panayi, 'Refugees in Twentieth century Britain: A Brief History', in Vaughan Robinson, ed., *The International Refugee Crisis: British and Canadian Responses* (London, 1993), p. 105.

41 Kathy Burrell, 'War, Cold War and the New World Order: Political Borders and Polish Migration to Britain', 'History in Focus', Issue 11, http://www.history/ ac.uk/ihr/Focus/Migration/articles/burrell.html. See also Krystyna Iglicka, *Poland's Post-war Dynamic of Migration* (Aldershot, 2001), pp. 42–3, 100.

42 Kushner and Knox, *Refugees*, pp. 355–74.

43 Home Office, Department of Work and Pensions, H. M. Revenue and Customs and Department for Communities and Local Government, 'Accession Monitoring Report, May 2004–June 2006'; Kathy Burrell, 'Introduction: Migration to the UK from Poland: Continuity and Change in East-West Mobility', in Kathy Burrell, ed., *Polish Migration to the UK in the 'New' Europe After 2004* (Farnham, 2009), pp. 1–11.

44 Vic George and Geoffrey Millerson, 'The Cypriot Community in London', *Race*, vol. 8 (1967), p. 277; Panayi, 'Refugees', p. 107.

45 Geoff Dench, *Maltese in London: A Case Study in the Erosion of Ethnic Consciousness* (London, 1975), p. 28.

46 Lucio Sponza, 'Italians in War and Post-war Britain', in Johannes Dieter-Steinert and Inge Weber-Newth, eds, *European Immigrants in Britain* (Munich, 2003), p. 189.

47 Colpi, *Italian Factor*, p. 135.

48 Kathy Burrell, *Moving Lives: Narratives of Nation and Migration among Europeans in Post-war Britain* (Aldershot, 2006), p. 8.

49 See 2001 Census.

50 Johannes-Dieter Steinert and Inge Weber-Newth, *Labour and Love: Deutsche in Großbritannien nach dem Zweiten Weltkrieg* (Osnabrück, 2000), pp. 46, 62, 116.

51 Ceri Peach, 'Empire, Economy, and Immigration: Britain 1850–2000', in Paul Slack and Ryk Ward, eds, *The Peopling of Britain: The Shaping of a Human Landscape* (Oxford, 2002), p. 269.

52 See the 2001 Census.

53 Arnold R. Watson, *West Indian Workers in Britain* (London, 1942); Margaret Byron, *Post-war Caribbean Migration to Britain: The Unfinished Cycle* (Aldershot, 1994), p. 77.

54 Byron, ibid., p. 78; 2001 Census.

55 Byron, ibid., pp. 79, 171.

56 Ibid., p. 80.

57 Ng, *Chinese in London*, p. 2; James L. Watson, 'The Chinese: Hong Kong Villagers in the British Catering Trade', in Watson, ed., *Between Two Cultures: Migrants and Minorities in Britain* (Oxford, 1977), p. 182.

58 Ceri Peach, 'South Asian Migration and Settlement in Great Britain, 1951–2001', *Contemporary South Asia*, vol. 15 (2006), pp. 134–6; Peach, 'Empire', p. 269.

59 Peach, 'Empire', p. 269; 2001 Census; Dylan Nichols, *What Are You Doing Here? The Question of Australians in London* (Brighton, 2007); Alice Bloch, 'Zimbabweans in Britain: Transnational Activities and Capabilities', *Journal of Ethnic and Migration Studies*, vol. 34 (2008), pp. 287–305; David Conradson and Alan Latham, 'Friendship, Networks and Transnationality in a World City: Antipodean Transmigrants in London', *Journal of Ethnic and Migration Studies*, vol. 31 (2005), pp. 287–305; Kristine Krause, 'Transnational Therapy Networks Among Ghanaians in London', *Journal of Ethnic and Migration Studies*, vol. 34 (2008), pp. 235–7.

60 Kushner and Knox, *Refugees*, pp. xv, 289–354, 375–95; Panayi, 'Refugees', pp. 107–8; Alice Bloch, *The Migration and Settlement of Refugees in Britain* (Basingstoke, 2002), p. 45; Kathy Spellman, *Religion and Nation: Iranian Local and Transnational Networks in Britain* (Oxford, 2004), p. 38.

61 JoAnn McGregor, ' "Joining the BBC (British Bottom Cleaners)": Zimbabwean Migrants and the UK Care Industry', *Journal of Ethnic and Migration Studies*, vol. 33 (2007), p. 805.

62 Fred Halliday, *Arabs in Exile: Yemeni Migrants in Urban Britain* (London, 1992), pp. 4–5.

63 Peach, 'Empire', p. 269; 2001 Census.

64 E. G. Ravenstein, 'The Laws of Migration', *Journal of the Royal Statistical Society*, vols 48 and 52 (1885 and 1888).

65 See, for instance: Ian R. G. Spencer, *British Immigration Policy: The Making of Multi-Racial Britain* (London, 1997); Kathleen Paul, *Whitewashing Britain: Race and Citizenship in the Post-war Era* (Ithaca, NY, 1997); Randall Hansen, *Citizenship and Immigration in Post-war Britain* (Oxford, 2000); James Hampshire, *Citizenship and Belonging: Immigration and the Politics of Demographic Governance in Post-war Britain* (Basingstoke, 2005).

66 Bernard Gainer, *The Alien Invasion: The Origins of the Aliens Act of 1905* (London, 1972); Bernard Porter, *The Refugee Question in Mid-Victorian Politics*

(Cambridge, 1979); Andreas Fahrmeier, *Citizens and Aliens: Foreigners and the Law in Britain and the German States, 1789–1870* (Oxford, 2000); Vaughan Bevan, *The Development of British Immigration Law* (London, 1986); London, *Whitehall and the Jews*.

67 Mary Chamberlain, *Narratives of Exile and Return* (London, 1997); Katy Gardner, *Age, Narrative and Migration: The Life Course of Bengali Elders in London* (Oxford, 2002); Burrell, *Moving Lives*.

68 Burrell, ibid., p. 25.

69 Chamberlain, *Narratives*, p. 5.

70 Enda Delaney, 'Transnationalism, Networks and Emigration from Post-war Ireland', *Immigrants and Minorities*, vol. 23 (2005), pp. 425–9.

71 Kathleen Neils Conzen, *Immigrant Milwaukee, 1836–1860: Accommodation in a Frontier City* (London, 1976), pp. 34–42. Delaney, ibid., pp. 428–9, analyses the newness of the transnational approach.

72 The circumstantial evidence consists of marriage registers and records of those assisted by charitable organizations in mid-nineteenth century London for which see Panayi, *German Immigrants*, p. 57.

73 Klaus J. Bade, *Migration in European History* (Oxford, 2003).

74 See, for example, Dirk Hoerder, *Labor Migration in the Atlantic Economies: The European and North American Working Classes during the Period of Industrialization* (London, 1985).

75 Stephen Castles and Mark J. Miller, *The Age of Migration: International Population Movements in the Modern World*, 3rd edn (Basingstoke, 2003).

76 Michael R. Marrus, *The Unwanted: European Refugees in the Twentieth Century* (Oxford, 1985).

77 See, for instance: Bade, *Migration in European History*; Dirk Hoerder and Leslie Page Moch, eds, *European Migrants: Global and Local Perspectives* (Boston, MA, 1996); Leslie Page Moch, *Moving Europeans: Migration in Western Europe Since 1650*, 2nd Edn (Bloomington and Indiana, 2003); Panikos Panayi, *Outsiders: A History of European Minorities* (London, 1999).

78 See, for instance, Massimo Livi-Bacci, *A Concise History of World Population*, 2nd Edn (Oxford, 1977); Ray Hall, 'Stabilizing Population Growth: The European Experience', in Philip Sarre and John Blanden eds, *An Overcrowded World? Population, Resources and the Environment* (Oxford, 2000), pp. 109–60; http://www.un.org/esa/population/publications/sixbillion/sixbillion.htm, UN Department of Economics and Social Affairs, Population Division, 'The World at Six Billion'.

79 See the classic, D. V. Glass, *Population Policies and Movements in Europe* (London, 1940).

80 Brenda Collins, 'The Origins of Irish Immigration to Scotland in the Nineteenth and Twentieth Centuries', in T. M. Devine, ed., *Irish Immigrants and Scottish Cities in the Nineteenth and Twentieth Centuries* (Edinburgh, 1991), p. 2.

81 John E. Knodel, *The Decline of Fertility in Germany, 1871–1939* (Princeton, 1974), p. 32.

82 Luigi di Comite, 'Aspects of Italian Emigration, 1881–1915', in Ira D. Glazier and Luigi De Roza, eds, *Migration Across Time and Nations: Population Mobility in Historical Context* (London, 1986), p. 150.

83 Salo W. Baron, *The Russian Jew Under Tsars and Soviets* (London, 1964), p. 76.

84 Panayi, *German Immigrants*, pp. 38–9.

85 See contributions to Klaus J. Bade, ed., *Population, Labour and Migration in 19th and 20th Century Germany* (Leamington Spa, 1987).

86 George and Millerson, 'Cypriot Community', p. 278; Floya Anthias, *Ethnicity, Class, Gender and Migration: Greek Cypriots in Britain* (Aldershot, 1992), pp. 6–7.

87 There is a large literature on the role of population growth in the Caribbean summarized by Lorna Chessum, *From Immigrants to Ethnic Minority: Making Black Community in Britain* (Aldershot, 2000), pp. 26–30.

88 See contributions to Bade, *Population, Labour and Migration.*

89 Clive, Trebilcock, *The Industrialization of the Continental Powers, 1780–1914* (London, 1981).

90 Stephen Castles, et al., *Here for Good: Western Europe's New Ethnic Minorities* (London, 1984); Timothy J. Hatton and Jeffrey G. Williamson, *The Age of Mass Migration: Causes and Economic Impact* (Oxford, 1998).

91 Walter D. Kamphoefner, 'At the Crossroads of Economic Development: Background Factors Affecting Emigration from Nineteenth Century Germany', in Glazier and De Roza, *Migration Across Time*, pp. 174–201; Brenda Collins, 'Proto-Industrialization and Pre-Famine Emigration', *Social History*, vol. 7 (1982), pp. 127–46.

92 Frank Neal, 'South Wales, the Coal Trade and the Irish Famine Refugee Crisis', in Paul O'Leary, ed., *Irish Migrants in Modern Wales* (Liverpool, 2004), pp. 9–33.

93 Frank Neal, *Black '47: Britain and the Irish Famine* (Basingstoke, 1998), pp. 123–56.

94 This figure is from Lynn Hollen Lees, *Exiles of Erin: Irish Immigrants in Victorian London* (Manchester, 1979), p. 39.

95 MacRaild, *Irish Migrants*, p. 32.

96 Lees, *Exiles of Erin*, p. 39.

97 Ruth-Ann Harris, *The Nearest Place that Wasn't Ireland: Early Nineteenth Century Irish Labour Migration* (Ames, IO, 1994), pp. 188–9.

98 Panayi, *German Immigrants*, pp. 42–3.

99   Simon Taylor, *A Land of Dreams: A Study of Jewish and Caribbean Migrant Communities in England* (London, 1993), pp. 87–90.

100 The document entitled 'Unemployment in the West Indies' is quoted in Panikos Panayi, *The Impact of Immigration: A Documentary History of the Effects and Experiences of Immigrants and Refugees in Britain Since 1945* (Manchester, 1999), pp. 38–40.

101 Panikos Panayi, *Spicing Up Britain: The Multicultural History of British Food* (London, 2008), pp. 168–9.

102 Angus Fraser, *The Gypsies* (Oxford, 1995).

103 Walter Goffart, *Barbarian Tides: The Migration Age and the Later Roman Empire* (Philadelphia, PA, 2006).

104 See, for instance, Philip M. Taylor, *The Distant Magnet: European Migration to the USA* (London, 1971), pp. 131–66.

105 M. A. Jones, 'The Role of the United Kingdom in the Transatlantic Emigrant Trade, 1815–1875' (unpublished University of Oxford D. Phil thesis, 1955); Panayi, *German Immigrants*, pp. 61–5.

106 Frank Neal, 'Liverpool, the Irish Steamship Companies and the Famine Irish', *Immigrants and Minorities*, vol. 5 (1986), p. 30.

107 Neal, *Black '47*, p. 50.

108 Ibid., pp. 51–88.

109 David Fitzpatrick, *Irish Emigration, 1801–1921* (Dublin, 1984), p. 23.

110 Panayi, *German Immigrants*, pp. 44–5, 61–7; Kirchberger, *Aspekte deutsch-britischer Expansion*, pp. 29–55; Manz, *Migranten und Internierte*, pp. 27–30.

111 Harold Pollins, *Hopeful Travellers: Jewish Migrants and Settlers in Nineteenth Century Britain* (London, 1991), p. 25.

112 Bill Williams, *The Making of Manchester Jewry, 1740–1875* (Manchester, 1985), p. 176.

113 Visram, *Asians in Britain*, pp. 14–33; Fisher, *Counterflows*, pp. 32–41, 65–71, 137–78.

114 Gardner, *Age*, pp. 91–4; Carole Adams, ed., *Across Seven Seas and Thirteen Rivers: Life Stories of Pioneer Sylhetti Settlers in Britain* (London, 1987).

115 See, especially, Mike and Trevor Phillips, *Windrush: The Irresistible Rise of Multi-Racial Britain* (London, 1998).

116 Julius Isaac, *British Post-war Migration* (Cambridge, 1954), pp. 144–59; Adams, *Across Seven Seas*, pp. 15–66.

117 Mimi Sheller and John Urry, 'The New Mobilities Paradigm', *Environment and Planning A*, vol. 38 (2006), pp. 207–26.

118 Castles and Miller, *Age of Migration*, p. 29.

119 Bloch, *Migration and Settlement of Refugees*, p. 46.

120 See, for instance, Neal, 'South Wales'.

121 Marrus, *Unwanted*, p. 3.

122 For a discussion of the concept of the refugee, see, for instance: Kushner and Knox, *Refugees*, pp. 11–16; Danièle Joly, *Haven or Hell? Asylum Policies and Refugees in Europe* (London, 1996), pp. 1–16; and Kay and Miles, *Refugees or Migrant Workers?*, pp. 1–10.

123 Rosemary Ashton, *Little Germany: Exile and Asylum in Victorian England* (Oxford, 1986), pp. 25–55; Christine Lattek, *Revolutionary Refugees: German Socialism in Britain, 1840–1860* (London, 2006); Panayi, *German Immigrants*, pp. 78–83.

124 Eric Hobsbawm, *Age of Extremes: A Short History of the Twentieth Century* (London, 1994), pp. 6–7.

125 Cahalan, *Belgian Refugee Relief*; E. Hatch, 'Belgian Refugees in the United Kingdom', *Quarterly Review*, vol. 446 (1916), pp. 188–214; John Horne and Alan Kramer, *German Attrocities, 1914: A History of Denial* (London, 2001).

126 See below p. 63.

127 Gerhard Hirschfeld, ed., *Exile in Great Britain: Refugees from Hitler's Germany* (Leamington Spa, 1984).

128 Martin Conway and José Gotovich, eds, *Europe in Exile: European Exile Communities in Britain, 1940–45* (Oxford, 2001).

129 Steinert and Weber-Newth, *Labour and Love*, pp. 32–46, 78–115.

130 Sponza, 'Italians in War and Post-war Britain', pp. 188–9.

131 Krzysztof Marchlewicz, 'Continuities and Innovations: Polish Emigration after 1849', in Freitag, *Exiles*, pp. 103–20; Norman Davies, 'The Poles in Great Britain, 1914–1919', *Slavonic and East European Review*, vol. 50 (1972), pp. 63–4.

132 John Slatter, ed., *From the Other Shore: Russian Political Emigrants in Britain, 1880–1917* (London, 1984).

133 Panayi, 'Refugees', p. 100; Norman Stone and Michael Glenny, *The Other Russia* (London, 1990), p. xvi.

134 See, for instance, Baron, *Russian Jew*, pp. 63–98; Schapiro, 'Russian Background'; Raphael Mahler, 'The Economic Background of Jewish Emigration from Galicia to the United States', *YIVO Annual of Jewish Social Science*, vol. 7 (1952), pp. 255–67; Kushner and Knox, *Refugees*, pp. 19–22; Lloyd P. Gartner, *The Jewish Immigrant in England, 1870–1914*, 3rd edn (London, 2001), pp. 15–23.

135 Margaret C. Wicks, *The Italian Exiles in London, 1816–1848* (New York, 1968); Porter, *Refugee Question*, p. 16; Freitag, *Exiles*.

136 Colin Holmes, *John Bull's Island: Immigration and British Society, 1871–1971* (Basingstoke, 1988), p. 35.

137 Dorothy Legarreta, *The Guernica Generation: Basque Refugee Children of the Spanish Civil War* (Reno, NV, 1984); Knox and Kushner, *Refugees*, pp. 103–25.

138   Marrus, *Unwanted*, p. 297.

139   Eugene Kulischer, *Europe on the Move: War and Population Changes, 1917–1947* (New York, 1948), p. 305.

140   See, for instance: Jerzy Zubrzycki, *Polish Immigrants in Britain: A Study of Adjustment* (The Hague, 1956); Sword, Davies and Ciechnowski, *Formation of the Polish Community*; Thomas Lane, *Victims of Stalin and Hitler: The Exodus of Poles and Balts to Britain* (Basingstoke, 2004); Kathy Burrell, 'War, Cold War and the New World Order: Political Borders and Polish Migration to Britain', 'History in Focus', Issue 11, http://www.history/ac.uk/ihr/Focus/Migration/articles/burrell.html.

141   Lane, ibid.; Kay and Miles, *Refugees or Migrant Workers?*; J. A. Tannahill, *European Volunteer Workers in Britain* (Manchester, 1958); Elizabeth Stadulis, 'The Resettlement of Displaced Persons in United Kingdom', *Population Studies*, vol. 5 (1952), pp. 207–37.

142   Kushner and Knox, *Refugees*, pp. 241–61; Panayi, 'Refugees', pp. 104–5.

143   Yasmin Khan, *The Great Partition: The Making of India and Pakistan* (London, 2007); Peach, 'South Asian Migration'.

144   Valerie Marrett, *Immigrants Settling in the City* (Leicester, 1989), pp. 13–29; William G. Kuepper, G. Lynne Lackey and E. Nelson Swinerton, *Ugandan Asians in Great Britain: Forced Migration and Social Absorption* (London, 1975).

145   Peter Loizos, *The Heart Grown Bitter: A Chronicle of Cypriot War Refugees* (Cambridge, 1981); Anthias, *Ethnicity*, p. 6.

146   Carol Dalglish, *Refugees from Vietnam* (London, 1989).

147   Joly, *Haven or Hell?*, pp. 86–9; Kushner and Knox, Refugees, pp. 289–92.

148   Panayi, 'Refugees', pp. 107–8.

149   Francis Fukuyama, *The End of History and the Last Man* (London, 1992).

150   UNHCR, *The State of the World's Refugees: In Search of Solutions* (Oxford, 1995), pp. 19–20.

151   Bloch, *Migration and Settlement of Refugees*, pp. 8–12; Tony Kushner, *Remembering Refugees: Then and Now* (Manchester, 2006).

152   See Chapter 5 below.

153   Peter Mathias, *The First Industrial Nation: The Economic Transformation of Britain, 1700–1914* (London, 2001).

154   Rosemary Sales, 'Secure Borders, Safe Haven: A Contradiction in Terms?', *Ethnic and Racial Studies*, vol. 28 (2005).

155   Stephen Castles and Godula Kosack, *Immigrant Workers and Class Structure in Western Europe* (London, 1973), pp. 27–8.

156   Muhammad Anwar, *The Myth of Return: Pakistanis in Britain* (London, 1979), p. 25.

157 Heinrich Dorgeel, *Die Deutsche Colonie in London* (London, 1881), pp. 17–21.

158 See Chapter 3.

159 J. A. Jackson, *The Irish in Britain* (London, 1963), p. 82.

160 Robert Miles, *Racism and Migrant Labour* (London, 1982), p. 123.

161 Jeffrey Williamson, 'The Impact of the Irish on British Labour Markets during the Industrial Revolution', in Roger Swift and Sheridan Gilley, eds, *The Irish in Britain, 1815–1939* (London, 1989), p. 160.

162 B. M. Kerr, 'Irish Seasonal Migration', pp. 365–80; Morgan, *Harvesters and Harvesting*, pp. 76–87.

163 See, for instance, Trevor Wilson, *The Myriad Faces of War: Britain and the Great War, 1914–1918* (Cambridge, 1986), pp. 215–31, 519–30.

164 Cahalan, *Belgian Refugee Relief*, p. 249.

165 Kenneth Little, *Negroes in Britain: A Study of Racial Relations in English Society*, 2nd Edn (London, 1972).

166 'The Transfer of Irish Workers to Great Britain', *International Labour Review*, vol. 48 (1943), pp. 338–42; Delaney, *Demography*, pp. 112–59.

167 Watson, *West Indian Workers*.

168 Kay and Miles, *Refugees or Migrant Workers?*; Stadulis, 'Resettlement of Displaced Persons'; Tannahill, *European Volunteer Workers*.

169 See below.

170 Sales, 'Secure Borders'.

171 See, for instance, Ulrich Herbert, *A History of Foreign Labour in Germany, 1880–1980: Seasonal Workers/Forced Laborers/Guest Workers* (Ann Arbor, MI, 1990), pp. 193–235.

172 Isaac, *British Post-war Migration*, pp. 194–5.

173 Sponza, 'Italians in War and Post-war Britain', p. 196.

174 Xavier Lannes, 'International Mobility of Manpower in Western Europe', *International Labour Review*, vol. 73 (1956), p. 14.

175 Panayi, *Impact*, pp. 38–9.

176 Chessum, *Immigrants to Ethnic Minority*, p. 32; Panayi, ibid., pp. 41–2; Peach, 'Empire', p. 268.

177 Peach, ibid.; Taylor, *A Land of Dreams*, p. 100.

178 See contributions to Burrell, *Polish Migration to the UK*.

179 See, for instance, Castles and Miller, Age *of Migration*, pp. 21–9; Robin Cohen, *Migration and Its Enemies: Global Capital, Migrant Labour and the Nation State* (Aldershot, 2006); Timothy J. Hatton and Jeffrey G. Williamson, eds, *Migration and the International Labor Market* (London, 1994).

180 Porter, *Refugee Question*, p. 3.

181 T. W. E. Roche, *The Key in the Lock: Immigration Control in England from 1066 to the Present Day* (London, 1969); Thomas W. Perry, *Public Opinion, Propaganda and Politics in Eighteenth Century England: A Study of the Jew Bill of 1753* (Cambridge, MA, 1962); Vaughan Bevan, *The Development of British Immigration Law* (London, 1986), pp. 50–8.

182 See: W. L. Burn, *The Age of Equipoise: A Study of the Mid-Victorian Generation* (London, 1964); Geoffrey Best, *Mid-Victorian Britain, 1851–1875* (London, 1971); Martin Hewitt, ed., *An Age of Equipoise? Reassessing Mid-Victorian Britain* (Aldershot, 2000).

183 G. R. Searle, *A New England? Peace and War, 1886–1918* (Oxford, 2004).

184 Fahrmeier, *Citizens and Aliens*.

185 Ibid., pp. 102–3; Bevan, *Development of British Immigration Law*, pp. 58–64.

186 Porter, *Refugee Question*, pp. 3, 86.

187 Neal, *Black '47*, pp. 123–76.

188 Bernard Gainer, *The Alien Invasion: The Origins of the Aliens Act of 1905* (London, 1972).

189 Jill Pellew, 'The Home Office and the Aliens Act, 1905', *Historical Journal*, vol. 32 (1989), pp. 369–85.

190 Bevan, *Development of British Immigration Law*, pp. 70–1.

191 Panayi, *Enemy*, pp. 47–8; J. C. Bird, *Control of Enemy Alien Civilians in Great Britain, 1914–1918* (London, 1986), pp. 14–16; Kushner and Knox, *Refugees*, pp. 44–54, 64–76; Colin Holmes, *A Tolerant Country? Immigrants, Refugees and Minorities in Britain* (London, 1991), pp. 26–7.

192 London, *Whitehall and the Jews*; Kushner, *Remembering Refugees*, pp. 141–80; A. J. Sherman, *Britain and Refugees from the Third Reich* (London, 1973).

193 The history of immigration legislation from 1948–81 can be traced in: Hansen, *Citizenship and Immigration*; Paul, *Whitewashing Britain*; Spencer, *British Immigration Policy*; Hampshire, *Citizenship and Belonging*, pp. 16–48; David Steel, *No Entry: The Background and Implications of the Commonwealth Immigrants Act, 1968* (London, 1969); and John Solomos, *Race and Racism in Britain* (Basingstoke, 1993), pp. 61–77.

194 Geoffrey K. Fry, *The Growth of Government: The Development of Ideas about the Role of the State and the Machinery and Functions of Government in Britain Since 1780* (London, 1979); Peter Hennesy, *Whitehall* (London, 1990).

195 Bloch, *Migration and Settlement of Refugees*; Kushner, *Remembering Refugees*; Vaughan Robinson, Roger Anderson and Sako Musterd, *Spreading the 'Burden'? A Review of Policies to Disperse Asylum Seekers and Refugees* (Bristol, 2003); Sales, 'Secure Borders', p. 445; Michael Dummett, *On Immigrants and Refugees* (London, 2001).

196 Sales, ibid.

197 Panayi, *Outsiders*, pp. 129–46; Paul, *Whitewashing Britain*.

198 Burrell, *Polish Migration to the UK*.

199 Robin Cohen, *Frontiers of Identity: The British and the Others* (Harlow, 1994), pp. 125–7.

200 *The Independent*, 14 August 2003.

201 Stephen Castles, 'Why Migration Policies Fail', *Ethnic and Racial Studies*, vol. 27 (2004), pp. 205–27.

202 Castles and Miller, *Age of Migration*, pp. 26–7.

203 See, for instance: P. Karsten, 'Irish Soldiers in the British Army, 1792–1922: Suborned or Subordinate', *Journal of Social History*, vol. 17 (1983), pp. 33–64; C. L. Joseph, 'The British West Indies Regiment, 1914–1918', *Journal of Caribbean History*, vol. 2 (1971), pp. 94–124; Reynolds, *Rich Relations*; Graham A. Smith, *When Jim Crow Met John Bull: Black American Soldiers in World War II Britain* (London, 1987).

204 Ashton, *Little Germany*; Gottfried Niedhardt, ed., *Großbritannien als Gast- und Exilland für Deutsche im 19. und 20. Jahrhundert* (Bochum, 1985); Lattek, *Revolutionary Refugees*.

205 Panayi, *German Immigrants*, pp. 56–60, 122–6, 130–1, 133–4; Kirchberger, *Aspekte deutsch-britischer Expansion*; Manz, *Migranten und Internierte*.

206 Lucio Sponza, *Italian Immigrants in Nineteenth Century Britain* (Leicester, 1988), pp. 36–51, 75.

207 Ibid., pp. 62–75, 141–61; John E. Zucchi, *The Little Slaves of the Harp: Italian Child Street Musicians in Nineteenth-Century Paris, London and New York* (London, 1992), pp. 76–110.

208 Colin Hughes, *Lime, Lemon and Sarsaparilla: The Italian Community in Wales, 1881–1945* (Bridgend, 1991), p. 47.

209 Andrew Wilkin, 'Origins and Destinations of the Early Italo-Scots', *Association of Teachers of Italian Journal*, no. 29 (1979), pp. 52–61.

210 Anne J. Kershen, *Strangers, Aliens and Asians: Huguenots, Jews and Bangladeshis in Spitalfields, 1660–2000* (London, 2005).

211 *Select Committee on Emigration and Immigration (Foreigners)* (London, 1888), p. 69.

212 Szeming Sze, 'Chinese Students in Great Britain', *Asiatic Review*, vol. 27 (1931), pp. 311–20; May, 'Chinese in Britain'.

213 J. A. G. Roberts, *China to Chinatown: Chinese Food in the West* (London, 2002), pp. 172–6; Susan Chui Chie Baxter, 'A Political Economy of the Ethnic Chinese Catering Industry' (University Aston Ph.D Thesis, 1988), pp. 107–12; *The Times*, 2 October 1961; Ng, *Chinese in London*, pp. 36–8.

214 Watson, 'The Chinese', pp. 184–91.

215 Chamberlain, *Narratives*.

216 Stuart B. Philpott, *West Indian Migration: The Montserrat Case* (London, 1973).

217 Byron, *Post-war Caribbean Migration*, pp. 69–72.

218 Colin Clarke, Ceri Peach and Steven Vertovec, eds, *South Asians Overseas: Migration and Ethnicity* (Cambridge, 1990); Hugh Tinker, *The Banyan Tree: Overseas Emigration from India, Pakistan and Bangladesh* (Oxford, 1977).

219 Peach, 'South Asian Migration', p. 136.

220 Gurharpal Singh and Darshan Singh Tatla, *Sikhs in Britain: The Making of a Community* (London, 2006), pp. 31–8.

221 Fisher, Lahiri and Thandi, *South Asian History of Britain*, p. 164.

222 Anwar, *Myth of Return*, pp. 27–46; Pnina Werbner, *The Migration Process: Capital, Gifts and Offerings among British Pakistanis* (Oxford, 1990); Badr Dahya, 'Pakistanis in Britain: Transients or Settlers?', *Race*, vol. 14 (1973), pp. 243–8.

223 Kershen, *Strangers, Aliens and Asians*, pp. 43–8; Gardner, *Age*.

224 Ravenstein, 'Laws of Migration'.

225 See contributions to Bade, *Population, Labour and Migration*.

Three paths to integration? Geography, demography and economics

Patterns of integration?

Taking a long-term perspective on Europe during the nineteenth and twentieth centuries, Leo Lucassen recently returned to the issue of integration in an attempt to explain the change in the position of migrant groups over time. He concluded his volume by suggesting that post-war arrivals will probably make their way up the social and economic ladder and will 'blend into western European societies, adding to it new flavours and colours, as so many migrants have done in the remote and recent past'.[1] Lucassen's book includes two case studies from Britain in the form of the nineteenth-century Irish and the post-war West Indians. The measures of integration which he uses include changes in geographical concentration, the incidence of intermarriage and social mobility linked to employment. Lucassen finds it difficult to come to firm conclusions about the Irish due to lack of sources, although he essentially concludes that integration must have occurred because the Irish became increasingly invisible.[2] This supports the assertions made by M. A. G. Ó Tuathaigh in his now classic article on the Irish in nineteenth-century Britain, which suggested that it 'would be wrong' to view the experience of this group as a 'static picture' because 'in the second half of the nineteenth century and, at a moderately increasing pace from the 1880s, there was some demonstrable improvement in terms of both jobs and of living conditions'.[3] When dealing with Caribbean migrants to Britain Lucassen concludes that a 'significant number . . . were confronted with unemployment, bad housing and racism', but that many of the descendants have 'fared well' in terms of 'upward mobility, decent housing, and high intermarriage rates'.[4]

The long-term perspective taken by scholars such as Lucassen and Ó Tuathaigh allows them to establish, as historians, that change, in the settlement patterns, demographic structure and economic and social position of the lives of migrants, takes place over time. This contrasts with the approach of many post-war social scientists, particularly those examining the position of West Indians and their offspring. From Michael Banton, in his classic study of *The Coloured Quarter*,[5] through the work of scholars such as Ruth Glass[6] and Sheila Patterson,[7] with their equally weighted titles, to the research of John Rex[8] and John Solomos,[9] observing the position of the second generation from the 1960s to the 1980s, it appears that African Caribbeans in Britain remain trapped in a ghetto of deprivation. In essence, these scholars, focusing upon particular moments in time from the 1950s until the 1980s almost inevitably come to gloomy conclusions. Similarly, most of the scholarship on the nineteenth-century Irish focuses upon this group as one experiencing poverty and deprivation, without taking a longer term perspective.[10] The historiography of the nineteenth-century Irish, dominated by the three Swift and Gilley volumes and focusing upon the first generation,[11] seems largely unaware of the fate of their offspring.[12]

Jewish historiography, in contrast, does not fizzle out in the early twentieth century. Much research has certainly concentrated upon the Eastern European immigrants who arrived at the end of the nineteenth century and who had similar inner city experiences of deprivation to the Irish and West Indians.[13] Yet numerous other scholars have taken a much longer term perspective, which has allowed them to trace the social and economic change which took place in the community over centuries, as movement out of the ghetto became a feature of the various Jewish waves which moved to Britain from the readmission of the middle of the seventeenth century.

Historians of Anglo-Jewry also realize the complexity of the group which they study, precisely because of the different waves which have formed it, from the predominantly Iberian and Dutch Jews of the seventeenth and eighteenth centuries, through to the increasingly Eastern European arrivals of the Victorian and Edwardian years to the refugees from Nazism. The long-term studies of Anglo-Jewry demonstrate two essentials in the evolution of the community. First, that it has developed as a result of migration from a variety of geographical locations and quite distinct religious practices. Just as importantly, the studies of scholars such as Lipman, Alderman, Rubinstein and Endelman have also shown that the migrants who moved to Britain had varying socio-economic backgrounds, work experiences and settlement patterns. Migration from the Russian Pale of Settlement in the late Victorian period, which involved working in a clothing sweatshop followed by movement to the London suburbs and social mobility to the highest social classes for subsequent generations, represents one paradigm. Yet the arrival of predominantly middle class Jews escaping from the Nazis during the 1930s, represents another. Numerous scholars have established the complexity of Jewish experiences in Britain, both in terms of identities and in terms of social and economic lives and mobility.[14]

The historiography of the nineteenth-century German community also reveals a complicated picture and also points to the fact that full integration never occurred. This particular migrant group suffered a fairly unique fate in comparison with all the others which have lived in Britain over the last two centuries, comparable with that of medieval Jewry. In fact, the history of the Germans in nineteenth-century Britain mirrors that of their Jewish compatriots in Germany in the sense that racism virtually eliminated them during the First World War. Any integration which occurred ceased in 1914, followed by mass deportation.[15] Nevertheless, a focus upon the Victorian and Edwardian period reveals a complex community, shaped by its origins. The historiography of this minority has demonstrated that it never constituted one community. Instead, Germans tended to move to Britain as specific groups often to work in particular occupations. This meant that Germans found themselves located on all parts of the economic and social spectrum from beggars to merchant bankers. Consequently, an examination of residential patterns reveals Germans in London from the poor East End through middling Islington to wealthy Sydenham.[16] The German community of nineteenth-century Britain stresses the importance of social and economic origins in the history of migrant communities in Britain over the last two centuries. Those who entered as merchant bankers, for instance, tended to remain in the social group in which they entered, while those who came with little money and found themselves residing in the East End, working in the sugar baking business, are unlikely to have experienced much social mobility, although some integration may have occurred as a result of marriage with native women.

The history of 'Asian' communities in Britain after the Second World War also emphasizes different experiences. While the concept of Asian ethnicity may have developed by the 1980s,[17] Asians in Britain have a variety of origins which play a large role in determining their social and economic lives. A relative lack of intermarriage (certainly in comparison with African Caribbeans) may bind Mirpuris, Sylhettis, Gujuratis and Punjabis together as Asians (although they tend to marry within their own group), but little else does. Members of these distinct communities have tended to reside next to each other in urban locations up and down the country. These groups collectively and individually may also tend to suffer higher rates of unemployment than wider society as a whole, yet, at the same time, they also have a considerably higher incidence of self employment (as do most post-war migrant groups). Yet notable differences exist between the educational attainments and social position of those of Mirpuri or Sylhetti origin and those from high caste Gujarati groups.[18]

Migrants as a whole clearly do not conform to particular patterns in terms of their geography, demography and economics. Perhaps the most important factor determining their lives once within the country consists of their social status before arriving in Britain. Pakistanis who moved to work in northern factories, for instance, have tended to remain within the lower classes, as have their offspring. As John Rex has demonstrated, birth in the ghetto for all ethnic groups largely influences their future life chances.[19] In contrast, a German who entered Britain as a merchant banker in the second half of the nineteenth century would have had quite different life chances, employment experiences and residential patterns, at least until 1914. Social mobility certainly does take place, although it often does so over generations, as the classic example of the Russian Jewish arrivals of the late nineteenth century illustrates.

The discussion below will demonstrate that no single paradigm explains the geography, demography and economics of migrants in Britain. One of the most tempting consists of Lucassen's cautious integration approach, which, if applied to those migrants or (more likely) their descendants finding themselves in middle class occupations over time has much to offer. However, the Irish and African Caribbeans covered by Lucassen provide just two examples of numerous migrants who have moved to Britain since 1800. Marion Berghahn's study of the middle class German Jews fleeing the Nazis offers quite a different picture.[20]

Geographical distribution on a national scale

Residential patterns of migrants in Britain do not therefore all fit into the classic pattern of emergence from the ghetto, because not all migrant groups initially moved there. Before examining issues such as geographical concentration, segregation and movement to the suburbs, we can first of all take a broader view of the distribution of migrants in Britain on a nationwide scale. This broader perspective demonstrates increasing dispersal in the post-war period to cities which had previously had little experience of foreign settlement, especially the Midlands and London outside the East and West End; newcomers and their offspring have almost constructed many parts of London since 1945.

Nevertheless, to suggest, for instance, that the East End acted as the sole magnet for migrants before 1945 simplifies reality. Certainly, this part of London has unique characteristics in the variety of migrant groups which it has attracted. Anne Kershen's study of Spitalfields, stretching from the end of the seventeenth century to the present, focused upon the experiences of Huguenots, Eastern European Jews and Sylhettis.[21] Yet other significant groups have lived in the East End including the Irish, who made up more than ten per cent of the population of Whitechapel in 1851.[22] Similarly, Germans focused upon the East End from the eighteenth century until their expulsion during the First World War,[23] while the Chinese counted a significant settlement in Limehouse.[24] Since 1945 those groups who have settled in the East End have included, in addition to Sylhettis, the Maltese and Somalis.[25]

Nevertheless, as the historiography of both the Jews and the Irish in Britain before 1945 has demonstrated, these two groups found themselves located throughout the country. To begin with the former, in his classic study of *The Rise of Provincial Jewry* Cecil Roth demonstrated how the readmitted Jews who had initially concentrated on London had, by the beginning of the nineteenth century, spread to 44 locations throughout the British Isles.[26] On closer inspection, however, some of these locations literally counted a handful of individuals. To give the example of Coventry, Roth struggled to persuade us of the presence of Jews and did not really provide any convincing numbers.[27] In fact, he points out that some of the communities which he describes had disappeared.[28]

The late nineteenth-century influx from Eastern Europe certainly increased the Jewish population of Britain, although, once again, it remained concentrated in particular locations. The most important of these consisted of the East End of London in Whitechapel and Stepney, but significant communities also evolved in the Gorbals area of Glasgow, the Leylands area of Leeds and Cheetham Hill in Manchester. Settlements also developed in ports connected with the transatlantic emigrant trade, including Liverpool, Hull and Newcastle, while 'second city Jewry' also took off in Birmingham. Similarly, the Jewish communities of South Wales had also expanded. During the inter-war years, Jews began to move out of their initial settlements as social mobility took place. Jewish East Enders, for instance, now began to migrate to a variety of locations, generally in the east and north London suburbs, including Hackney, Stoke Newington, Palmers Green, Chingford, Golders Green, Hendon and Finchley, although movement had also taken place to other parts of the capital. At the same time, a migration also began to occur to seaside resorts such as Bournemouth and Blackpool.[29] Despite the increase in population, which had taken place as a result of the Eastern European influx of the late nineteenth century, as well as subsequent demographic increase and dispersal, most of the British population would probably still have had limited interaction with an increasingly dispersed but still concentrated minority, which, nationwide stood at about 370,000 by the outbreak of the Second World War.[30]

In contrast, taking the nineteenth and early twentieth centuries together, the Irish became more ubiquitous than the Jews, partly due to their greater numbers, which counted over 800,000 people in 1861 and over half a million in 1931, a figure which simply includes those born in Ireland and not the second generation.[31] At the same time, the Irish fitted much more comfortably into the British labour market, fuelling the industrial revolution in the same way as the rest of the British population, in contrast to Eastern European Jews, who tended to find employment with their own countrymen.[32] Certainly, the Irish also developed concentrations in particular parts of the country, especially the big cities such as London, Glasgow, Birmingham, Manchester, Liverpool, Leeds, Edinburgh, Cardiff and Newcastle. But they also counted significant numbers in smaller locations,[33] of quite a different magnitude to the handful of Jews outlined by Cecil Roth. In the town of Newport, for instance, the Irish made up 10.7 per cent of the population in 1851, counting 2,069 from 19,323 individuals.[34] They certainly remained highly concentrated in the initial stages of settlement, although would subsequently disperse. However, in contrast to any other migrant group before 1945 the Irish also made an appearance in the countryside, as temporary harvesters. In the 1860s they 'were still very active in certain counties' including Northumberland, Yorkshire, Cheshire, Shropshire, Worcestershire, Warwickshire, Gloucestershire, Wiltshire, East Anglia, Essex and Lincolnshire.[35] At the same time, Irish navvies also worked in the countryside.[36] Irish migrants had therefore lived in much of the country before 1945, either as seasonal labourers or more permanent settlers, although the latter, in the short run at least, remained highly concentrated.

Most of the other significant groups who moved to Britain by World War Two focused upon London. This applies particularly to the 50–60,000 German immigrants in the late Victorian and Edwardian period, fifty per cent of whom always lived in the capital, with much smaller concentrations in major northern cities such as Liverpool, Manchester, Hull and Bradford.[37] The Italian community showed a similar concentration upon the capital (of between 5,000 and 10,000) throughout the nineteenth and early twentieth centuries, with smaller concentrations in Edinburgh, Glasgow, Liverpool, Manchester and South Wales.[38] Most of the smaller European groups tended to concentrate on central London.[39] Black, Asian and Chinese communities, composed of sailors, who often remained temporarily, often focused upon port areas including Cardiff, Liverpool and East London next to the Thames.[40]

Migrants had certainly settled throughout the country before 1945. While most groups had significant settlemenents in distinct parts of London, the Irish resided all over Britain. Ethnic concentrations of particular groups continue after the Second World War, but two significant developments occur. First, within London, migrants and their offspring moved out of the East and West End heartland where they had previously focused and now caused the expansion of many inner and outer London suburbs. Secondly, newcomers, especially those from beyond Europe, also settled in areas which had previously had limited experience of migration, particularly parts of the Midlands and the North.

While some migrants had moved out of the central London heartland before 1945, especially in the case of the settlement of wealthier nineteenth-century Germans and socially mobile Jews during the interwar years, many parts of the capital had little experience of migration before 1945. Part of the explanation for the growth of settlement in the capital's suburbs lies in the fact that migration expanded as population within them grew, especially as social housing increased.[41] Certainly, a variety of groups have continued to settle in the East End, largely because of its cheap housing.[42]

From the 1950s migrants from the Commonwealth began to reside in new areas of the capital relatively untouched by foreigners before the Second World War, as West Indians developed concentrations in two new locations, Brixton and Notting Hill.[43] Nevertheless, as Ruth Glass pointed out in 1960, these remained the heartlands of the community with members also residing elsewhere in the capital, although still largely within west and south London.[44] Since the 1960s some movement has occurred to north and east London, especially to Brent, Hackney and Haringey and particularly Tottenham within the latter.[45]

The development of South Asian communities in Britain, meanwhile, took off slightly later as migrants from India, Pakistan, Bangladesh and East Africa arrived in significant numbers during the 1960s and 1970s. Particular patterns have developed here, with individual groups focusing upon particular parts of London. Thus Sikhs have concentrated in the Southall heartland, while Gujuratis have settled slightly further north in Wembley, with another concentration around Tooting. These all represent suburbs of London which have expanded in the twentieth century and which developed in the post-war period largely as a result of immigration. On the other hand, Sylhetti settlement has focused upon the long-standing immigrant area of Tower Hamlets. Pakistani communities, meanwhile, have largely evolved outside the capital.[46]

Irish settlement in post-war London certainly differs from the mid nineteenth century focus upon Whitechapel, St Giles and Southwark.[47] The new communities have tended to reside in north and north-west London, especially Brent, Camden, Islington and Ealing. If an Irish heartland in London exists, it consists of Kilburn.[48] Of other 'white' groups, Jewish settlement has increasingly moved further and further out into the suburbs as upward mobility has brought this group to the top of the social scale.[49] The post-war Greek Cypriot settlement has predominantly focused upon North London, initially in inner London in Camden Town, although its members have increasingly moved to the northern suburbs, initially Haringey, but then further out to Enfield. Nevertheless, like most of the post-war migrant groups, while Greek Cypriots have concentrations, they are represented in most London boroughs from Hackney, one of the poorest, to Barnet, one of the richest.[50]

By the beginning of the twenty-first century London had become a truly global city. On the one hand it counts residents from throughout the world within it, not simply the major groups outlined above. At the same time, while concentrations of particular communities focus upon specific areas, all parts of the capital, especially Newham, Brent, Islington, Haringey, Tottenham and Ealing, now count a significant number of migrants and their descendants. Post-war London was built upon and expanded to a large extent as a result of international migration.[51]

The same applies to the provincial conurbations of Manchester and Birmingham, while cities such as Wolverhampton, Bradford, Blackburn and Leicester have also evolved largely as a result of immigration. In view of the numbers and level of dispersal of the Irish in nineteenth-century Britain, it seems difficult to speak of areas newly influenced by immigration after 1945. Yet this does appear the case because of the larger volume of immigration, the level of difference of newcomers, entrepreneurial activity and the fact some newcomers have not yet integrated.[52]

The change seems difficult to deny for a town such as Leicester. Some Irish immigration had occurred both before the Second World War and in its immediate aftermath, but the Victorian settlement remained small in scale.[53] In fact, while some migration from a variety of locations towards Leicester occurred in the early post-war years, only from the 1970s did the movement of Asians really take off so that ethnic minorities now make up about 35–40 per cent of its population, completely different from the few thousand Irish people who settled in the Victorian years.[54]

A similar situation exists in some northern cities. In Bradford, for instance, Muslims, mostly Mirpuris, made up 17 per cent of the population in 2002.[55] Similarly, as Vaughan Robinson demonstrated from the 1980s, South Asian settlement also moved towards Lancashire. He examined the West Midlands, especially Wolverhampton, with an important concentration of Sikhs, and Birmingham, which housed a variety of groups, including Pakistanis.[56]

Yet let us go back to the middle of the nineteenth century and we find an even higher concentration of migrants in some of these cities in the form of the Irish. In 1851, for instance, Bradford counted an Irish born population of 9,581, making up 26 per cent of the total. Although by 1901, as the population of Bradford grew to 279,767, the number of Irish born fell,[57] such figures provide no indication of Irish ethnicity amongst the second and subsequent generations, which censuses since 1991 have recorded. Similarly, as Roger Swift has demonstrated, the Irish made up 17 per cent of the population of Wolverhampton in 1871.[58] On the other hand Birmingham counted an Irish born population of a maximum of 8,873 in 1852, making up just 4.9 per cent of the total in contrast to the 206,800 people who classed themselves as belonging to Black and ethnic minorities in the city by 1991 (21.5 per cent of the population), which excludes the 38,000 Irish born in the city by around this time.[59]

We can conclude this discussion comparing the dispersal of migrant communities before and after 1945 with a number of observations. Firstly, in view of the fact that more migrants have moved to Britain since 1945 than before, it is inevitable that they have, collectively, become more widespread than either the Irish or Jews before 1945. Yet this remains a blanket observation. While post-war migrants, especially South Asians, may have settled in cities and areas relatively untouched by immigration, some areas which witnessed a large scale settlement of Irish, have on the other hand, remained relatively monocultural in the post-war period. The major focus for the Irish influx of the nineteenth century consisted of Liverpool, which had an Irish born population making up between 12.6 and 22.3 per cent of the total between 1841 and 1891, a situation not approached in the post-war years, probably because of the importance of Liverpool as a passenger port in the nineteenth century, which it no longer held after 1945.[60] Similarly, the vast scale of Irish migration to Scotland and Wales has not replicated itself during the post-war period, even though some influxes have occurred to traditional areas of settlement such as Cardiff and Glasgow.[61]

The inevitability of ghettoization?

At the end of the twentieth century the Labour government, reacting to a groundswell of racism, had become conscious of the concentration of migrants in urban locations and decided to introduce a policy to disperse 'asylum seekers' to areas and towns which did not count significant numbers of migrants.[62] The government was therefore trying to prevent one of the inevitabilities of migrant settlement. The development of migrant networks has meant that new arrivals have followed their already settled friends or relatives.[63]

Scholars of American immigration history such as Kathleen Neils Conzen or Stanley Nadel have stressed migrant concentration,[64] as have a variety of social scientists working on recent settlement in Britain such as Muhamad Anwar and Pnina Werbner, to give just the example of those who have worked on Pakistanis.[65] Such concentration proves important for the formation of ethnic communities.[66] Similarly, despite the attempts of the state to disperse refugees in recent decades, this policy has hardly happened. Instead, it has tended to open up refugee concentrations in particular parts of cities.[67] At the same time, public housing initiatives have also tended to have a similar effect in the sense that allocations have often kept particular ethnic groups together.[68] Government policy and the inevitabilities of transnational migration represent two factors which lead to the concentration of populations in particular parts of cities. A third consists of the difficulties of affording decent housing, which has, throughout British history, pushed migrants into particularly poor locations, from which they eventually move out. At the same time, as underlying economic factors have determined so much migration to Britain, many newcomers have settled near their places of work.[69]

That concentration of migrants has taken place throughout British history seems indisputable, whether referring to the Irish, Jews, West Indians or, increasingly in recent decades, South Asian Muslims. Much of the hostility which migrants face revolves around their apparent refusal to mix, indicated by this residential concentration. Ted Cantle saw this as one of the factors which prevented community cohesion, leading to ethnic conflict in northern cities in the summer of 2001.[70] Ceri Peach even attempted to assess whether contemporary Britain has ghettoes, but concluded that 'the American ghetto model of hypersegregation is not present'. He did, however, notice significant concentrations amongst Pakistanis and Bangladeshis, explained by chain migration and the desire to reside next to members of the same group to continue religious practice. But this did not apply to African-Caribbeans. Writing in the middle of the 1990s Peach concluded that: 'Ghettos on the American model do not exist and, despite an unfavourable economic position and substantial evidence of continuing discrimination, the segregation trend amongst the Black Caribbean population in London is downwards.'[71] This links with a statement by Kathleen Conzen, who, referring to the situation in the USA, wrote in 1979, that 'two generations after the last of the great waves of European immigration . . . brooding churches often bear the only witness to immigrant neighbourhoods that once were'.[72]

If we combine the assertions of Peach, Conzen and Lucassen it would appear that residential concentration, particularly in the poor inner city, represents an early temporary phase in the history of any group due to a combination of economic, political and cultural factors. While Lucassen and Peach, writing about the post-war West Indian migration display some caution about the extent to which segregation had declined by the beginning of the twenty-first century, it seems easier to suggest that such patterns have disappeared for those groups which settled in the nineteenth century.

Following from contemporary observers, much literature on the Irish in Victorian Britain has focused upon the concentrated nature of their settlement within the inner city. This observation began with nineteenth-century writers, most notably Friedrich Engels on Manchester but also others such as Leon M. Faucher, who, referring to Manchester in the 1840s, described the Irish as 'the most dirty and unhealthy portion of the population, their dwellings are the most dirty and unhealthy and their children the most neglected'.[73] Such views partly followed from official descriptions of the Irish in Britain, including one appendix from the Royal Commission on the Condition of the Poorer Classes in Ireland from 1836, which wrote of the Irish settling in 'the cheapest dwellings which can be procured' which meant that 'they collected in the lowest, dampest, dirtiest, most unhealthy, and ruinous parts of the town'. Just as significantly, the description claimed that: 'The Irish settled in England associate little with the natives, except on occasions when their work throws them together' and formed 'a distinct community in the midst of the English'. The report explained 'this separation' as 'owing partly to the difference of habits, partly to the differences of religious persuasion, partly to the difference of country, and in some cases the language' as well as the unwillingness of the 'natives' to 'mix with them'.[74]

Much of the scholarship on the Irish in nineteenth-century Britain has stressed this segregation. Liverpool provides one of the starkest examples. Frank Neal, for example, has demonstrated that the Irish here concentrated in fourteen political wards, in which they constituted between 8.4 and 47.2 per cent of the population. In Stockdale Street in St Bartholmew's ecclesiastical district, the Irish made up 90.3 per cent of residents, while Neal also found high concentrations in streets in Vauxhall and the North End.[75] Colin Pooley has confirmed that segregation in Liverpool continued until the 1870s as a result of economic and cultural factors.[76] However, he has also questioned the extent of this segregation and those scholars who set out to prove the existence of ghettos, demonstrating that a significant percentage of the population lived outside the 'ghettos' by 1871.[77]

Those historians of the Irish in Victorian Britain who have moved out of the nineteenth century have included Steven Fielding, who doubted the degree of segregation during the mid Victorian period. He demonstrated how the 56 per cent of Roman Catholics residing in poor working class districts in Manchester in the late nineteenth century had declined to 30 by 1939, although he partly explained this as a result of slum clearance.[78] Lynne Lees explained the movement of the Irish out of their inner London districts by pointing to the 'transformation of the city centre to a manufacturing area' which 'led more and more people to move to outer districts'.[79] John Hickey, meanwhile, also demonstrated how the Irish moved out of their original areas of settlement in Cardiff.[80]

The few studies of the Irish which have taken the longer perspective do suggest dispersal over time. The same certainly happened to the nineteenth-century Germans, even before their ethnic cleansing of the First World War. This group had a more diverse social structure than the Irish. Some evidence exists to suggest that middle class merchants had ethnic concentrations, but an examination of the London Germans demonstrates that they lived throughout the capital by the outbreak of the First World War. Certainly, two major concentrations based on the East and West End had developed, as recognized by contemporary observers. While the latter emerged in the late Victorian years, the former had evolved from the eighteenth century. German working class settlement reached its peak here towards the end of the nineteenth century, but had begun to decline by 1914 due to housing schemes to improve the area and the influx of Eastern European Jews, together with some social mobility, which sent Germans further east.[81]

Jewish concentration in late Victorian and Edwardian Britain replicated, to some extent, the forced ghetto in the Russian Pale of Settlement,[82] although, in the new surroundings, no legal restrictions forced such concentration.

This new influx represented just one strand of Anglo-Jewry at the end of the nineteenth century, adding to the already established communities which had emerged since the middle of the seventeenth. Wealthy Sephardic Jews had already settled in the West End by the beginning of the nineteenth century. During the Victorian period members of the Ashkenazi community moved out of the City towards similar areas, as well as to Islington, St John's Wood and Maida Vale. Less wealthy Jews migrated to Dalston and Hackney. Nevertheless, a significant concentration continued in the City and its immediate surroundings in the East End.[83]

The influx of the late Victorian and Edwardian period essentially created a new Jewish community in Britain, whose most obvious manifestations included the level of ethnic concentration. The poor Ashkenazi Jews from the Pale of Settlement moved into inner city areas to develop settlement patterns similar to those of their Irish predecessors. The East End represented their true heartland so that in 1911 43,925 of the 63,105 Russians (overwhelmingly Jews) recorded in the census for England and Wales, lived in the East End borough of Stepney, meaning that it housed up to 70 per cent of newly arrived Jews. In 1889 East London accounted for 90 per cent of the capital's Jews.[84] Such inner city concentrations also developed in other big cities where the new Eastern European arrivals settled. In Glasgow, for instance, about 4,000 out of 6,000 Jews resided in the Gorbals.[85]

The concentration which characterized the late Victorian and Edwardian periods broke down after the First World War. By the early 1930s only 60 per cent of the capital's Jewish population resided in east London. Even within this part of the metropolis dispersal occurred away from Stepney, where only 52 per cent of Jewish families now lived, towards Hackney, Bethnal Green, Stoke Newington, Shoreditch and Poplar, as well as to areas outside east London.[86]

After the Second World War, as Jewish social mobility continued apace, further dispersal occurred to the outer London suburbs. The decline of the Jewish population in Britain, partly as a result of exogamy,[87] suggests that those who stopped practising their religion would have moved out of the newly emerging areas of Jewish settlement such as Redbridge. In addition to the move towards north-east London, which finds explanation in a gradual migration northwards out of the East End, the other major emerging concentration stretched from Golders Green and Hendon towards Edgware and, in recent years, has even extended into Hertfordshire, especially Radlett. Significant concentration does take place so that a survey from the 1980s found that 60 per cent of all Jews in Barnet lived in six of the twenty electoral wards in the borough, suggesting a level of concentration similar to the Irish in the middle of the nineteenth century for those Jews who still identify themselves as such. Similarly, one third of Jews in Manchester had moved to the northern districts of Whitefield and Prestwich as the Cheetham Hill area disappeared as a significant area of Jewish settlement.[88]

The major migrant groups of the nineteenth century in the form of the Irish and Jews therefore have a complex history. On the one hand, dispersal has clearly taken place, particularly in the case of the latter, where it has occurred fairly rapidly. Similarly, the inner city Irish ghettos had also disappeared by the inter-war years, partly due to redevelopment. While London Jews from Eastern Europe remained heavily focused upon Stepney in the decades before the Great War, this 'ghetto' had begun to unravel itself by the 1920s. Some evidence suggests that Jews moved *en masse* to particular parts of north east and north-west London, where concentration allowed the opening up of new religious institutions,[89] but this *bloc* migration not only ignores those Jews who had 'lapsed', but also those who moved to other parts of the capital.[90] Irish and Jewish migration demonstrated concentration, but its extent remains questionable, while dispersal remains indisputable.

The 'ghettos', which developed amongst post-war migrants remain in the early stages of their history and there seems no reason to believe that they will not go the same way as their Jewish and Irish predecessors in the sense that their residents will both disperse and move en bloc to suburban regions. Most South Asian residential concentrations are less than four decades old, while the West Indian ones, which show more signs of breaking up, go back to the 1950s.

Studies of West Indian migration to Britain have certainly pointed to the concentration of newcomers in particular locations, even based on their island of origin. In the 1970s Stuart Philpott estimated that 'well over 3,000' of the 4,000 Montseratians in Britain lived in London, especially Stoke Newington, Hackney and Finsbury Park, inner city areas where other West Indians lived and worked in skilled or unskilled labouring, transport or factory work. The settlement patterns also linked with the transnational organization of the migration process so that newcomers resided near or with the people who assisted their passage.[91] Peach pointed to a similar combination of factors when examining the settlement of all West Indians to Britain during the 1950s and 1960s. While demonstrating the existence of concentrations in London and Birmingham, he asserted that dispersal occurred as early as 1961 and also asserted that West Indians demonstrated a similar level of concentration to the less visible but more numerous Irish group of the time.[92] While John Rex in particular has devoted attention to the social segregation of immigrants (Black and Asian) in inner city areas,[93] which became most evident in the urban riots of the early 1980s,[94] other surveys point to a variety of settlement patterns, confirming the findings of Peach. An analysis of the 1991 census by the Policy Studies Institute demonstrated that 37 per cent of Caribbeans resided in local authority wards with less than 5 per cent of their own ethnic group, while 37 per cent lived in those with over 20, of whom only 3 per cent lived in wards with 25 per cent or more Caribbean population. This gives a mean figure of 9 per cent and demonstrates significant variations in residence patterns, suggesting integration.[95] Caribbean concentrations have also developed outside the first areas of settlement. By the early 1990s out-migration occurred from inner London boroughs such as Hackney and Lambeth towards Enfield.[96]

By the beginning of the twenty-first century, following the events of 11 September 2001, inter-ethnic conflict in northern cities in the same summer and the bombs on the London tube in July 2005, Asian communities, more particularly those of Islamic faith, had become the most symbolic of an exclusivist and highly concentrated ethnic group, resembling the Jews and Irish before them. On closer inspection, however, South Asians, like their Irish and Jewish predecessors, certainly did not all live in 'the ghetto'.

In view of the specific origins and organized nature of Asian migration to Britain, focused settlements inevitably evolved, often in industrial areas, as in the case of Mirpuris moving to Bradford or Rochdale.[97] Asian migrants have tended to purchase inner city property, which they viewed as an investment, as quickly as possible. Pnina Werbner has demonstrated this process amongst Pakistanis in Manchester, while Anwar has shown the same development in Rochdale.[98] While this may represent the most common paradigm for the settlement of South Asians in Britain, it is certainly not the only one. Migration to Leicester, for instance, had followed this pattern during the 1960s, but a change occurred during the early 1970s, following the expulsion of Asians from Uganda by Idi Amin. In fact, some of the refugees from Uganda initially found themselves residing in camps before moving to Leicester, where they often had contacts, despite the attempts of the Uganda Resettlement Board and Leicester City Council to prevent movement to the city.[99] Settlement focused upon a few inner city wards from the 1960s, while some parts of Leicester have remained largely white. By the 1980s movement began to take place out of the inner city towards the 'higher-status suburb of Oadby'.[100] Similarly, the initial Pakistani concentrations which emerged in the central wards of Manchester in the 1960s had already begun to move into the 'inner suburbs' by the end of the 1980s, representing a fairly rapid dispersal similar to the experiences of east London

Jews half a century earlier.[101] In London South Asians moved out of inner London Boroughs such as Brent towards Harrow and Redbridge. In the latter, over two thirds lived in five southern wards adjacent to Newham, rather than in the wealthier northern ones.[102]

Despite the migration of South Asian groups which has taken place out of the inner cities and towards the suburbs, ethnic clustering continues. Most research suggests that Indians represent the least concentrated South Asian group (although more so than African-Caribbeans, Chinese or Irish), followed by Pakistanis and Bangladeshis. Segregation occurs more typically in northern and midland cities including Leicester, Bradford and Leeds. A combination of religious and economic factors contribute to this situation so that poorer Bangladeshis and Pakistanis are more likely to wish to reside near a mosque in contrast to, in some cases, more middle class Indians. The Policy Studies Institute survey from the early 1990s suggested that Indians and Bangladeshis resided, on average, in an area where 13 per cent of their group lived, while the figure for Pakistanis stood at 14 per cent.[103]

Evidence on settlement patterns of South Asians therefore remains complex. While concentration has taken place since the 1960s, it seems that ghettoization, as a rule, has not, although exceptions exist in specific locations.[104] Nevertheless, taking a perspective that incorporates the history of migrant settlement to Britain during the past two hundred years, there seems no reason to view South Asian settlement as in any way unusual, just a few decades after Indians, Bangladeshis and Pakistanis began to arrive in the country. From the point of view of residence, integration has occurred. While it may appear slow, it resembles Irish and Jewish settlement patterns.

Demography

Exogamy may also provide an indication of integration as does the break up of the extended family unit. Lucassen cautiously suggests that the former indicates that the assimilation process has begun.[105] Before examining the extent to which inter-ethnic marriage and relationships take place, some attention needs to focus upon the demographic structures of migrants who have moved to Britain. Most communities have displayed a relatively even gender balance, if not in the short-run, as in the case of the first South Asian arrivals, then certainly over time. Male dominated communities therefore usually consist of temporary migrants, working in specific occupations, such as merchant shipping during the nineteenth century. The importance of families has reflected the situation in society as a whole, although, with the increasing break up of white families,[106] migrant groups may now have become unusual in this way. While the accommodation of extended families in single residential units may have represented the norm for the first generation, their descendants increasingly move away from this pattern to reflect wider society. Exogamy becomes common amongst the descendants of migrants rather than the settlers themselves, although this pattern varies from one ethnic group to another.

At least one community appears to have undergone the ultimate form of assimilation in the sense that its members intermarried to such an extent that they actually disappeared. This predominantly male group consisted of the Black community which existed in the early nineteenth century, although the research of Norma Myers suggests that, rather than disappearing, this community may simply have slipped out of the public gaze following the abolition of slavery.[107]

For most of the next century and a half Black and Asian people consisted mostly of males partly due to the involvement of people from all over the world in the British merchant navy. By the 1850s about 5,000–6,000 'lascars and Chinese seamen found themselves in British ports.'[108] Nevertheless, some Indian women did come to Britain, as nurses and nannies to British families, although they would not have had much contact with Lascars.[109] The Chinese also had an uneven gender ratio with 338 males to 49 females in 1901 and 1,747 males to 187 females in 1931.[110] Black people counted a predominance of males until the middle of the twentieth century, whether they consisted of sailors, workers imported to help in both of the War efforts, students or political activists present in Britain in connection with the rise of Pan-Africanism.[111]

One European group which demonstrated an uneven demography in Britain during the nineteenth century consisted of Italians. Apart from the presence of a significant number of child musicians,[112] Lucio Sponza has calculated that women never made up more than 30 per cent of the Italian community in England and Wales between 1861 and 1911. As a result of such uneven figures Sponza demonstrated that families with an English, rather than Italian, wife predominated in the middle of the nineteenth century, while some Italians married Irishwomen and those of other nationalities. Such unions represented 'a contributing factor to the process of sedentarization' of Italian male migrants in Britain.[113]

Mixed relationships also took place between the overwhelmingly male non-European migrants and native women, leading to much concern in the press and amongst academics during the inter-war period.[114] In his study of the Bute Town area of Cardiff in the late 1930s and early 1940s Kenneth Little analyzed the parentage of '200 children, mainly in attendance at the largest school of the area'. He concluded that while 25 per cent of fathers consisted of 'Whites', the rest were made up of 19 per cent West Indians, 23 per cent West Africans, 14 per cent Arabs and 19 per cent 'Somalis, Maltese, Indians, Greeks, etc.' In contrast, the mothers consisted of 81 per cent white, 11 per cent 'Anglo-Negroid' with the remainder made up of 'Anglo-Chinese, Egyptians, Somalis, etc'.[115]

Smaller communities have therefore generally demonstrated a predominance of males over females, inevitably leading to inter-ethnic relationships. The larger nineteenth-century groups showed a more even gender ratio, although, as integration occurred, the second and subsequent generations almost certainly practiced exogamy. German males always outnumbered females between 1861 and 1911, although to a lesser extent than the communities considered above, so that women constitute between 31 and 40 per cent of the total. More married than single Germans lived in Britain and children, whether born in Germany or Britain, were therefore equally normal amongst this group. Unions with English partners certainly took place as indicated by the marriage registers of St George's German Lutheran Church in Whitechapel which demonstrated that, by the period 1883–96, 24.4 per cent of unions included a non-German husband or wife.[116]

The Eastern European Jewish migration to Britain during the late nineteenth and early twentieth centuries transformed the demography of Anglo-Jewry. Whereas the established community had marriage and fertility patterns resembling those of wider society, the new arrivals had considerably higher birth rates than their English neighbours until the inter-war years. This explains the rise in the Jewish population to a peak figure of perhaps 450,000 Jews by the 1950s. Immigration statistics suggest that more males then females entered the country in the late Victorian and Edwardian years, although a considerable number of children also arrived. Nevertheless, as early as 1911, about 22 per cent of Russian born men under 45 had non-Russian wives. Despite this high rate of intermarriage, the community grew. The post-war history of Anglo-Jewry demonstrates full integration in demographic terms. By 1980 British Jews had a low fertility rate and a high proportion of old people. Consequently, the number of Jews had declined to 259,927 by the 2001 census. Exogamy also continued and would now, in view of declining fertility, have a significant effect. The number of synagogue marriages therefore fell from 1,830 in 1965 to 1,031 by 1992.[117]

The Irish migrants of the nineteenth century display similar demographic characteristics to the Jews. Males seem to have predominated, although the discrepancy remained fairly small. In the case of London women appear to have outnumbered men in the middle of the century. Families were common, although significant percentages of the Irish were single according to local census statistics. The size of Irish households exceeded that of their neighbours, especially following the Famine influx, when a household could contain a nuclear group, extended family and lodgers. Nevertheless, this pattern increasingly changed over time. In the case of Liverpool the mean number of persons per house in 1851 stood at 9.4 and 7.2 for the Irish and non-Irish population respectively, but by 1871 the figures had evened out to 7.6 and 7.3.[118]

The decline of the size of the Irish community by the First World War points to the fall of immigration, but also suggests exogamy. As early as 1851 28.3 per cent of Irish married couples in Gateshead included an English or Scottish partner.[119] This certainly became normal in some of the smaller Irish communities such as Stafford, Bristol or York. But exogamy remained less common in the more populous community in Manchester, where the Roman Catholic Church opposed mixed marriages and where, presumably, more Roman Catholic partners presented themselves, especially in a city where the Church lay at the centre of a whole network of educational, social, religious and philanthropic organizations. The growth of the Roman Catholic population and the Church which supported it in Britain finds explanation in the fact that Irish people and their descendants married each other. The continuing increase in the number of Roman Catholics after the Second World War partly results from the further influx of people from Ireland.[120] Ultimately, choice of partners in Britain remains personal for this group as for members of all other ethnic minorities although the availability (or lack) of members of the same ethnicity, plays a role.

Demographic patterns of post-war migrants, like those before 1945, vary from one group to another. One relatively unusual group consists of the Irish because women have made the majority of the migrants, a situation which goes back to the late nineteenth century and continues into the inter-war years.[121] Some German women entered the country as the brides of members of the British occupying forces who administered their towns and cities in the immediate aftermath of the Second World War.[122] On the other hand, another European group, Greek Cypriots, had a fairly even demography. While some migration of single people took place, these individuals usually wedded members of their own community through a system of marriages arranged by members of their extended families. In other cases Greek Cypriots arrived as families either as a whole, or with the male making the first move followed by his wife and children. While exogamy remained unusual in the first generation it has become increasingly common in the children and grand-children of the migrants and, because of the small size of the community and the fact that no large reserve exists in a distant homeland (as the population of Cyprus totals just over 800,000) it seems conceivable that this group may disappear from Britain at some time during this century.[123]

Even the much larger West Indian community has declined significantly in terms of first generation immigrants, due to mortality and return migration, although a close examination of Black Caribbean ethnicity demonstrates growth so that Black Caribbeans totalled 565,876 people according to the 2001 census, making up 1 per cent of the population of the UK. Nevertheless, this does not represent a significant increase from an estimate by Ceri Peach from the 1970s which suggested that 548,000 people of West Indian origin lived in Great Britain. The other interesting figure from the 2001 census consists of the number of people describing themselves as mixed, which had reached 677,117, many of whom would have had one Black Caribbean and one white parent. The early history of West Indian migration to Britain actually demonstrated a fairly even demographic structure, although, as in the case of some other post-war communities, women and children followed men. Relationships between West Indian men and women have remained complex, reflecting both the situation in the Caribbean and the situation of wider white society in Britain. Consequently, the nuclear two parent and two child family has represented just one norm, although many people of African-Caribbean origin have viewed marriage as the ideal. By 1984 a total of 31 per cent of West Indian households consisted of lone parent families compared with ten per cent of Whites. By 2001 Black Caribbeans actually displayed the highest rates of single person households amongst any ethnic group, at 38 per cent. In addition, Black Caribbeans also had a high incidence of inter-ethnic relationships and marriages, whether compared with other groups in the UK or with Black people in the USA. According to one research project 40 per cent of 'native born Black Caribbean' males had a native white partner, although even the figure for foreign born males of this community stood at nearly 18 per cent. A tolerant attitude amongst both Black and white people towards such relationships facilitated by the lack of ghettoization of this minority (especially in comparison with the USA) which allows working and social relationships to develop, offers one of the main explanations for this high rate of inter-ethnic relationships.[124]

South Asian immigrants in Britain have displayed a different demographic history from their Black Caribbean counterparts. In 1956 93 per cent of Pakistani and Bangladeshis in Britain consisted of males, while the figure for Indians stood at 73 per cent. These male migrants intended to work and send remittances back to their families with the ultimate aim of returning home. Consequently, during the 1950s and 1960s in particular all-male households evolved amongst the different South Asian communities. One landlord usually owned these homes, although some had more than one owner. In any case, once tenants had saved enough money, they went on to purchase their own property. The gender and age structure of the South Asian communities changed over time, when, rather than returning home, many sent for their wives and families. Thus, by 1974, the proportion of males fell to 65 per cent for Pakistanis and 56 per cent for Indians, leading to the development of more traditional family household units. Pnina Werbner has actually written of 3 phases in the lifestyle and housing of South Asians from single men to young families to 'extended, complex 3 generational families'. Ugandan refugees did not follow this path, as they arrived as families. In demographic terms the South Asian community has not declined due to a lower rate of return migration, the importation of brides from the homeland and a relative lack of exogamy, certainly in comparison with Black Caribbeans. The 2001 census suggested that only 6 per cent of Indians, 4 per cent of Pakistanis and 3 per cent of Bangladeshis had married out, although this figure would probably not count unions between different groups of South Asians and would not take into account differences between the various generations. Despite the marriage choices which individuals make, South Asian communities remain strong and it proves difficult to predict their demographic future.[125]

FIGURE 6 A mixed 'race' wedding, 2006. Alamy images

Demographic and geographic patterns precisely reveal the fact that individual members of particular groups make choices about their residence and choice of partners. Ethnic communities simply do not function as blocks because the members which make them up make their own choices about their identity, in which decisions about residence and marriage partner are important and reflect their general perception of their position within and relationship to British society.[126]

Economics

Like all else about the history of millions of migrants and their offspring in Britain over the past two centuries, it proves impossible to make generalizations about their economic and social position. An examination of contemporary Britain would help to illustrate this point. Many indicators suggest that Bangladeshis and Pakistanis fall at the bottom of the economic and social ladder and that Poles who have recently migrated live in some of the worst housing conditions. On the other hand, some of the richest people in contemporary Britain consist of foreigners, symbolized by the ownership of football clubs or even by the footballers playing in the Premier League. Similarly, socio-economic indicators since the 1960s have suggested that the Jewish minority has a considerably higher social status than British society as a whole. Meanwhile, Indians or Chinese people may have higher unemployment rates than the 'White British', yet a larger percentage of their populations work as professionals.[127]

This diversity in the economic and social position of immigrants in British society does not simply represent a contemporary phenomenon. Examining the mid-Victorian period we might point to the contrast between established Anglo-Jewry, some of whose members had reached the higher echelons of British society, and the mass of the labouring Irish, firmly within the working classes. Yet even these prove generalizations because of the social and economic diversity of Jews in Britain during the Victorian and Edwardian years: while social mobility may have taken place, so did the migration of poor newcomers from Eastern Europe.[128] Similarly, Lynn Hollen Lees recognized that the Irish in mid nineteenth-century London included a 'small number of middle-class' people, mostly Protestant, who 'chose the metropolis for its professional and educational opportunities', together with 'craftsmen' who 'travelled to London for training and job opportunities'. But she recognizes that the largest group consisted of 'rural labourers and small farmers who lacked skills' and fell into the industrial proletariat both here and in the rest of the country.[129] The Germans constituted perhaps the most diverse migrant group in Victorian and Edwardian Britain, at least to the same extent as Jews, ranging from beggars to millionaires.[130]

While many indicators, especially in contemporary Britain, may emphasize the low social and economic status of migrant communities, diversity amongst individual groups and between them, also strikes us. This contradicts the view put forward by much social science research of the 1970s, led by Castles and Miles, which, focusing upon the Irish in the middle of the nineteenth century and the recruitment of migrants to Europe in the decades after the Second World War, could only stress the working class status of such newcomers.[131] More recently, Castles and Miller have recognized the movement of the highly skilled,[132] as has Adrian Favell in an analysis of migration within the European Union, with one focus upon London.[133]

The original work of Castles paid limited attention to the social mobility of post-war migrants in Europe.[134] Lucassen has more recently recognized upward movement amongst Black Caribbeans (while also accepting high rates of unemployment),[135] although, as a result of the dearth of research in this area, has struggled to see the same pattern amongst the Irish.[136] The classic example of social mobility over a long time period consists of Eastern European Jews, moving from a concentration upon manual employment in the footwear and clothing industries in the inner city at the end of the nineteenth century, to a range of middle class occupations by the end of the twentieth.[137]

As in the case of residence patterns, diversity and social mobility reflect the reality of immigrant economic and social patterns in Britain over the past two centuries. One method of social mobility consists of the opening up of small businesses. While restaurants, especially in post-war Britain, aim to serve the ethnic majority,[138] the residential concentration which occurs amongst migrant groups also allows the development of ethnic economies, which have a considerable degree of independent sustainability. Such ethnic economies become apparent amongst the Jewish communities from the end of the nineteenth century and continue amongst South Asians one hundred years later. However, these patterns do not replicate themselves across all ethnic groups so that such economic activity remains relatively under-developed amongst the Irish and Black Caribbean groups, for example.

A series of explanations present themselves for these developments and contrasts. Religion plays a role in two ways. First, in the case of Jews and South Asians, dietary rules necessitate the development of shops and suppliers to provide acceptable foods, which leads to the evolution of a whole series of businesses to provide either kosher, halal or vegetarian products. While this factor may explain the absence of an Irish and African Caribbean food industry of any size, it cannot account for the growth of German food in London before the First World War.[139] Religion also functions in another way in the sense that it provides rooting and drive for ethnic entrepreneurs who find mainstream avenues of professional success closed to them because of racism and therefore turn to business. This theory originates in Max Weber and R. H. Tawney in their explanation of the role of non-conformists in the rise of capitalism.[140] W. D. Rubinstein, meanwhile, demonstrated that a significant percentage of the very wealthy in Britain since the eighteenth century have consisted of outsiders, especially Jews, in fields such as banking and chemicals. He also stressed the role of religion.[141] On the other hand, in his study of entrepreneurship amongst Eastern European Jewish immigrants who moved to Britain at the end of the nineteenth century, Andrew Godley drew a relationship between levels of assimilation and entrepreneurship.[142] A recent study of Asian business success again has its origins in Weber. It stresses racism, leading Asians to self-employment; the role of foreign religions; and the fact that some Asian migrants, especially those from East Africa, had previous experience of running businesses.[143] The size of the immigrant market has also played a role in business success amongst immigrants in Britain, especially in the case of Asians, who can now potentially reach two million people if they concentrate upon producing foods or clothes simply aimed at people with origins in south Asia, although they often branch out to reach the British market, as happened in the case of Tilda Rice, for example.[144] On the local level a city with an Asian population of over 100,000 clearly provides a significant market. A study of Leicester in the late 1970s, with a population of 100,000 Asians after the large influx from Uganda, drew a clear link between the size of this ethnic group and an increase in the number and percentage of businesses owned by immigrants, including food shops.[145] However, Asian business success remains relative, especially for a small grocer serving members of his own community in the inner city. By the early twenty-first century some indicators suggested a decline in Asian self-employment due to a series of factors including the reluctance of the second generation to continue the hard work of their parents and the opening of smaller outlets by supermarket chains.[146] At the same time, those who do not open up businesses find themselves suffering higher unemployment rates than the population as a whole.[147] A final factor, when considering the presence of economically successful migrants in Britain, needs to move away from religion, entrepreneurship and markets to point to the fact that British immigration policy has welcomed those who have had their own means.[148]

As with residence and demography, we again need to stress diversity both between different migrant groups and within them so that, throughout the past two centuries, migrants have varied from beggars to millionaires. Certainly, some groups have greater variations than others. The Victorian and Edwardian German community counted one of the most diverse, while, according to much of the literature, the Irish consisted of a mass of workers, who underwent a slow process of social mobility.

Research on the Irish stresses their working class occupations in the Victorian period. Some of the migrants engaged in activities below even unskilled manual employment, including prostitution and thieving, as Frank Neal demonstrated in Liverpool.[149] Neal has also stressed the destitution, disease and hardship faced by the Irish famine migrants upon arrival in British ports in the late 1840s.[150] The Victorian journalist and social commentator Henry Mayhew wrote about the 10,000 'street-Irish' in London in the early 1850s, who sold a variety of products ranging from nuts, fruit and fish to 'lucifer matches and watercress'. On the one hand such activity might suggest an entrepreneurial spirit but Mayhew pointed out that Irish people involved themselves in street selling because of the unavailability of labouring work all year round. He also claimed that 'the majority of the Irish street-sellers of both sexes beg'.[151] Elizabeth Malcolm has researched the presence of the Irish in English asylums in the second half of the nineteenth century and linked this with poverty and prejudice.[152]

Lees confirms Mayhew's observation about the economic activities of the Irish in nineteenth-century London as they 'were channelled into the bottom ranks of the capital's social and economic hierarchy' where they struggled for survival but formed a 'vast pool of casual labour upon which such industries as transportation, construction and food distribution developed'.[153] Beyond the capital the Irish found themselves playing a particular role as navvies helping to construct the railways and acting as industrial fodder for textile factories. In 1841 up to 10 per cent of navvies in Britain came from Ireland.[154] The Irish proved particularly important in textile production in Yorkshire and Lancashire, where they received low wages for long hours. In Bradford factories they carried out a variety of tasks. Elsewhere in the north of England the Irish worked as casual workers in the Cleveland ironstone field and in a wide variety of occupations in Tyneside. In Scotland Irish occupations mirrored those further south. Navvies helped to construct docks, harbours and railways. They also carried out unskilled or semi-skilled jobs in shipyards, docks, factories, distilleries, potteries and gasworks. Other Irishmen worked as miners, especially in the Lanarkshire coalfield. In south Wales the Irish became involved in a variety of occupational activities, especially of an unskilled nature.[155] Meanwhile, domestic service accounted for more than one third of occupied Irish women during the nineteenth century.[156]

Finally, despite their apparent concentration upon inner city ghettos, the Irish also remained uniquely important in the countryside as agricultural labourers for much of the nineteenth century, usually of a seasonal variety. In the 1830s they helped with the hay and corn harvests, sometimes arriving alone and sometimes bringing their begging children. A total of 57,651 Irish harvesters arrived in Britain in 1841. A general decrease occurred during the course of the nineteenth century as emigration to the USA grew. Some permanent settlers worked in agriculture as in the case of York where the Irish helped in chicory production.[157]

The first generation Irish in nineteenth-century Britain therefore found themselves overwhelmingly employed in manual work, often of an unskilled variety. Yet, as Lynn Lees has demonstrated, a middle class community also existed, admittedly small in number. In Liverpool around 6.5 per cent of the Irish population may have worked in 'professional and intermediate occupations' including merchants and bankers.[158]

It seems inevitable that some social mobility would have taken place amongst the offspring of the mid-Victorian migrants, yet Handley, in his study of *The Irish in Modern Scotland*, could write that 'Throughout the second half of the nineteenth century, the vast majority of Irish immigrants and the first, second and third generation of those who had settled in the country in the early decades of the century took their places in the industrial army that laboured at unskilled and semi-skilled jobs'.[159] This reflects the fact that native Britons also increasingly became proletarianized during the course of the nineteenth century.[160] But a certain amount of social mobility must have taken place amongst the Irish, so that the middle class community which developed had 'risen from the ranks'. This group included 'publicans and shopkeepers', although, in contrast, for instance, to South Asians in late twentieth-century Britain, there remained a dearth of the latter. Unfortunately, the historians of the economic integration of the nineteenth-century Irish have not taken their narratives into the twentieth.[161]

The Victorian German community of the nineteenth century offers a remarkably different pattern of economic activity from the Irish. Although the ethnic cleansing of the Great War halted social integration, much had occurred by then. Germans came in far smaller numbers and often migrated as part of an occupational chain migration. Little evidence exists to suggest that they found themselves employed in unskilled factory employment. The exception would consist of the sugar bakers, carrying out hard physical work and labouring for long hours and little pay in the East End of London and Liverpool.[162] Yet the majority of the Germans in London before the First World War found themselves towards the bottom of the British class structure and poverty remained widespread amongst them. Unlike the Irish the majority of Germans worked in a variety of skilled occupations. These included tailoring in London. Germans became particularly important as waiters by the Edwardian period so that they made up about ten per cent of this occupational group. German street musicians, usually moving to Britain in the summer, also characterized Victorian street life. A significant German middle class also developed, again composed of distinct occupational groups. In the first place, small tradesmen and shopkeepers, especially bakers, barbers and butchers had become ubiquitous, particularly in London. While they served the population as a whole, the emergence of an ethnic economy in the East and West End of London, despite the much smaller size of this group in comparison with the Irish, allowed food shops, selling German bread and meats, to flourish.[163] Foreign correspondence clerks formed another section of the German middle classes in Britain.[164] In addition, a stream of teachers, governesses and academics flowed to the country with particular skills. Governesses, for instance, could offer instruction in music and foreign languages.[165] Bankers, engineers and textile merchants also migrated to a state with greater business opportunities, which recognized and accepted their entrepreneurial skills.[166]

Social integration and mobility proves difficult to measure amongst the Victorian and Edwardian Germans. Most probably remained in the class to which they were born, while others returned home to Germany, either because they had entered Britain temporarily or because they faced deportation during the Great War. Certainly, many businessmen who had moved to the country as representatives of other firms or on their own went on to establish their own companies.[167] Some of these took British nationality, indicated by the 6,836 naturalized Germans according to the 1911 census. Although the Great War meant that they faced a social boycott, those who had become naturalized managed to survive into the 1920s, in contrast with their poorer compatriots, who retained German nationality and therefore had their property confiscated.[168]

Italian immigration to Britain does not have such a dramatic episode in its history, at least not until the Second World War. Much of the movement which occurred during the nineteenth century consisted of lower class manual occupational groups involved in activities such as street music. A handful found employment in distinct skilled occupations such as barometer and thermometer making. Others worked as unskilled labourers.[169] Italians also became involved in various aspects of catering and food provision including the ice cream trade. Some migrants started off selling penny ices in the streets of Victorian Britain and eventually moved on to buy ice cream carts

FIGURE 7 Italian stores in London, 1907. Image by © Hulton-Deutsch Collection/Corbis

and vans in the twentieth century.[170] Italians also became involved in restaurant work by the First World War. Many simply found employment as waiters, while others would, by 1945, have established their own eateries.[171] Something of a watershed occurred in the history of Italian integration in Britain during the Second World War. While the community did not face the strength of hostility endured by the Germans between 1914 and 1918, Italian men and women faced internment which meant that many shops and catering establishments suffered.[172]

A new predominantly working class Italian group arrived in the 1950s.[173] However, continuities exist as evidenced by the social mobility and integration which occurred amongst some families from the end of the nineteenth century, as well as in the post-war period. Catering Empires such as that established by Charles Forte have their origins in migration before the First World War.[174] At the same time, Italian migration in recent decades has become increasingly skilled.[175]

Perhaps the most complicated long standing group of all, but also the one which demonstrates the most obvious social mobility over the past two centuries, consists of the Jews. The complexity of this minority in purely social terms lies in the fact that it has evolved as a result of several waves of immigration. During the Victorian period increasingly established Anglo-Jewry consisted of both Sephardic and Ashkenazi Jews who had migrated from southern, central and Eastern Europe from the readmission of the middle of the seventeenth century. Lower down the social scale the increasing migration from Eastern Europe created a new community by the Edwardian years whose members began to experience some social mobility before 1914. They moved through the generations from labourers working in sweatshops to the professions in a century. The initial ghettoization, as well as subsequent geographical movement *en masse* to the suburbs, meant that a classic ethnic economy developed. Finally, a more middle class group fled from the Nazis and moved to the country during the 1930s, although many of its members would initially end up in occupations below their professional and educational standing.

By the early nineteenth century a middle and upper class Jewish community had already become established both within London and beyond. Leeds, for instance, housed Jewish artisans, traders and craftsmen.[176] A similar situation developed in Cardiff during the course of the Victorian period, where Jews worked in a wide variety of occupations.[177] Some of these middle class members of provincial Victorian Jewry originated in itinerant traders who had previously peddled their goods through the streets, while others had come directly to establish or work in businesses from the continent, particularly from Germany.[178] The top of the Jewish social ladder in mid-Victorian Britain included stock brokers, merchant bankers and large scale merchants, followed by smaller manufacturers.[179] Even a Jewish aristocracy had emerged during the Victorian period, while a few Jews had begun to move into the legal and medical professions, despite facing prejudice.[180] Endelman has demonstrated that 'radical assimilation' occurred amongst both native and foreign born middle and upper class Jews during the Victorian years, which meant a move towards Christianity.[181] However, all accounts of Victorian Jewry also point to the existence of a substantial poor group which had not experienced much integration, consisting of both new nineteenth-century arrivals and the descendants of earlier settlers who had not experienced significant social mobility. Bill Williams has described this population as a 'flotsam of peddlers and petty criminals'.[182]

The peak in the influx of immigration from Eastern Europe at the end of the nineteenth century meant a change in the social and occupational structure of the Jewish communities of Britain. The established middle class group displayed hostility to the newcomers believing they might undermine their position.[183] The classic occupations of the Eastern European immigrants, concentrated in the inner cities, revolved around garment manufacture. By 1911 'about half of all Russians, Poles and Rumanians in England and Wales were engaged in some branch or other of the clothing trades, including footwear and headwear'. In east London, where tailoring, as elsewhere, proved particularly important, the figures stood even higher.[184] As con-temporaries recognized, much of the employment in this sector occurred in 'sweatshops' and involved migrants exploiting members of their own community, although a trade union movement evolved to counter such exploitation.[185]

The concentration of Jews in particular locations allowed the develop-ment of distinct ethnic economies, revolving particularly around food pro-vision as dictated by dietary rituals. Jewish butchers and bakers, advertising in the *Jewish Chronicle*, became particularly visible. These would survive into the post-war period, moving out of the East End with the Jewish population to the suburbs. They would, however, decline dramatically by the end of the twentieth century as kosher observance fell.[186]

This move away from the observance of dietary rules represented one aspect of the acculturation process, also characterized by upward social mobility, which would bring the descendants of the Eastern European Jews to the top of the British social and economic ladder by the 1960s and 1970s. Some members of this group had already begun establishing businesses by the outbreak of the First World War, especially in clothing and food.[187] Working class occupations predominated during the inter-war years, but a shift occurred away from clothing towards industries such as cabinet and cigarette making. Women increasingly worked in the clerical sphere. Some movement also took place into the professions, especially law, medicine, dentistry and accountancy.[188]

Social mobility increased significantly in the post-war period. The refugees from Nazism came from overwhelmingly middle class backgrounds. While some may not have pursued their original employment in the short run, the two seminal studies of these refugees take a celebratory attitude towards their history in Britain, pointing to their success after the Second World War, which had meant a period of internment for some.[189] By 1961 up to 44 per cent of Jews fell into the middle classes. By 1978 almost 95 per cent of Redbridge Jewry owned their homes, compared with 55 per cent of the British population as a whole.[190] An analysis of the 2001 census demon-strated that Jews had considerably better educational qualifications than the rest of British society. Consequently, they found themselves concen-trated in middle class occupations. While around 11 per cent of the whole population worked in the professions, the figure for this group stood at 23 per cent.[191] Bill Rubinstein has also demonstrated the movement of Jews into various strands of the British elites, pointing to 14 Jewish Cabinet ministers between 1945 and 1995 and 45 members of the Royal Society in 1975. Jewish-born writers have included Harold Pinter, Tom Stoppard and

Arnold Wesker. This community has also impacted upon popular culture as evidenced by the Jewish origins of figures such as Frankie Vaughan, Helen Shapiro, Mike and Bernie Winters and Marc Bolan.[192]

Jewish social mobility has taken place over the course of a century if the focus remains upon Eastern European Jews and even longer if the analysis includes other members of this community. We might therefore expect few of the post-war migrants to have attained the same level of economic success in a few decades. But economic indicators remain contradictory, both between and within individual groups. Social status, occupation and income upon arrival in Britain play a significant role in determining the level of economic success of both migrants and their offspring.

An examination of the post-war period as a whole demonstrates that migrants and their descendants have found employment in all occupational activities from top to bottom. Many researchers have pointed to the fact that they also experience higher levels of unemployment (caused largely by prejudice and ghettoization) than the population as a whole. In the early 1960s Black people in Britain already had a greater chance of finding themselves without a job than white society.[193] By the economic recession of the 1970s and 1980s the second generation, especially those of South Asian and Caribbean origin, experienced higher unemployment rates than the white population, reflecting the experience of their parents,[194] a pattern which remains until the present. While only 5 per cent of white British males faced unemployment in 2002–3, the figure stood at between 13 and 17 per cent for South Asians and Black people.[195]

Despite the need to focus upon and emphasize unemployment, this contradicts many other economic statistics on migrant employment in the post-war years, which demonstrate the importance of migrants in the British economy.[196] The Labour Force Survey revealed that 10 per cent of employees in Britain in 2004 were born in another country, a figure which excludes the descendants of migrants.[197] Throughout the post-war years a series of groups have entered the country to work in predominantly working class occupations. This movement began with the arrival of the Irish and Eastern Europeans from the late 1940s followed by African Caribbeans and South Asians, and, most recently, Poles. British immigration policy, determined, to some extent, by the needs of the British economy, has facilitated this process.[198] Yet other economic indicators also point to the fact that some post-war migrants have a relatively high level of economic success. These include figures on self employment and education. While Pakistanis may have higher rates of unemployment than whites, they also have considerably higher levels of self-employment. Statistics on educational achievement reveal even more contradictions. While the Irish, Chinese and Indian populations had some of the highest proportions of their populations with degrees, around a fifth of these groups had no qualifications.[199]

An individual analysis of a few of the groups who have moved to Britain since 1945 may help to unravel some of these contradictions. The two major waves of Poles have migrated towards predominantly working class occupations, often involving a loss of status. Certainly, some social mobility subsequently took place, as indicated by statistics such as house purchase.[200] Although around 40 per cent of those who made their way to Britain in the two years following the accession of Poland to the EU in May 2004 found employment in 'administration, business and management', the rest worked in more solidly working class employment such as agriculture, food, fish and meat processing, hospitality and catering and manufacturing.[201]

Members of the Greek Cypriot community in Britain have worked in a wide variety of occupations since the 1950s. As early as 1966 a total of 19.6 per cent of this group were self-employed, when the figure for the population as a whole stood at 7.1 per cent. Nevertheless, many of the self-employed exploited their own countrymen and women, particularly in the field of clothing manufacture, resembling the picture amongst Eastern European Jews before the First World War. Greek Cypriots played a particularly important role in catering. While many have opened up their own restaurants, others laboured for years as waiters or cooks, for example. A move into the professions and away from long hours of manual labour has occurred amongst the descendants of the migrants.[202]

African-Caribbean employment reveals patterns of general improvement over the decades, although, once again, the picture remains far from straightforward. Lucassen used this group as one of his case studies in his study of immigrant integration in Britain. He pointed to the fact that the first migrants tended to work in manual and low skilled employment and that their offspring tended to suffer high levels of joblessness, especially in the 1980s. However, he suggests an improvement in their social and economic position in recent years.[203] Lucassen's analysis of this group precisely illustrates the way in which the long term approach allows a move away from the focus upon one particular moment, especially during the 1980s, taken by scholars such as Solomos and Rex, which tended to reveal the wretchedness of the economic and social position of, especially, African-Caribbean youth, who participated in the 1980s inner city riots, leading to the development of concepts of an underclass.[204] We should certainly not dismiss such research because many social and economic statistics demonstrate that African-Caribbeans remain disadvantaged.

Although the Black migrants who moved to Britain before 1945 have little relation with those who arrived from the late 1940s, it proves instructive to briefly examine the position of these earlier arrivals. The majority of those who lived in Victorian Britain tended to fall into the lower social economic groups. Mayhew identified some 'Ethiopian serenaders',[205] while Michael Banton pointed to the presence of 'negro beggars' in London.[206] The most durable Black group consisted of sailors, originating both in Africa and the West Indies and living in port cities, including Liverpool, the East End of London and Cardiff.[207] Some increase occurred during the two World Wars counting seamen, soldiers and munition workers.[208] Middle class Black people included students and political activists, mostly from Africa.[209]

Those who arrived from the Caribbean in the late 1940s generally found themselves at the bottom of the social and economic ladder, employed in manual occupations and experiencing higher rates of unemployment than the majority population because of the potency of racism.[210] Many of the newcomers experienced a loss of social status because of this prejudice. Although only 22 per cent of West Indian migrants had worked in unskilled or semi-skilled jobs in the Caribbean, this figure rose to 63 per cent in Britain. Almost 90 per cent of West Indian professional and skilled workers could only find manual work in London.[211] Sheila Patterson identified a range of industries and factories which employed West Indians in South London during the early 1960s including food and soft drinks manufacture, the garment trade and building and construction.[212] Others found public sector jobs including transport. By 1958 4,000 worked for London Transport.[213] Despite this type of employment which involved working with people on a face-to-face basis, West Indians rarely served in retail outlets until the 1960s because shopkeepers feared that customers might stay away.[214] This racial prejudice, which has persisted until the present, despite the passage of a series of measures since the 1960s to prevent it,[215] also meant that West Indians did not experience the same levels of promotion as their colleagues, whether they worked in the private or public sector, especially before the introduction of equality legislation.[216] Such prejudice lay behind the fact that migrants from the Caribbean experienced higher levels of unemployment than natives. Companies such as London Transport implemented a redundancy policy of 'last in, first out'.[217] Therefore, as early as 1961 West Indian males in London endured an unemployment rate of 6 per cent compared with 3.2 per cent for men born in England.[218]

The children of West Indian immigrants faced similar experiences to their parents. During the 1960s, while youth employment offices could find unskilled work for 'coloured school leavers' they had greater difficulty in placing them in skilled occupations, clerical positions and even in shop work, which involved dealing with the public.[219] Many studies also revealed the failure of the education system as the overwhelmingly white teaching profession viewed West Indian children with hostility or indifference.[220] At the same time the fact that many Black children grew up in the inner city has meant that they have also attended the worst schools.[221] Even today, they still have the worst levels of achievement amongst all ethnic groups.[222] Consequently, Black youth has experienced higher rates of unemployment. This position as a virtual underclass focused upon the inner city has played a central role in the greater levels of criminality amongst Black males in Britain.[223]

While people of West Indian origin may still represent a generally underprivileged group, changes have taken place. The high levels of inter-marriage and the increasing geographical dispersal of the descendants of the migrants has meant improvement. A Black middle class has developed,[224] while some of the most successful sportsmen in Britain have African-Caribbean origins.[225] Nevertheless, these represent minorities, especially the latter. Those who remain in the inner city face a difficult future similar, in economic and social terms, to their parents and grandparents.

The experiences of Asians and their descendants also display some bleak facts, although, in view of the complexity of the origins of those who make up this group, it proves difficult to demonstrate any clear pattern. Both Black and Asian people experience racism, which has meant that they also find themselves with higher rates of unemployment and, in the case of Bangladeshis and Pakistanis, with low rates of educational achievement. Yet, on the other hand, they also have higher rates of self-employment, while Indians demonstrate some of the best levels of educational achieve-ment. Part of the reason for the contradictions lies in the different caste origins of the original migrants.

Like African-Caribbeans in Britain, Asian settlement does not begin after 1945, although it clearly takes on a completely different magnitude in the post-war years. Those resident before the Second World War include a diversity of occupational groups, as recognized by a range of scholars including Rozina Visram and Shompa Lahiri. The title of the first edition of Visram's classic study of the pre-1945 history of Asians in Britain, *Ayahs, Lascars and Princes*, points to this diversity. In reality, the second of these groups of generally temporary and poor residents who focused upon ports, outnumbered other South Asian populations in the country during the nineteenth century. Nevertheless, Visram has pointed to the presence of Asian MPs, suffragettes and other political activists, although these remain individuals. During the First World War 1.27 million Indians fought on the Western Front, although only a few thousand of those injured made it to Britain. During the inter-war years a maximum of 8,000 Indians may have lived in Britain. An Indian working class appears to have emerged, especially amongst those involved in the docks and shipping, while others found employment in catering. Indian hawkers and peddlers also became visible. At the same time, by the end of the Second World War as many as 1,000 Indian doctors may have lived in Britain, laying the foundation for the post-war migration of this group. Some Indians also moved to Britain during the Second World War, especially from Mirpur, in order to work in factories in big cities such as Birmingham because of the labour shortage caused by conscription.[226]

This diversity remains after the Second World War. Indians who moved to Britain as professionals often retained their status. However, while Indians as a whole may have the best educational qualifications after the Chinese and one of the highest rates of professional employment, they also display a higher unemployment rate than the 'White British'. The Bangladeshi and Pakistani community, more heavily concentrated in the inner city, has some of the highest unemployment rates, as well as the largest percentage of people without qualifications, explained by their social origins as agricultural workers. On the other hand, Pakistanis have by far the highest self-employment rate at 23 per cent.[227]

These contemporary patterns reflect the diverse migrant origins of South Asians in Britain, as well as the residence of many Bangaldeshis and Pakistanis in the inner city, where they moved to carry out manual employment, which accounted for around four fifths of these groups in the early 1970s.[228] Since that time, an increasing number of Pakistanis, as well as other South Asian groups, have moved into self-employment, although this partly results from the racism they face in other forms of employment. While some Asian businessmen may have become multi millionaires,[229] most operate companies making small profits.[230] At the same time, the children of Bangladeshi and Pakistani parents, concentrated in the inner city, have tended to have similar employment experiences to those from African Caribbean backgrounds, certainly during the era of high unemployment in the 1980s.[231] Those South Asians who have done well in Britain have often migrated to professional occupations and come from higher castes.[232] One of the most notable success stories, now celebrated even by the right-wing press,[233] consists of Ugandan Asians many of whom already had business experience in Uganda.[234]

Economic integration of Asians in Britain therefore proves highly complex because of the diversity of groups concerned. In some ways, different types of integration have occurred. Those whose parents worked in manual occupations have not experienced the same level of economic success as those from higher caste backgrounds. Self-employment may offer one particular form of economic activity favoured by South Asians, but it neither suggests integration, especially in the case of those who open up grocery stores where their own group lives, nor does it lead to a comfortable middle class lifestyle, as many of these businesses make small profits.

The Chinese community, while smaller in scale and not quite as diverse, has similar experiences to South Asians. This group also counted small numbers before 1945, with concentrations in port towns, where some had arrived as sailors and where others had opened up small businesses including grocery stores, laundries and the first Chinese restaurants.[235] The growth of the post-war Chinese community mirrored the spread of the Chinese

FIGURE 8 An elderly man passes the front of a store selling Chinese goods in London's Soho district, *c.* 1934, Soho, London, Image © E.O. Hoppé/CORBIS

restaurant and Chinese food, although, like their Indian counterparts, few of those involved in this trade have made significant profits.[236] At the same time, Chinese people experience unemployment rates higher than those of the White British. However, they also demonstrate the best levels of educational success at school.[237]

The inevitability of integration?

Reaching conclusions about the geography, demography and economics of the millions of migrants and their offspring in Britain over the past two hundred years proves highly problematic. Nevertheless, we can make a series of assertions. First, migrant communities do not remain trapped in a time warp of ghettoization and poverty, even though the move out of such initial living conditions may take generations. The mid-nineteenth-century Irish migrants provide one of the best examples of the gradual escape from 'the ghetto', while the Jews provide one of the most 'textbook' instances.

A focus upon Jews, however, also indicates that while the geographic ghetto may dissipate over time, the late nineteenth-century Eastern Europeans tended to move as a group towards the outskirts of London. This has also happened in the case of South Asian groups, as the example of Leicester and the move to the Oadby suburb has demonstrated. But while Leicester may demonstrate some of the highest levels of segregation in the country, many social surveys have pointed to the increasingly dispersed nature of the members of the communities which evolved in the post-war years. If dispersal in housing patterns provides an indication of integration, then most groups in Britain, certainly over generations, have experienced some integration.

The demographics of migrant groups demonstrate variations. On the one hand some communities have originated from predominantly male settlers, especially in the case of South Asians, reunited with their wives and children who subsequently followed them. Other groups have tended to move as families from the Irish through the Jews to West Indians and Greek Cypriots. Relationships and families in Britain often tend to reflect patterns in the homeland, so that those who originate in states with well founded concepts of families, such as Cyprus, continue this pattern, while West Indians have often had more informal relationships. The British environment also takes its toll over time. Intermarriage and inter-ethnic relationships, a clear indicator of integration, gradually become a fact of life, although it becomes the norm for some groups sooner than for others. At the same time, fertility patterns also gradually mirror those of the majority population.

The economic position of migrant communities also points to diverse patterns. Over the past two hundred years it remains undeniable that immigrants have undertaken some of the worst employment for the lowest pay and have experienced the worst unemployment rates. This represents the most common, but not the only, paradigm. Some migrants have moved to Britain with money, skills and qualifications, especially over recent decades. While contemporary statistics may demonstrate high rates of unemployment, some of the wealthiest people in Britain, welcomed by the government, are also migrants. At the same time, social mobility also takes place. The case of Eastern European Jews best demonstrates this process in action, although the move from working in East End sweatshops to professional employment occurred over the course of a century in some cases, involving up to four generations.

Integration therefore remains a slow process. Focusing upon the Irish in the 1850s or West Indians in the 1960s simply confirms the fact that many immigrants initially find themselves in difficult circumstances. Equally, over time and through generations, convergence with the norms of the population as a whole occurs. The example of the nineteenth-century migrants suggests that social mobility also needs a long time period. While some post-war migrant communities have demonstrated this process in action, there remains a long way to go before some of them reach the same social and economic status as much of the majority population.

Notes and references

1   Leo Lucassen, *The Immigrant Threat: The Integration of Old and New Migrants in Western Europe since 1850* (Urbana and Chicago, 2005), p. 213.

2   Ibid., p. 49.

3   M. A. G. Ó Tuathaigh, 'The Irish in Nineteenth Century Britain: Problems of Integration', *Transactions of the Royal Historical Society*, vol. 31 (1981), p. 156. See also Paul O'Leary, *Immigration and Integation: The Irish in Wales, 1789–1922* (Cardiff, 2000).

4   Lucassen, *Immigrant Threat*, p. 141.

5   Michael Banton, *The Coloured Quarter: Negro Immigrants in a British City* (London, 1955).

6   Ruth Glass, *Newcomers: The West Indians in London* (London, 1960).

7   Sheila Patterson, *Dark Strangers: A Sociological Study of the Absorption of a Recent West Indian Migrant Group in Brixton, South London* (London, 1963).

8 See, for instance, John Rex, *The Ghetto and the Underclass: Essays on Race and Social Policy* (Aldershot, 1988).

9 John Solomos, *Black, Youth and the State: The Politics of Ideology and Policy* (Cambridge, 1988).

10 See, for instance: W. J. Lowe, *The Irish in Mid-Victorian Lancashire: The Shaping of a Working Class Community* (New York, 1989); and Frances Finnegan, *Poverty and Prejudice: A Study of Irish Immigrants in York, 1840–1875* (Cork, 1982).

11 Roger Swift and Sheridan Gilley have edited three important books in the form of: *The Irish in the Victorian City* (London, 1985); *The Irish in Britain, 1815–1939* (London, 1989); and *The Irish in Victorian Britain: The Local Dimension* (Dublin, 1999).

12 But see Steven Fielding, *Class and Ethnicity: Irish Catholics in England, 1880–1939* (Buckingham, 1993), who, however, tackles the survival of Catholic identity rather than changes in social and economic position.

13 The classic studies are: Lloyd P. Gartner, *The Jewish Immigrant in England, 1870–1914* (London, 1960); John A. Garrard, *The English and Immigration, 1880–1910* (London, 1971); Bernard Gainer, *The Alien Invasion: The Origins of the Aliens Act of 1905* (London, 1972).

14 The most important long-term studies of Anglo-Jewry revealing these complexities include: Geoffrey Alderman, *Modern British Jewry* (Oxford, 1992); W. D. Rubinstein, *A History of the Jews in the English Speaking World: Great Britain* (Basingstoke, 1996); Todd M. Endelman, *The Jews of Britain, 1656–2000* (London, 2002); and V. D. Lipman, *A History of the Jews in Britain Since 1858* (Leicester, 1990).

15 See Chapter 5 below.

16 See: Panikos Panayi, *German Immigrants in Britain during the Nineteenth Century, 1815–1914* (Oxford, 1995); Stefan Manz, *Migranten und Internierte: Deutsche in Glasgow, 1864–1918* (Stuttgart, 2003); and Ulrike Kirchberger, *Aspekte deutsch-britischer Expansion: Die Überseeinteressen der deutschen Migranten in Großbritannien in der Mitte des 19. Jahrhunderts* (Stuttgart, 1999).

17 The concept of Asian identity and ethnicity receives full attention in Chapter 4.

18 See the discussion below.

19 Rex, *Ghetto*.

20 Marion Berghahn, *German-Jewish Refugees from Nazi Germany* (Oxford, 1988).

21 Anne J. Kershen, *Strangers, Aliens and Asians: Huguenots, Jews and Bangladeshis in Spitalfields, 1660–2000* (London, 2005).

22 Lynn Hollen Lees, *Exiles of Erin: Irish Immigrants in Victorian London* (Manchester, 1979), p. 57.

23 Panikos Panayi, *German Immigrants in Britain during the Nineteenth Century, 1815–1914* (Oxford, 1995), pp. 26–7, 93–100; Panikos Panayi, 'Anti-German

Riots in London During the First World War', *German History*, 7 (1989), vol. 7, pp. 194–7.

24 John Seed, 'Limehouse Blues: Looking for Chinatown in the London Docks, 1900–40', *History Workshop Journal*, Issue 62 (2006), pp. 58–85.

25 Geoff Dench, *Maltese in London: A Case Study in the Erosion of Ethnic Consciousness* (London, 1975); Geoff Dench, Kate Gavron and Michael Young, *The New East End: Kinship, Race and Conflict* (London, 2006); David J. Griffiths, 'Fragmentation and Consolidation: The Contrasting Cases of Somali and Kurdish Refugees in London', *Journal of Refugee Studies*, vol. 13 (2000), pp. 281–302; John Eade, *Placing London: From Imperial Capital to Global City* (Oxford, 2000).

26 Cecil Roth, *The Rise of Provincial Jewry: The Early History of the Jewish Communities in the English Countryside* (London, 1950), pp. 110–11.

27 Ibid., pp. 52–3.

28 Ibid., p. 26.

29 Gartner, *Jewish Immigrant in England*, pp. 145–6; Henrietta Adler, 'Jewish Life and Labour in East London', in Sir Hubert Llewellyn Smith, ed., *New Survey of London Life and Labour*, vol. 6 (London, 1934), pp. 271–2, p. 296; Lipman, *History of the Jews in Britain*, pp. 206–9; Ursula Henriques, *The Jews of South Wales: Historical Studies* (Cardiff, 1993).

30 Lipman, ibid., p. 205.

31 Panikos Panayi, *Immigration, Ethnicity and Racism in Britain, 1815–1945* (Manchester, 1994), pp. 51–2.

32 See below.

33 See, for instance, Swift and Gilley, *Irish in Victorian Britain*.

34 Chris Williams, ' "Decorous and Creditable": The Irish in Newport', in Paul O'Leary, ed., *Irish Migrants in Modern Wales* (Liverpool, 2004), p. 55.

35 D. Morgan, *Harvesters and Harvesting, 1840–1900* (London, 1982), p. 76; Sarah Barber, 'Irish Migrant Agricultural Labourers in Nineteenth Century Lincolnshire', *Saothar*, vol. 8 (1982), pp. 10–23.

36 J. H. Treble, 'Irish Navvies in the North of England, 1830–50', *Transport History*, vol. 6 (1973), pp. 227–47.

37 Panayi, *German Immigrants*, pp. 92–107.

38 Lucio Sponza, *Italian Immigrants in Nineteenth Century Britain* (Leicester, 1988), pp. 322–5; Terri Colpi, *The Italian Factor: The Italian Community in Great Britain* (Edinburgh, 1991), p. 74.

39 Panayi, *Immigration*, pp. 56–7.

40 See, for instance, Kenneth Little, *Negroes in Britain* (London, 1972); Seed, 'Limehouse Blues'; J. Salter, *The East in the West or Work Among the Asiatics and*

Africans in Britain (London, 1896); Diane Frost, *Work and Community Among West African Migrant Workers Since the Nineteenth Century* (Liverpool, 1999), pp. 29–103.

41 Panikos Panayi, 'Cosmopolis: London's Ethnic Minorities', in Andrew Gibson and Joe Kerr, eds, *London from Punk to Blair* (London, 2003), pp. 67–71; Malcolm Harrison, Deborah Phillips, Kusminder Chahal, Lisa Hunt and John Perry, *Housing, 'Race' and Community Cohesion* (Coventry, 2005).

42 Dench, Gavron and Young, *New East End*.

43 Edward Pilkington, *Beyond the Mother Country: West Indians and the Notting Hill White Riots* (London, 1988); Patterson, *Dark Strangers*.

44 Glass, *Newcomers*, pp. 32–40.

45 Richard Skellington, *'Race' in Britain Today*, 2nd Edn (London, 1996), p. 58.

46 Panayi, 'Cosmopolis'; Gurharpal Singh and Darshan Singh Tatla, *Sikhs in Britain: The Making of a Community* (London, 2006), pp. 62–3; Muhamad Anwar, *British Pakistanis: Demographic, Social and Economic Position* (Coventry, 1996), pp. 16–19; Kershen, *Strangers*.

47 Seán Hutton, 'The Irish in London', in Nick Merriman, ed., *The Peopling of London: 15,000 Years of Settlement from Overseas* (London, 1993), p. 119.

48 Bronwen Walter, 'Contemporary Irish Settlement in London: Women's Worlds, Men's Worlds', in Jim Mac Laughlin, ed., *Location and Dislocation in Contemporary Irish Society: Emigration and Identities* (Cork, 1997), pp. 67–8; Judy Chance, 'The Irish in London: An Exploration of Ethnic Boundary Maintenance', in Peter Jackson, ed., *Race and Racism: Essays in Social Geography* (London, 1987), pp. 142–60.

49 Barry A. Kosmin and Caren Levy, *The Work and Employment of Suburban Jews: The Socio-Economic Findings of the 1978 Redbridge Jewish Survey* (London, 1981).

50 Robin Oakley, *Changing Patterns of Distribution of Cypriot Settlement* (Coventry, 1987).

51 Panayi, 'Cosmopolis'; Merriman, *The Peopling of London*.

52 See below.

53 Graham Davis, The Irish in Britain, 1815–1914 (Dublin, 1991), pp. 175–6.

54 Gurharpal Singh, 'Multiculturalism in Contemporary Britain: Reflections on the "Leicester Model"', in John Rex and Gurharpal Singh, eds, *Governance in Multicultural Societies* (Aldershot, 2004), p. 57; Valerie Marrett, *Immigrants Settling in the City* (Leicester, 1989), pp. 1–5; Margaret Byron, *Post-war Caribbean Migration to Britain: The Unfinished Cycle* (Aldershot, 1994), pp. 75–7.

55 Humayun Ansari, *'The Infidel Within': Muslims in Britain Since 1800* (London, 2004), p. 173.

56 Vaughan Robinson, *Transients, Settlers and Refugees: Asians in Britain* (Oxford, 1986). See also Singh and Tatla, *Sikhs in Britain*, pp. 62–3; and Anwar, *British Pakistanis*, pp. 20–6.

57 C. Richardson, 'Irish Settlement in Mid-Nineteenth Century Bradford', *Yorkshire Bulletin of Economic and Social Research*, vol. 20 (1968), p. 41.

58 Roger Swift, 'Anti-Catholicism and the Irish Disturbances: Public Order in Mid-Victorian Wolverhampton', *Midland History*, vol. 9 (1984), p. 88.

59 Carl Chinn, ' "Sturdy Catholic Emigrants": The Irish in Early Victorian Birmingham', in Swift and Gilley, *Irish in Victorian Britain*, pp. 52, 58; Skellington, *'Race'*, p. 58.

60 Frank Neal, *Sectarian Violence: The Liverpool Experience, 1819–1914* (Manchester, 1988), p. 9.

61 For Wales see: O'Leary, *Immigration and Integration*; and Charlotte Williamson, Neil Evans and Paul O'Leary, eds, *A Tolerant Nation? Exploring Ethnic Diversity in Wales* (Cardiff, 2003). For the Irish in nineteenth-century Scotland see J. E. Handley: *The Irish in Scotland, 1798–1845* (Cork, 1943); and *The Irish in Modern Scotland* (Cork, 1947). For Scotland more recently see Scottish Office Central Research Unit Papers, 'Ethnic Minorities in Scotland', June 1983.

62 Vaughan Robinson, Roger Anderson and Sako Musterd, *Spreading the Burden: A Review of Policies to Disperse Asylum Seekers and Refugees* (Bristol, 2003).

63 See above Chapter 2.

64 Kathleen Neils Conzen, 'Immigrants, Immigrant Neighbourhoods, and Ethnic Identity: Historical Issues', *Journal of American History*, vol. 66 (1979), pp. 603–15; Stanley Nadel, *Little Germany: Ethnicity, Religion and Class in New York City, 1845–80* (Urbana and Chicago, 1990).

65 Pnina Werbner, *The Migration Process: Capital, Gifts and Offerings among British Pakistanis* (Oxford, 1990), pp. 11–49; Muhammad Anwar, *The Myth of Return: Pakistanis in Britain* (London, 1979).

66 See Chapter 4 below.

67 Deborah Phillips, 'Moving Towards Integration: The Housing of Asylum Seekers and Refugees in Britain', *Housing Studies*, vol. 21 (2006), pp. 539–53.

68 See, for instance, Jeff Henderson and Valerie Khan, 'Race, Class and the Allocation of Public Housing in Britain', *Urban Studies*, vol. 21 (1984), pp. 115–28.

69 As an introduction to these issues see E. D. Huttman, 'Housing Segregation in Western Europe: An Introduction', in E. D. Huttman, W. E. Blanco and S. Saltman, eds, *Urban Housing: Segregation of Minorities in Western Europe and the United States* (London, 1991), pp. 21–39.

70 Ted Cantle, *Community Cohesion: A New Framework for Race and Diversity* (Basingstoke, 2005), pp. 198–201.

71 Ceri Peach, 'Does Britain Have Ghettos?', *Transactions of the Institute of British Geographers*, New Series, vol. 21 (1996), pp. 232–4. See also Nissa Finney and Ludi Simpson, *'Sleepwalking to Segregation?' Challenging Myths About Race and Immigration* (Bristol, 2009).

72 Conzen, 'Immigrants', p. 603.

73 Leon M. Faucher, *Manchester in 1844: Its Present Condition and Future Prospects* (London, 1844), p. 28.

74 *Royal Commission on the Conditions of the Poorer Classes in Ireland, Appendix G, The State of the Irish Poor in Great Britain* (London, 1836), pp. xi, xiv.

75 Neal, *Sectarian Violence*, pp. 10–15.

76 Colin G. Pooley, 'The Residential Segregation of Migrant Communities in Mid-Victorian Liverpool', *Transactions of the Institute of British Geographers*, New Series, vol. 2 (1977), pp. 364–82.

77 Colin G. Pooley, 'Segregation or Integration? The Residential Experience of the Irish in Mid-Victorian Britain', in Swift and Gilley, *Irish in Britain*, pp. 60–83.

78 Fielding, *Class and Ethnicity*, pp. 27–33.

79 Lees, *Exiles of Erin*, p. 60.

80 John Hickey, 'Irish Settlement in Nineteenth Century Cardiff', in O'Leary, *Irish Migrants in Modern Wales*, pp. 34–53.

81 Panayi, *German Immigrants*, pp. 93–100; Manz, *Migranten und Internierte*, pp. 41–3.

82 See Salo W. Baron, *The Russian Jew Under Tsars and Soviets*, 2nd Edn (London, 1964), pp. 63–74.

83 Lipman, *History of the Jews in Britain*, pp. 14–15; Endelman, *Jews of Britain*, pp. 94–5.

84 Panayi, *Immigration*, p. 55.

85 Murdoch Rogers, 'Glasgow Jewry: The History of the City's Jewish Community', in Billy Kay, ed., *Odyssey: Voices from Scotland's Recent Past* (Edinburgh, 1982), p. 113.

86 Adler, 'Jewish Life', pp. 271–2, 296; Lipman, *History of the Jews in Britain*, pp. 207–8.

87 See below.

88 Endelman, *The Jews of Britain*, pp. 230–1; Stanley Waterman and Barry Kosmin, 'Ethnic Identity, Residential Concentration and Social Welfare: The Jews in London', in Jackson, *Race and Racism*, pp. 263–4; *Jewish Chronicle*, 13 July 2005; David Graham, Marlena Schmool and Stanley Waterman, *Jews in Britain: A Snapshot from the 2001 Census* (London, 2007), pp. 23–37.

89 See Chapter 4 below.

90 Waterman and Barry Kosmin, 'Ethnic Identity', p. 261.

91 Stuart B. Philpott, 'The Montserratians: Migration Dependency and the Maintenance of Island Ties in England', in James L. Watson, ed., *Between Two Cultures: Migrants and Minorities in Britain* (Oxford, 1977), p. 108.

92 Ceri Peach, *West Indian Migration to Britain: A Social Geography* (London, 1968), pp. 84–8.

93 John Rex, 'The Social Segregation of the Immigrant in British Cities', *Political Quarterly*, vol. 39 (1968), pp. 15–24.

94 John Benyon and John Solomos, eds, *The Roots of Urban Unrest* (Oxford, 1987).

95 Tariq Modood, et al., *Ethnic Minorities in Britain: Diversity and Disadvantage* (London, 1997), p. 188.

96 Deborah Phillips, 'Black Minority Ethnic Concentration, Segregation and Dispersal in Britain', *Urban Studies*, vol. 35 (1998), p. 1686.

97 Verity Saifullah Khan, 'The Pakistanis: Mirpuri Villagers at Home and in Bradford', in Watson, *Between Two Cultures*, pp. 57–76; Anwar, *Myth of Return*, pp. 17–61.

98 Werbner, *Migration Process*, pp. 15–49; Anwar, ibid., pp. 28–35.

99 John Martin and Gurharpal Singh, *Asian Leicester* (Stroud, 2002), pp. 10–11; E. Nelson Swinerton, William G. Kueper and G. Lynne Lackey, *Ugandan Asians in Great Britain* (London, 1975); Marrett, *Immigrants Settling in the City*.

100 Martin and Singh, ibid., pp. 16–20; Phillips, 'Black Minority Ethnic Concentration', p. 1687.

101 Werbner, *Migration Process*, pp. 15–49.

102 Phillips, 'Black Minority Ethnic Concentration', p. 1687.

103 Modood, *Ethnic Minorities in Britain*, p. 188.

104 See the following: ibid.; Peach, 'Does Britain Have Ghettos?'; Ron Johnston, James Forrest and Michael Poulsen, 'Are there Ethnic Enclaves/Ghettos in English Cities', *Urban Studies*, vol. 39 (2002), pp. 591–618; John Stillwell and Deborah Phillips, 'Diversity and Change: Understanding the Ethnic Geographies of Leeds', *Journal of Ethnic and Migration Studies*, vol. 32 (2006), pp. 1131–52.

105 Lucassen, *Immigrant Threat*, pp. 136–7.

106 As an introduction to such issues see, for instance: John Haskey, Kathleen Kiernan, Patricia Morgan and Miriam E. David, *The Fragmenting Family: Does it Matter?* (London, 1998); and Graham Allan and Graham Crow, *Families, Households and Society* (Basingstoke, 2001).

107 Norma Myers, *Reconstructing the Black Past: Blacks in Britain, 1780–1830* (London, 1996). Assimilationist perspectives include: Peter Fryer, *Staying Power: The History of Black People in Britain*, pp. 235–6; and James Walvin, *Black and White: The Negro and English Society, 1555–1945* (London, 1973), pp. 189–201.

108 Rosina Visram, *Asians in Britain: 400 Years of History* (London, 2002), p. 33.

109 Visram, *Asians in Britain*, pp. 50–4.

110 Panayi, *Immigration*, p. 60.

111 Fryer, Staying Power, pp. 237–367.

112 John E. Zucchi, *The Little Slaves of the Harp: Italian Child Street Musicians in Nineteenth-Century Paris, London and New York* (London, 1992), pp. 76–110.

113 Sponza, *Italian Immigrants*, pp. 58–60.

114 Paul B. Rich, *Race and Empire in British Politics* (Cambridge, 1990), pp. 130–5.

115 Little, *Negroes in Britain*, pp. 108–9.

116 Panayi, *German Immigrants*, pp. 108–10.

117 S. Rosenblaum, 'A Contribution to the Study of the Vital and other Statistics of the Jews in the United Kingdom', *Journal of the Royal Statistical Society*, vol. 68 (1905), pp. 525–62; Adler, 'Jewish Life', pp. 283, 294; Barry A. Kosmin, 'Nuptiality and Fertility Patterns of British Jewry, 1850–1980: An Immigrant Transition?', in D. A. Coleman, ed., *Demography of Immigrant and Minority Groups in the United Kingdom* (London, 1982), pp. 245–61; Bernard Wasserstein, *Vanishing Diaspora: The Jews in Britain Since 1945* (London, 1996), pp. viii, 74; Rubinstein, *History of the Jews*, pp. 418–19; Graham, Schmool and Waterman, *Jews in Britain*, pp. 39–50.

118 John Haslett and W. J. Lowe, 'Household Structure and Overcrowding Among the Lancashire Irish, 1851–1871', *Histoire Social*, vol. 10 (1977), pp. 45–58; Finnegan, *Poverty and Prejudice*, pp. 72–4; David Large, 'The Irish in Bristol in 1851: A Census Enumeration', in Swift and Gilley, *Irish in the Victorian City*, pp. 51, 53; Lees, *Exiles of Erin*, pp. 48–51.

119 Frank Neal, 'A Statistical Profile of the Irish Community in Gateshead: The Evidence of the 1851 Census', *Immigrants and Minorities*, vol. 27 (2009), p. 66.

120 Fielding, *Class and Ethnicity*; Lucassen, *Immigrant Threat*, pp. 46–8; Walter, 'Contemporary Irish Settlement in London', pp. 61–93; A. E. C. W. Spencer, 'Catholics in Britain and Ireland', in Coleman, *Demography*, pp. 211–43; John Herson, 'Migration, "Community" or Integration? Irish Families in Victorian Stafford', in Swift and Gilley, *Irish in Victorian Britain*, pp. 156–89.

121 Walter, ibid., p. 65; Louise Ryan, 'Passing Time: Irish Women Remembering and Re-Telling Stories of Migration to Britain', in Kathy Burrell and Panikos Panayi, eds, *Histories and Memories: Migrants and their History in Britain* (London, 2006), pp. 191–209.

122 Inge Weber-Newth, 'Bilateral Relations: British Soldiers and German Women', in Louise Ryan and Wendy Webster, eds, *Gendering Migration: Masculinity, Feminity and Ethnicity in Post-War Britain* (Ashgate, 2008), pp. 53–70.

123 Floya Anthias, *Ethnicity, Class, Gender and Migration: Greek Cypriots in Britain* (Aldershot, 1992), pp. 7–8; Kathy Burrell, *Moving Lives: Narratives of Nation and Migration among Europeans in Post-war Britain* (Aldershot, 2006), pp. 10–11; Pamela Constantinides, 'The Greek Cypriots: Factors in the Maintenance of Ethnic Identity', in Watson, *Between Two Cultures*, pp. 269–300; Panikos Panayi, 'One Last Chance: Masculinity, Ethnicity and the Greek Cypriot

Community of London', in Pat Kirkham and Janet Thumin eds, *You Tarzan: Masculinity, Movies and Men* (London, 1993), pp. 146–52.

124 Glass, *Newcomers*, pp. 15–20; Patterson, *Dark Strangers*, pp. 298–307; Colin Brown, *Black and White Britain: The Third PSI Survey* (Aldershot, 1984), pp. 28, 35–9; Office for National Statistics, *Focus on Ethnicity and Identity* (London, 2005), pp. 1–2, 5; Suzanne Model and Gene Fisher, 'Unions Between Blacks and Whites: England Compared with the USA', *Ethnic and Racial Studies*, vol. 25 (2002), pp. 728–54; Sharon Beishon, Tariq Modood and Satnam Virdee, *Ethnic Minority Families* (London, 1998); Susan Benson, *Ambiguous Ethnicity: Interracial Families in London* (Cambridge, 1981).

125 Robinson, *Transients, Settlers and Refugees*, pp. 32–3, 225; Office for National Statistics, *Focus on Ethnicity and Identity*, p. 4; Roger Ballard and Catherine Ballard, 'The Sikhs: The Development of South Asian Settlements in Britain', in Roger Ballard, ed., *Desh Pradesh: The South Asian Presence in Britain* (London, 1994), pp. 21–56; Werbner, *Migration Process*, pp. 21–7; Ceri Peach, 'South Asian Migration and Settlement in Great Britain, 1951–2001', *Contemporary South Asia*, vol. 15 (2006), pp. 136–7.

126 See Chapter 4 below for identity.

127 Office for National Statistics, *Focus on Ethnicity and Identity*, pp. 9–10; Rubinstein, *History of the Jews*, p. 400; Brendan O'Neill, 'How Migrants Really Live', *New Statesman*, 4 June 2007, pp. 28–30; http://business.timesonline.co.uk/tol/business/specials/rich_list; Will Hutton, 'Greed Will be the Death of Football', *Observer*, 30 September 2007.

128 V. D. Lipman, *A Social History of the Jews in England, 1850–1950* (London, 1954), pp. 65–80.

129 Lees, *Exiles of Erin*, pp. 53–4.

130 Panayi, *German Immigrants*, pp. 110–44.

131 Stephen Castles and Godula Kosack, *Immigrant Workers and Class Structure in Western Europe* (London, 1973), pp. 57–115; Robert Miles, *Racism and Migrant Labour* (London, 1982), pp. 121–50.

132 Stephen Castles and Mark J. Miller, *The Age of Migration: International Population Movements in the Modern World*, 3rd edn (Basingstoke, 2003), pp. 170–2.

133 Adrian Favell, *Eurostars and Eurocities: Free Movement and Mobility in an Integrating Europe* (Oxford, 2008).

134 Stephen Castles, *Here for Good: Western Europe's New Ethnic Minorities* (London, 1987), pp. 137–9.

135 Lucassen, *Immigrant Threat*, pp. 130–4.

136 Ibid., pp. 35–40.

137 See below pp. 113–15.

138 Panikos Panayi, *Spicing Up Britain: The Multicultural History of British Food* (London, 2008), pp. 162–76.

139 Ibid., pp. 40–64, 124–50.

140 Max Weber, *The Protestant Ethic and the Spirit of Capitalism* (Originally 1904, London, 1976 Edn); R. H. Tawney, *Religion and the Rise of Capitalism* (London, 1926).

141 W. D. Rubinstein, *Men of Property: The Very Wealthy in Britain since the Industrial Revolution* (London, 1981), pp. 144–75.

142 Andrew Godley, *Jewish Immigrant Entrepreneurship in New York and London, 1880–1914: Enterprise and Culture* (Basingstoke, 2001).

143 Hilary Metcalf, Tariq Modood and Satnam Virdee, *Asian Self-Employment: The Interaction of Culture and Economics in England* (London, 1996).

144 Panayi, *Spicing*, p. 206.

145 Howard E. Aldrich, John C. Carter, Trevor P. Jones and David McEvoy, 'Business Development and Self-Segregation: Asian Enterprise in Three British Cities', in Ceri Peach, Vaughan Robinson and Susan Smith, eds, *Ethnic Segregation in Cities* (London, 1981), p. 172.

146 Trevor Jones, 'Small Asian Businesses in Retreat? The Case of UK', *Journal of Ethnic and Migration Studies*, vol. 29 (2003), pp. 485–500.

147 Mark S. Brown, 'Religion and Economic Activity in the South Asian Population', *Ethnic and Racial Studies*, vol. 23 (2000), pp. 1035–61.

148 Louise London, *Whitehall and the Jews, 1939–1948: British Immigration Policy and the Holocaust* (Cambridge, 2000), p. 122, points out that 'Financial support was of the utmost importance' for those Jews wishing to enter Britain just before World War Two, if it meant an offer of work or support from a sponsor.

149 Frank Neal, 'A Criminal Profile of the Liverpool Irish', *Transactions of the Historic Society of Lancashire and Chesire,* vol. 140 (1990), pp. 160–99.

150 Frank Neal, *Black '47: Britain and the Irish Famine* (Basingstoke, 1998).

151 Henry Mayhew, *London Labour and the London Poor, Vol. 1* (originally 1861, London, 1968), pp. 104–20.

152 Elizabeth Malcolm, ' "A Most Miserable Looking Object": The Irish in English Asylums, 1850–1901: Migration, Poverty and Prejudice', in John Belchem and Klaus Tenfelde, eds, *Irish and Polish Migration in Comparative Perspective* (Essen, 2003), pp. 121–32.

153 Lees, *Exiles of Erin*, pp. 88–95.

154 Treble, 'Irish Navvies'.

155 J. M. Werly, 'The Irish in Manchester, 1832–49', *Irish Historical Studies*, vol. 17 (1973), pp. 345–58; Richardson, 'Irish Settlement', pp. 51–5; T. P. MacDermott, 'Irish Workers in Tyneside in the Nineteenth Century', in Norman McCord, ed., *Essays in Tyneside Labour History* (Newcastle-upon-Tyne, 1977), pp. 154–77; Malcolm Chase, 'The Teeside Irish in the Nineteenth Century', *Labour History Review*, vol. 57 (1992), pp. 14–17; Handley, *Irish in Scotland,* pp. 54–62, 84, 109,

117; Handley, *Irish in Modern Scotland*, pp. 134–6; A. B. Campbell, *The Lanarkshire Miners* (Edinburgh, 1979), pp. 178–204; Paul O'Leary, 'Skill and Workplace in an Industrial Economy: The Irish in South Wales', in Belchem and Tenfelde, *Irish and Polish Migration*, pp. 63–74.

156 David Fitzpatrick, ' "A Peculiar Tramping People": The Irish in Britain, 1801–70', in W. E. Vaughan, ed., *A New History of Ireland*, vol. 5 (Oxford, 1989), pp. 641–2.

157 J. A. Jackson, *The Irish in Britain* (London, 1963), pp. 74–6; Davis, *Irish in Britain*, pp. 96–101; E. J. T. Collins, 'Migrant Labour in British Agriculture in the Nineteenth Century', *Economic History Review*, vol. 29 (1976), pp. 48–52; Finnegan, *Poverty and Prejudice*, p. 28.

158 John Belchem, 'Class, Creed and Country: The Irish Middle Class in Victorian Liverpool', in Swift and Gilley, *The Irish in Victorian Britain*, pp. 190–211; Ó Tuathaigh, 'The Irish in Nineteenth Century Britain', pp. 155–6.

159 Handley, *Irish in Modern Scotland*, pp. 134–5.

160 Donald M. MacRaild and David E. Martin, *Labour in British Society, 1830–1914* (Basingstoke, 2000); Neville Kirk, *Change, Continuity and Class: Labour in British Society, 1850–1920* (Manchester, 1998).

161 Belchem, 'Class, Creed and Country', p. 193. See also: Ó Tuathaigh, 'The Irish in Nineteenth Century Britain', pp. 155–7; and Fielding, *Class and Ethnicity*, pp. 29–30.

162 Hans Rössler ' "Die Zuckerbäcker waren vornehmlich Hannoveraner": Zur Geschichte der Wanderung aus dem Elbe-Weser-Dreieck in die Britische Zuckerindustrie', *Jahrbuch der Männer vom Morgenstern*, vol. 81 (2003).

163 Panayi, *German Immigrants*, pp. 123–34; Panayi, *Spicing*, pp. 55–9.

164 Gregory Anderson, 'German Clerks in England, 1870–1914: Another Aspect of the Great Depression Debate', in Kenneth Lunn, ed., *Hosts, Immigrants and Minorities: Historical Responses to Newcomers in British Society* (Folkestone, 1980), pp. 222–62.

165 Panayi, *German Immigrants*, pp. 134–8; Manz, *Migranten und Internierte*, pp. 87–110.

166 Stanely D. Chapman, 'Merchants and Bankers' in Werner E. Mosse, et al., eds, *Second Chance: Two Centuries of German-Speaking Jews in the United Kingdom* (Tübingen, 1991), pp. 335–46; Panayi, ibid., pp. 139–42; Manz, ibid., pp. 48–86; Stefan Manz, Margrit Schulte Beerbühl and John R. Davis, eds, *Migration and Transfer from Germany to Britain, 1660–1914* (Munich, 2007).

167 Panayi, ibid., pp. 140–2.

168 See: ibid.; and Manz, *Migranten und Internierte*, pp. 231–95.

169 Sponza, *Italian Immigrants*, pp. 62–93.

170 Lucio Sponza, 'Italian "Penny Ice-Men" in Victorian London', in Anne J. Kershen, ed., *Food in the Migrant Experience* (Aldershot, 2002), pp. 17–41;

Panayi, *Spicing*, pp. 76–8; Colin Hughes, *Lime, Lemon and Sarsaparilla: The Italian Community in Wales, 1881–1945* (Bridgend, 1992), pp. 13–58.

171   Panayi, ibid., pp. 83–8.

172   Colpi, *The Italian Factor*, pp. 99–129.

173   Ibid., pp. 192–7; Anthony Rea, *Manchester's Little Italy: Memories of the Italian Colony of Ancoats* (Manchester, 1988).

174   Charles Forte, *Forte: The Autobiography of Charles Forte* (London, 1986).

175   Donna R. Gabaccia, *Italy's Many Diasporas* (London, 2000), pp. 164–5.

176   Ernest Krausz, *Leeds Jewry: Its History and Social Structure* (Cambridge, 1964), p. 1.

177   Ursula Henriques, 'The Jewish Community of Cardiff, 1813–1914', *Welsh History Review*, vol. 14 (1988), pp. 267–79.

178   V. D. Lipman, 'The Origins of Provincial Anglo-Jewry', in Aubrey Newman, ed., *Provincial Jewry in Victorian England* (London, 1978), pp. 1–12.

179   Lipman, *A Social History of the Jews*, pp. 27–8.

180   Endelman, *The Jews of Britain*, pp. 99–100; John Cooper, *Pride Versus Prejudice: Jewish Doctors and Lawyers in England, 1890–1990* (Oxford, 2003), pp. 11–42.

181   Todd M. Endelman, *Radical Assimilation in English Jewish History, 1656–1945* (Bloomington and Indianapolis, 1990), pp. 73–143.

182   Bill Williams, *The Making of Manchester Jewry, 1740–1875* (Manchester, 1976), p. 57.

183   Bill Williams, ' "East and West': Class and Community in Manchester Jewry, 1850–1914', in David Cesarani, ed., *The Making of Modern Anglo-Jewry* (Oxford, 1990), pp. 15–33; Eugene C. Black, *The Social Politics of Anglo-Jewry, 1880–1920* (Oxford, 1988).

184   Geoffrey Alderman, *Modern British Jewry* (Oxford, 1992), p. 121.

185   Joseph Buckman, *Immigrants and the Class Struggle: The Jewish Immigrant in Leeds, 1880–1914* (Manchester, 1983); Anne J. Kershen, *Uniting the Tailors: Trade Unionism Amongst the Tailors of London and Leeds, 1870–1939* (London, 1995).

186   Panayi, *Spicing*, pp. 46–55, 133–41.

187   Ibid.; Godley, *Jewish Immigrant Entrepreneurship*, pp. 54–6.

188   Adler, 'Jewish Life and Labour', pp. 283–7; Lipman, *A History of the Jews in Britain Since 1858*, pp. 212–13.

189   Gerhard Hirschfeld, ed., *Exile in Great Britain: Refugees from Hitler's Germany* (Leamington Spa, 1984); Mosse, *Second Chance*.

190   Rubinstein, *History of the Jews*, p. 400.

191   Graham, Schmool and Waterman, *Jews in Britain*, pp. 79–98.

192   Rubinstein, *History of the Jews*, pp. 402–5.

193   Castles and Kosack, *Immigrant Workers*, p. 90.

194   Malcolm Cross, 'Ethnic Minority Youth in a Collapsing Labour Market: The UK Experience', in Czarina Wilpert, ed., *Entering the Working World: Following the Descendants of Europe's Immigrant Labour Force* (Aldershot, 1988), pp. 56–88.

195   Office for National Statistics, *Focus on Ethnicity and Identity*, p. 9.

196   Dudley Baines, 'Immigration and the Labour Market', in Nicholas Crafts, Ian Gazeley and Andrew Newell, eds, *Work and Pay in Twentieth Century Britain* (Oxford, 2007), pp. 330–52.

197   Christian Dustmann and Francesca Fabbri, 'Immigrants in the British Labour Force', *Fiscal Studies*, vol. 26 (2005), p. 424.

198   See Chapter 2.

199   Office for National Statistics, *Focus on Ethnicity and Identity*, p. 9.

200   Sheila Patterson, 'The Poles: An Exile Community in Britain', in Watson, *Between Two Cultures*, pp. 219–21.

201   Home Office, Department of Work and Pensions, H. M. Revenue and Customs and Department for Communities and Local Government, 'Accession Monitoring Report', 22 August 2006, p. 23.

202   Anthias, *Ethnicity, Class, Gender*; E. J. B. Rose, et al., *Colour and Citizenship: A Report on British Race Relations* (London, 1968), pp. 154–8; Zena Theodorou and Sav Kyriacou, 'Cypriots in London', in Merriman, *Peopling of London*, pp. 98–105.

203   Lucassen, *Immigrant Threat*, pp. 130–6.

204   Rex, *Ghetto*.

205   Mayhew, *London Labour*, pp. 190–4.

206   Michael Banton, *The Coloured Quarter* (London, 1955), p. 26.

207   Little, *Negroes in Britain*; Diane Frost, ed., *Ethnic Labour and British Imperial Trade: A History of Ethnic Seafarers in the UK* (London, 1995).

208   Fryer, *Staying Power*, pp. 294–7, 358–67.

209   Edward Scobie, *Black Britannia: A History of Blacks in Britain* (Chicago, 1972), pp. 141–151.

210   Racism receives full consideration in Chapter 5.

211   Pilkington, *Beyond the Mother Country*, pp. 31–2; Glass, *Newcomers*, p. 31.

212   Patterson, *Dark Strangers*, pp. 101–30.

213   Ron Ramdin, *The Making of the Black Working Class in Britain* (Aldershot, 1987), p. 197.

214   Clifford S. Hill, *How Colour Prejudiced is Britain?* (London, 1971), p. 53.

215   See Chapter 6.

216 Lorna Chessum, *From Immigrants to Ethnic Minority: Making Black Community in Britain* (Aldershot, 2000), pp. 133–40.

217 Patterson, *Dark Strangers*, p. 97.

218 R. B. Davison, *Black British Immigrants to England* (London, 1966), p. 89.

219 Hill, *How Colour Prejudiced is Britain?* p. 138.

220 Two classic studies on this subject are: Bernard Coard, *How the West Indian Child is Made Educationally Subnormal in the British School System: The Scandal of the Black Child in Schools in Britain* (London, 1971); and Tony Sewell, *Black Masculinities and Schooling: How Black Boys Survive Modern Schooling* (Stoke-on-Trent, 1997).

221 Mohan Luthra, *Britain's Black Population: Social Change, Public Policy and Agenda* (Aldershot, 1997), pp. 185–202.

222 Office for National Statistics, *Focus on Ethnicity and Identity*, p. 8.

223 See, for instance, John Benyon, ed., *Scarman and After: Essays Reflecting on Lord Scarman's Report, The Riots and their Aftermath* (Oxford, 1984).

224 Sharon J. Daye, *Middle Class Blacks in Britain: A Racial Fraction of a Class Group or a Class Fraction of a Racial Group* (Basingstoke, 1994).

225 Ernest Cashmore, *Black Sportsmen* (London, 1982).

226 The above paragraph is based upon: Visram, *Asians in Britain*; and Michael H. Fisher, Shompa Lahiri and Shinder S. Thandi, *A South Asian History of Britain: Four Centuries of Peoples from the Indian Sub-Continent* (Oxford, 2007), pp. 95–158.

227 Office for National Statistics, *Focus on Ethnicity and Identity*, pp. 8–10.

228 Anwar, *Myth of Return*, p. 46.

229 Andrew Bryson, 'Britain's Richest Asians', *Daily Telegraph*, 19 April 2006.

230 Monder Ram, David Smallbone, David Deakins and Trevor Jones, 'Banking or "Break-Out": Finance and the Development of Ethnic Minority Businesses', *Journal of Ethnic and Migration Studies*, vol. 29 (2003), p. 663.

231 Cross, 'Ethnic Minority Youth', p. 72.

232 http://www.dalits.nl/pdf/noescape.pdf, Dalit Solidarity Network UK, 'No Escape: Caste Discrimination in the UK', 2006.

233 Tony Kushner, *Remembering Refugees: Then and Now* (Manchester, 2006), p. 34.

234 Metcalf, Modood and Virdee, *Asian Self-Employment*.

235 J. P. May, 'The Chinese in Britain', in Colin Holmes, ed., *Immigrants and Minorities in British Society* (London, 1978), pp. 111–24; John Seed, 'Limehouse Blues'; K. C. Ng, *The Chinese in London* (Oxford, 1968), pp. 1–19; Maria Lin Wong, *Chinese Liverpudlians: A History of the Chinese Community in Liverpool* (Birkenhead, 1989).

236 Panayi, *Spicing*, pp. 168–72.

237 Office for National Statistics, *Focus on Ethnicity and Identity*, pp. 8–9.

CHAPTER 4

Ethnicity, identity and Britishness

From national and ethnic blocks to individuals

The residential, demographic and economic patterns of migrant communities have demonstrated that, if studied over time, some type of integration inevitably occurs, even though its speed and nature vary from one group to another. Integration also takes place with regard to the relative relationships between ethnic minorities, their lands of origin and their place of settlement, which might be described as cultural adaptation, indicated by changes, for instance, in dress and food. While first generation migrants may have the closest connections with their country of origin, we might expect their descendants to increasingly develop what we might describe as hybrid identities, using elements of both the homeland and the environment into which they were born.

In contemporary Britain, individuals have created their own identities, recognized in both popular and academic circles. One of the main forms of identification in a society in which over ten per cent of the population can point to immediate migrant origins, consists of ethnicity, recognized as a category in censuses since 1991.[1] However, the situation was certainly not always thus, especially for historians, who tended to ignore ethnicity as a category, especially at the height of Marxist class analyses of British society during the course of the 1960s and 1970s. M. A. G. Ó Tuathaigh took issue with E. P. Thompson's assertion in the classic *Making of the English Working Classes* that 'the Irish were never pressed back into ghettoes. It would have been difficult to have made a people who spoke the same language and were British citizens under the Act of Union into a subject minority'.[2] From the perspective of the mass of work on ethnicity since Thompson first published his book in 1976 (especially that which has focused upon the Irish in Britain) his assertion seems, at best, naïve and, at worst, arrogant, as he appears to dismiss the existence of Irish ethnicity in the Victorian period. He does, however, recognize the distinctiveness of the Irish, devoting 16 out of 908 pages to them. Other mainstream British historians have ignored ethnicity and continue to do so.[3]

Much early research on migrant communities, following the study of the process of migration, tended to look at ethnicity as a block phenomenon, with limited study of individual lives. The modern historiography of the Irish in nineteenth-century Britain, which evolved from the middle of the 1970s, points to the way in which the study of migrant ethnicity emerged. Without overtly dealing with ethnicity, integration or individual choice, those historians of the Irish who tackled their identity or, more accurately, their ethnic organizations, tended to focus upon two central issues. First, the rise of the Roman Catholic Church in Britain as a mass organization for the first time since the Reformation in order to service the spiritual needs of the new migrants.[4] And, secondly, the relationship between migrants and politics, whether with the British mainstream,[5] the Irish Nationalist movement in Britain,[6] or the evolution of sectarianism,[7] as the Irish communities consisted of both Protestants and Roman Catholics. While the study of sectarianism accepted that the Irish were not one simple mass, most of the earlier research remained ungendered and predominantly male and did not study individual lives. This is perhaps an inevitability in view of the absence of any significant sources which could reveal the reality of second generation dual identity in late nineteenth-century Liverpool or Manchester, for instance. By the 1990s, as the concept of ethnicity had increased in importance in social science studies of migration and had begun to gain currency as immigrants also began to attract attention from historians, two important studies appeared using this idea written by Steven Fielding and Mary Hickman. Both, however, still took a block approach and focused upon religion and politics.[8]

In fact, the whole concept of ethnicity essentially works on the premise of blocks of people. The introduction to one of the seminal works on the subject, by Nathan Glazier and Daniel P. Moynihan, talks significantly of 'ethnic groups'. Glazier and Moynihan recognize the way in which they are also interest groups in a political sense so that those who speak for such entities, from Hungarian nationalists in central Europe in 1848, to West Indians in 1960s Britain, seek some recognition for the groups they represent, whether this means creating a new nation state or simply gaining some rights revolving around equal treatment from the British state.[9]

This approach, taken to its extreme, might suggest instrumentalism by those who lead ethnic groups. But all ethnicity has some sort of real basis. We might accept the statement of David Mason that 'most academic commentators and policy makers would stress some sort of cultural distinctiveness as the mark of an ethnic grouping'.[10] But what exactly constitutes this cultural distinctiveness?

Clearly, for those recognized as ethnic minorities in recent British history,[11] the key issue consists of their migrant origins, which lie outside the UK. In this sense, much of the constructed ethnicity looks back to the homeland, whether this consists of the growth of newspapers, political activity or religion. The last two represent the main ways in which the 'official' ethnicity of a group evolves, illustrated throughout the recent history of immigrant settlement in Britain from the German political organizations and churches of the Victorian period,[12] to the rise of organized Islam and the political groups around it.[13] Nevertheless, religion and politics throw up new problems. Politics in particular remains very much a voluntary activity and involves personal choice. Whether taking the example of Germans in nineteenth-century Britain or contemporary Muslims, those who regard themselves as constituting members of these two ethnic groups, have choices open to them. These range, in the case of Germans, from Marxists to extreme nationalists and, in the case of Muslims, from jihadists to actors in the mainstream British political process. Religion proves just as problematic. Not only does information about Church or mosque attendance prove difficult to find, different types of Christianity and Islam have emerged in Britain, harking back to the homeland.

The link with the place of origin requires further examination, as it provides an important root but certainly cannot suggest what happens in the land of settlement. The idea of Islam in Britain proves problematic, for instance. Not only do Muslims differ in their religious practices but they also originate in different parts of the world including Africa, South Asia and the Middle East.[14] Pakistanis who moved to Britain from the 1950s are unlikely to have seen themselves as having some sort of international Islamic identity, although they realized that their religion did have adherents globally. By the beginning of the twenty-first century, these Pakistani migrants and their offspring, as well as finding themselves connected with a religious ethnic group in Britain, have become recognized as what can be described as either a racial or regional group in the form of Asians or South Asians. Part of the explanation for the existence of this latter group lies in the fact that it has almost become a legal category along racial terms indicated by equal opportunities questionnaires and the existence of a census category of Asians.[15]

The evolution of such ethnicities may well have originated in the wishes of British Asian intellectuals and scholars, taking us back to Glazier and Moynihan. For instance, while the authors of *A South Asian History of Britain* may recognize the diversity of the peoples about whom they write, they also begin their book with the assertion that 'People of South-Asian descent collectively comprise the largest ethnic minority in Britain today.'[16]

Pakistanis in contemporary British society therefore possess a range of identities based upon ethnicity either assigned or available to choose as a label on an individual basis. Homeland therefore only acts as one root for the development of ethnicities in Britain or anywhere else. Diasporas clearly exist on a global level[17] but, they also become constructed and 'imagined' on the local level in particular environments.[18] The assertion of Benedict Anderson about imagined national communities as artificial constructs also applies to ethnic groups, whether they claim to represent everyone in a particular nation state or, more arrogantly still, they claim to speak for members of their 'community' wherever they may live anywhere in the world. Anderson's assertion that people of one nationality could never meet more than a handful of members of the same group applies both to nationalities and to ethnic groups.[19] Both nation states and ethnic minorities are artificial constructs with political motivation behind them.

Migrants and their descendants in Britain therefore have a variety of ethnicities which they can choose depending upon a range of factors such as land of origin, religion and political affiliation. In addition, class, gender and place of birth also help to determine adherence or even allegiance. Social science scholarship has therefore, in recent decades, increasingly moved away from the idea of block ethnicities towards the concept of identity, which works upon an individual basis.[20] Such an approach has a variety of advantages. First, it takes us away from both the nation state and the ethnic group. Individuals can now have multiple identities. This is eloquently explained by Avtar Brah in the introduction to her *Cartographies of Diaspora*. Brah points to her own life history as a woman born in the Punjab, who grew up in Uganda, studied in America and found herself living in Britain after Idi Amin's expulsion of Asians in 1972. She could therefore be Indian, African, Punjabi or British, to give just four identities.[21] 'Twice migrant' groups such as East African Asians in Britain[22] might appear to have more identities open to them than other individuals of migrant origin, yet an examination of any group would reveal a similar complexity. Clearly, such an assertion would apply to a group formed by a series of migratory movements with a variety of ethnic origins such as Jews in late nineteenth- and twentieth-century Britain.[23] But it would also apply to apparently more uniform groups such as Italians in recent British history, as revealed, for instance, by Ann-Marie Fortier, who questioned the concept of an Italian community.[24]

Individuals may regard themselves as having an identification dependent upon the surroundings in which they find themselves. This particularly applies to the second and subsequent generations, who find themselves caught between two cultures. This choosing of identity according to situation can even lead to different types of behaviour, whether it consists of choice of dress[25] or choice of food inside and outside the home.[26]

As with personal motivations for migration,[27] it proves easier to establish identities upon an individual basis in contemporary Britain than it does in the nineteenth century. The reason for this once again lies in the use of oral history methodology, which allows an interrogation of the individual subject. Scholars, for example, of the Irish in Victorian Britain, have few personal accounts upon which they can draw. Those who have written about ethnicity have therefore inevitably focused upon ethnic blocks, especially organized around religion and politics. In contrast, scholars such as Katy Gardner or Kathy Burrell can directly interrogate the subjects which they have in front of them about identity. Gardner and Burrell, while recognizing that their subjects have multiple identities, have chosen to utilize trans-nationalism as a tool of analysis. This allows a recognition of the fact that migrants in Britain, whether they consist of Bangladeshis in the East End of London for Gardner or Europeans in Leicester for Burrell, have relationships with both their land of settlement and their land of origin. This approach recognizes the fact that migrants and their descendants have personal networks and connections which transcend the nation state. While they may live in a particular state, their lives and experiences are not contained within that political entity. This is partly because of the personal connection with the homeland, the role of kinship. The migrants and their descendants have different life experiences from their ethnically British neighbours. They can perpetuate this ethnicity in contemporary society by the wide availability of communications, whether aeroplanes, which allow them to return home on a regular basis, telephones, or satellite television and newspapers, by which they experience their everyday lives partly through events in their homelands, as well as in Britain. The newness of such lives, however, seems questionable. An examination of the German community in nineteenth-century Britain would demonstrate the countless newspapers which had developed covering a whole range of stories from both Germany and Britain, appealing to a variety of interest groups. But the transnational approach also allows the recognition that migrant lives involve multiple journeys, not only backwards and forward, but also, as in the case of Avtar Brah, through multiple locations. Ultimately, transnationalism allows an acceptance of the fact that individuals affected by the migration process have allegiances, outlooks and personal identities which transcend the artificial boundaries imposed by the unitary nation state.[28]

Therefore, whatever approach we take, migrants and their descendants clearly identify themselves in a variety of ways connected with their lands of origin, their lands of settlement and their own lived experiences. Over time, we might argue that the descendants of migrants adapt British norms. Just as their economic, demographic and residential patterns suggest integration, so, in the same way, do other aspects of their lives, whether language, religious practice, dress or food. For example, the Eastern European Jewish community who settled in the East End of London and other inner city areas in the decades leading up to the First World War moved out of the ghetto in a physical sense and experienced social mobility and married people from other groups. In addition, their language has increasingly become English (especially for those growing up and educated in Britain), they have adopted western dress, drifted away from religion to the same extent as the majority population, and have increasingly eaten the foods of wider society.[29] Perhaps the clearest indication of the acceptance of Britishness lies in the fact that Jews became over-represented in the armed forces in both World Wars.[30]

Despite the small minority of militant anti-British migrants and their descendants who may have lived in Britain over the last two centuries, the vast majority of people accept their passport nationality. However, the concept of Britishness has increasingly become (what US public opinion and scholarship previously called) 'hyphenated' in recent decades.[31] Migrant groups now see themselves as Black British or British Asian, for example. This concept did not exist for most ethnic communities before 1945, except for Anglo-Jewry, probably the longest running community perceived as having a dual identity, although (as we have seen) the concept of just a dual identity simplifies reality.[32] On the other hand, nineteenth-century Germans did not develop the concept of British Germans.[33] The Irish, meanwhile, appear to have remained Irish.[34] In both cases the second and subsequent generations do not appear to have felt the need to develop a hyphenated identity, even though they underwent the integration process common to all migrants and their descendants.

In recent decades the concept of dual ethnicity has taken off. This especially applies to Black and Asian newcomers who often see themselves as Black and British and Asian and British on both an institutional and individual level. But Marion Berghahn's study of German Jewish refugees from Nazi Germany carried the title of *Continental Britons*.[35] One explanation for the emergence of dual identity may lie in the level of hostility which post-war migrant groups have faced, forcing them to justify their loyalty to Britain, while emphasizing their ethnic origins. Yet animosity towards migrant communities has not significantly increased in the post-war period.[36] A more persuasive argument consists of the acceptance of Britain as a plural society in a post-imperial world, emphasized by the presence of millions of people of Black and Asian origin by the twenty-first century. This acceptance partly arises from the fact that people with imperial origins have always possessed voting rights and have participated in the political process and have therefore managed to stress their difference. Public intellectuals of Asian and Black origin have further emphasized this dual identity. According to a series of scholars Britishness has now come to incorporate a variety of ethnic groups, moving away from a more narrowly defined idea of this nationality in which whiteness or long standing British genealogy determined who constituted the in and out groups.[37]

The acceptance by post-war migrants and their descendants of their status as Britons partly emerges from the fact that those with origins in the Empire and Commonwealth have always possessed British Nationality. Similarly, the fact that nationality in Britain works on the concept of *jus solis*, has also facilitated this process.[38] The German migrants of the nineteenth century, for instance, may have constituted foreign nationals but they could become naturalized while their descendants would acquire British nationality, meaning that many would end up fighting for Britain when the First World War broke out.[39] The same applied to those of Italian origin, who found themselves in the British Army between 1939 and 1945.[40]

Ethnicity, identity and Britishness amongst migrants and their descendants raises complex issues. In the first place, just as scholars of nationalism have demonstrated that the nation state remains diverse, so, in the same way, have those working upon ethnicity in recent decades. If ethnic groups exist, then their individual members constitute them. While they may have similar life experiences, each of these individuals may view their relationship to both their ethnic group and British society in a unique way. At the same time, a perspective which covers a period of two hundred years also needs to recognize the fact that change occurs from one generation to another. Just as economics and demography suggest integration, so do personal identities, as measured in forms of behaviour such as language use, food consumption and dress.

Ethnicity and personal identity have therefore operated upon two different levels. On the one hand, virtually all ethnic groups of any significance have established their own organizations during the past two centuries, some of which are extremely durable, as witnessed by the survival of the reborn Roman Catholic Church, which emerged to serve the mass Irish migration of the Victorian period. In fact, religion forms both the major source of ethnic organization and personal identity since 1800. The recent rise of Islam follows well established patterns of nineteenth-century migrant communities, whether the Irish, Germans, Italians or Jews. Politics has represented the other major organizational tool for migrant groups over the past two hundred years, if not for personal identity. Refugees in Britain often wish to continue their previous activity. At the same time, as the centre of an Empire, many migrants from the colonies partly developed their own nationalism in Britain, whether Irish, Indians or Africans. However, as class has proved such a vital factor in British history over the last two centuries, newcomers have often either moved into mainstream politics or have developed their own left-wing groupings. More recently, a link appears to have evolved between politics and religion in the form of Islamic extremism, although Irish nationalism clearly had a root in Roman Catholicism.

In addition to these homeland based roots of ethnic organization, new forms of ethnicity have also evolved in post-war Britain. Perhaps the best example and the most artificial consists of South Asian ethnicity, which brings together a whole variety of groups with diverse religions and geographical origins. The bodies which hold Sikhs, Hindus and South Asian Muslims together include newspapers and radio stations. Food, dress and language act as a cement on the level of everyday relations between these groups.[41] South Asian ethnicity does not necessarily differ significantly from, for instance, 'German-ness', in which newspapers played an important role in developing the idea of a German minority in Britain.[42]

But this officially constructed ethnicity backed up by the building blocks of churches, temples, political parties and newspapers, provides limited information on how individuals of migrant origin perceive themselves. The development of the Roman Catholic Church or of Islam in Britain suggests that many people from Ireland or Pakistan have practised their religion, although many others almost certainly have not. Some lapse in religious practice also occurs through generations. Indicators of personal identity such as language use, dress and food help to indicate changes over time, moving closer to British norms.

When considering ethnicity and identity, as well as their relationship with Britishness, we therefore need to bear the following issues in mind. First, ethnic groups and organizations use elements from both the land of origin and the homeland to develop hybrids. Second, ethnic organizations do not speak for everybody. While some minorities have official organs which claim to represent them, subgroups also emerge, as evidenced by the history of Anglo-Jewry. Thirdly, while some ethnic organizations may survive for hundreds of years, they also evolve. This becomes clearer when ethnicity and identity are examined upon an individual process. The change from the norms of the homeland to those of Britain, usually taking place through generations, serves as one of the best indicators of integration, whether measured through language, dress or food.

Religion

While contemporary Britain may have developed into a secular society, as evidenced by church attendance,[43] this generalization masks both the importance of religion during the past two centuries as a whole[44] and its centrality for both the majority of the population before 1945 and ethnic minorities since the Victorian era. Scholars of immigration in the USA have long recognized the importance of faith. Oscar Handlin wrote that 'The very process of adjusting immigrant ideas to the conditions of the United States made religion paramount as a way of life'.[45] Similarly, Will Herberg, who laid particular stress upon religion as a signifier of ethnicity, claimed that the 'first concern of the immigrants . . . was with their churches',[46] or at least it concerned those who felt that they should care for the spiritual needs of what they regarded as their flock. Frederick C. Luebke, meanwhile, claimed that the Germans of the nineteenth century 'identified themselves first of all as Catholics, Lutherans, Evangelicals, Mennonites, or Methodists, and only secondarily (sometimes only incidentally) as Germans'.[47]

Luebke's assertion seems bold, but may contain much truth in view of the evolving nature of German nationalism, especially in the diaspora in the century leading up to the First World War.[48] More problematic may be the fact that it proves difficult to measure the extent of religious practice and church attendance, which, while it may not give the lie to Luebke's assertion, suggests that we should treat it with caution. Another classic text on nineteenth-century European migration to the USA, by Jay P. Nolan, asserted that while immigrants reproduced 'the type of religion with which they were familiar in the old country . . . for some it was an active spiritual life centred on the parish; for others it was an indifferent attitude toward religion, and the immigrant parish was hard-pressed to change these patterns of tradition'.[49] Similarly, Lynn Lees, writing about the Irish in nineteenth-century London claims that 'most migrants as well as their English-born children took part in the major Catholic rituals marking birth and probably death but . . . far fewer had either the opportunity or the interest to sustain the pattern of regular parochial devotions recommended to them by their priests'.[50] Clearly individual choice plays a determining role in the extent to which each person of migrant origin practises their own religion.

Nevertheless, faith has remained central in the collective and individual identities of virtually all migrant communities in Britain during the last two centuries, including Italians, Germans and the Irish before 1945, together with Greek Cypriots and many West Indians after the Second World War. Some communities and individuals primarily identify themselves as a religious group. The best example in recent British history consists of the Jews, who, since the readmission of the seventeenth century, have developed all of the paraphernalia of organized religion. But Anglo-Jewry consists of a complexity of religious groups, who differentiate themselves according to area of origin, religious practice and class. The picture is equally complex for those post-war migrants originating in South Asia. For practising Pakistani, Bangladeshi and Indian Muslims, together with Hindus and Sikhs, religion can play a central role in their lives. However, more than one form of Islam exists in Britain, while Hinduism partly revolves around caste. About a fifth of Muslims in Britain do not originate in South Asia.[51] Even some of those originating in South Asia have moved to Britain via East Africa or even the West Indies, a fact which also applies to Hindus and Sikhs.[52]

Todd Endelman has written: 'Traditional Judaism is an all-embracing way of life. It does not occupy a segment of the observant Jew's daily or weekly routine but provides the framework in which, in theory, he or she lives all of his or her life.'[53] The same applies to Islam and Sikhism, but a minority of adherents of any of these three faiths in Britain would have led such exemplary and disciplined religious lives, especially if they moved outside 'the ghetto'. While Judaism, Islam and Sikhism may demand the most from their adherents, they resemble the other religions which have established themselves in Britain over the past two centuries in terms of the sophistication of their organization. This spreads beyond the building and opening of official places of worship to incorporate other aspects of the lives of adherents. Whether Roman Catholicism, Judaism or Islam, each of these faiths have opened up schools, philanthropic bodies and social organizations. While, on the one hand, such developments suggest a desire to hold on to members of the flock, the establishment of bodies such as youth and sporting clubs also point to an adaptation of conditions in the new environment. It is not simply these large religions which have behaved in such a way but also smaller faiths such as the German Evangelical Church during the nineteenth century.

A focus upon some of these religions helps to illustrate the ways in which they have used the opportunity of the evolution of a migrant community to establish the paraphernalia associated with them. At the same time we can also see the process of adaptation. Similarly, the complexity of apparently unified religion will also become apparent. Finally, despite the efforts of religious leaders, their words often fall upon deaf ears.

The evolution of the Roman Catholic Church during the nineteenth century provides a starting point for investigating the complexity of migrant religious identity and practice in modern Britain. The influx of Irish migrants transformed the Roman Catholic Church from 'a small, proud, rich, and unpopular body', consisting of the descendants of those individuals who had not converted to Protestantism during the Reformation, together with prominent members of the European establishment, into 'a large, prudent, poorer and popular body, with a vast majority of Irish adherents'.[54] Missionaries played a large role in this process. In London such efforts received financial support from wealthy Catholics in the city, foreign ambassadors and contributions from abroad. Jesuits, nuns and monks played a role in this process.[55] The re-establishment of the Roman Catholic Church on a national level in mainland Britain, following a gap of 265 years in 1850 and coming on the heels of Catholic Emancipation in 1829, formed the background of the growth of the Roman Catholic religion in England. From 29 September 1850 'England became an ecclesiastical province with an archbishop and twelve . . . bishops, taking their titles from their own sees', whose number quickly rose to fourteen.[56]

The renaissance of the Roman Catholic Church in mainland Britain took place against the background of a religious revival in Ireland. Donald MacRaild has suggested that 'post-Famine Ireland experienced a "devotional" revolution, whereby the spread of modern communications, the penetration of the English language and, most importantly, the destruction of traditional peasant society paved the way for an assertion of liturgical practice and richer visual symbolism'.[57] The number of priests in Ireland increased from 2,150 ministering to a population of 6.5 million in 1840, a ratio of 1:3,000, to 3,700 for 3.3 million, making a ratio of 1:900.[58]

This contrasted 'with a worsening ratio of clergy to people in England, where all the Churches struggled in vain to cope with a rapidly expanding and increasingly urban population'.[59] Nevertheless, starting from a situation of a virtually non-existent Roman Catholic Church in the early nineteenth century, the newly established religion, in purely numerical terms, witnessed a burgeoning during the Victorian period. For instance, the 18 parishes staffed by 47 priests in Lancashire in 1846 had increased to 45 parishes with

FIGURE 9 Irish Roman Catholic celebration in East London before the First World War, London Metropolitan Archives

129 priests by 1870.[60] As early as the 1840s between 110,000 and 125,000 Irish Catholics lived in London.[61] The total number of Irish Catholics in Britain during the Victorian period, consisting of both the migrants and their descendants, may have reached 1.2 million.[62]

But what do such bald figures suggest about Irish Catholic identity in Victorian Britain? Irish Catholic ethnicity and personal identity did not simply manifest itself in church attendance, but also participation in a whole series of social events, which could almost control the whole lives of believers. As Steven Fielding has written, Catholicism did not just comprise 'a vague feeling of belonging, but also included a bureaucratic institution with its own set of interests, which were articulated and enforced by appointed officials – the Hierarchy and the clergy'. He has described Roman Catholic priests in Manchester, who predominantly consisted of Irish born immigrants throughout the nineteenth and early twentieth centuries, as 'policemen of the faith', who wanted 'the laity to passively obey their will'.[63] Donald MacRaild has written of the 'sense of respect, even awe', in which most Roman Catholics held their priests during the nineteenth century.[64]

The positive attitude which Irish Catholics in Britain may have had towards their priests did not necessarily translate into Church attendance. While virtually all Catholic children in London during the 1830s underwent baptism, only 10 per cent of Roman Catholics 'fulfilled their Easter duties in 1837'.[65] Levels of church attendance appear to have stood at between 25 and 30 per cent amongst the Catholic population of the capital. Around a quarter of Irish Catholics in Cardiff may have 'performed their Easter duty in the period 1841 to 1861', while only 10 per cent of those in Liverpool practised their faith, according to Graham Davis.[66] Frank Neal, on the other hand, has suggested a much higher figure, reaching 90 per cent of the Roman Catholic working class in Liverpool in 1853.[67] Perhaps we can accept a figure somewhere in between suggested by John Belchem, who claims that 'only' 43 per cent of Catholics in the city 'attended Mass regularly in 1865'. He also asserts that 'the Liverpool Irish maintained an exalted notion of their own religion and a sovereign contempt for the "haythen", by whom they were surrounded'.[68]

Church attendance seems difficult to measure and the figures prove contradictory, but the growth of the parishes and the respect for the priest suggests that the Church played a significant role in the life of Irish Catholics in nineteenth-century Britain. But this influence did not manifest itself simply in the direct power of religion, but also in the development of a whole range of organizations, which aimed at influencing the everyday lives of the migrants, leading Donald MacRaild to write of 'social Catholicism'.[69] Fielding has suggested that although the Church aimed at the spiritual wellbeing of its adherents, it felt that 'it also needed to control the mind and body, and consequently sought to dominate the life of every Catholic'.[70]

Irish Catholics falling upon hard times would have come into contact with representatives of their Church almost immediately after arrival in Britain. As well as looking after the welfare of the newcomers, Catholic philanthropic organizations also aimed at incorporating them into the expanding Church and effectively constituted missionary organizations.[71] New establishments developed aimed at specific aspects of the lives of the Irish Catholic community in Britain, particularly the prevention of drinking. In London such groups included the Total Abstinence Society and the Catholic Association for the Suppression of Drunkenness, while a Scottish equivalent consisted of the Catholic Temperance Movement.[72] In Liverpool, the Catholic Church had established 'a micro-welfare state' by the 1920s incorporating schools, nurseries and hostels. Philanthropic organizations included the Catholic Women's League and the Catholic Social Guild.[73]

However, the most important instrument for the maintenance of Irish Catholicism in Britain consisted of schools, an attempt by both the local and national Roman Catholic hierarchy to inculcate Irish and Catholic values into schoolchildren, even though a fully national scheme did not develop.[74]

On the local level, schoolchildren of Irish Catholic origin came into contact with religious education. In Liverpool about 22,369 Irish schoolchildren in the city, one in eight of the local population, received a Roman Catholic education by the 1870s.[75] Similarly, about 13 per cent of schoolchildren in Manchester went to Catholic schools just before the outbreak of the First World War.[76] The inculcation of the correct values into children did not simply take place in the classroom, but also through Roman Catholic youth organizations, which had emerged by the end of the nineteenth century. In Manchester they included the Catholic Lads' Clubs and the Catholic Boys' Brigade, partly reactions against similar mainstream organizations.[77] Similarly, in Dundee the Roman Catholic Church had established a variety of bodies for children by the outbreak of the First World War including a Home for Catholic Working Boys and a nursery.[78]

The overwhelming majority of work on the Irish in Britain has focused upon the Victorian period, which makes it difficult to measure the extent to which the Roman Catholic organizations continued to hold an influence after 1918 as well as the extent to which the Catholic faith survived. Mary Hickman claims that priests actually increased their influence after 1921 because the creation of an Irish Free State took the attention of the migrant community away from the politics of Home Rule.[79] But in Dundee concern had risen in the early 1920s about 'leakage from the Church' especially towards left-wing politics.[80] However, a strong Roman Catholic identity survived into the inter-war years in Liverpool, with a population of 95,000 practising this religion. Sixteen churches still functioned and could attract thousands of people at Easter. A whole range of organizations continued to survive into this period.[81] Similarly, Church attendance in Manchester remained constant in at least one place of worship, St Wilfrid's in Hulme, during the inter-war years, which even sent out missions. On the other hand, while 41 per cent of adolescents had connections with the Catholic youth organizations in 1918, this figure had fallen to 28 per cent by 1940.[82]

Some 'leakage' may have taken place in the inter-war years, but the Irish arrivals after 1945 gave the Roman Catholic Church the opportunity to reinvigorate itself. The extent of apostasy seems questionable in view of the fact that the number of Catholics in Britain grew to around 5 million by the 1970s. While migrants from Europe may partly explain the rise from the two million Roman Catholics of the 1920s, 'the majority of the increase was a direct outcome of Irish settlement'.[83] Enda Delaney has demonstrated that missionary activity, of a similar nature to that which occurred in the Victorian period, also took place in the cities in which the new Irish migrants settled during the post-war years, as they often focused upon areas which had little experience of previous Irish settlement. The missions had some success as surveys demonstrated significant levels of church attendance, although the figures varied from one investigation to another, just as they had during the nineteenth century.[84] Perhaps most significantly of all, for Catholic, if not specifically Irish identity, the number of children attending Roman Catholic schools had increased during the post-war years, because they could now receive state funding.[85]

Religion has played a central role in the maintenance of Irish Catholic identity during the last two centuries, especially in the years before 1945. After the Second World War, much writing on Irish Catholics suggests that they have assimilated, or at least become invisible, because of the racialization of identity, which has made Black and Asian people more noticeable, meaning that the Irish and their descendants have increasingly assimilated into white British society,[86] a theory questioned by scholars such as Louise Ryan and Bronwen Walter.[87] It seems tempting to speak of a Roman Catholicism after 1945 representing a residual Irish identity, from which the Irish element has lessened in importance in comparison with the Victorian period in particular, when Catholicism had the same status in public discourse as Islam at the start of the twenty-first century.[88] However, in recent decades, something of a rediscovery of secular Irishness has also taken place in Britain. In any case, Roman Catholicism always represented one face of Irishness in Britain, as politics, especially during the nineteenth century, also played a key role.[89]

Just as importantly, a significant percentage of Irish migrants have not even consisted of Roman Catholics, but Protestants. As many Protestants as Roman Catholics may have left Ireland in the century after 1815 to emigrate worldwide, while a quarter of the Irish in Victorian Britain may have consisted of Protestants focused especially upon Liverpool and the West of Scotland.[90] But the research carried out upon the ethnic identification of this group has revealed little about religious practice. It has focused, instead, upon the evolution of an anti-Catholic political identity epitomized by the Orange Order.[91]

Like the Irish, religion has proved of central importance for Germans and Italians. During the Victorian and Edwardian years a whole series of German Protestant Churches opened in Britain, focused primarily upon London. As in the case of the Roman Catholic Irish, they had a range of educational and philanthropic activity connected with them. If any sort of German national identity existed in Britain on a national scale before 1914 then it did so along religious lines. One German Roman Catholic Church also existed in London during the nineteenth century, suggesting that other German Catholics attended Irish churches elsewhere in the country. Interestingly, the German Churches represent the main continuities between the migrants of the nineteenth century and more recent arrivals. While the Germanophobia and consequent ethnic cleansing of the First World War may have removed most traces of the German community, the racists spared places of worship. Actually establishing religious attendance in the case of Germans, as with any other ethnic minority in Britain over the last two centuries, proves problematic. A census of church attendance in London in 1905 suggested that only 745 people attended one of the 15 places of worship available to Germans on the relevant Sunday morning, while the figure reached 777 in the evening. Considering a London German population of around 27,000, this represents a lower percentage than any of the figures given for Irish Catholic worship. Nevertheless, there seems no reason to dismiss Luebke's statement about the importance of religion in the German diaspora during the nineteenth century, particularly because of the central role of German philanthropy and education in the everyday lives of many poorer Germans. These philanthropic organizations did much to create the illusion of a unified German community in Britain before 1914 as it involved the rich giving to the poor. In reality, certainly in London, the different social classes of Germans worshipped in their own churches, whether in the poor East End or wealthier areas such as Islington or Forest Hill, although provincial churches probably attracted a wider social spectrum as only one existed in many locations. While religion may have played a role in German identification, it divided as much as united Germans, not only because of the social distinctions but also because Germans practised different religions.[92] Apart from Protestants and Roman Catholics, German Jews also lived in Britain. They did not tend to use their own synagogues before 1914 and do not appear to have developed a uniquely German religious Jewish identity. But they had an impact upon both 'Orthodox' and 'Progressive' Judaism in the nineteenth and twentieth centuries. A significant percentage of the refugees from Nazism, meanwhile, viewed themselves as secular, having already undergone decades of acculturation and assimilation in the German environment.[93]

Italians in Britain resemble the Germans in the sense of constituting a European group in which religion played an important role in creating a sense of community. Like the German Churches, those which developed for Italian Catholics in the nineteenth century tended to survive into the twentieth. Also like their German counterparts, they had their own philanthropic organizations. While the Italian community, like all those under consideration, consisted of a variety of groups, a shared Roman Catholic religion has tended to serve as an important unifying factor crossing areas of origin and class. Although the extent of worship remains difficult to measure, a survey from the middle of the 1990s revealed that three-quarters of Italians viewed themselves as religious, while about a third attended church about once a week. A total of 96 per cent of women questioned in the same survey claimed that their children had been baptised.[94]

No discussion of religion as a factor in ethnic identity in Britain over the last two centuries can ignore the Jewish community. Superficially, Jews in Britain, like their co-religionists elsewhere, may have a primarily religious ethnicity, but area of origin also plays a significant role. Similarly, social class has also helped to determine Jewishness in the British case, although this links with area of origin and wave of migration. In addition, again connected with continental antecedents, the type of religious practice also helped to divide Anglo-Jewry into different subgroups. As scholars such as Geoffrey Alderman and Bill Williams have stressed, it proves difficult to speak of one Jewish community over the last two centuries.[95] A long term approach helps an analysis of declining Jewish religious practice.

At the start of the nineteenth century the main factor dividing Jews in Britain consisted of area of origin, with the Sephardic community originating in Spain and Portugal in decline. The Ashkenazi group would continue to grow into the second half of the nineteenth century as a result of immigration from central and eastern Europe. The Sephardic community had developed a wide range of charitable activities, particularly educational, since the end of the seventeenth century, focused upon London, but counted fewer synagogues than the Ashkenazi.[96] The construction of a synagogue, whether in London or in the provinces, signified the 'arrival' of a Jewish community. Together with the major central London Ashkenazi congregations which had established themselves around the Western, the Hambro and Great Synagogues, places of worship evolved in suburban locations and in the provinces. In Cardiff, for instance, a synagogue first opened in a rented room during the 1850s appointing a minister followed by a school in the 1860s.[97] By the middle of the nineteenth century Ashkenazi Jewry, reflecting developments on the continent, had begun to divide into Orthodox and Reform, indicated by the opening of distinct synagogues by those who wanted a more liberal interpretation of rituals, most symbolically the West London Synagogue in 1840.[98]

Despite the many divisions of Anglo-Jewry by this time, the middle of the nineteenth century also witnessed an attempt to develop formal national representative bodies reflecting both the increased confidence of Anglo-Jewry and the organization of the campaign for Jewish emancipation. The Board of

Deputies, originating in the middle of the eighteenth century, represents the most all-encompassing of these bodies, as it had both a political and religious function and claimed to stand for all of the different Jewish communities.[99] At the same time the Chief Rabbinate, formally established during the 1840s, attempted to provide a unity of religious service and rituals for Orthodox congregations.[100] In 1870 there followed the foundation of the United Synagogue, which aimed at keeping the London congregations together as Jews moved into the suburbs.[101] Jewish education and charitable activity grew during the Victorian period, consolidating developments which occurred from the readmission of the seventeenth century. 'The number of pupils in Jewish day schools rose from about 2,000 in the early 1850s to 5,687 in London and 2,127 in the provinces in the early 1880s'.[102]

What relationship did members of established Victorian Jewry have with their religion? The establishment of the communal structures tells us little about patterns of worship or maintenance of Jewishness. V. D. Lipman interrogated the census of all worship in Britain carried out on the weekend of 28–9 March 1851 and came to the conclusion that, using his estimate of the Jewish population of '35,000 souls in 1851', about 3,000 'or rather less than ten per cent of the Jewish population' actually attended services, which appears lower than figures for Roman Catholics. Part of the explanation may lie in the existence of 'unsynagogued' congregations outside London,[103] but it also seems tempting to suggest that a process of continuing assimilation, including conversion, occurred. However, Endelman suggests that conversion remained unusual, suggesting, instead, that 'the decline of Judaism within the native middle class . . . proceeded . . . from a . . . general disinclination to consider religion of any kind to be a critical element in the routine of daily life'.[104]

Mid Victorian Jewry therefore remained a diverse community with a centralizing tendency at the top. While the number of synagogues continually increased in both London and the provinces, the level of religious practice appears to have remained low. Dramatic changes occurred as a result of the late nineteenth-century influx from Eastern Europe, which created conflict between the newcomers and the various groups of established Anglo-Jewry. The new arrivals established their own synagogues, independent *hebroth* or *chevrot*, 'in any back- or upstairs-room, attic, or hut that could be found fit for the purpose', as they could not afford the luxurious surroundings of their established co-religionists.[105] These places of worship developed organically where the migrants settled, counting scores in the East End of London and twenty in Liverpool. In Glasgow *ad hoc* synagogues emerged in Oxford Street and South Portland Street in the Gorbals, together with a religious school with a roll of about 400.[106] The emergence of so many places of worship suggests that the newcomers had a strong wish to practice their own religion and had little desire to enter the synagogues which serviced the established community. They faced so much hostility that something of a schism emerged between the two groups in the decades leading up to the First World War. This partly manifested itself in the establishment of the Federation of Synagogues in 1887 to hold together the new *chevroth* and *hebroth*.[107] The mutual distrust did not simply revolve around religious practice, but also class, area of origin, outward appearance and numbers so that the established community feared that the influx of so many newcomers who settled in 'ghettos' would lead to an upsurge of antisemitism which would undermine the gains they had made during the nineteenth century. The immigrants also established their own religious schools, continuing practices in Eastern Europe. But in these early days religious practice appears haphazard and the 1905 census of religious worship in London suggested an attendance of about 25 per cent of the capital's Jews,[108] considerably higher than the figure for Germans.

FIGURE 10 Boys from the Jewish Free Boys' School, work on a model railroad that they built in their woodworking and metalsmithing shops. Bishopsgate, London. Image © Hulton-Deutsch Collection/CORBIS

The divisions amongst Anglo-Jewry survived into the inter-war years, while Jewish religious practice continued to decline. Rosalyn Livshin demonstrated this decrease amongst many second generation Jews by the 1920s, partly as a result of the influence of secular Jewish social and sporting organizations, while others could not attend synagogue services because of working on Saturday or because 'religion seemed to be altogether meaningless and irrelevant in the conditions in which they found themselves'.[109] Nevertheless, as Jews moved out of the inner city and into the suburbs, they opened new synagogues, symbolized in London by the development of the Hendon congregation.[110] In fact, the number of synagogues in England and Wales increased from about 150 in 1901 to 250 in 1921 and 350 in 1940.[111] Bill Rubinstein has argued that in religious terms, 'the old and new Jewries were successfully blending into a dominant Anglo-Jewish religious style and characteristic pose' during the interwar years, symbolized by the increasing strength of the United Synagogue, which attracted the upwardly mobile Jews of Eastern European origin.[112] However, the Federation of Synagogues remained, while some provincial and London congregations maintained independence from any of the national groupings.[113]

Anglo-Jewry reached its numerical peak in the immediate post-war years. The period since 1945 has meant a gradual decline in religious adherence, as well as a continuing factionalism amongst Jewish groups who increasingly refused to work with each other. The four main congregations which have emerged have consisted of Sephardic, Reform, Orthodox and the expanding Ultra-Orthodox, around the Union of Orthodox Hebrew congregations. Some indications of communal life, such as education, both full-time and after-school, supported by both the state and private funds, as well as charitable activity, suggest a strengthening of the religious aspects of the Jewish community, at least in the earlier post-war decades. However, figures which deal with attendance at synagogue services during the 1990s point to the fact that 26 per cent of Jews from mainstream Orthodox families never attended any, while 47 per cent went once or twice a year or for particular occasions. Meanwhile, the annual average number of religious marriages had declined from 1,830 per year in the late 1960s to 1,031 by 1992. By the beginning of the twenty-first century a large percentage of London's Jews saw themselves as having a secular rather than a religious identity, linked to the lack of religious practice and also to the section of Anglo-Jewry to which they saw themselves aligned, with the more Orthodox describing themselves as more religious.[114]

One way of measuring the decline of religious Judaism and the development of Britishness amongst those descendants of the Eastern European migrants consists of food patterns. While kosher practice may have reached a peak in the immediate post-war years, it has seen a decline since that time, indicated by the decrease in the number of kosher butchers. The changing contents of Jewish plates in Britain points to the Anglicization of the descendants of the Eastern Europeans, who move away from consuming the food of their Ashkenazi homeland such as 'liver balls', 'einlauf', 'kreplech' and 'stuffed necks' to eating the same products as the wider population by as early as the 1930s including egg mayonnaise, sardines, roast beef, roast lamb and mint sauce, together with strained prunes, apples or pears. These trends would continue into the post-war period, indicated by the fact that the handful of officially recognized kosher restaurants existing in Britain today, include those which market themselves as Italian and Chinese.[115]

Bill Rubinstein has pointed to the fact that Jews have increasingly become incorporated into the higher echelons of British society in virtually all fields of life ranging from science to politics to entertainment.[116] Names such as Nigel Lawson, Marc Bolan or Claire Rayner point to the way in which Jews have simply become part of mainstream British society with an apparently purely British identity, even though Nigel Lawson and his daughter would regard themselves as Jewish, certainly in a secular sense.[117]

Anglo-Jewry provides an example of a complex group with multiple identities developing as a result of a series of waves of immigration. It is also a highly centralized community, represented by a complexity of bodies. The social mobility of the descendants of the newcomers who arrived at the end of the nineteenth century finds reflection in the increasing integration into British norms, epitomized most clearly by the overrepresentation of Jews in the armed forces during both World Wars.

While South Asian migrants may have brought the most visible religions into Britain amongst those communities which have developed in the post-war years, faith also plays a role for others, especially Greek Cypriots. Greek Orthodox Churches have existed in London since the seventeenth century. St Sophia, opened by Greek merchants in 1878, served as the main focus for migrants from Cyprus in the immediate post-war years. There followed other places of worship, especially in the main areas of settlement including Camden Town and Kentish Town. By the 1990s the number of Greek Orthodox Churches in London and its suburbs had increased to 32, while others existed to serve the small communities of Greek Cypriots outside the capital. Most of these simply took over vacated Anglican churches. Writing in the early 1990s Floya Anthias asserted that the majority of Greek Cypriots maintained Christmas, New Year, Easter and weddings, baptisms, funerals and memorials. Older women represent the mainstay of the church, while

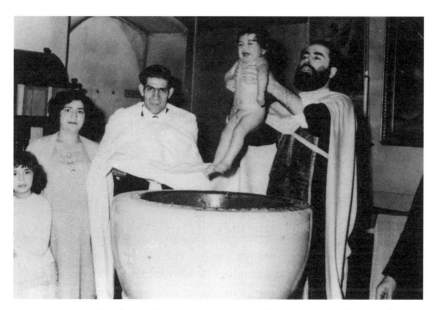

FIGURE 11 Greek orthodox christening in London, 1963, author's own photograph

men attend less frequently. The church plays an important role in the life-cycle of Greek Cypriots in Britain. Unlike the other migrant religions, it has not developed a significant welfare organization, with the main activity consisting of Sunday schools. The church represents an important ethnic focus for those Cypriots not linked to any particular community organization.[118]

The most visible of the new migrant religious identities in post-war Britain and those which count the largest numbers of adherents originate in South Asia in the form of Hinduism, Sikhism and Islam. At least some of the adherents of all of these religions have roots in former British India, although some have moved via sojourns in Africa and elsewhere. Islam remains the most complex religion both because its adherents do not consist purely of South Asians but also, and partly because of this, it represents the most diverse in terms of religious practice. It is also the largest and most organized of the new post-war religions in Britain, with a sophisticated welfare organization, as well as the one that has become most politicized.

While Hinduism, Sikhism and Islam may have witnessed rapid expansion after 1945, their adherents already lived in London during the Victorian years, although they had difficulty practising their respective religions because of the hostility which they faced. In fact, because of animosity combined with the attention which they received from missionaries, a few conversions to Christianity occurred amongst Indians in Britain during the nineteenth century. One of the most famous converts consisted of Duleep Singh, the last 'Maharaja' of the Punjab who moved to Britain in 1854 after the East India Company took over his land. However, he subsequently went back to his own religion upon returning to India, but appears to have converted to Christianity again on his deathbed in Paris, suggesting a use of religion for utilitarian motives. The efforts of Joseph Salter and other missionaries to convert Lascars in the East End of London appear to have had limited success. But it proved difficult to continue the practice of the original South Asian religions, at least in an organized manner. A few mosques had appeared in London by the outbreak of the First World War including one in Woking with a burial ground. A congregation had also developed in Liverpool as the result of the efforts of a convert to the Islamic faith.[119]

Further development of organized religious practice occurred amongst South Asians during the inter-war period. The Central Hindu Association and the Hindu Association of Europe had come into existence by the 1930s. These carried out a range of welfare, social and religious activities.[120] The first Sikh *Gurdwara* appears to have opened in a house in Shepherd's Bush in London in 1911 and served as the focal point for the community in Britain: some worshippers would travel hundreds of miles to attend services during the major religious festivals, especially *Vaisakhi*.[121] The Islamic religion witnessed the most significant development during the inter-war years, with several mosques opening in London. Humayun Ansari has detailed the way in which everyday religious practice occurred amongst both South Asian and Middle Eastern migrants in the early twentieth century. Marriages, often involving a white partner, took place with either a Muslim or a Christian blessing, while some migrants, often seamen, preferred to keep a distance from white society because of the hostility which they often faced and so they could continue their religious practices more easily.[122]

In view of the small numbers of their practitioners, Hinduism, Sikhism and Islam remained minor religions in Britain before the Second World War, with little organization and little opportunity for their adherents to carry out the strict religious practice characteristic of the homeland. The large scale migration of South Asians from the 1960s, like the arrival of the Irish in the nineteenth century, would dramatically transform this situation. Despite apparently constituting the third largest religious group in Britain,[123] with some spectacular places of worship, above all the Swaminarayan Temple in Neasden,[124] Hindus appear to have the lowest religious profile amongst the South Asian religious groups. This probably finds explanation in the fact that no political issue has united the whole

FIGURE 12 Avtar Singh Deogan before and after arriving in Britain in the early 1960s, author's own photographs

community in the same way in which the wearing of traditional dress has brought together Sikhs or the Iraq War has unified Muslims. Just as Muslims and Sikhs are constituted by a variety of sub-groups, Hindus are divided by area of origin, religious practice and caste, which make the development of a unified Hindu voice highly problematic.[125] One way in which some sort of a unified community comes together lies in the development of religious festivals, especially Diwali in Leicester, which can bring together crowds of up to 60,000 people.[126]

Sikhs also constitute a diverse community. In the first place, caste plays a role. At the same time, while some Sikhs have migrated directly from India, others have moved via East Africa. The emergence of *gurdwaras* illustrates the visible 'arrival' of this community in Britain. In the initial stages of the migration process, the all male households 'rarely practiced religious rituals and, if anything, they scorned the idea of doing so'.[127] These early settlers 'tended to avoid overt symbols of the faith' and most 'opted for a clean-shaven appearance' and rarely wore their turbans.[128] However, as one Sikh girl, complaining about having to revert to traditional dress, having previously worn English clothes, suggested, following the arrival of 'hordes of Punjabis',[129] men and women turned to the clothing associated with their religion above all, in the case of men, the beard and the turban and, in the case of women, the *salwar kamiz* (trouser suit). Nevertheless, the story does not end with the Sikh community reverting to homeland dress *en masse* at some stage during the course of the 1960s. Generation, situation, individual and family religious adherence as well as personal choice, have all played a large role in determining whether Sikhs wear their traditional dress. As Parminder Bhachu has written, Sikh women are as much influenced by their locality within England as by English fashions as a whole. Sikh women in the early 1990s appeared Brummie in their clothing and accents in the same way that women from Camden looked Camdenian.[130] Such developments contrast with the 'turban campaigns' whereby individual Sikhs successfully asserted their right to wear their traditional headdress working on the buses and driving motorcycles. Singh and Tatla have actually identified four 'turban campaigns'.[131]

A contrast also exists between the rise of the gurdwaras, some of which compare with the grand architecture of both similar buildings in India and the most spectacular church buildings in Britain, and the decreasing levels of religious adherence. The increase in the number of temples essentially points to the growth in the Sikh population of Britain since the 1950s, as well as their improving economic position, as much of the finance for the buildings comes from donations. Whereas the early arrivals used makeshift buildings such as school halls and houses, increasing numbers of purpose built locations have emerged in recent decades so that the number of *gurdwaras* has grown from 1 in 1951 to 214 by 2001. With one survey claiming that 39 per cent of Sikhs attended services at least once a week, this seems a remarkably high level of religious adherence. *Gurdwaras* have attempted to retain their flocks by community activities such as scouting groups, while the need for the translation of services has also arisen.[132] Although Sikhs may appear to have high levels of religious attendance, this should not cover the diversity of the communities and individuals which make up this religious group.

Superficially, the rise of Islam in Britain since the 1940s would also suggest high levels of religious practice amongst those who adhere to this faith. The early settlers had to practise their religion as best they could, symbolized by the fact that they could not obtain halal meat. While some individuals during the 1950s and 1960s simply ate locally available food, others tried to avoid this in one of three ways. In the first place, they could turn to kosher butchers as Islamic doctrine allowed the consumption of such meat. Secondly, they could purchase live chickens and then make them halal at home by slaughtering them whilst reciting prayers. Thirdly, some migrants simply ate vegetables rather than consume meat provided by

English butchers. In the longer term South Asian Muslims would solve their dietary problems as their numbers increased and a market emerged. By the 1970s and, more especially, the 1980s, halal meat became increasingly available as the number of butchers selling it in British inner cities, supervised by the Halal Food Authority, established in 1994, increased.[133] On the other hand, while the availability of religiously acceptable foods kept pace with the growth of the Muslim population, changes in consumption patterns reflect the integration of the second and subsequent generations. The ultimate symbol of this consists of the 'Full Muslim' halal breakfast, consumed before sunrise during Ramadan.[134]

Changes in food patterns reflect the integration process, which has affected the descendants of the South Asian migrants who arrived from the 1950s. However, much research has focused upon the apparent separation of Islamic communities. One indication of this apparent separation lies in the institutionalization of Islam. The early post-war arrivals worshipped in mosques in makeshift accommodation such as terraced houses indicated by the opening of the first place of worship in Bradford in 1959, which attracted a variety of different sects. In the long run, however, not only did Bradford become dominated by one particular group from the Punjab, but the number of mosques in the city had increased to 34 by 1989, with several different traditions unified, to some extent, by the Bradford Council of Mosques, established in 1981.[135] Such developments mirror the national picture so that the 18 registered mosques from 1983 had increased to 338 by 1985, while a further growth has occurred since then to perhaps 1,300.[136] At the same time a whole series of national organizations have also developed in Britain, reflecting the range of Muslim sects and interests in the country, not simply from South Asia, but also from other parts of the world. The numerous Islamic organizations have also focused upon specific interest groups such as youth and women.[137] Many mosques have educational activities attached to them. In fact, by 2007 a total of 100 independent and seven state funded schools existed in Britain, leading to claims that such institutions would perpetuate ethnic difference and division.[138] Placing the evolution of Islamic institutions in the historical context of the development of the Jewish and Irish Catholic communities over the last two centuries there seems nothing particularly unique about the development of Islamic institutions.

The practice of the Islamic faith works at the individual and family level as scholars such as Pnina Werber and Katy Gardner have demonstrated. Werbner has especially focused upon Manchester and has shown how specific rituals, performed especially by women, take place in the home.[139] Katy Gardner, meanwhile, in interviews she carried out with elderly Bengalis in

Tower Hamlets, demonstrated that they have become increasingly religious with age, which she explains in two ways. First, the 'growing Islamicization' of pockets of Britain, especially the East End of London, which has made religious practice easier. Second, aging led the elderly men she interviewed to consider their mortality and therefore think more about religion than their previous worries of work and money.[140]

However, a picture of the growth of an all-encompassing religion, which has apparently fully incorporated all Muslims in Britain, needs balancing against the realities of multicultural Britain, in which assimilation and integration take place. The increasing use of Islamic dress by women born in Britain may suggest otherwise, although some claim that wearing it makes them feel liberated and confirms their identity.[141] On the other hand, only a small minority of Muslim men regularly wear Islamic dress.[142] Integration rather than assimilation appears the norm amongst British Muslims.

Religion has played a key role for a variety of groups in Britain over the last two centuries, above all Irish Catholics, Jews, Sikhs and Muslims, whose primary identification revolves around their faith. The evolution of community organizations has, in all cases, facilitated the practice of these new religions in Britain. While the long-term history of the Irish and Jews suggest an inevitable lessening of identification along religious grounds, it seems too early to come to conclusions about the South Asian communities which have emerged in recent decades.

Politics

Politics has also played a key role in the perpetuation of ethnic difference in Britain over the last two centuries, especially for active refugees who have fled persecution in their homeland. Classic examples include the exiles from the continental repression of the nineteenth century, especially following the failure of the 1848 revolutions, and those who fled from Nazism. Similarly, politically active wealthy migrants from the Empire who arrived in Britain from the late Victorian period also continued their campaigning in their new surroundings. In addition, members of the more populous groups have also involved themselves in political activity, either continuing to support homeland causes, as the classic example of the Victorian Irish would suggest, or participating in new activities, sometimes as a reaction against racism, as the East End Jews fighting the British Union of Fascists during the 1930s would indicate. More recently, Islamist politics have partly evolved as a form of resistance to racism, although such activity also developed in response to international developments involving the perceived victimization of Muslims. As indicated by the actions of a small number of Islamic youths in London during 2005, violence has also represented a form of political consciousness in Britain, dating back to the Irish in the middle of the nineteenth century, but also manifesting itself in the inner city riots of the 1980s, which particularly involved African-Caribbean young men. In contrast to the activities on the street, many migrants and their descendants become incorporated into mainstream political processes, an important indicator of integration and facilitator of multiculturalism.[143]

Refugees and migrants have participated in a whole range of political activities in Britain since the early nineteenth century. Those involved in home-land politics perpetuate a form of consciousness distinct from mainstream processes in Britain and therefore develop their own political ethnicity. Such individuals, including exiles from nineteenth century continental repression or African and Asian sojourners before 1945, look forward to returning home to continue with their political activity. On the other hand, the entry of ethnic minorities into mainstream politics provides a clear indication of integration. In between lie the newly constructed forms of political activity, often reactions against racism and often resulting in violence.

In the nineteenth century a whole series of political exiles found them-selves in Britain wishing to continue activities which they had pursued on the continent. Many had little desire to remain in exile, even though they may have made the most of their time in Britain to help them with their campaigning, as Margaret C. Wicks demonstrated in her study of Italian refugees in London during the early nineteenth century. However, some of the educated elites she covered did settle in Britain and secured prestigious employment.[144]

As a result of expulsion and the desire for the creation of a 'free' Poland, much political activity has taken place amongst Poles in Britain since the Victorian period, most of whom, until the influx of the twenty-first century, had migrated at least partially due to German and Russian oppression. During the 1840s some Polish exiles had joined a group called the Fraternal Democrats of all Nations, which, as the name suggests, unified refugees from a range of European states in a type of collective refugee ethnicity. In addition, the Polish Democratic Committee and the Democratic Committee for Poland's Regeneration also came into existence during this decade, receiving support from English radicals. Furthermore, tiny Polish socialist societies also emerged during the 1850s.[145] During the First World War Poles in Britain who stressed their Polishness (as opposed to Jewishness) campaigned for the formation of a Polish state at the end of the conflict, establishing the Polish Information Committee, although, as Norman Davies demonstrated, a series of factions evolved in London.[146] The Polish Government and Army in Exile who found themselves in Britain during the Second World War clearly identified themselves along political lines, although, as during the Great War, some splintering occurred, determined partly by attitudes to the Soviet takeover. Rather bizarrely, the anti-Communist Polish government in exile continued to have its own President until 1990. Nevertheless, only a minority of the post-war community remained involved in exile politics, establishing, instead, a whole range of other organizations.[147] In her work on Poles in post-war Leicester Kathy Burrell examined 'Polish spaces', such as ex-servicemen's clubs,[148] but focused especially upon the way in which her interviewees remembered the Polish national past and homeland arguing that the problem of returning to a Communist Poland gave added impetus to the development of a transnational identity for the migrants.[149]

At the end of the nineteenth century, as autocracy grew in the last days of the Tsarist Empire, London became a centre of political activity for Russian exiles, the most famous of whom consisted of Lenin. Numerous groupings came into existence including the Society of Friends of Russian Freedom, which brought together revolutionaries and their British sympathizers. The Russian Revolutions of 1917 sent many of the exiles back home, although others would follow during the 1920s as a result of Soviet repression, the most famous of whom, in this case, consisted of Trotsky.[150]

One of the most politically active national communities in Britain from the middle of the nineteenth to the middle of the twentieth centuries consisted of Germans. They splintered into a variety of sub-groupings who had moved to Britain for a range of reasons and identified themselves according to causes ranging from Communism to Nazism in the period as a whole. While some simply saw their time in Britain as a temporary phase, others spent the majority of their lives in the country.

German political exiles began to move to Britain during the 1830s and, following the failure of the 1848 revolutions, which sent over a significant number of refugees of various political persuasions, a series of distinct groupings would emerge. Internecine strife occurred on the extreme left, partly revolving around the question of support for Karl Marx. One of the longest lasting left-wing groups was the German Workers Educational Association. The importance of London as a centre of Communist revolutionary activity is indicated by the 1864 foundation of the First International. Marx and Engels spent their lives in Britain after fleeing from the failure of the 1848 revolutions, although Engels had migrated partly in connection with his father's business interests. A further wave of left-wing refugees would move to Britain following Bismarck's introduction of the Anti-Socialist Laws in

1878. Yet more exiles followed subsequently including Edward Bernstein, who brought his *Sozialdemokrat* newspaper with him and, in 1895, the anarchist Rudolf Rocker, who would eventually find himself interned during the First World War.[151] More left-wing political activists would follow to London after the Nazi seizure of power.[152] Some of these would have consisted of Jews, establishing their own organizations, most famously the Association of Jewish Refugees, which campaigned on their behalf for decades after 1945.[153] The Germanness and political beliefs of left-wing refugees from central Europe remained inseparable in many cases.

The same applies to those primarily liberal and nationalistically minded exiles from the 1848 revolutions including Gottfried Kinkel, Karl Heinrich Schaible, Arnold Ruge and Carl Blind, who established a whole series of German newspapers in London during the middle of the nineteenth century, including *Der Deutsche Eidgennose*, edited by Blind and aiming at 'the over-throw of tyranny in Germany'.[154]

In addition, right-wing German political activity developed in Britain from the end of the nineteenth century to the Nazi period. In the late Victorian and Edwardian years the rising nationalistic confidence in Germany found reflection in the German community which lived in Britain, demonstrated by the fact that bodies such as the German Colonial Society and the German Navy League had branches in London and Glasgow.[155] Meanwhile, the inter-war years saw the Nazification of much German activity in Britain.[156]

Although Jews may have fled from Eastern Europe partly as a result of persecution from their homeland, their activity in their new environment became quickly concerned with the conditions which they now faced, rather than with the plight of the Jews which they had left behind. The main reason for the difference between eastern European Jewish and German political identification probably lies in the fact that many of the Germans fled because of their political activity, rather than because they formed part of a large group persecuted because of their ethnicity. In essence the German refugees simply continued campaigning for the same issues in London that they had done on the continent, whereas many Jewish newcomers of the Victorian and Edwardian period became politicized for the first time.

Established Anglo-Jewry devoted attention to the plight of the Jews in both Eastern Europe before 1914 and Nazi Europe after 1933: the old com-munity established a whole series of organizations to assist them. The extent of this support has caused some debate, with several historians pointing to the fact that Jews already resident in Britain, cared as much about the con-sequences of the influx of thousands of Jewish newcomers upon the rise of antisemitism and therefore their own position, as they did about supporting refugees from continental European repression.[157] Nevertheless, Anglo-Jewry established a range of organizations to help those Jews remaining in Europe both before 1914 and during the 1930s and 1940s. In the late nineteenth century, these included the Mansion House Fund, set up in 1882 to protest against Russian treatment of Jews and to help refugees both in England and on the continent. Similarly, during the 1930s a series of organizations had similar aims including the Central British Fund for German Jewry and the Jewish Refugees Committee. Many of these groups primarily aimed at easing the plight of the refugees upon their arrival in a new environment. The Poor Jews Temporary Shelter established in 1885 may provide an example of such an organization, but it would not allow residents to stay for more than two weeks. In fact, most sojourners consisted of transmigrants on their way to the USA. On the other hand, those bodies established during the 1930s accepted that many of the people they assisted would remain for the long term. During both refugee movements Anglo-Jewish initiatives aimed as much at facilitating integration and anonymizing the obvious Jewishness of the newcomers as they did at providing assistance.[158]

However, just as the newly arrived Jewish refugees from Eastern Europe followed a separate path from the established community in religious terms, so, in the same way, in the short-term at least, they established their own political groupings. In the longer run Jewish migrants have become absorbed in mainstream politics.[159] In the short term Jews who had fled Tsarist oppression joined political groupings which would help to ease their wretched social position and help to fight everyday antisemitism. This particularly meant Jewish trade unions, especially those in the tailoring trades, in order to fight against exploitation by fellow Jews, pointing to the fact that class solidarity proved more important than ethnic identification with Jewish employers.[160] By the 1930s Jewish consciousness in the East End of London became more directly political, responding to the threat posed by antisemitic fascist activity. Some Jews joined the Communist Party and participated in anti-fascist demonstrations culminating in the 'Battle of Cable Street' in October 1936 when, under the influence of the British Communist Party, 100,000 anti-fascists (many of them local East End Jews) stood up to 1,900 fascists.[161] Other Jews in late nineteenth and early twentieth century Britain preferred to follow a different transnational political ideology in the form of Zionism, which had taken off throughout Europe by 1900. A series of international groups had branches in Britain, while home grown products included the Zionist Organization, established in 1897. The English Zionist Federation, which had fifty branches by 1914, counted 30,000 members by 1921, as well as 234 affiliated bodies.[162] There seem close similarities between those Jews who looked to return to Israel in early twentieth century Britain and those Muslims who have become politically radicalized by international Islamic movements a hundred years later, with both looking for their political inspiration beyond British shores. Nevertheless, this only represents one political identity. The majority of Jews and Muslims have become fully integrated in mainstream political processes, facilitated by their nationality and consequent voting rights.[163]

The same also applies to the Irish in Britain following the extension of the franchise at the start of the twentieth century because they have always had the right to vote, even though, following the formation of the Irish Free State in 1921, they no longer possessed British nationality.[164] During the Victorian period they found themselves as part of the mass of disenfranchised working class voters who turned to means other than the ballot box to make their voices heard. Such methods included participation in political pressure groups, especially those campaigning for Home Rule, and violence, especially revolving, in the case of Protestants, around the Orange Order. But the Irish also became incorporated into mainstream politics, especially as the franchise widened during the course of the nineteenth and early twentieth centuries.

Much campaigning certainly took place in the British mainland for the purpose of establishing an independent Irish state. As early as 1840 a Repeal Association campaigned for the abolition of the Act of Union between Britain and Ireland.[165] The Irish Confederates became a more important body during this decade, with close links to the Chartists. They reached a peak of activity during 1848, especially in Liverpool, Manchester and Bradford. But they came under close surveillance and repression during the year of revolution, disappearing in 1848.[166]

However, from the 1850s a more violent variation of Irish nationalism surfaced in the form of the Fenian Irish Republican Brotherhood (IRB), a transnational organization with a headquarters in New York carrying out activity in both Ireland and the British mainland. The IRB aimed at overthrowing British rule by violence and may have counted as many as 80,000 members in the United Kingdom in 1865, despite strong opposition towards it from the Roman Catholic Church. It reached a peak of activity in 1867 and 1868 with an attempt to seize Chester Castle, a failed Irish rising, a raid on a Manchester police cart transporting IRB prisoners and the bombing of Clerkenwell jail, which, instead of freeing Fenian inmates, killed twenty residents who lived nearby. Such activity led 22,000 Irish people in London to present a petition declaring their loyalty to Queen Victoria in 1868.[167] While violence died down after this time, a subsequent reorganization of

Fenian activity resulted in an attack on Salford Barracks and Liverpool Town Hall in 1881, the latter of which damaged the building, while the former killed a seven year old boy. Further bombings occurred in this second phase of the 'dynamite war', carried out by Irish-Americans until 1887.[168]

Irish Nationalism also manifested itself in less violent organizations during the late Victorian years, especially amongst the Lancashire community, focused upon Liverpool. These included the National Brotherhood of St Patrick during the 1860s.[169] More importantly, the Home Rule Confederation of Great Britain, formed in 1870, counted numerous branches and thousands of members throughout the country during the 1870s and 1880s.[170] The peak of pre-First World War nationalist activity came with the development of the Irish National League of Great Britain from 1883, which, like its predecessors, worked with a leadership based in Ireland.[171] Irish nationalists remained strong in Liverpool at the beginning of the twentieth century where they counted, 'at various times, 10,000 members in 17 active branches, shared the government of the city for three years, formed the official opposition in the Council as late as 1922 with 23 members and had the wholehearted support' of the immigrant population.[172] While the Irish in Britain volunteered *en masse* to fight in the First World War, the Irish rebellion of 1916 found support in mainland Britain.[173]

Organized Irish Catholic activity in Britain displayed a strong streak of loyalty to the homeland, although participation in mainstream politics also played a role in the integration of this group, from the Chartists to the Liberal and Labour parties.[174] As well as this formalized political activity, Irish Catholics and Irish protestants developed a form of political consciousness which manifested itself in inter-ethnic conflict on the streets, with a focus upon the big cities where they lived cheek by jowl, especially Liverpool and Glasgow. Behind this conflict lay the Orange Order, originally established in County Armagh in 1795 and forming its first branch in Liverpool in 1819, where it became especially prominent. It also had heartlands in Manchester and Scotland, particularly in Glasgow and Edinburgh, where large numbers of Protestants lived. As with Irish nationalism, this group therefore formed part of a transnational movement with activity throughout the British Isles during the nineteenth century. Although it may have had an air of respectability, certainly in terms of its organization, its members also fought Roman Catholics in the streets, especially in Liverpool, Glasgow and Edinburgh, where sectarian violence became endemic during the nineteenth century. While both the Orange Order and rioting may have declined after the First World War, sectarianism certainly did not, illustrated not just by the survival of the 'Old Firm' football rivalry in Scotland, but also, for instance, in the fact that anti-Catholicism played a role in anti-Italian riots in Edinburgh in June 1940, following Mussolini's declaration of War on Britain.[175]

The Irish in Britain after the First World War and into the decades after 1945 have increasingly become integrated into mainstream British politics. A pattern of Catholic support for the Labour Party and Protestant backing for the Conservative and Unionist Party developed, although this does not tell the whole picture.[176] The 1930s also witnessed an IRA bombing campaign which affected Liverpool, Coventry, London, Birmingham and Manchester. While, like its nineteenth century predecessors, it did not tend to involve members of the Irish community in Britain, about 200 Irishmen marched through London in support of IRA prisoners the day after several bombs went off in the capital.[177] The IRA bombings at the end of the twentieth century received relatively little support amongst the Irish in Britain, even though sections of mainstream British society did not distinguish between the IRA bombers from Ireland and the Irish community in Britain during the peaks of bombing.[178] The post-war community voted on issues within Britain rather than those in the homeland, which meant that, as a pre-dominantly working class group, they tended to opt for the Labour party and became important in constituency activities in the areas in which they settled.[179]

Although the nineteenth-century Black and Asian migrants did not become involved in the level of political activity of the Irish, in view of their small numbers, politics played a role in their identification. Indeed, many individuals and groups moved from the higher echelons of South Asian, West Indian and African societies to London in order to develop political consciousness. From 'the 1850s, in ever increasing numbers, African traders, chiefs, lawyers and doctors sent children to Britain from Sierra Leone and the Gold Coast for higher education, a few also coming from Lagos and the Oil Rivers'. This led to the formation of the Gold Coast Aborigines Protection Society, which sent deputations to London in order to attempt to improve the position of its people in Britain.[180] The later nineteenth century also saw the beginnings of formalized Pan-Africanism, especially with the establishment of the African Association in London in 1897. The leading figure in this group actually consisted of the African-American Henry Sylvester Williams. It aimed at encouraging 'a feeling of unity' and facilitating 'friendly inter-course among Africans in general', as well as protecting 'the interests of all subjects claiming African descent' throughout the British Empire.[181] Three years later there followed the Pan-African Conference, which also met in London, attended by both Africans and African Americans, to discuss the position of Black people globally. It resulted in the transformation of the African Association into the Pan-African Association, which aimed at improving the position of Africans throughout the world. However, the organization remained short-lived because the Black population of London consisted especially of transient students, while the group received limited support from white political parties.[182] New pan-African groupings came into existence in inter-war Britain, including the African Progress Union, established in 1918, while, two years later, the second Pan-African Congress opened in Central Hall, Westminster, leading, after sessions in Brussels and Paris, to the formation of the Second Pan-African Association.[183] The West African Students Union, emerging specifically in inter-war London, developed into an instrument of African nationalism.[184] The League of Coloured Peoples became perhaps the most significant Black political grouping in London during the 1920s and 1930s, led by a Jamaican doctor, Harold Moody, with its own journal the *Keys*. Established in London in 1931, it aimed at improving the position of its members and of Black people throughout the world but fizzled out following the death of Moody in 1947.[185]

The development of Black political consciousness in early twentieth century London resembles the activities of refugees who made their way to Britain in the Victorian period because in both cases such consciousness brought together educated individuals with a common cause. In this sense the closest similarity lies with the formation of the International[186] whereby those with common concern for one particular group (the working classes or Black people) claim to represent their interests throughout the world. The Black political activists anticipated later developments because they created a new identity from a diverse set of people, whose common interest consisted of their skin colour and African origins. Thus the concept of Black ethnicity in Britain, which would witness further development after 1945, originated at the beginning of the twentieth century as the result of the efforts of a combination of educated Africans, African Americans and West Indians.

A political ethnicity reflecting specific origins emerged amongst South Asian settlers in Britain before 1945. In the first place, a variety of groups campaigning for Indian independence developed including the India League, which counted white members, and the London branch of the Indian National Congress.[187] Rosina Visram, meanwhile, has described the activities of Lascars to improve their position during the inter-war years.[188] More specifically, the Sikh-based Indian Workers Association also surfaced in Coventry during the 1930s.[189] In addition, a Pan-Islamic Society came into existence as early as 1903, renamed the Central Islamic Society in 1910, with the aim of removing 'misconceptions prevailing among non-Muslims regarding Islam and Muslims'.[190]

As a result of their British citizenship and consequent voting rights, the vast majority of post-war Commonwealth immigrants and their descendants have fallen into mainstream politics, displaying particular support for the Labour Party.[191] Nevertheless, the level of discrimination faced by ethnic minorities from South Asia and the Caribbean, as well as a continued interest in homeland politics, has meant the development of a series of political organizations, as well as more direct action on the streets in the form of rioting and protest.

One of the most significant bodies from the Caribbean has consisted of the West Indian Standing Conference, established in 1959 as an umbrella organization to support the interests of new arrivals and those facing discrimination.[192] Nevertheless, West Indian politically based consciousness has also operated on a more informal level in Britain. Les Back, working upon one London community, has written about the emergence of a hybrid national identity in an area he studied, revolving around skin colour and which also incorporated white ethnic groups.[193] At the same time, we also need to recognize the emergence of a Black political ethnicity in Britain, in which gender plays a central role.[194] Furthermore, Sheila Patterson pointed to the presence of an admittedly small number of Rastafarians in London by the end of the 1950s,[195] who would develop further in subsequent decades.[196] One of the most significant manifestations of informal Black political consciousness, born out of the resentment of years of discrimination and unemployment, consisted of the inner city riots which took place during the 1980s. Although a variety of ethnic groups participated in the events in London, Bristol and other big cities, they became closely related with Black youth, partly because the Thatcher government and parts of the press which supported the Conservatives focused upon race rather than disadvantage as the main cause of the disturbances.[197] The fact that Black youth participated in street violence suggests that they had adapted the behaviour of the disenfranchised in Britain from previous decades and centuries.[198] In fact, the actions of Black youth in Britain during the 1980s has direct twentieth century precedents both in the 1919 race riots and in the Nottingham and Notting Hill disturbances of 1958. While Black people essentially constituted the victims of violent racism on these occasions, they fought back both in 1919 and 1958.[199]

Disaffection with social and economic conditions also played a role in the emergence of radical Islam at the end of the twentieth century,[200] as witnessed especially in the inner city riots of 2001, in which, like their

Jewish and Black predecessors earlier in the twentieth century, northern Muslim youth stood up to white racists.[201] Nevertheless, such behaviour, together with other forms of resistance, notably the bombing of the London underground in 2005, represents part of a transnational Islamic diasporic consciousness which essentially emerged in the aftermath of the Iranian revolution of 1979 and had its first manifestation in Britain during the 'Rushdie Affair' in the late 1980s when Muslims took to the streets in order to burn the *Satanic Verses*, which they viewed as an affront to Islam.

Focusing specifically upon this action, Tariq Modood has claimed that the background to the book burning of January 1989 consisted of the fact that South Asian Muslims 'form a virtual underclass in Britain', which he supports with a series of social and economic indicators.[202] While the situation may not be so straightforward, because of the economic success of some Muslims,[203] his general assertion about the economic deprivation faced by this group as a factor in causing politicization remains true and is accepted by other scholars.[204] However, Pnina Werbner has dismissed social and economic causation, asserting, instead, that 'the Muslim response to the *Satanic Verses* was not an instance of an underprivileged underclass confronting the priest of an alien "high culture"'. Instead, she sees it as a confrontation 'between *equal* aesthetic communities, each defending its own high culture: not "popular" versus "high", or "low" versus "high" but "high" versus "high"'.[205] Werbner essentially sees Islamic political consciousness in Britain as a clash of two equally confident ideologies in the form of the liberal ideal versus Islam, which explains the level of hostility between the two. Issues of morality, lifestyle and world view also help to explain the level of animosity of Muslims towards mainstream society. As Alison Shaw has written, 'Many Pakistanis hold a low opinion of western social and sexual morality . . . They often cite Britain's high divorce rate and the increasing proportion of illegitimate births as evidence of the low moral standards of the west',[206] an issue which fuelled the reaction to the *Satanic Verses*.

However, the road from the first Pakistani arrivals of the 1950s and 1960s to the events of July 2005 remains complex. The early settlers established their own pressure groups such as the Pakistani Welfare Association, which, following the cessation of Bangladesh, gave rise to the Bangladeshi Welfare Association. In essence, such bodies represented the first generation. During the 1970s their descendants established their own youth centres and football clubs, partly with the assistance of state funding. Groups such as the Bangladeshi Youth Front also emerged. Meanwhile, a whole series of Islamic organizations evolved, although most of these had a primarily religious purpose.[207] While the publication of the *Satanic Verses* represents an important turning point, international events also played a role on the road to July 2005, including the Iranian revolution of 1979, which offered a template of a political movement based upon Islam. Meanwhile, the first US led war against Iraq led to the development of fervent global anti-western hostility amongst Muslims, especially as the main political ideology opposing the USA, in the form of Soviet Socialism, virtually died in the aftermath of the collapse of the USSR. The invasion of Afghanistan and Iraq created a feeling of international victimhood and brotherhood amongst many vulnerable and already politically active second and third generation British Muslims, who had accepted radical Islamic ideologies.[208]

Although the bombers of July 2005 represent the most extreme positions amongst British Muslims, public opinion surveys reveal opposition to British foreign policy against Islamic countries amongst this community.[209] The Sikh community in Britain, with the same geographical origins as many Muslims, offers a contrast to Islamic political activity. Sikhs constitute part of an international diaspora based on religion, with one ultimately distinct geographical origin in the Punjab.[210] Some religious radicalism has developed amongst them seen, for instance, in the hostility towards a play in Birmingham in 2004, *Behzti*, which suggests sexual immorality in a *gurdwara*. Similarly, a movement for an independent Sikh state, Khalistan, also had support in Britain during the 1980s and 1990s. On the other hand, the class based Indian Workers Association thrived into the post-war years.[211] Perhaps because British foreign policy never targeted Sikhs abroad or perhaps because they suffer less deprivation in Britain than Muslims, Sikh political activity has never become as radicalized as its Islamic equivalent.

We need to conclude this section by stressing the fact that the major migrant communities in Britain, from the Irish onwards have always become incorporated into mainstream politics. We also need to re-emphasize the fact that similarities exist especially between Irish, Jewish and Islamic political activity. All became victims of racism and, initially at least, found themselves at the bottom of the class ladder. All could call upon an international religion, vilified by the mainstream in Britain,[212] as the basis for their political activism, whether Irish nationalism, Zionism or radical Islam.

Cultural identities

Both political and religious activity, while they may change in the new environment, form a definite link with the land of origin. Attending religious services or participating in activities revolving around organized religion represent one way in which the first generation wishes to maintain identification with the past. The same applies to political activity attached to the homeland. In the longer term both religion and politics increasingly become symbols of hybrid Britishness. Indicators of identity connected with popular or high culture suggest more clearly and earlier that the integration process has begun. This could apply, for instance, to sport, although, even here, some loyalty to the homeland survives.[213] Aspects of everyday life demonstrate similar paradigms. Food undergoes a fairly rapid process of integration, even though, in the short run, newly arrived migrant communities have the desire to eat the foods of their homeland.[214] In the longer term, all migrant diets indicate traces of British influence. On the other hand, post-war migrants can maintain contact with a fairly 'pure' form of culture in their own homeland because of the development of cinema and satellite television, allowing them to live hybrid, transnational lives.[215]

The Irish in Britain over the past two centuries provide indications of changing cultural identities, especially in the twentieth century and, even more so, in the years since 1945, when religion and politics declined in importance, in contrast with the Victorian period. In the case of this community, one aspect of their everyday lives which suggests an easy path into Britishness throughout the past two centuries consists of their food patterns, which remain too similar to the norms of wider society to act as an indicator of difference.[216] Nevertheless, this remains something of an anomaly, certainly before 1945, because other aspects of their lives, in addition to religion and politics, certainly suggest difference, at least in the short run. Michael Dewey focused upon Irish burial rituals in early nineteenth-century urban Britain, which combined 'a mixture of orthodox religion, superstition and pagan survivals'. He examined the wake, which 'has social, psychological and practical implications' including the reinforcement of 'the solidarity of the social group'.[217] Another ritual, which begins to develop during the nineteenth century and becomes a mass phenomenon for Irish communities throughout the world during the twentieth century, providing a clear indication of the development of transnationalism, consists of the spread of St Patrick's Day celebrations.[218]

Sport provides one of the most interesting aspects of Irish identity in Britain although it has connections with both religion and politics. Two interesting paths have developed. In the first place, Gaelic sports, linked with the Irish nationalist movement, suggest that a distinct identity has survived, independent of any British influences. Football, on the other hand, points to an indentification which has emerged through participation in the people's game. The Gaelic Athletic Association (GAA), established in 1884, represented the sporting arm of a late nineteenth-century nationalist project, under the leadership of the Gaelic League, which wished to see the spread of Gaelic ideals and the Gaelic language not simply amongst the population of Ireland, but also Irish Catholics in the diaspora.[219] A London branch of the Gaelic Athletic Association had opened by 1896 and Irish sports would certainly take off in the capital in the early twentieth century,[220] as well as spreading to other Irish communities including Liverpool[221] and Manchester. Fielding, however, describes activities in the latter as 'feeble' because of the necessity to speak Gaelic in order to participate in hurling and Gaelic football, pointing to the ethnic exclusiveness of the Gaelic League, which would find difficulty succeeding amongst a diasporic community.[222] This, however, appears to contrast with the situation in Scotland, where Joseph M. Bradley has outlined the history of the GAA from the end of the nineteenth century to the present.[223] Irish sports, minus the linguistic test, survived well into the twentieth century so that sixty GAA clubs existed in London by the 1960s, while Birmingham had it own Gaelic Football League.[224]

But the Irish also participated in the most mainstream of British sports in the form of football. In Scotland the cities of Glasgow, Edinburgh and Dundee have football clubs which have functioned around the principle of the perpetuation of the Protestant/Catholic distinctiveness which had emerged in these cities during the course of the nineteenth century. Indeed, writing at the beginning of the twenty-first century, using the testimony of Glasgow Celtic supporters he interviewed, Joseph M. Bradley has gone as far as to state that supporting this football club represents a way in which the descendants of the migrants who made their way to Britain during the nineteenth century have continued to display their Irish identity, demonstrated most clearly by the waving of the Irish tricolour. Such assertions root football in Glasgow against a sectarian divide which manifests itself in other aspects of life in the city.[225] However, Bradley has also tackled the issue of football as an agent of assimilation.[226] This would appear its role in English cities with Irish communities such as Liverpool, despite the fact that Irish football clubs evolved here.[227]

Sport represented just one way in which organized Irish ethnicity has evolved in Britain since the Victorian period. Ó Tuathaigh has written of a 'full spectrum of immigrant associations' by the end of the nineteenth century dedicated not just to sport but also to Irish music and song which 'constituted a mosaic of ties binding the immigrant community to the homeland'.[228] The Irish press has also played a role in this process.[229]

In the post-war period Irish identities appear to have undergone a fairly rapid integration and assimilation process, although football and

FIGURE 13 Schiller Anstalt in Victorian Manchester. Sue Coates, 'Manchester's German Gentlemen: Immigrant Institutions in a Provincial City, 1840–1920', *Manchester Region History Review*, vol, 5 (1991–2)

sectarianism in Scotland warn against such an easy generalization. The first generation inevitably hold on closer to the land of their birth, as demonstrated by both Bronwen Walter and Louise Ryan in their accounts of Irish women in Britain.[230] But this association with home becomes increasingly less common amongst the second and subsequent generations, partly because they remain largely invisible (if we ignore names) in contrast with ethnic minorities from beyond Europe. Perhaps the absence of large scale Black and Asian migration to Scotland helps to account for the continuing importance of nineteenth-century patterns of ethnic identity.[231]

While religion and politics have played key roles for German identities in Britain from the nineteenth century, activity independent of these two roots has also evolved. In the Victorian period Germans established all sorts of *Vereine* (societies), especially at the higher end of the social scale, which had, as their main area of interest, activities which included sport, theatre and music. The German *Turnverein* became particularly important for the German community of London. For the working classes pubs and skittle alleys proved especially attractive.[232] By 1914 the German beer hall had become an important area of socialization for the community in the capital. In fact, while no dietary restrictions existed for Germans, they differed significantly from the Irish because they purchased not only a variety of German lagers, but also a wide range of sausages and other German delicacies.[233] In the interwar years a variety of activities developed amongst the different groups of migrants of German origin who lived in Britain. Some restaurants had survived the ethnic cleansing of the First World War, while a range of newspapers also resurfaced.[234] The refugees from Nazism established a whole variety of support and cultural activities during the inter-war years including those which focused upon theatre and cabaret. Many of these would survive into the post-war period.[235] The Germans who arrived after 1945, especially professionals, had less concern about actively maintaining their ethnic identities. The mass of ethnic organizations which had developed during the Victorian years did not resurface, partly because of the absence of a geographically concentrated community. However, some of the German churches survived the First World War and would continue to exist. At the same time, while Germans who arrived after 1945 may not have participated in the sort of ethnic activity of their predecessors, they certainly had not lost their sense of German identity and their connection with their land of birth, even in the case of those women who had married Englishmen and who accepted their dual identity.[236]

Wendy Ugolini, following Anne-Marie Fortier, has recently blown apart the issue of ethnic identification amongst the Italian community in Britain and has revealed the complex issues of dual identity amongst the second generation. The picture painted especially by Terri Colpi during the 1990s focused upon a fairly monolithic group with continuities from the early nineteenth century until the post-war period, although she certainly acknowledged the northern Italian origins of those migrants who arrived before 1945 compared to those from the south after the Second World War. Writing before the issue of individual identity had moved fully to the centre of studies of migration and ethnicity, Colpi focused upon the associational culture of the Italian community, which did not allow an investigation of the subtleties of individual identification.[237] In contrast, Ugolini, examining Scotland (especially Edinburgh), carried out interviews to reveal the complexities of the Italian community in Britain, especially during the Second World War. Ugolini takes particular offence to the idea of a unified victim group, which experienced the Second World War through the sinking of the *Arandora Star* and internment.[238] Instead, focusing especially upon the second generation, she demonstrated their dual identity, particularly through the fact that many fought in the British army, sometimes even on Italian soil.[239]

Kathy Burrell has confirmed the complexity of Italian identities in post-war Britain, with her focus upon transnationalism, as well revealing the same patterns for Poles and Greek Cypriots. While members of these communities may live in Britain, many of their memories and aspects of their everyday lives, such as television watching and newspaper reading, especially through publications in Britain, lie rooted in their place of birth.[240] Once again, Burrell, like Ugolini, adds a personal dimension, through oral history, to the earlier studies of Greek Cypriots and Poles, which tended to focus upon their associational culture. For instance, over thirty newspapers have existed for the Greek Cypriot community in Britain, the most important of which consists of the still surviving *Parikiaki*, which contains an English language section for the second and subsequent generations.[241] By the 1990s numerous associations existed for Cypriots in Britain including community centres receiving public funding, village societies, women's organizations, a Thalassaemia Society and at least one theatre group.[242] Clearly, Greek Cypriots like other communities, have seen a change in their identities through different generations. A good indication of this transition, again pointing to the complexity of multiple identities, consists of language use amongst the second and subsequent generations. While Standard Modern Greek represents the official language of Greece and Cyprus, Greek Cypriots and their children in London speak the dialect of Cyprus. This spoken medium also incorporates English words, meaning that the London Greek Cypriot community has developed its own unique language, which neither people from Greece or Cyprus fully understand. This language reflects the migratory history of the group which speaks it.[243]

Jewish language patterns in Britain remain equally complex, partly because of the different geographical origins of Jews in Britain. Those who arrived from Eastern Europe in the late Victorian and Edwardian years spoke Yiddish, which served as the language of communication for the migrants, whether in everyday life or in publications, as newspapers emerged. However, once Yiddish speaking schoolchildren entered an English classroom they, like pupils from all over the world, began the process of integration, which increasingly meant the decline of Yiddish language use and its replacement by English as the normal medium of communication amongst the second generation by the inter-war years.[244] Those who arrived as refugees during the 1930s, some of them children without their parents, also had to change from using German to English.[245]

Just as the German Jewish refugees from Nazism established their own social and cultural organizations, so did the exiles from the Tsars. Associational activity before the First World War reflects the class divisions of Anglo-Jewry and some of the organizations came into existence because the established community wished to quickly Anglicize the newcomers. For middle class German Jewish migrants of the Victorian period the move into British circles proved relatively straightforward partly because they had already become acculturated into mainstream German society and consequently did not regard religion as an important barrier.[246] By the outbreak of the First World War integrated Anglo-Jewry had established organizations which confirmed its Anglicized and middle class status. These included literary and musical societies in, for instance, Newcastle, Glasgow, Merthyr and Cardiff in addition to the countless similar organizations in London.[247]

The new arrivals from Tsarist Russia did not instantly gravitate towards such institutions but, instead, either formed their own, or participated in activities set aside for them by the established community. Sport proved a particularly important tool in the latter sense. Mirroring the activities of groups such as the Scouts and the Catholic Lads' Clubs, with the aim of placing potentially disaffected youth on a straight and narrow path, bodies such as the Jewish Lads' Brigade, the Brady Street Boys' Clubs, the West Central Lads' Club and the Stepney Lads' Club (all formed between 1895 and 1900) had a similar aim.[248] Sport proved especially important in the integration process. To take the example of football in London, not only did Jewish leagues come into existence before the First World War, but, in the longer term, supporting some of larger professional football teams, especially Arsenal and Tottenham, which had certainly occurred amongst Jews on a significant scale by the 1930s, proved an important method of entry into mainstream society. The participation in football spectating on a Saturday also reflected a decline in synagogue attendance.[249] The new arrivals also established their own cultural groupings, rather than participating in those opened for them by established Anglo-Jewry or simply following mainstream activity. For instance, Yiddish theatres had emerged in the East End of London by 1914, the most significant of which consisted of the Yiddish People's Theatre opened in 1912, with space for 1,500 people.[250]

A literary culture also developed amongst Jews in Britain. One indication of this consists of the newspaper scene, which resembles the German equivalent in the sense that numerous publications came and went. These reflected the tensions in Anglo-Jewry as many of the papers represented a particular viewpoint. Those which appeared in Yiddish in the late nineteenth and early twentieth century clearly aimed at the newcomers from Eastern Europe. In Glasgow alone 'one Yiddish newspaper after another folded' and they became unsustainable by the 1930s as the use of this language declined.[251] By the end of the nineteenth century two Jewish newspapers had established themselves on a national scale in the form of the *Jewish World* and the *Jewish Chronicle*. While the former folded during the inter-war years, the latter became the journalistic voice of established Anglo-Jewry. In addition, it also played an important role in constructing Jewishness with columns on a variety of aspects of Jewish life in Britain, such as cooking.[252] While many of the Jewish social and cultural organizations which had developed during the course of the Victorian and Edwardian years disappeared as integration and assimilation proceeded, the *Jewish Chronicle*, together with much of the religious paraphernalia, survived as the main indicators of the continued existence of Anglo-Jewry. A Jewish literary scene, focusing upon Jewish topics, had also developed by the end of the nineteenth century, epitomized by the work of Israel Zangwill, and subsequently emerging to incorporate other writers who have developed themes beyond the ghetto as Anglo-Jewry has experienced social mobility.[253]

Those groups who had arrived from beyond Europe had also begun to develop social and cultural activities before 1945, although these did not take off until the mass migration of the post-war period. The few Chinese people who lived in Britain before the Second World War made the handful of restaurants which existed an important centre of social activity, especially in the community which had emerged in Limehouse in the East End of London. The level of difference between English and Chinese food would partly help to explain this, as would the small size of this community. Chinatown also gained a reputation as an opium smoking area during the Victorian era and both natives and immigrants from China participated in this activity so that 'opium dens' served a similar purpose to the restaurants as centres of socialization. Some organizations also emerged including those amongst Chinese students, together with Chinese Schools for children born in Britain. Despite the increase in the numbers of Chinese after the Second World War this group has not developed the same sort of associational culture as Asians and Black people. One of the reasons for this lies in the dispersed nature of the community, many of whom run isolated restaurants in locations throughout the country. But some organized cultural activity has developed in the few Chinatowns which have emerged, above all in Soho in London although a recent wave of Chinese migration has meant that the Soho pattern has begun to emerge in other urban centres.[254]

Towards the end of the twentieth century a new kind of identity had emerged in Britain amongst the descendants of immigrants from India and Pakistan: British Asian. This new identity merges together all of the different groups which make it up, not only those who originate in the sub-continent, but also those who came via Africa and elsewhere. The pressures towards the creation of this new secular hyphenated identity include a collective experience amongst its members of discrimination, as well as feelings of more similarity with each other than with mainstream white British society. Other drivers which have led to the emergence of this new identity include the acceptance by the state of Asians as a demographic category, although the government also recognizes the various sub-groups which make up British Asian. Just as importantly, British Asian has emerged as a cultural category, demonstrated by the existence of both *Eastern Eye*, a newspaper which appeals to all of the different sub-groups and the emergence of BBC Asian Network, a publicly funded all day radio channel. These organs deal both with collective experiences and those of the individual groups which make up British Asians. Dress and food also play an important role. While these two factors may divide South Asian ethnic groups because of their connection with religion, they also allow the development of a national market in these goods because a level of similarity exists. In the case of food, while the different South Asian religions may have varying attitudes to meat consumption, they consume similar spices, resulting in a level of collective food identity.[255]

The importance of religion in South Asian identities means that the family remains central. Writers on South Asian Muslims in Britain have especially pointed to the marginalization of women in the public sphere, which means that their identity links closely with their activities in the home and their families.[256] Nevertheless, this seems too simplistic in view of the number of South Asian women, of all faiths, who have entered the public sphere.[257]

Second and subsequent generations of South Asians have also experienced integration. While schools which teach the language of the land of origin have developed, connected especially with religious institutions, English becomes the main medium of communication fairly rapidly, meaning a decline in speaking the tongue of the homeland. However, children have the opportunity to also learn Indian languages through evening classes.[258] Similarly, ninety Sikh newspapers have appeared in England since 1964, the vast majority of them published in Punjabi.[259] Hybrid identities have emerged amongst the second and subsequent generations, indicated especially by the development of Bhangra music with origins in the Punjab, but developing a life of its own in the British environment.[260] At the same time Bengali youth in Britain have developed Bangla music which has emerged out of Banglatown in the East End of London.[261] Ikhlaq Din, in a study of Pakistani youth in Bradford, has demonstrated that the second generation here listen to a range of US, British and Asian music ranging from rap to religious pieces.[262] But transnationalism guarantees continual contact with South Asia, epitomized by watching Bollywood films, which act as a particularly important bonding mechanism for women.[263] The evolution of international television stations, most notably ZTV, also maintains a diasporic identity,[264] although this goes hand in hand with watching US and British films, which most young Asians prefer.[265]

The process of hybridization appears even clearer amongst African-Caribbeans in Britain. Part of the reason for this lies in the fact that, in contrast to South Asians, West Indians had already accepted their Britishness in the Caribbean, with many of them viewing their move to Britain as a migration to the mother country.[266] At the same time the numerous children of interracial relationships develop a complex identity.[267] Upon arrival in British cities community based upon aspects of Caribbean identity certainly developed. As in the case of South Asians, one of the reasons for this lay in the level of hostility they faced, which forced them together, both geographically and culturally. Community centres and ex-servicemen's associations had already developed in Brixton by the early 1960s, while sport, especially cricket, proved of particular significance, both for those who played it and those who supported the West Indies when they toured England.[268]

During the second half of the twentieth century a Black ethnicity evolved in Britain, primarily political in nature, which could also incorporate Africans.[269] Newspapers such as *Voice* play a role in perpetuating this identity, which also has a transnational cultural aspect. For West Indians this would not only incorporate the Caribbean, where family ties exist and towards which travel and holidays occur,[270] but also the USA. Such developments have given rise to the concept of the Black Atlantic, meaning that an international Black popular culture has evolved, revolving especially around music, with a main base in the USA but with offshoots in Britain and the Caribbean.[271] The British aspect of this diasporic culture draws from the local environment, reflected both in everyday relationships and in the emergence of distinctive forms of popular culture.[272]

Conclusions

The migration process creates hybrid identities. While the first generation may have a closer connection with the homeland, they also find themselves affected by their surroundings. We might see the development of migrant communities in Britain as demonstrating the move from ethnicity to Britishness, but this new form of identity incorporates elements of the homeland for individuals.

The most important building block for the development of ethnicity in recent British history has consisted of religion in the sense that it has appeared the most unchanging. Three of the most significant ethnic communities in Britain over the last two centuries, in the form of Irish Catholics, Jews and Muslims, have evolved from a religious identification. Politics has also proved important for all of these groups because their most fervent adherents have felt an allegiance to another state, Ireland, or an international political movement in the form of Zionism or pan-Islamism.

The transnational paradigm, especially when considering the groups which have evolved since 1945 offers a useful tool in a consideration of ethnicity in Britain. For Poles, Indians and African-Caribbeans, for example, contact with the homeland proves important. While members of these three groups may feel fully integrated into British society, reading foreign language newspapers, watching films from the land of origin or listening to international music points to their ethnic origins and suggests a desire to hold on to them.

While early studies on ethnicity may have revolved around the concept of blocks of people, more recent research, based especially upon oral history, has demonstrated the simplicity of this older approach. Although Islam may have established itself as one of the fastest growing religions in Britain after 1945, it proves difficult to measure mosque attendance on an individual basis, while the same applies to Roman Catholic and Jewish religious practice over the last two centuries. Similarly, the political organizations which have emerged amongst apparently unitary groups simply represent sections of them. The Germans demonstrate the variety of different political persuasions held by any national minority. At the same time, continuing with politics, most migrant communities simply participate in the mainstream in the same way as the wider British population.

Individuals choose the extent to which they practise their ethnicity, but, over generations, they eventually become British, often in a hybrid or hyphenated manner. Cultural integration seems more inevitable than economic integration, which remains problematic because of the strength of racism. The adoption of English as the primary language of communication as a result of schooling in Britain provides the clearest indication of this process. At the same time dress and, in particular, food, undergo a change in the new environment.

The certainties of the homeland become less secure in Britain. While some members of communities try to re-establish what they view as the norms of their land of origin, not everyone of the same ethnic origin follows the same path. All ethnic communities in Britain contain both sub-groups and, ultimately, individuals. The individuals choose the extent to which they practise the norms of the homeland, which become increasingly less likely in the second and subsequent generations. Hybrid British identities emerge in which elements of both the 'home', the new environment and, in some cases, an international diasporic consciousness, combine. While all of these new identities might suggest diaspora, they also point to Britishness.

Notes and references

1 David Coleman and John Salt, 'The Ethnic Group Question in the 1991 Census: A New Landmark in British Social Statistics', in Coleman and Salt, eds, *Ethnicity in the 1991 Census*, Vol. 1, *Demographic Characteristics of the Ethnic Minority Population* (London, 1996), pp. 1–32.

2 M. A. G. Ó Tuathaigh, 'The Irish in Nineteenth Century Britain: Problems of Integration', *Transactions of the Royal Historical Society*, vol. 31 (1981), p. 150; E. P. Thompson, *The Making of the English Working Classes* (London, 1982 reprint), p. 480.

3 See Chapter 1.

4 The work of Sheridan Gilley is especially important here. See, for instance: 'The Roman Catholic Mission to the Irish in London, 1840–1860', *Recusant History*, vol. 10 (1969–70), pp. 123–45; 'The Roman Catholic Church and the Nineteenth-Century Irish Diaspora', *Journal of Ecclesiastical History*, vol. 35 (1984), pp. 188–207; 'Catholic Faith of the Irish Slums: London, 1840–70', in H. J. Dyos and M. Wolff, eds, *The Victorian City: Images and Realities* (London, 1973), pp. 837–53.

5 See, for instance: Rachel O'Higgins, 'The Irish Influence in the Chartist Movement', *Past and Present*, no. 20 (1961), pp. 83–96; Dorothy Thompson, 'Ireland and the Irish in English Radicalism before 1850', in James Epstein and Dorothy Thompson, eds, *The Chartist Experience: Studies in Working-Class Radicalism and Culture, 1830–1960* (London, 1982), pp. 120–59; John McCaffrey, 'The Irish Vote in Glasgow in the Late Nineteenth Century: A Preliminary Survey', *Innes Review*, vol. 21 (1970), pp. 306.

6 The classic work is Alan O'Day, *The English Face of Irish Nationalism* (Dublin, 1977). But see also, for instance, Bernard O'Connell, 'Irish Nationalism in Liverpool, 1873–1923', *Eire Ireland*, 10 (1975), pp. 24–37.

7 The classic works include: Tom Gallagher, *The Uneasy Peace: Religious Tension in Modern Glasgow, 1819–1940* (Manchester, 1987); Frank Neal, *Sectarian Violence: The Liverpool Experience, 1819–1914* (Manchester, 1988); and Donald MacRaild, *Faith, Fraternity and Fighting: The Orange Order and Irish Migration in Northern England, c.1850–1920* (Liverpool, 2005).

8 Mary Hickman, *Religion, Class and Identity: The State, the Catholic Church and the Education of the Irish in Britain* (Aldershot, 1995); Steven Fielding, *Class and Ethnicity: Irish Catholics in England, 1880–1939* (Buckingham, 1993).

9 Nathan Glazier and Daniel P. Moynihan, 'Introduction', in Nathan Glazier and Daniel P. Moynihan, eds, *Ethnicity: Theory and Experience* (Cambridge, MA, 1975), pp. 1–26.

10 David Mason, *Race and Ethnicity in Modern Britain*, 2nd edn (Oxford, 2000), p. 12.

11 As opposed to the national minorities of Scots or Welsh.

12 Panikos Panayi, *German Immigrants in Britain during the Nineteenth Century, 1815–1914* (Oxford, 1995).

13 See, for example, Philip Lewis, *Islamic Britain: Religion, Politics and Identity among British Muslims* (London, 2002).

14 See, for instance, Danièle Joly, *Britannia's Crescent: Making a Place for Muslims in British Society* (Aldershot, 1995).

15 Coleman and Salt, 'Ethnic Group Question'.

16 Michael H. Fisher, Shompa Lahiri and Shinder Thandi, *A South Asian History of Britain* (Oxford, 2007), pp. xi–xxii. While Fisher is an American, Lahiri and Thandi are British South Asians.

17 Robin Cohen, *Global Diasporas: An Introduction* (Abingdon, 1999).

18 Pnina Werbner, *Imagined Diasporas among Manchester Muslims* (Oxford, 2002).

19 Benedict Anderson, *Imagined Communities: Reflections on the Origin and Spread of Nationalism* (London, 1991).

20 As an introduction see, for instance, Jonathan Rutherford, ed., *Identity: Community, Culture, Difference* (London, 1990); and Stuart Hall and Paul du Gay, eds, *Questions of Cultural Identity* (London, 1996).

21 Avtar Brah, *Cartographies of Diaspora: Contesting Identities* (London, 1996), pp. 1–10.

22 Parminder Bhachu, *Twice Migrants: East African Sikh Settlers in Britain* (London, 1985).

23 See, for instance, David Cesarani, ed., *The Making of Modern Anglo-Jewry* (Oxford, 1990); Todd M. Endelman, *The Jews of Britain, 1656–2000* (London, 2002); David Feldman, *Englishmen and Jews: Social Relations and Political Culture, 1840–1914* (London, 1994).

24 Anne-Marie Fortier, *Migrant Belongings: Memory, Space, Identity* (Oxford, 2000).

25 Parminder Bhachu, 'Culture, Ethnicity and Class Among Punjabi Sikh Women in 1990s Britain', *New Community*, vol. 17 (1991), pp. 408–9.

26 David Graham, *Secular or Religious: The Outlook for London's Jews* (London, 2003), p. 14.

27   See Chapter 2.

28   Steven Vertovec, 'Transnationalism and Identity,' *Journal of Ethnic and Migration Studies*, vol. 27 (2001), pp. 573–82; Katy Gardner, *Age, Narrative and Migration: The Life Course of Bengali Elders in London* (Oxford, 2002), pp. 14–18; Kathy Burrell, *Moving Lives: Narratives of Nation and Migration among Europeans in Post-war Britain* (Aldershot, 2006), pp. 110–12; Panayi, *German Immigrants*, pp. 180–3.

29   Rosalyn Livshin, 'The Acculturation of the Children of Immigrant Jews in Manchester, 1890–1930', in Cesarani, *Making of Modern Anglo-Jewry*, pp. 79–96; David Graham, Marlena Schmool, and Stanley Waterman, *Jews in Britain: A Snapshot from the 2001 Census* (London, 2007); Panikos Panayi, *Spicing Up Britain: The Multicultural History of British Food* (London, 2008), pp. 46–55, 133–41.

30   Tony Kushner, *The Persistence of Prejudice: Antisemitism in British Society during The Second World War* (Manchester, 1989), pp. 122–6.

31   See, for instance, Frederick C. Luebke, *Germans in the New World: Essays in the History of Immigration* (Urbana and Chicago, 1990).

32   Endelman, *Jews of Britain*; Geoffrey Alderman, *Modern British Jewry* (Oxford, 1992).

33   Panayi, *German Immigrants*.

34   Standard works on the Irish in Victorian Britain have not dealt with their Britishness, tying in with the lack of work on their integration overall. See, for example, Donald MacRaild, *Irish Migrants in Modern Britain, 1750–1922* (Basingstoke, 1999); Graham Davis, *The Irish in Britain* (Dublin, 1991); Fielding, *Class and Ethnicity*.

35   Marion Berghahn, *Continental Britons: German Jewish Refugees from Nazi Germany* (Oxford, 1988).

36   See Chapter 5 below.

37   See, for instance: Paul Ward, *Britishness Since 1870* (London, 2004), pp. 113–40; and Harry Goulbourne, *Ethnicity and Nationalism in Post-Imperial Britain* (Cambridge, 1991).

38   See Chapter 6.

39   Such individuals included Robert Graves, for which see, *Goodbye to All That* (Harmondsworth, 1985).

40   See Wendy Ugolini, 'Communal Myths and Silenced Memories: The Unremembered Experience of Italians in Scotland During World War Two' (University of Edinburgh Ph.D thesis, 2006).

41   See Brah, *Cartographies of Diaspora*.

42   Panayi, *German Immigrants*, pp. 145–200.

43   Steve Bruce, *Religion in Modern Britain* (Oxford, 1995).

44 Ibid.

45 Oscar Handlin, *The Uprooted: The Epic Story of the Great Migration that Made the American Peoples*, 2nd edn (London, 1979), p. 105.

46 Will Herberg, *Protestant-Catholic-Jew: An Essay in American Religious Sociology* (Chicago, 1983), p. 14.

47 Frederick C. Luebke, *Bonds of Loyalty: German Americans and World War I* (De Kalb, IL, 1974), pp. 34–5.

48 See, for instance: Harold James, *A German Identity: 1770 to the Present Day* (London, 1994).

49 Jay P. Nolan, *The Immigrant Church: New York's Irish and German Catholics, 1815–1865* (London, 1975), p. 58.

50 Lynn Hollen Lees, *Exiles of Erin: Irish Immigrants in Victorian London* (Manchester, 1979), p. 182.

51 Lewis, *Islamic Britain*, p. 14.

52 Ibid., pp. 58–60; Steven Vertovec, 'Caught in an Ethnic Quandary: Indo-Caribbean Hindus', in Roger Ballard, ed., *Desh Pradesh: The South Asian Presence in Britain* (London, 1994), pp. 272–90; Bhachu, *Twice Migrants*.

53 Todd M. Endelman, ' "Practices of a Low Anthropological Level": A Schechita Controversy of the 1950s', in Anne J. Kershen, ed., *Food in the Migrant Experience* (Aldershot, 2002), p. 81.

54 David Fitzpatrick, ' "A Particular Tramping People": The Irish in Britain, 1801–70', in W. E. Vaughan, ed., *A New History of Ireland*, vol. 5 (Oxford, 1989), p. 651.

55 Sheridan Gilley, 'Roman Catholic Mission'; Lees, *Exiles of Erin*, pp. 175–93.

56 John Denvir, *The Irish in Britain* (London, 1892), pp. 160–1.

57 MacRaild, *Irish Migrants*, p. 80.

58 Graham Davis, *The Irish in Britain, 1815–1914* (Dublin, 1991), p. 130.

59 Ibid.

60 W. J. Lowe, *The Irish in Mid-Victorian Lancashire: The Shaping of a Working Class Community* (New York, 1989), p. 113.

61 Lees, *Exiles of Erin*, p. 180.

62 Davis, *Irish in Britain*, p. 140.

63 Fielding, *Class and Ethnicity*, pp. 38, 43, 44.

64 MacRaild, *Irish Migrants*, p. 88.

65 Lees, *Exiles of Erin*, p. 180.

66 Davis, *Irish in Britain*, p. 140.

67 Neal, *Sectarian Violence*, p. 127.

68 John Belchem, *Irish, Catholic and Scouse: The History of the Liverpool-Irish, 1800–1939* (Liverpool, 2007), p. 91.

69 MacRaild, *Irish Migrants*, p. 91.

70 Fielding, *Class and Ethnicity*, p. 56.

71 See, for instance, Gilley, 'Roman Catholic Mission'.

72 Lees, *Exiles of Erin*, p. 192; J. E. Handley, *The Irish in Scotland, 1798–1945* (Cork, 1943), p. 246.

73 Frank Boyce, 'Irish Catholicism in Liverpool between the Wars', *Labour History Review*, vol. 57 (1992), pp. 17–20.

74 Hickman, *Religion, Class and Identity*.

75 Hugh Heinrick, *A Survey of the Irish in England* (London, 1872), pp. 92–3.

76 Fielding, *Class and Ethnicity*, p. 62.

77 Ibid., pp. 65–6.

78 W. M. Walker, 'Irish Immigrants in Scotland: Their Priests, Politics and Parochial Life', *Historical Journal*, vol. 15 (1972), pp. 655–6.

79 Hickman, *Religion, Class and Identity*, p. 231.

80 Walker, 'Irish Immigrants in Scotland', p. 666.

81 Boyce, 'Irish Catholicism in Liverpool'.

82 Fielding, *Class and Ethnicity*, pp. 50, 67.

83 Enda Delaney, *The Irish in Post-war Britain* (Oxford, 2007), p. 134. See also A. E. C. W. Spencer, 'Catholics in Britain and Ireland', in D. A. Coleman, ed., *Demography of Immigrant and Minority Groups in the United Kingdom* (London, 1982), pp. 211–43.

84 Delaney, ibid., pp. 149–59.

85 Ibid., pp. 156–9; Hickman, *Religion, Class and Identity*, pp. 238–48.

86 Martin Mac an Ghaill, 'The Irish in Britain: The Invisibility of Ethnicity and Anti-Irish Racism', *Journal of Ethnic and Migration Studies*, vol. 26 (2000), pp. 137–47.

87 Louise Ryan, 'Who Do You Think You Are? Irish Nurses Encountering Ethnicity and Constructing Identity in Britain', *Ethnic and Racial Studies*, vol. 30 (2007), pp. 416–38; Bronwen Walter, *Outsiders Inside: Whiteness, Place and Irish Women* (London, 2001).

88 See Chapter 5.

89 See below.

90 MacRaild, *Irish Migrants*, pp. 100–8; Davis, *Irish in Britain*, p. 140.

91 See below.

92 Panayi, *German Immigrants*, pp. 91–3, 148–79; Stefan Manz, *Migranten und Internierte: Deutsche in Glasgow, 1864–1918* (Stuttgart, 2003), pp. 165–70,

197–230; Susanne Steinmetz, 'The Germans Churches in London, 1669–1914' and Lothar Kettenecker, 'The Germans After 1945', in Panikos Panayi, ed., *Germans in Britain Since 1500* (London, 1996), pp. 49–71, 195–6.

93   See: the essays by Julius Carlebach and Albert H. Friedlander in W. E. Mosse, et al., eds, *Second Chance: Two Centuries of German-Speaking Jews in the United Kingdom* (Tübingen, 1991), pp. 405–35; and Berghahn, *Continental Britons*.

94   Lucio Sponza, *Italian Immigrants in Nineteenth Century Britain* (Leicester, 1988), pp. 22–3, 133–40; Azadeh Medaglia, *Patriarchal Structures and Ethnicity in the Italian Community in Britain* (Aldershot, 2001), pp. 98–99; Fortier, *Migrant Belongings*, pp. 30, 107–14.

95   Alderman, *Modern British Jewry*; Bill Williams, ' "East and West": Class and Community in Manchester Jewry, 1850–1914', in Cesarani, *Making of Modern Anglo-Jewry*, pp. 15–33.

96   V. D. Lipman, 'A Survey of Anglo-Jewry in 1851', *Transactions of the Jewish Historical Society of England*, vol. 17 (1951–2), pp. 174–5.

97   Lipman, ibid.; Cecil Roth, *The Rise of Provincial Jewry: The Early History of the Jewish Communities in the English Countryside* (London, 1950); Ursula Henriques, 'The Jewish Community of Cardiff, 1813–1914', *Welsh History Review*, vol. 14 (1988), pp. 282–3.

98   Endelman, *Jews of Britain*, pp. 110–11.

99   Alderman, *Modern British Jewry*, pp. 44–8.

100   Ibid., pp. 38–43; W. D. Rubinstein, *A History of the Jews in the English Speaking World: Great Britain* (Basingstoke, 1996), pp. 89–90.

101   Alderman, ibid., pp. 85–9; Aubrey Newman, *The United Synagogue, 1880–1970* (London, 1977).

102   V. D. Lipman, *A History of the Jews in Britain Since 1858* (Leicester, 1990), p. 29.

103   Lipman, 'Survey of Anglo-Jewry in 1851', p. 186.

104   Todd M. Endelman, *Radical Assimilation in English Jewish History, 1656–1945* (Bloomington and Indianapolis, 1990), p. 97.

105   Alderman, *Modern British Jewry*, pp. 142–5.

106   Murdoch Rodgers, 'Glasgow Jewry: The History of the City's Jewish Community', in Billy Kay, ed., *Odyssey: Voices from Scotland's Recent Past* (Edinburgh, 1982), p. 113; Kenneth E. Collins, *Second City Jewry: The Jews of Glasgow in the Age of Emancipation, 1790–1919* (Glasgow, 1990), pp. 48–9.

107   Alderman, *Modern British Jewry*, p. 154.

108   Endelman, *Jews of Britain*, pp. 148–50.

109   Livshin, 'Acculturation', pp. 90–3.

110   Geoffrey Alderman, *The History of the Hendon Synagogue* (London, 1978).

111   Lipman, *History of the Jews in Britain*, p. 218.

112   Rubinstein, *History of the Jews*, pp. 234–5.

113   Endelman, *Jews of Britain*, pp. 220–2.

114   Endelman, *Jews of Britain*, pp. 239–40; Rubinstein, *History of the Jews*,
pp. 408–23; Graham, *Secular or Religious*; Stanley Waterman and Barry Kosmin,
'Ethnic Identity, Residential Concentration and Social Welfare: The Jews in
London', in Peter Jackson, ed., *Race and Racism: Essays in Social Geography*
(London, 1987), pp. 254–71.

115   Panayi, *Spicing Up Britain*, pp. 46–55, 133–41; Endelman, 'Practices'.

116   Rubinstein, *History of the Jews*, pp. 402–5.

117   For the Jewishness of Nigella Lawson see Gilly Smith, *Nigella Lawson: The
Unauthorised Biography* (London, 2005), pp. 3–17, 200–10.

118   Floya Anthias, *Ethnicity, Class, Gender and Migration: Greek Cypriots in Britain*
(Aldershot, 1992), pp. 124–5; Michael Constantinides, *The Greek Orthodox
Church in London* (Oxford, 1933); Vic George and Geoffrey Millerson,
'The Cypriot Community in London', *Race*, vol. 8 (1967), p. 290; Pamela
Constantinides, 'The Greek Cypriots: Factors in the Maintenance of Ethnic
Identity', in James L. Watson, ed., *Between Two Cultures: Migrants and Minorities
in Britain* (Oxford, 1977), pp. 186–7; Zena Theodorou and Sav Kyriacou,
'Cypriots in London', in Nick Merriman, ed., *The Peopling of London: 15,000
Years of Settlement from Overseas* (London, 1993), pp. 102–4.

119   Gurharpal Singh and Darshan Singh Tatla, *Sikhs in Britain: The Making of a
Community* (London, 2006), pp. 44–5; Humayun Ansari, *'The Infidel Within':
Muslims in Britain Since 1800* (London, 2004), pp. 82–4; Fisher, Lahiri and
Thandi, *South Asian History of Britain*, pp. 95–101; Rosina Visram, *Asians in
Britain: 400 Years of History* (London, 2002), pp. 57–64, 103–4.

120   Fisher, Lahiri and Thandi, ibid., p. 149; Visram, ibid., p. 298; Rashmi Desai,
Indian Immigrants in Britain (London, 1963).

121   Singh and Tatla, *Sikhs in Britain*, pp. 71–2.

122   Ansari, *'Infidel Within'*, pp. 92–144. Richard I. Lawless, *From Ta'izz to Tyneside:
An Arab Community in the North-East of England during the Early Twentieth
Century* (Exter, 1995), pp. 174–236, examines such processes on a local level.

123   Fisher, Lahiri and Thandi, *South Asian History of Britain*, p. 208.

124   Ceri Peach, 'Social Geography: New Religions and Ethnosuburbs – Contrasts
with Cultural Geography', *Progress in Human Geography*, vol. 26 (2002), p. 256;
Daily Telegraph, 19 August 1995.

125   See: Fisher, Lahiri and Thandi, *South Asian History of Britain*, pp. 208–11; and
the contributions of Rachel Dwyer, Shrikala Warrier and Kim Knott to Ballard,
Desh Pradesh.

126   John Martin and Gurharpal Singh, *Asian Leicester* (Stroud, 2002), p. 12.

127   Roger Ballard and Catherine Ballard, 'The Sikhs: The Development of South
Asian Settlements in Britain', in Watson, *Between Two Cultures*, p. 37.

128 Singh and Tatla, *Sikhs in Britain*, p. 127.

129 Quoted in Arthur Wesley Helweg, *Sikhs in England: The Development of a Migrant Community* (Oxford, 1979), p. 54.

130 Bhachu, 'Culture, Ethnicity and Class', pp. 408–9.

131 Singh and Tatla, *Sikhs in Britain*, pp. 127–35.

132 Ibid., pp. 69–93; Roger Ballard, 'Differentiation and Disjunction Among the Sikhs', in Ballard, *Desh Pradesh*, pp. 109–16.

133 Panayi, *Spicing Up Britain*, pp. 143–4; Ansari, *'Infidel Within'*, pp. 354–5.

134 *Guardian*, 10 October 2006.

135 Philip Lewis, 'Being Muslim and Being British: The Dynamics of Islamic Reconstruction in Britain', in Ballard, *Desh Pradesh*, pp. 58–87.

136 Lewis, *Islamic Britain*, p. 13; *The Times*, 29 March 2008.

137 Ansari, *'Infidel Within'*, pp. 340–88.

138 Marie Parker-Jenkins, 'Equal Access to State Funding: The Case of Muslim Schools in Britain', *Race, Ethnicity and Education*, vol. 5 (2002), pp. 273–89; Nasar Meer, 'Muslim Schools in Britain: Challenging Mobilisations or Logical Developments?', *Asia Pacific Journal of Education*, vol. 27 (2007), pp. 55–71.

139 Pnina Werbner, *The Migration Process: Capital, Gifts and Offerings among British Pakistanis* (Oxford, 1990), pp. 151–71.

140 Gardner, *Age, Narrative and Migration*, pp. 109–13.

141 Fadwa El Guindi, *Veil: Modernity, Privacy and Resistance* (Oxford, 1999).

142 Ansari, *'Infidel Within'*, p. 215.

143 Ethnic minorities in the mainstream political process receive attention in Chapter 6.

144 Margaret C. Wicks, *The Italian Exiles in London, 1816–1848* (New York, 1968).

145 T. Grzbienowski, 'The Polish Cause in England a Century Ago', *Slavonic Review*, vol. 11 (1932), pp. 81–7; Peter Brock, 'Polish Democrats and English Radicals, 1832–1862: A Chapter in the History of Anglo-Polish Relations', *Journal of Modern History*, vol. 25 (1953), pp. 139–56; Peter Brock, 'The Polish Revolutionary Commune in London', *Slavonic and Eastern European Review*, vol. 35 (1956), pp. 116–28.

146 Norman Davies, 'The Poles in Great Britain, 1914–19', *Slavonic and Eastern European Review*, vol. 50 (1972), pp. 63–89.

147 Wojciech Rojek, 'The Government of the Republic of Poland in Exile, 1945–92', in Peter D. Stachura, ed., *The Poles in Britain, 1940–2000: From Betrayal to Assimilation* (London, 2004), pp. 33–47; Jan E. Zamojski, 'The Social History of Polish Exile (1939–1945): The Exile State and the Clandestine State', in Martin Conway and José Gotovich, eds, *Europe in Exile: European Exile*

Communities in Britain, 1940–45 (Oxford, 2001), pp. 183–211; Jerzy Zubrzycki, *Polish Immigrants in Britain: A Study of Adjustment* (The Hague, 1956), pp. 108–9.

148   Kathy Burrell, 'Homeland Memories and the Polish Community in Leicester', in Stachura, ibid., pp. 79–82.

149   Burrell, *Moving Lives*.

150   John Slatter, ed., *From the Other Shore: Russian Political Emigrants in Britain, 1880–1917* (London, 1984); Barry Hollingsworth, 'The Society of Friends of Russian Freedom: English Liberals and Russian Socialists', *Oxford Slavonic Papers*, vol. 3 (1970), pp. 45–64; Colin Holmes, 'Trotsky and Britain', *Society for the Study of Labour History Bulletin*, vol. 39 (1979), pp. 33–8; Norman Stone and Michael Glenny, *The Other Russia* (London, 1990).

151   Panayi, *German Immigrants*, pp. 82–3, 194–6; Rosemary Ashton, *Little Germany: Exile and Asylum in Victorian England* (Oxford, 1986), pp. 56–138; Christine Lattek, *Revolutionary Refugees: German Socialism in Britain, 1840–1860* (London, 2006); Rudolf Rocker, *The London Years* (London, 1956).

152   Anthony Glees, *Exile Politics during the Second World War: The German Social Democrats in Britain* (Oxford, 1982).

153   Ronald Stent, 'Jewish Refugee Organizations', in Mosse, *Second Chance*, pp. 594–8; Berghahn, *Continental Britons*, pp. 156–67.

154   Ashton, *Little Germany*, pp. 139–87; Panayi, *German Immigrants*, pp. 182, 195.

155   Panayi, ibid., pp. 197–8; Manz, *Migranten und Internierte*, pp. 185–97.

156   James J. and Patience P. Barnes, *Nazis in Pre-War London, 1930–1939: The Fate and Role of German Party Members and British Sympathisers* (Brighton, 2005).

157   See, for instance, Alderman, *Modern British Jewry*, pp. 117–20, 276–82; Eugene C. Black, *Social Politics of Anglo-Jewry, 1880–1920* (Oxford, 1988).

158   Alderman, ibid., pp. 113, 117–18; William D. and Hilary L. Rubinstein, *Philosemitism and Support in the English-Speaking World for Jews, 1840–1939* (Basingstoke, 1999), pp. 43–4; Stent, 'Jewish Refugee Organizations', pp. 579–94; Anne J. Kershen, *Strangers, Aliens and Asians: Huguenots, Jews and Bangladeshis in Spitalfields, 1660–2000* (London, 2005), p. 119; Norman Bentwich, *They Found Refuge: An Account of British Jewry's Work for the Victims of Nazi Oppression* (London, 1956).

159   See, especially, the two volumes by Geoffrey Alderman on this subject: *The Jewish Community in British Politics* (Oxford, 1983); and *London Jewry and London Politics, 1899–1986* (London, 1989). Jews in mainstream politics receive full consideration in Chapter 6.

160   Joseph Buckman, *Immigrants and the Class Struggle: The Jewish Immigrant in Leeds, 1880–1914* (Manchester, 1983); Anne J. Kershen, *Uniting the Tailors: Trade Unionism Amongst the Tailors of London and Leeds* (Ilford, 1995).

161   See: Tony Kushner and Nadia Valman, eds, *Remembering Cable Street: Fascism and Anti-Fascism in British Society* (London, 2000); Elaine R. Smith, 'Jewish

Responses to Political Antisemitism and Fascism in the East End of London', in Tony Kushner and Kenneth Lunn, eds., *Traditions of Intolerance: Historical Perspectives on Fascism and Race Discourse in Britain* (Manchester, 1989), pp. 53–71; Henry Srebrnik, *London Jews and British Communism* (London, 1995).

162 Gideon Shimoni, 'Poale Zion: A Zionist Transplant in Britain 1905–1945', *Studies in Contemporary Jewry*, vol. 2 (1986), pp. 273–4; Paul Goodman, *Zionism in England, 1899–1949* (London, 1949); Stuart A. Cohen, *English Zionists and British Jews: The Communal Politics of Anglo-Jewry, 1895–1920* (Princeton, 1982); Geoffrey Alderman, 'The Political Impact of Zionism in the East End of London Before 1940', *London Journal*, vol. 9 (1983), pp. 35–8.

163 See Chapter 6.

164 Delaney, *Irish in Post-war Britain*, p. 191.

165 Davis, *Irish in Britain*, p. 170.

166 MacRaild, *Irish Migrants*, pp. 136–8; Lowe, *Irish in Mid-Victorian Lancashire*, pp. 182–9.

167 MacRaild, ibid., pp. 138–42; Lowe, ibid., pp. 189–98; John Newsinger, *Fenians in Mid-Victorian Britain* (London, 1994); Patrick Quinlivan and Paul Rose, *The Fenians in England, 1865–1872* (London, 1982).

168 Belchem, *Irish, Catholic and Scouse*, pp. 176–80; K. R. M. Short, *The Dynamite War: Irish-American Bombers in Victorian Britain* (Dublin, 1979).

169 Gerard Moran, 'Nationalists in Exile: The National Brotherhood of St Patrick in Lancashire, 1861–5, in Roger Swift and Sheridan Gilley, eds, *The Irish in Victorian Britain: The Local Dimension* (Dublin, 1999), pp. 21–35.

170 MacRaild, *Irish Migrants*, pp. 143–4; John Denvir, *The Irish in Britain* (London, 1892), p. 267.

171 Fielding, *Class and Ethnicity*, p. 80.

172 Bernard O'Connell, 'Irish Nationalism in Liverpool, 1873–1923', *Eire Ireland*, vol. 10 (1975), p. 24.

173 Belchem, *Irish, Catholic and Scouse*, pp. 249–96; MacRaild, *Irish Migrants*, pp. 150–3.

174 See Chapter 6.

175 MacRaild, *Faith*; Tom Gallagher, *Edinburgh Divided: John Cormack and No Popery in the 1930s* (Edinburgh, 1987), pp. 150–2; Gallagher, *Uneasy Peace*; Neal, *Sectarian Violence*; Bill Murray, *The Old Firm: Sectarianism, Sport and Society in Scotland* (Edinburgh, 2000).

176 Graham Walker, 'The Orange Order in Scotland Between the Wars', *International Review of Social History*, vol. 37 (1992), pp. 177–206.

177 Belchem, *Irish, Catholic and Scouse*, pp. 312–14; Delaney, *Irish in Post-war Britain*, pp. 118–19; Tim Pat Coogan, *The IRA*, 2nd edn (London, 1994), pp. 113–31;

Gary McGladdery, *The Provisional IRA in England: The Bombing Campaign, 1973–1997* (Dublin, 2006), pp. 29–45.

178 Anti-Irish prejudice in Britain during the 1970s is covered in Chapter 5 below. For the Irish bombing campaigns see: Coogan, ibid., pp. 385–9, 513–32; and McGladdery, ibid., pp. 56–225.

179 Delaney, *Irish in Post-war Britain*, pp. 191–4.

180 Hans Werner Debrunner, *Presence and Prestige: Africans in Europe: A History of Africans in Europe Before 1918* (Basel, 1979), pp. 369–72.

181 Ron Ramdin, *The Making of the Black Working Class in Britain* (Aldershot, 1987), pp. 49–50.

182 Ibid., pp. 52–5; Immanuel Geiss, *The Pan-African Movement* (London, 1974), pp. 177–92; Peter Fryer, *Staying Power: The History of Black People in Britain* (London, 1984), pp. 281–7.

183 Geiss, ibid., pp. 240–9.

184 Ibid., pp. 297–303; Hakim Adi, *West Africans in Britain, 1900–1960: Nationalism, Pan-Africanism and Communism* (London, 1998).

185 Ibid., pp. 100–29; Roderick J. MacDonald, 'Dr Harold Arundel Moody and the League of Coloured Peoples, 1931–1947: A Retrospective View', *Race*, vol. 14 (1973), pp. 291–310; Edward Scobie, *Black Britannia: A History of Blacks in Britain* (Chicago, 1972), pp. 141–52.

186 Julius Braunthal, *History of the International, 1864–1914* (London, 1966).

187 Fisher, Lahiri and Thandi, *South Asian History of Britain*, pp. 136–7.

188 Visram, *Asians in Britain*, pp. 225–53.

189 Singh and Tatla, *Sikhs in Britain*, p. 96.

190 Ansari, *'The Infidel Within'*, pp. 84–92.

191 See Chapter 6 below.

192 Ramdin, *Making of the Black Working Class*, pp. 410–15, 426–30.

193 Les Back, *New Ethnicities and Urban Culture: Racisms and Multiculture in Young Lives* (London, 1996), pp. 51–62.

194 Julia Sudbury, *'Other Kinds of Dreams': Black Women's Organizations and the Politics of Transformation* (Abingdon, 1998).

195 Sheila Patterson, *Dark Strangers: A Sociological Study of the Absorption of a Recent West Indian Migrant Group in Brixton, South London* (London, 1963), pp. 352–5.

196 Ernest Cashmore, *Rastaman: The Rastafarian Movement in England* (London, 1979).

197 John Benyon and John Solomos, eds, *The Roots of Urban Unrest* (Oxford, 1987); Michael Rowe, *The Racialization of Disorder in Twentieth Century Britain* (Aldershot, 1998); Ceri Peach, 'A Geographical Perspective on the 1981 Urban

Riots in England', *Ethnic and Racial Studies*, vol. 9 (1986), pp. 396–411; Harris Joshua, Tina Wallace and Heather Booth, *To Ride the Storm: The 1980 Bristol 'Riot' and the State* (London, 1983).

198 See, for instance: E. P. Thompson, 'The Moral Economy of the English Crowd in the Eighteenth Century', *Past and Present*, no. 50 (1971), pp. 76–136; George Rudé, *The Crowd in History: A Study of Popular Disturbances in France and England* (London, 1985); John Benyon, 'Interpretations of Civil Disorder', in Benyon and Solomos, ibid., pp. 25–6.

199 See Panikos Panayi, ed., *Racial Violence in Britain in the Nineteenth and Twentieth Centuries*, (London, 1996).

200 Nasar Meer, 'The Politics of Voluntary and Involuntary Identities: Are Muslims in Britain an Ethnic, Racial or Religious Minority?', *Patterns of Prejudice*, vol. 42 (2008), pp. 61–81.

201 See, for instance: Ash Amin, 'Unruly Strangers? The 2001 Urban Riots in Britain', *International Journal of Urban and Regional Research*, vol. 27 (2003), pp. 460–4.

202 Tariq Modood, *Multicultural Politics: Racism, Ethnicity and Muslims in Britain* (Edinburgh, 2005), p. 103.

203 See Chapter 3 above.

204 See, for instance: Katy Gardner and Abdus Shukur, ' "I'm Bengali, I'm Asian and I'm Living Here": The Changing Face of British Bengalis' in Ballard, *Desh Pradesh*, pp. 162–3; Tahir Abbas, 'A Theory of Islamic Political Radicalism in Britain: Sociology, Theology and International Political Economy', *Contemporary Islam*, vol. 1 (2007), p. 111; Brah, *Cartographies of Diaspora*, pp. 49–66.

205 Werbner, *Imagined Diasporas*, p. 110.

206 Alison Shaw, *Kinship and Continuity: Pakistani Families in Britain* (London, 2000), p. 266.

207 Ansari, *'The Infidel Within'*, pp. 340–88; John Eade, 'The Search for Wholeness: The Construction of National and Islamic Identities Among British Bangladeshis', in Anne J. Kershen, ed., *A Question of Identity* (Aldershot, 1998), pp. 136–59.

208 Werbner, *Imagined Diasporas*, pp. 153–83; Abbas, 'Theory'.

209 See, for instance, *Sunday Telegraph*, 1 February 2006.

210 Darshan S. Tatla, *The Sikh Diaspora: The Search for Statehood* (London, 1999).

211 John De Witt, *Indian Workers' Association in Britain* (London, 1969); Singh and Tatla, *Sikhs in Britain*, pp. 94–121, 138–42; Sasha Josephides, 'Principles, Strategies and Anti-Racist Campaigns: The Case of the Indian Workers' Association', in Harry Gouldbourne, ed., *Black Politics in Britain* (Aldershot, 1990), pp. 115–29.

212   See Chapter 5 below.

213   Jeremy MacClancy, ed., *Sport, Identity and Ethnicity* (Oxford, 1996); Grant Jarvie, ed., *Sport, Racism and Ethnicity* (London, 1991).

214   Panayi, *Spicing Up Britain*.

215   See, for instance, Vertovec, 'Transnationalism and Identity'; and Burrell, *Moving Lives*.

216   Panayi, *Spicing Up Britain*, pp. 44–6.

217   Michael Dewey, 'The Survival of an Irish Culture in Britain', *Irish Historical Studies*, vol. 20 (1982), pp. 25–6, 31–2.

218   Mike Cronin and Daryl Adair, *The Wearing the Green: A History of St Patrick's Day* (London, 2002).

219   Mike Cronin, *Sport and Nationalism in Ireland: Gaelic Games, Soccer and Irish Identity Since 1884* (Dublin, 1999).

220   John Hutchinson and Alan O'Day, 'The Gaelic Revival in London, 1900–22: Limits of Ethnic Identity', in Swift and Gilley, *Irish in Victorian Britain*, pp. 254–76.

221   Belchem, *Irish, Catholic and Scouse*, p. 286.

222   Fielding, *Class and Ethnicity*, p. 17.

223   Joseph M. Bradley, *Sport, Culture, Politics and Scottish Society: Irish Immigrants and the Gaelic Athletic Association* (Edinburgh, 1998).

224   Delaney, *Irish in Post-war Britain*, p. 172.

225   Joseph M. Bradley, 'Marginal Voices: Football and Identity in a Contested Space', in Kathy Burrell and Panikos Panayi, eds, *Histories and Memories: Migrants and their History in Britain* (London, 2006), pp. 234–52. For more on football and sectarianism in Scotland generally see, for instance, Murray, *Old Firm*.

226   Joseph M. Bradley, 'Integration or Assimilation? Scottish Society, Football and Irish Immigrants', *International Journal of the History of Sport*, vol. 13 (1996), pp. 61–79.

227   See, for instance, David Kennedy and Peter Kennedy, 'Ambiguity, Complexity and Convergence: The Evolution of Liverpool's Irish Football Clubs', *International Journal of the History of Sport*, vol. 24 (2007), pp. 894–920.

228   Ó Tuathaigh, 'Irish in Nineteenth Century Britain', p. 164.

229   See, for instance, Owen Dudley Edwards and Patricia J. Storey, 'The Irish Press in Victorian Britain', in Roger Swift and Sheridan Gilley, eds, *The Irish in the Victorian City* (London, 1985), pp. 158–78.

230   Walter, *Outsiders Inside*; Ryan, 'Who Do You Think You Are?'.

231   Mac an Ghaill, 'Irish in Britain'.

232   Panayi, *German Imigrants*, pp. 179–90; Sue Coates, 'Manchester's German
      Gentlemen: Immigrant Institutions in a Provincial City, 1840–1920',
      Manchester Region History Review, vol. 5 (1991–2), pp. 21–20; Christiane
      Eisenberg, '"German Gymnastics" in Britain, or the Failure of Cultural
      Transfer', in Stefan Manz, Margrit Schulte Beerbühl and John R. Davis, eds,
      Migration and Transfer from Germany to Britain, 1660–1914 (Munich, 2007),
      pp. 141–5; Jonathan Westaway, 'The German Community in Manchester,
      Middle Class Culture and the Development of Mountaneering in Britain',
      English Historical Review, vol. 124 (2009), pp. 571–604.

233   Panikos Panayi, 'Sausages, Waiters and Bakers: German Migrants and Culinary
      Transfer to Britain', in Manz, Beerbühl and David, ibid., pp. 149–53.

234   James J. and Patience P. Barnes, 'London's German Community in the Early
      1930s', in Panayi, *Germans in Britain since 1500*, pp. 131–46.

235   See, for instance: J. M. Ritchie, *German Exiles: British Perspectives* (New York,
      1997); Berghahn, *Continental Britons*, pp. 150–67; Günter Berghaus, 'The
      Emigres from Nazi Germany and their Contribution to the British Theatrical
      Scene', in Mosse, *Second Chance*, pp. 297–314.

236   Kettenacker, 'Germans After 1945', pp. 187–208; Johannes-Dieter Steinert
      and Inge Weber-Newth, *Labour and Love: Deutsche in Großbritannien nach dem
      Zweiten Weltkrieg* (Osnabrück, 2000), pp. 271–91.

237   Terri Colpi, *The Italian Factor: The Italian Community in Great Britain*
      (Edinburgh, 1991).

238   See Chapter 5.

239   Wendy Ugolini: 'Reinforcing Otherness? Edinburgh's Italian Community and
      the Impact of the Second World War', *Family and Community History*, vol. 1
      (1998), pp. 57–69; and 'Memory, War and the Italians in Edinburgh: The Role
      of Communal Myth', *National Identities*, vol. 8 (2006), pp. 421–36. See also
      Fortier, *Migrant Belongings*.

240   Burrell, *Moving Lives*.

241   Anthias, *Ethnicity, Class, Gender and Migration*, pp. 285–9.

242   Sasha Josephides, 'Associations Amongst the Greek Cypriot Population in
      Britain', in John Rex, Daniele Joly and Czarina Wilpert, eds, *Immigrant
      Associations in Europe* (Aldershot, 1987), pp. 42–61. For Polish associational
      activity see, for instance, Patterson, 'The Poles: An Exile Community in Britain',
      in Watson, *Between Two Cultures*, pp. 225–30.

243   Evienia Papadaki and Maria Roussou, 'The Greek Speech Community', in
      Safder Allandina and Viv Edwards, eds, *Multilingualism in the British Isles:
      The Older Tongues and Europe* (London, 1991), pp. 189–201.

244   Anne J. Kershen, 'Mother Tongue as a Bridge to Assimilation?: Yiddish and
      Sylhetti in East London', in Kershen, ed., *Language, Labour and Migration*
      (Aldershot, 2000), pp. 13–20; Livshin, 'Acculturation', pp. 86–90.

245 Stefan Howald, 'Everyday Life in Prewar and Wartime Britain', in Marian Malet and Anthony Grenville, eds, *Changing Countries: The Experience and Achievement of German-Speaking Exiles from Hitler in Britain, 1933 to Today* (London, 2002), pp. 106–9.

246 Endelman, *Radical Assimilation*, pp. 114–43.

247 Henriques, 'Jewish Community of Cardiff', p. 294; Collins, *Second City Jewry*, pp. 42–3; *Jewish Year Book, 1903–4* (London, 1903).

248 Lipman, *History of the Jews*, pp. 107–8; Sharman Kadish, *'A Good Jew and a Good Englishman': The Jewish Lads' and Girls' Brigade, 1895–1995* (London, 1995); Susan L. Tananbaum, 'Ironing Out the Ghetto Bend: Sports and the Making of Modern British Jews', *Journal of Sport History*, vol. 31 (2004), pp. 53–75.

249 Dave Dee, ' "Your Religion is Football!" Soccer and the Jewish Community in London, 1900–1960' (unpublished De Montfort University MA Thesis, 2007).

250 Chain Bermant, *Point of Arrival: A Study of London's East End* (London, 1975), p. 199.

251 Rodgers, 'Glasgow Jewry', p. 118.

252 David Cesarani, *The Jewish Chronicle and Anglo-Jewry, 1841–1991* (Cambridge, 1994).

253 Joseph H. Udelson, *Dreamer of the Ghetto: The Life and Works of Israel Zangwill* (London, 1990); Bryan Cheyette, ed., *Contemporary Jewish Writing in Britain and Ireland: An Anthology* (London, 1998).

254 Virginia Berridge, 'East End Opium Dens and Narcotic Use in Britain', *London Journal*, vol. 4 (1978), pp. 3–28; John Seed, 'Limehouse Blues: Looking for Chinatown in the London Docks', *History Workshop Journal*, vol. 62 (2006), pp. 58–85; Szeming Sze, 'Chinese Students in Great Britain', *Asiatic Review*, vol. 27 (1931), pp. 311–20; Kwee Choo Ng, *The Chinese in London* (London, 1968); James L. Watson, 'The Chinese: Hong Kong Villagers in the British Catering Trade', in Watson, *Between Two Cultures*, pp. 195–200; Anthony Shang, 'The Chinese in London', in Merriman, *Peopling of London*, pp. 88–97; Wai-ki E. Luk, 'Chinese Ethnic Settlements in Britain: Spatial Meanings of an Orderly Distribution', *Journal of Ethnic and Migration Studies*, vol. 34 (2009), pp. 575–99.

255 See Brah, *Cartographies*; Fisher, Lahiri and Thandi, *South Asian History*; N. Ali, V. S. Kalra and S. Sayyid, eds, *A Postcolonial People: South Asians in Britain* (London, 2006); John Hamlett, Adrian R. Bailey, Andrew Alexander and Gareth Shaw, 'Ethnicity and Consumption: South Asian Shopping Patterns in Britain, 1947–75', *Journal of Consumer Culture*, vol. 8 (2008), pp. 91–111.

256 Werbner, *Imagined Diasporas*, pp. 203–10; Shaw, *Kinship and Continuity*, pp. 58–60, 171–5; Amrit Wilson, *Finding a Voice: Asian Women in Britain* (London, 1981).

257 See Chapter 6.

258 Robert Jackson and Eleanor Nesbitt, *Hindu Children in Britain* (Stoke-on-Trent, 1993), pp. 147–65.

259 Singh and Tatla, *Sikhs in Britain*, pp. 186–95.

260 Ibid., pp. 198–204.

261 Kershen, *Strangers, Aliens and Asians*, pp. 69–70; Gardner and Shukur, ' "I'm Bengali" ', pp. 160–1.

262 Ikhlaq Din, *The New British: The Impact of Culture and Community on Young Pakistanis* (Aldershot, 2006), pp. 31–6.

263 Divya P. Tolia-Kelly, 'A Journey Through the Material Geographies of Disapora Cultures: Four Modes of Environmental Memory', in Burrell and Panayi, *Histories and Memories*, pp. 159–65.

264 Rajinder Kurmar Dudrah, 'British South Asian Identities and the Popular Cultures of British Banghra, Bollywood Film and Zee TV in Birmingham' (unpublished University of Birmingham Ph.D Thesis, 2001).

265 Din, *New British*, pp. 86–9.

266 See, for instance, Mary Chamberlain, *Narratives of Exile and Return* (London, 1997), pp. 70–90.

267 Barbara Tizard and Ann Phoenix, *Black White or Mixed Race: Race and Racism in the Lives of Young People of Mixed Parentage* (London, 2002), pp. 42–55.

268 Patterson, *Dark Strangers*, pp. 270–3; Lorna Chessum, *From Immigrants to Ethnic Minority: Making Black Community in Britain* (Aldershot, 2000), pp. 228–47; Mike and Trevor Phillips, *Windrush: The Irresistible Rise of Multi-Racial Britain* (London, 1998), pp. 100–3.

269 Ramdin, *Making of the Black Working Class*.

270 Tracey Reynolds, 'Caribbean Families, Social Capital and Young People's Diasporic Identities', *Ethnic and Racial Studies*, vol. 29 (2006), pp. 1087–1103.

271 Winston James, 'Migration, Racism and Identity Formation: The Caribbean Experience in Britain', in Winston James and Clive Harris, eds, *Inside Babylon: The Caribbean Diaspora in Britain* (London, 1993), pp. 231–87; Paul Gilroy, *The Black Atlantic: Modernity and Double Consciousness* (London, 1993); Harry Goulbourne, *Caribbean Transnational Experiences* (London, 2002).

272 Back, *New Ethnicities*; Reynolds, 'Caribbean Families'.

CHAPTER 5

Xenophobia and racism

Racism, social scientists and historians

By the middle of the 1980s the study of racism in Britain had become established in the mainstream of sociological discourse and had also begun to attract serious attention from historians. The original students of the settlement of Black people in Britain, such as Kenneth Little, Sheila Patterson and Michael Banton took a rounded view of the experiences of Black people, focusing upon their economic lives and their interaction with white people, including relationships between men and women. These scholars recognized that part of the everyday lives of Black people in Britain consisted of coping with discrimination in its various forms, whether in the attempt to find employment or in the endeavour to interact with members of the opposite sex.[1] During the course of the 1960s and into the 1970s social scientists increasingly moved towards the study of 'race relations', as indicated, for instance, through the publication of Anthony Richmond's study of Bristol in 1973,[2] following on from the similar use of this phrase by leading sociologists such as Michael Banton and John Rex in the 1969 report on *Colour and Citizenship* edited by E. J. B. Rose.[3] This approach began to move away from the concept of Black people as individual actors and towards the idea of a group which faced blanket racism. By the 1980s this racism based approach began to dominate social science research. Younger researchers, particularly in the form of the Marxist inspired Robert Miles and John Solomos published a series of British state centred volumes focusing upon the way in which British government and society made the position of Black people in particular almost intolerable.[4] Tariq Modood has increasingly moved into the centre of the study of racism in contemporary Britain focusing especially upon Muslims, although the range of his work covers the whole ethnic minority experience[5] reflecting the move away from the Marxist inspired master narrative of the inevitability of ethnic exclusion in a capitalist society to examine the subtleties of identities and inter-ethnic relations.

Something of a full cycle has therefore occurred in the study of racism in Britain, caused by a number of developments. The earliest scholars, using case studies such as Cardiff,[6] Stepney[7] or Brixton[8] wrote on the initial stages of immigration, examining the first processes of interaction between black and white people. Despite the emergence of the race relations paradigm, many scholars continued to focus upon local case studies such as Sparkbrook,[9] Bristol,[10] and Nottingham.[11] Certainly, their work became increasingly negative about the position and life chances of ethnic minorities, as well as the all pervasive nature of state and popular discrimination.

The reality of the marginalization of ethnic minorities, particularly those of African-Caribbean, but, increasingly, Asian origin, drove the research focus away from inter-ethnic relations towards racism. The Notting Hill riots of 1958 followed by the rise of Powellism in the late 1960s represented some of the earliest reality checks for anyone who may have had any illusions about the intolerant nature of British society. The increasing racialization of immigration laws from the 1960s and the officially recognized existence of police racism by the 1980s confirmed the all pervasive nature of dis-crimination in British society. However, events outside Britain such as the growing US media focus upon the position of Black people across the Atlantic also fuelled the British interest in the position of 'coloured' minorities in their midst.[12] At the same time a series of Marxist inspired scholars, above all Stephen Castles, placed the British experience into the pattern of the emergence of ethnic minorities in Europe during the post-war period. Two of his major studies stressed the position of migrants and their descendants at the bottom of the social scale where they faced discrimination because they had moved to western Europe in order to carry out employment which the ethnic majority shunned. Not only did they become marginalized because of their ethnicity but also because of their class. As a Marxist analysing a capitalist system of social and economic relations, migrants remained a commodity.[13] Interestingly, the more recent work of Castles has moved away from this deterministic approach, reflecting the decline of the Marxist master narrative.[14] Nevertheless, the reality of racism in Britain remains.

Historians developed their study of racism in a similar, but not identical, way to their social science brethren. Something of a breakthrough occurred during the late 1970s, especially revolving around the work of Colin Holmes, although studies which appeared from the 1960s had certainly accepted the racist nature of British society. Holmes focused especially upon antisemitism, publishing his seminal work in this field in 1979,[15] which not only provided the influence for subsequent studies of antisemitism in Britain, but also inspired emerging scholars of immigration to study other experiences of hostility, not least because he acted as their Ph.D. supervisor.[16] Holmes followed *Anti-Semitism in British Society* with two general volumes on immigration in Britain, one of which focused specifically upon the question of British tolerance.[17] In contrast to some of the theoretical Marxist influenced social science writing on racism and the position of migrants in British society, Holmes took an empirically informed, balanced and considered approach to his themes, often making international comparisons in the century in which racial ideologies had controlled much of Europe. But his work on antisemitism in particular left historians in no doubt about the importance of racism in British history.

Holmes did not operate in a vacuum. Although the nineteenth- and early twentieth-century scholars of the history of Anglo-Jewry had paid relatively little attention to antisemitism, preferring, instead, to write accounts which focused upon the settlement and integration of this community into wider British society, as epitomized by the work of Cecil Roth,[18] the study of anti-semitism in Britain began to take off during the 1960s. The first studies focused particularly upon reactions to the Jewish immigration of the late nineteenth century. Bernard Gainer[19] and Lloyd P. Gartner[20] approached the subject differently from John Garrard, more clearly influenced by the racism faced by new arrivals from the Commonwealth and Empire so that his book actually compares the two influxes.[21] In essence, Holmes took the work of these three scholars forward into the inter-war period, but also examined the more widespread nature of antisemitism towards wealthier Jews, as well as its literary manifestations. Similarly, and predating Holmes by a year, Gisela C. Lebzelter published a volume on inter-war political antisemitism.[22]

Those who had worked upon the Irish in Britain had always focused upon the animosity which they had faced. This applies even to the Victorian commentator John Denvir, while Handley also had this as one of the themes of his studies of the Irish in Scotland.[23] The increasing attention which the Irish attracted from the 1970s and 1980s included hostility, especially in the form of sectarian violence, as one of its key themes.[24]

Similarly, the study of colour based racism in British history had also taken off by the 1980s. Jim Walvin, who worked on the general theme of Black people in Britain, focused upon hostility towards them,[25] although the most important scholar in this sense consisted of Peter Fryer.[26] Other historians, some of them specializing in Africa, examined the issue of the evolution of the idea of racism in Victorian society.[27]

By the end of the 1980s and into the 1990s racism had become a significant area of historical research in Britain, even though the mainstream profession still tended to ignore it. Key themes which emerged during this period included internment, especially during the Second World War, but also the Great War. A plethora of studies appeared on the former, written by a combination of professional historians and journalists.[28] The studies of the Second World War focused upon both Jews and Italians.[29] Similarly, an upsurge in the study of racial violence in recent British history also occurred.[30] Following on from social scientists, and the earlier study by Gainer on the emergence of the Aliens Act of 1905, historians also turned their attention to the development of immigration and nationality law.[31] A series of more general books also touched upon Britain's history of racism.[32] An important publication aiming at a wider audience consisted of Robert Winder's *Bloody Foreigners* in 2004, although its superficial and broad historical sweep make it of limited value to serious students.[33] By this time, some of the scholars who had played a large role in the study of hostility towards minorities began to take a more circumspect and balanced approach, paying as much attention to positive as negative responses, as evidenced by some of the work of Tony Kushner,[34] although his book on attitudes towards refugees remained scathing.[35]

Xenophobia and racism in modern British history

A plethora of publications over the past three decades in particular have therefore demonstrated that migrants and their offspring in Britain have faced a wide range of manifestations of hostility over the last two centuries. But, as Colin Holmes has written, although 'there is abundant evidence of the hostile attitudes and treatment which immigrants, refugees and related minorities have endured in Britain . . . it would be an error, nevertheless, to portray Britain as a country in which these groups faced unremitting hostility'.[36]

Social scientists, dealing particularly with Black and Asian people, increasingly felt comfortable with the use of the concept of racism to describe all aspects of the hostility faced by ethnic minorities from the Empire and Commonwealth in the post-war period, without suggesting any biological determinism of the type which characterized Nazi Germany between 1933–45. Scholars such as Solomos, Miles and Layton-Henry essentially refer to hostility based upon colour, arguing that the British state had racialized the newcomers as a result of immigration policy and the more general concern of both state and society with colour.[37]

Historians might deal with the same type of everyday and state hostility as Solomos, Miles, Rex and others, but as many of them write against the shadow of Nazism and its consequences, they do not use the term racism so freely. At the same time, the concept of racism is sometimes inappropriate, as in the case of the everyday attacks which the Irish faced in the Victorian period, where the ideological driving force consisted of religion. Similarly, while Germans may have experienced some of the most intense hostility of any group during the First World War, this animosity had extreme nationalism as its driving force. On the other hand, when dealing with the history of hostility based upon colour, historians have tended to use the concepts of race and racism.[38] Antisemitism also lends itself to the concept of racism because of the racialization of Jews in Britain and Europe from the end of the nineteenth century.[39] Nevertheless, the main concern of those who opposed Jews in the East End of London before the First World War consisted of the perceived threat to housing and employment rather than their supposed racial inferiority, although members of the BUF who marched through the East End of London in the 1930s had awareness of racial ideas.

Scholars have approached racism in different ways. On the one hand, both social scientists and some historians have employed it to describe attitudes towards people of colour as well as using the concept of race as a general description of the interaction between British politics and society with post-war 'coloured' ethnic minorities. Historians have used race and racism more cautiously. In my own work, I have utilized racism in order to describe reactions to a variety of migrants over a long time period.[40] However, most historians of hostility towards ethnic minorities other than Black people have remained more cautious and have preferred to focus upon the specific form of hostility which exists, whether religion-based anti-Irish Catholic feeling, which also helps to explain negative attitudes towards Italians, nationalist inspired Germanophobia during the First World War, or antisemitism from the late nineteenth century. While extreme animosity towards the Irish, Germans and Jews argued that such groups had a biologically determined predisposition influencing the way they behaved, such views tended to simply affect a proportion of people who hated the Irish, Germans or Jews. It therefore seems more accurate to describe hostility towards most ethnic minorities in Britain over the last two centuries as xenophobia, or fear of strangers. One motivation behind such animosity usually consists of short-term press inspired negative views of newcomers and has affected all immigrants in Britain over the last two centuries, whether Irish, German, Jewish, Asian or Black. As a rule, the media usually focus upon one group at a time, in a quite obsessive manner. The more developed ideologies tend to evolve in racist circles and when a group has a presence in Britain over a long period of time.

Although totalitarian regimes tend to demonstrate top down racism, even in Nazi Germany individuals made their own choices about the extent to which they practised or resisted the dictates of a regime.[41] This applies even more so to the classic liberal democracy in the form of Great Britain. For the Marxist inspired social and political scientists, the state plays a central role in the creation of racism. One of the most powerful tools in racialization consists of immigration laws, which begin to exclude people according to their ethnic origin with the passage of the Aliens Acts of 1905 and then expand, especially after the Second World War, to keep out increasing numbers of undesirables according to the areas of the world from which they originate, especially if they have the 'wrong' skin colour. Nationality Laws have also helped to define Britishness during the twentieth century. By the 1980s social scientists and policy makers had also revealed the endemic nature of racism in British government bodies, whether the police, the judiciary or the immigration service. The Scarman report following the inner city riots of the 1980s brought these issues to the attention of a wider British public opinion.[42] Despite attempts to rid the police in particular of racism, this did not happen and, following the publication of the findings of the Stephen Lawrence Inquiry in 1999, the concept of institutional racism emerged in Britain.[43] It seems likely that official institutions have practised ethnic exclusionism throughout the past two centuries, but relatively little research exists from historians to support this assertion in comparison with more recent history.

Nevertheless, much research now exists to demonstrate that in times of stress, more specifically the two World Wars, the British state has introduced policies, which make it barely distinguishable from illiberal regimes on the continent. This becomes especially clear in the ethnic cleansing of British society of traces of Germany through property confiscation, internment and deportation during the First World War. The state also used internment, albeit briefly, in the Second World War, while the treatment of Irish and Muslim terrorist suspects in recent decades also points to British governments taking direct illiberal actions.[44]

Throughout the past two centuries British state policy towards ethnic minorities has had a symbiotic relationship with public attitudes, which have a series of manifestations. Inter-ethnic relationships on the ground prove difficult to measure. While friendships and relationships develop, much evidence points to overt hostility, most notably in the form of violence or rioting which has characterized British reactions to all migrant groups since the Victorian period.[45] The press have played a central role in the marginalization of minorities from the Irish through to 'asylum seekers'. Interestingly, while some publications may have managed to focus upon more than one outgroup at a time, since the early nineteenth century, and in fact, going back to the 'Jew Bill' of 1753,[46] the press has tended to focus upon one particular minority at any one time. Like the campaign for the repeal of the Jewish Naturalization Act of 1753, most of the periods of intense hostility have one particular aim in mind, especially during the twentieth century: the introduction of immigration legislation to exclude members of a particular minority. Thus the victims have changed from the mid nineteenth-century Irish, though late nineteenth-century Jews, Germans in the First World War, inter-war Jews, post-war Black and then Asian immigrants to 'asylum seekers'. At the same time as such anti-immigration campaigns occur, underlying racial ideologies and hostilities have also emerged, especially during the course of the nineteenth century and the inter-war years. The focus upon one particular group does not mean the disappearance of hostility towards other previous victims, who fade into the background. Antisemitism did not vanish during the First World War Germanophobia just as anti-Black and anti-Asian racism did not disappear at the end of the twentieth century when the press focused upon asylum seekers.

Public hostility towards ethnic minorities has also manifested itself in the job market, as stressed by social scientists such as Solomos, Miles and Rex focusing upon the Black community since the 1950s. While little research has examined the job market in any detail before the Second World War, the First World War resulted in mass sackings and strikes against German employees.[47]

Racist political groupings have existed in Britain throughout the course of the twentieth century, often feeding off press hostility in order to influence government on a particular piece of legislation. The Orange Order may not have specifically operated in this manner, but it did act as a focus for anti-Catholicism during the Victorian period. On the other hand, since the rise of the British Brothers League at the end of the nineteenth century, anti-immigrant parties have remained part of the political landscape, often influencing the mainstream because of the latter's fear of losing votes.

Racist violence has also remained a constant over the last two centuries. In fact, until the early 1960s, reflecting the violent modern history of Britain,[48] it became a feature of the landscape of inter-ethnic relations, whether between

Catholics and Protestants during the Victorian years, against C
the First World War, when the worst violence occurred, betv
gentiles from the late nineteenth century until the late 194(
Blacks and Whites from the First World War until the late
that time anti-immigrant riots have declined but attacks upc.. ..uividual
members of ethnic minorities have continued, especially illustrated by the
murder of Stephen Lawrence in 1993.

An examination of xenophobia and racism in Britain over the last
two centuries reveals that it has remained endemic. All ethnic minorities
have experienced a range of popular manifestations of hostility backed up
by institutional racism, which operates in a variety of ways. While particular
peaks of hostility have emerged, especially during war time, but also at times
of purportedly high immigration, a racist murmur has always characterized
the recent history of Britain, both official and unofficial.

Institutional racism

Following the publication of the Macpherson report in 1999 the concept
of institutional racism emerged in Britain, referring to the way in which
particular organizations in the British state, especially the police forces,
found themselves wracked with endemic discrimination, which meant that
they could 'not provide an appropriate and professional service to people
because of their colour, culture or ethnic origin'.[49] The report followed on
from post-war sociological research which had pointed to the existence of
official racism both in British institutions and in the structure of the British
state, notably nationality and immigration laws. In fact, the Scarman Report
of 1981 had already recognized police racism in areas with large Black
populations.[50] By the 1980s British society had full knowledge of the official
racism which existed within its midst, especially through the practices
of British institutions. Establishing the existence of such practices before
1945 proves problematic because of the absence of research into education,
policing and the courts. Instead, historians before 1945 have tended to focus
upon the most obvious and draconian examples of official racism about
which information has proved easiest to detect, especially internment and
repatriation during the two World Wars. The events of these conflicts
represent the worst examples of official racism and xenophobia in Britain
during the last two centuries and would not be repeated on such a scale
again after 1945, although internment without trial has occurred more
recently on a smaller scale against Muslims and Irish people. It seems likely
that racism amongst government institutions has existed throughout the

past two centuries but has become more visible under the intense scrutiny of recent decades. At the same time, immigration laws have always acted as an instrument to keep out undesirables, so that each of those passed since the 1905 Aliens Act has had a specific group in mind.

Underlying other manifestations of official ideology lies Britishness. Scholars such as Paul Ward may point to the increasingly inclusive nature of this concept since the arrival of immigrants from beyond Europe[51] while Robert Colls views it romantically.[52] But the idea of Britain lies behind much of the xenopbobia of the past two centuries, above all immigration and nationality laws, which aim to exclude outsiders regarded as not having the correct credentials to become British. Paul Gilroy wrote about the absence of Black in the Union Jack during the 1980s and 1990s, paying particular attention to the criminalization of Black people in both official and public discourse.[53] In the early nineteenth century there was certainly no Roman Catholic or Jewish in the Union Jack because these two groups did not even have the same civil rights as Protestants until the passage of the Catholic Relief Act of 1829 and the Jewish emancipation legislation later in the nineteenth century.[54] At the same time the First World War witnessed the emergence of a virulent Germanophobia in Britain which wanted to ethnically cleanse the country of any traces of the influence of the enemy.[55] During the conflict an official propaganda machine existed which officially sanctioned Germanophobia, especially in the period before the introduction of conscription in January 1916.[56] While this Germanophobia did not single out the Germans in Britain, the popular press certainly did.[57] Similarly, during the Second World War, the propaganda machine focused especially upon German Nazis and Italian fascists, as well as warning of the dangers of the enemy within, which helped to lead to the outbreak of violence against Italians in June 1940 and to the introduction of internment in the same month.[58] Outside the two World Wars the British state did not peddle this type of xenophobia. As a liberal democratic state many of the ideas of Britishness and the creation of concepts of outsiders come from the press, which plays a central role in the evolution of policy towards ethnic minorities in both peace and wartime, either by influencing governments to pass immigration legislation in peacetime or by pressuring the state to take draconian measures against them in wartime.[59]

Unlike racist regimes in other parts of Europe during the twentieth century, the British state has not overtly peddled racist ideology against migrant populations in its midst. Ideas put forward by the British government do not indicate a structurally racist regime, even though it remains structurally nationalist. Education may represent one area where racist ideas have circulated, as suggested by much research on the post-war decades, although scholars have not substantially examined the period before then. Mike Cole has tried to address the historical roots of racism in British education. He argues that mass schooling during the nineteenth century emerged as a result of the desire to continue British racial dominance within the Empire pointing to the development of Empire Day in schools and suggesting that imperial racist images moved into the curriculum.[60]

The large numbers of foreign schoolchildren arriving in Britain during the course of the 1960s faced a series of problems which led to their marginalization, especially in a traditional educational system which aimed at assimilation.[61] In the first place, they had to adjust to their new environment. Some simply found themselves herded together in one group with other foreign ethnicities as schools and teachers assumed that they were 'dunces' if they could not speak English. While special language classes may have evolved, the 'dunce class' represented the short-term solution. It partly consisted of those who could not speak English together with West Indians who spoke dialect.[62] The children had therefore arrived into a situation where teachers and education authorities had pre-existing concepts about immigrant children partly as a result of the ethnicity and social status of teachers in contrast to the pupils who confronted them.[63] Sometimes the racism manifested itself in direct ways. In one instance, a teacher at a school in Shepherds Bush asked a pupil why she did not draw herself wearing a grass skirt when producing a picture of life in the West Indies.[64] Some teachers resented the fact they taught 'the wrong children' as late as the end of the 1980s. With a predominantly middle class white profession teaching increasing numbers of children from ethnic minority backgrounds throughout the post-war period, relations between the two groups have suffered.[65] Part of the reason for the development of mutual animosity lay not only in the racism of many schoolteachers, but also in their patronizing attitudes.[66]

As well as the problem of disorientated children facing less than sympathetic teachers, local authorities had little idea about how to deal with the consequences of increasing numbers of ethnic minority children in their midst. Lorna Chessum has demonstrated that in Leicester, the local education authority, like many schoolteachers, viewed them as a problem. While initially pursuing an assimilationist approach, this then moved on to become an integrationist one, followed by a more cultural pluralist one.[67] By the 1970s and 1980s Black boys in particular had developed into the stereotype of troublemakers. Some teachers have directed them towards sport because this developed into one of the positive role models that had emerged for them by the 1970s and 1980s. Although Asians had more positive educational stereotypes attached to them as hardworking and passive, they also became problematized because of their foreign languages, and, increasingly by the twenty-first century, because of their religion, especially in the case of Muslims. By this time many so-called Muslim schools had become so because poorer Muslims remained in the inner city, while whites had moved away.[68]

Some curriculum change also occurred, as schools introduced multicultural elements.[69] However, the Thatcher and New Labour regimes, influenced by 'New Right' ideology, developed a concern with inculcating citizens with a sense of Britishness, leading to the introduction of a national curriculum and subsequently to courses in citizenship at secondary level. Subjects such as history proved especially important, with support from eminent academics such as Sir Geoffrey Elton who, in 1986, told a Historical Association lobby in the House of Lords that: 'Schools need more English history, more kings and bishops' and that the 'non-existent history of ethnic minorities and women leads to incoherent syllabuses'.[70] Although the National Curriculum introduced social history it continued to contain a large element of mainstream British history together with a study of major world events after 1900.[71] The development of citizenship education under New Labour appears an attempt to create a new type of Briton. While it supports concepts of pluralism and equal access to political power for all ethnic minorities, it ignores 'immigration rules that systematically discriminate against Black and Asian people' and 'a system of criminal justice that, at each stage, treats Black people more severely than their white counterparts'.[72]

The attempts by educators to incorporate ethnic minorities since the 1960s have resulted in some success as suggested by the attainment of educational qualifications, even though these remain uneven between one group and another.[73] While a move may have taken place away from the Empire Day celebrations of the early twentieth century and the overtly racist attitudes of many white middle class teachers of the early post-war decades, the education system still has an ideological function of creating British citizens.

Nothing could better illustrate the structurally racist nature of Britain than migration and nationality legislation. For most of the nineteenth century Britain had a fairly laissez-faire approach to immigration control against the background of economic and political security but also against the backdrop of emerging and rising racism. The racialization of people from beyond Europe did not impact upon anti-immigration legislation because they had not yet moved to Britain in large numbers. At the same time anti-Catholicism never had the power to exclude the Irish because the

Act of Union of 1801 created a unitary British and Irish state. However, the rise of antisemitism in the late Victorian period led to the passage of the Aliens Act of 1905 aimed at excluding Eastern European Jews. This Act also implemented much of the paraphernalia of aliens control which would develop during the course of the twentieth century including ports of disembarkation policed by immigration officers as well as the concept of undesirable aliens who could include 'lunatics' or 'idiots' and those who had convictions abroad.[74]

Nationality legislation in Victorian Britain remained 'a model of clarity' according to Andreas Fahrmeier, because it simply put forward the concept of *jus solis*, whereby 'every person born within the dominions of the crown no matter whether of English or of foreign parents', even when the latter were 'merely temporarily sojourning', obtained British citizenship. However, under medieval legislation, those of British parentage also had rights in Britain. The Naturalization Act of 1870 essentially formalized measures in this area.[75] Following Rogers Brubaker's classification of positive *jus solis* and negative *jus sanguinis*, we would come to the conclusion that Britain falls into the same positive historical category as France in contrast to Germany.[76] Nevertheless, while Britain pursued a liberal nationality regime in the nineteenth century, it still needs to be seen as one of the building blocks for excluding foreigners from the civil rights of wealthier Britons in an emerging rather than fully developed parliamentary democracy.

The First World War represents an important turning point in the development of nationality legislation. When the conflict broke out the British Nationality and Status of Aliens Act (1914) found itself making its way through Parliament. It confirmed the principle of *jus solis* for those born in the British Empire. Those who wished to become naturalized needed a 'good character' and 'an adequate knowledge of the English language' and had to take an oath of allegiance. However, the level of Germanophobia led to the passage of the British Nationality and Status of Aliens Act (1918), which allowed the Home Secretary to revoke naturalization certificates granted to Germans and, in one of the most blatantly xenophobic measures in modern British history, it would not allow the naturalization of any enemy alien for a period of ten years after the end of the War.[77]

The aftermath of the xenophobia of the First World War led to the passage of the Aliens Act of 1919, which formalized and extended the provisions of the measures passed in 1905 and 1914, helping to keep down immigration into the country at a time when large numbers of refugees emerged in Europe as a result of imperial collapse and rising intolerant regimes.[78] The British Nationality Act of 1948 perpetuated the principles of the 1914 legislation by continuing with the concept of imperial citizenship. While allowing settlement in the UK, this changed due to the racism which emerged during the course of the 1960s, leading to the immigration acts 1962, 1968 and 1971. Kathleen Paul, examining the racialization of immigration control during the early post-war years, has pointed to the fact that the 1948 measure made special provisions for the white and historically British Irish who 'were neither British subjects nor aliens but Irish citizens with all the rights and duties of British subjecthood' including the right to vote and stand for Parliament.[79] A further formalization and standardization occurred with the passage of the British Nationality Act of 1981, which repealed the automatic right of residence of Britons born outside the UK enshrined in 1948 and subsequently undermined by the immigration legislation of the 1960s and 1970s. Furthermore, it also diluted the principle of *jus solis* because children born to parents living in Britain as a result of illegal immigration or because they had overstayed their period of residence, did not automatically obtain British citizenship, although they could acquire it if they lived in the country for ten years continuously.[80]

In the late twentieth- and early twenty-first centuries, attention switched to asylum. Danièle Joly has written about the political construction of asylum following the end of the Cold War when European states developed a negative attitude towards movements which they could not control if they applied the 1951 UN Refugee Convention to them.[81] The Thatcher, Major and New Labour governments developed a variety of responses to this uncontrolled migration in a period when the state continued to expand its power. In the first place, using policies adopted during the Ugandan refugee crisis of the early 1970s, newcomers often found themselves directed to camps, if only temporarily. At the same time, responding to a hostile media, both national and local, as well as the stress which large scale settlement would place upon local authority resources, the government adopted a policy of dispersing refugees throughout the country. This also followed on from the work of the Uganda Resettlement Board, established in 1972. Dispersal often meant sending refugees away from the areas where they would have wished to settle near established communities, often in London, to locations which had little experience of foreign populations. These have included Sighthill in Glasgow and Caia Park in Wrexham in the twenty-first-century. Established communities resented the arrival of 'asylum seekers', leading to local tensions, violence and even murders. At the same time, the British state has also detained some people who have made asylum claims, some of them in prisons. Special centres opened for the purpose of housing those who did not automatically receive the right to enter Britain including

Campsfield House, near Oxford, which began operating in 1993. The number of people held in such establishments increased from just a handful in 1973 to over 3,000 by 1991. At the same time, those seeking asylum have also faced an assault on their rights to welfare entitlements.[82]

While it may seem tempting to view such developments as evidence of increasing racism and hostility towards refugees and migrants in Britain, they have historical precedents. Asylum narrowed from the mid-Victorian generosity which largely welcomed refugees, even though some dissenting voices existed even then.[83] David Feldman has asserted that the limitation of welfare payments to those claiming asylum represents a new departure as previous migrants have usually received treatment similar to that of natives.[84] Tony Kushner and Katherine Knox have conclusively demonstrated the meanness of asylum policy throughout the course of the twentieth century.[85] The 1905 Aliens Act really did mark a watershed, as it set a precedent, as the British state grew, of the necessity of a measure to control undesirable migratory movements. Nationality law has actually demonstrated relatively little change over the past two hundred years. While an element of *jus sanguinis* has entered the system since 1981, the principle of *jus solis* has essentially remained intact. The narrowing of citizenship rights from the whole Empire to Britain essentially followed the demise of imperialism. The recent introduction of citizenship tests and ceremonies for those wishing to become naturalized appears a new departure making it more difficult to become British,[86] yet this process never remained straightforward. The increasing level of control and the incessant introduction of new nationality and, more especially, immigration legislation since 1945 do represent new paths, partly explained by the growth of modern government as much as an increasingly racist and exclusivist British state. In essence, the use of nationality and immigration legislation, whatever boundaries it utilizes, remains a method of exclusion. Beginning with the 1905 Aliens Act, governments, responding to public opinion, have attempted to control the racial make-up of British citizenship and those who constitute the British population,[87] but they have often done so after significant demographic changes have already occurred. Immigration and nationality has become racialized, but not retrospectively because British governments have not carried out retrospective deportation. Nevertheless, deportation has characterized recent British history, particularly during the course of the twentieth century. The 1905 Aliens Act again set the precedent by allowing the Home Secretary to deport 'undesirables'.[88] One of the earliest mass deportations as a result of this measure affected hundreds of German gypsies who faced hostility wherever they went.[89]

However, the most significant expulsion in recent British history took place against the virulent Germanophobia of the First World War. The fact that the German community of Britain declined from 57,500 in 1914 to just 22,254 in 1919[90] suggests that this group experienced ethnic cleansing. This ties in with the other measures which Germans faced from both state and society[91] and does not differ significantly from other episodes of ethnic cleansing in Europe during the twentieth century.[92] Following the anti-Black riots of 1919 the government decided to blame the victim by carrying out a similar act. Repatriation committees came into existence in those cities with Black populations of any significance including Hull, South Shields, Glasgow, Cardiff, Liverpool, London and Salford. Despite the rioting faced by the small Black communities in these locations the government decided 'to remove the "threat" posed by Black sailors in ports across the country'.[93] Meanwhile, although the vast majority of the quarter of a million Belgian refugees who had entered Britain during the First World War returned home willingly, a small percentage found themselves forced to leave.[94]

The Second World War also witnessed a dramatic instance of deportation. While it affected fewer people than the Germans in the First World War, it has left a more obvious memory because of the fact that a community remained to commemorate these actions. In fact, as they affected two different groups in the form of Italians and German Jews, both have remembered the internment and deportation implemented in the spring of 1940.[95] About 8,000 Germans and Italians found themselves sent to Canada and Australia following the Cabinet decision to carry out deportation under Churchill's prompting in June 1940. One of the boats transporting prisoners to Canada, the *Arandora Star*, was sunk by a German submarine on 2 July, resulting in 700 deaths. It marked a turning point in the policy of internment and repatriation, as the Government did not see through the vindictive policies which affected the Germans in the First World War.[96]

In peacetime Britain after 1945 no mass expulsions have taken place. But as a result of the evolution and criminalization of the 'illegal immigrant', the deportation of individuals has become one of the everyday activities of the immigration service.[97] However, as enshrined in the series of Acts passed since 1905 some people do not even manage to cross British borders and face refusal of entry once they land at British ports and airports. During the 1980s, for instance, an increase occurred in the number of visitor refusals for people coming from the Caribbean.[98] In case any of the wrong type of people managed to make it through the net at points of entry, however, an Illegal Immigration Intelligence Unit had come into existence in 1973 and by the 1980s it carried out 'passport raids' amongst ethnic minorities.[99]

This has been superseded by the Orwellian sounding Immigration Service Enforcement Directorate, which counted around 500 staff by the beginning of the twenty-first century.[100] Asylum has also now become a complex process which can involve a judicial procedure for each individual case,[101] which can last for years.[102]

The operation of immigration control forms an important aspect of state racism in twentieth-century Britain. The expulsion of undesirables, whether individuals in peacetime, or groups in wartime, further emphasizes the importance of the composition of populations. However, much of the research carried out since the Scarman Report has focused upon the police and judiciary, regarded as one of the other central tenets of racist Britain in recent decades.

Evidence from the nineteenth and early twentieth centuries reveals similar examples of biased policing and convicting. Roger Swift pointed to the determination with which the police dealt with crime amongst the Irish during the Victorian period. He demonstrated that working class districts with heavy Irish concentrations faced surveillance, which led to resentment. Most importantly, anticipating subsequent developments, the Irish were more likely to face arrest than the rest of the population. Swift believes that the Irish faced such discrimination more because of class than ethnic prejudice 'although instances of anti-Irish sentiment were undoubtedly displayed by individual policemen against Irish immigrants from time to time'.[103] At the same time, as Bernard Porter has demonstrated, the evolution of the Metropolitan Police Special Branch during the nineteenth century partly emerged from the surveillance of suspected Irish bombers.[104] Meanwhile, Lucio Sponza pointed to police hostility towards Italians at the end of the nineteenth century.[105]

Relatively little information exists on the relations between the police and the Jewish community, although one article assumes a basically harmonious position in the East End of London.[106] On the other hand, Judge J. Rentoul asserted in 1909 that three quarters of the cases he tried consisted of 'aliens of the very worst type in their own country', including 'the Russian burglar, the Polish thief, the Italian stabber, and the German swindler'.[107]

In May 1915 the police became overwhelmed by the level of violence against Germans, although my own research on these events has not revealed any systematic or individual police prejudice, while the courts seemed to sentence those involved in the attacks appropriately. Nevertheless, the anti-German riots of the First World War took place against the background of a Gemanophobic state in which hostility towards Germans had essentially become legalized.[108] Jacqueline Jenkinson carried out detailed research into police and judicial attitudes towards Black people during the 1919 riots. She pointed to friction between the police and the Black settlements, as well as a tendency in Hull, Cardiff and Glasgow to arrest Blacks rather than whites. The courts, however, took a more even handed approach.[109] Richard Thurlow and D. S. Lewis, meanwhile, have pointed out that the police tended to come down more heavily upon Fascists than Jews in the East End of London during the 1930s.[110]

Research carried out upon police and judicial racism in recent decades has focused upon a series of issues. First, the mistreatment of minorities by the police. This links with uneven sentencing. At the same time, minority groups have faced over policing, indicated by stop and search tactics against Blacks and, more recently, Muslims. Furthermore, the police have failed to devote the same amount of attention towards crimes, especially of a racial nature, carried out against ethnic minorities as they have towards those faced by whites. Finally, the lack of Black and Asian police and judges facilitates much of the uneven treatment. While Black youth and Black people generally may have represented the main victims of a biased judiciary and police in Britain since 1945, the Irish and Muslims have had negative experiences because of the threat of IRA and Islamic terrorism.

Examples of police brutality exist in the years immediately after the end of the Second World War with the handling of violence between Black and white people in Liverpool in 1948, harking back to similar actions in 1919. The police solved the problem by 'removing the coloured minority' and arresting 60 Blacks and 10 whites. Black people also faced police violence in their own homes.[111] The police appear to have acted more fairly during the Notting Hill Riots, although some Black people felt that the police had not done enough to protect them against white rioters.[112]

Paul Gilroy suggested that until the 1970s senior police thinking did not link crime with immigrants to any great extent other than as a consequence of social deprivation.[113] But during the course of the 1970s and into the 1980s the police began to view criminality amongst Black youth as a particular problem, especially rioting and mugging, both sensationalized in the popular press. The police reacted in a heavy handed manner and developed new polices. These included the 'swamping' of some Black communities (especially Brixton) with large numbers of policemen, the use of stop and search tactics, and the establishment of the Special Patrol Group, which had particular powers to deal with disorder and acted in a particularly brutal manner, epitomized in the murder of Blair Peach during an antiracist rally in Southall in 1979. While the roots of Black youth criminality lay in social deprivation, the solution of heavy handed policing simply added to the problem, which acted as a major factor in the 'uprisings of July 1981' when police throughout the country faced attack from inner city youths of a variety of ethnic groups, following on from the Brixton disorder earlier that year. Despite the recommendations of the Scarman Report, heavy handed policing against Black people continued, symbolized by the death of Cynthia Jarrett during a search of her home in 1985, which sparked the Broadwater Farm riot in Tottenham in October of that year.[114]

One particular aspect of police racism which has received attention has consisted of the mistreatment of Black people following arrest, some of whom have died. As early as 1959 a Colonial Office document listed a series of complaints against police officers by West Indians. These included 'forceful entry', two cases of 'wrongful arrest' and two cases of 'assault' and 'brutality'.[115] By the 1980s the issue of Black deaths in custody began to receive public attention, although the police officers responsible did not usually face charges.[116] Clinton McCurbin serves as one example of such a death. He actually died in a Next retailing outlet in Wolverhampton in 1987, after two police officers strangled him.[117]

Irish and Asian people have faced specific forms of hostility from the police especially connected with their perceived link to terrorism. A Commission for Racial Equality report on discrimination against the Irish carried out by Bronwen Walter and Mary Hickman suggested that 25 per cent of those questioned had faced negative police reactions to their ethnicity.[118] The Prevention of Terrorism Act of November 1974 following the IRA Birmingham pub bombings earlier in that year allowed the police to hold suspects for up to seven days without trial, often leading to violence against them.[119] The need for results following the Guildford and Birmingham pub bombings in 1974 led to two of the greatest miscarriages of justice in peacetime British history, with the false conviction of the Guildford Four and the Birmingham Six, subsequently found innocent.[120] By the beginning of the twenty-first century, following the attacks of 11 September 2001, Muslims found themselves in a similar position to the Irish a few decades earlier, although even before 11 September a deterioration had taken place between police and Asian youth.[121] The events of 11 September have led to measures against Muslims in Britain. This has not only resulted in an extension of the period of time police can question suspects to 28 days, but also a curtailment of free speech and an increase in surveillance, which affects Muslims in particular, but also wider society as a whole. Those who even flirt with Islamic terrorism, whether through websites or even through discussions, can now find themselves at the Old Bailey for planning acts of terror.[122]

Apart from the heavy handed tactics faced by a variety of ethnic minorities since the 1950s, the police have not done enough to assist the members of minorities who have become victims of crimes, especially of a racist nature. During the 1970s, despite constant attacks by right-wing youths against Bengalis in the East End of London, the police responded slowly or not at all.[123] In a survey carried out in North Plaistow between 1988 and 1991, 70 people reported an incident of violent racism to the police, of whom 58 stated that police had attended the scene. However, almost half of the respondents remained unsatisfied with the police response, higher then the same figures for white people.[124] Despite signs of improvement during the course of the 1980s and 1990s, the most symbolic example of police failure to investigate a racial incident followed the murder of Stephen Lawrence in 1993. The fact that the Blair government established a national enquiry to examine the whole issue of the investigation of his murder and the relationship between police and ethnic minorities suggests that some progress had occurred since the 1970s, although the Scarman Report had previously failed to eradicate racism in police forces.[125]

Another key issue in relations between the police force and ethnic minorities, especially Blacks and Asians, remains the complete domination of this profession by members of the ethnic majority at all ranks. At the beginning of 1976 the Metropolitan Police counted only 39 Black officers out of a total force of 21,000.[126] Some increase has occurred since then, although by 1994 only 2,100 (or 1.6 per cent) of the 127,290 police officers in England and Wales consisted of members of ethnic minorities.[127] This under-representation has continued, especially in areas with a high percentage of Black and Asian people in their populations. For example, 3.3 per cent of officers in the Metropolitan Police in 1999 consisted of ethnic minorities at the time when they constituted 25.5 per cent of London's population.[128] Part of the reason for these low figures lies in the fact that Black, Asian and even Irish people who join the police face racism. Hickman and Walter gave the example of a woman 'working in a civilian job for the Metropolitan Police. Her boyfriend was Irish. She was told that unless she gave him up she would be moved from her job in a top security building. She gave up her job'.[129] In 1982 a lecturer from the Police Training College in Hendon leaked some essays written by recruits to the media (for which he lost his position) which included statements such as: 'quite frankly I don't have any liking whatsoever for wogs, nig nogs and Pakis'.[130] When Black and Asian people joined the forces they therefore had negative stereotypes assigned to them. In fact, few, if any, officers have not encountered racism.[131]

At the same time, the judicial system has revealed similar patterns. Part of the problem again lies in the ethnic make-up of judges. Of the 2,086 judges in 1995 only 29 came from ethnic minority backgrounds.[132] Consequently, the nearly all-white judiciary has tended to come down more heavily upon Black defendants than those with white skin, which helps to explain the increase in Black prisoners in the second half of the twentieth century.[133]

There seems little doubt that Britain has been a structurally racist state over the past two hundred years, whether this phrase refers to immigration and nationality law or policing. However, at times of extreme insecurity the British state has also carried out acts of extreme persecution. Arun Kundani, concerned about the undermining of individual liberty after 11 September, has written of *The End of Tolerance*. In view of the experiences of minorities during the two World Wars, particularly the First, we might argue that the atmosphere created by the 'War on Terror' repeats that fostered between 1914 and 1918 and 1939 and 1945. During these two conflicts the British state dispensed with peacetime concepts of civil liberties in order to fight war. While all sections of the population suffered, ethnic minorities, especially those regarded as the enemy within, found themselves especially hard hit.[134]

The most intolerant act of the Second World War consisted of internment. When the war broke out the 73,000 enemy aliens in Britain, most of them Jewish refugees, faced division into 3 categories, A, B and C, depending upon the level of their perceived threat. Those in A, about 600, faced immediate internment, while 6,200 in Category C faced no interference. The vast majority remained at liberty but faced some restrictions upon movement. The success of the Nazi spring offensive in 1940 and the Italian declaration of war on Britain on 10 June caused panic in popular and official circles, leading to the implementation of a policy of mass internment against the 'enemy within', meaning that 22,000 Germans and Austrians and 4,300 Italians may have faced a period of incarceration. This experience, while indicative of intolerance, remained relatively short lived, so that the number of internees had declined to 1,300 by August 1944. Most of them found themselves on the Isle of Man. The early release took place against the background of the fighting of an anti-fascist war.[135]

This contrasted with the Great War, when Britain became saturated with Germanophobia. While the mass deportation represents the most important aspect of the ethnic cleansing which ensued, the German community in Britain also faced complete confiscation of its property, ranging from the branches of the Deutsche or Dresdner Banks to the local butchers and

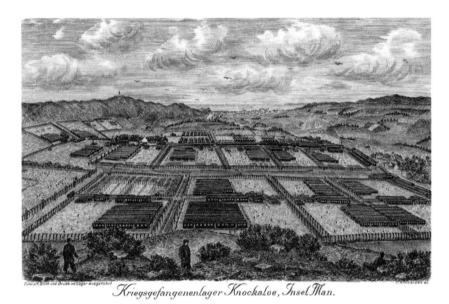

Kriegsgefangenenlager Knockaloe, Insel Man.

FIGURE 14 Knockaloe internment camp on the Isle of Man during the First World War, courtesy of Manx National Heritage

bakers found in high streets up and down the country. The proceeds of this property eventually went towards Germany's reparations payments under the Treaty of Versailles. At the same time mass internment of all enemy alien males took place from May 1915 until the conclusion of peace, reaching a peak of 32,440 in November 1915 and still totalling 24,255 when the conflict ended.[136]

Germans in the Second World War and, more especially, in the First World War, faced the full wrath of the British state. The experiences of the Great War resemble those of Nazi Germany, the Armenian Genocide or the war in Yugoslavia in the sense that the British state, backed up by a hostile press and elements of the extreme right, systematically cleansed Britain of German influence. But as in the case of the return of Jews to Germany after 1945,[137] Germans would return to Britain after 1919.[138]

'Friendly' minorities have also had to endure official wartime hostility, or at least indifference, but not on the same scale as enemy aliens. The approximately 150,000 Black American GIs in Britain during the Second World War arrived as part of a segregated army. The British government opposed them, although it gave in under pressure from the USA. Once in Britain official racism towards them ranged from government departments to local police forces.[139]

There seems little doubt that the British state over the past two centuries has had obvious elements of structural racism and xenophobia. During peacetime these characteristics have manifested themselves in the exclusion of those with the wrong ethnic credentials from the benefits of residence and citizenship in Britain. At the same time, as most clearly demonstrated by the treatment of African-Caribbeans by the police and judiciary from the 1950s structural racism also means official discrimination. In wartime the British state has resorted to extreme measures characteristic of other twentieth-century nation states.[140] While it did not carry out genocide, it certainly practised ethnic cleansing.

Ideologies, outsiders and their persecution

State xenophobia and racism go hand in hand with popular animosity, manifesting itself in the creation of outsiders (especially by the press), everyday hostility, the rise of racist political parties and violence. In a liberal democratic state, a groundswell of such hostility influences policy makers, especially during the course of the twentieth century, when Britain has operated upon universal suffrage.

Racist and xenophobic ideologies underlie concrete manifestations. While some outsiders such as Blacks and Jews have remained objects of fear for much of the past two centuries, the main focus of xenophobes has changed from the mid nineteenth-century Irish to the contemporary 'asylum seekers'. Nevertheless, while the major group of outsiders may change over time, the main reasons for hostility do not. In the first place, at the most basic level, demonstrated especially in press racism demanding a change in immigration laws, and resurfacing regularly since the campaign for the 1905 Aliens Act, lies the idea that newcomers compete for scarce resources, whether jobs, housing, welfare or women. Secondly, lies the alien nature of each specific group of outsiders determined by some apparently inherent characteristic which means that they threaten 'the British way of life'. Religion has remained of central importance to this discourse and has incorporated Roman Catholicism for much of the nineteenth century, Judaism from the late Victorian period to the Second World War and, most recently, Islam. Animosity becomes especially virulent in wartime, when particular groups of outsiders become associated with the enemy as potential traitors, illustrated by attitudes towards Germans and Jews during both World Wars and Muslims during the 'war on terror'. Finally, a variety of groups have become racialized over the past two centuries ranging from the Irish in the mid Victorian period through Jews from the end of the nineteenth century and Blacks and Asians throughout the previous two hundred years. The rise of European imperialism and the growth of scientific racism has helped to create such outsiders.

Racist and xenophobic ideologies operate on a variety of levels. The evolution of racism developed amongst 'informed opinion' from the middle of the nineteenth century encompassing professional academics, journalists, politicians and racial thinkers. Such scientific racism had reached its peak by the First World War and would begin to decline amongst intellectuals in Britain, as in the USA, by the inter-war years,[141] although its legacies would continue to influence much of the population into the post-war years. While scientific racism may have declined amongst educated opinion after 1945, other forms of xenophobia have not and continue to circulate both in right-wing intellectual publications such as the *Salisbury Review* and in more popular publications.[142] Part of this marginalization of outsiders operates upon literary and media stereotypes, which perpetuate historically rooted images.[143] In the context of spreading ideas and negative views of outsiders amongst British society over the last two centuries, the press has remained fundamentally important. Teun A. Van Dijk in particular recognized this for the 1980s,[144] while Elizabeth Poole and John E. Richardson have demonstrated the role of both the popular press and broadsheets in creating negative images of Muslims in contemporary Britain.[145] Tony Kushner has pointed to the role of the Daily *Mail* and the *Daily Express* in whipping up hostility to refugees both during the 1930s and at the beginning of the twenty-first century.[146] Similarly, newspapers and the periodical press played a central role both in the creation of Irish stereotypes in the nineteenth century[147] and in whipping up hysterical Germanophobia during the Great War.[148] Unlike the broadcast media, which have controls upon what they can transmit, newspapers for much of the last two centuries have written what they wished. Even after the passage of Race Relations legislation from the 1960s, the press has constantly vilified ethnic outsiders, continuing patterns firmly established by the middle of the nineteenth century. Before 1945 the print media could publish the most negative of headlines against the Irish, Germans and Jews.

The hostility towards the nineteenth-century Irish revolved around three key themes: anti-Catholicism, poverty and, towards the end of the Victorian period, following the development of Social Darwinism, racial stereotyping. From the Reformation and continuing with the evolution of the British nation state during the eighteenth century, anti-Catholicism remained central to Britishness. It focused not simply upon the Irish and their migrant representatives in Britain, but also upon French and Spanish neighbours.[149]

While the peak of such xenophobic anti-Catholicism may have occurred with attacks upon the Irish during the murderous Gordon Riots of 1780,[150] this ideology, drawing 'upon a tradition extending backwards to the Reformation and beyond . . . influenced the behaviour of all classes in English society in the nineteenth century'.[151] John Wolfe has pointed out that its most virulent form 'was to be found in the areas of Irish settlement, in Lancashire and the West of Scotland'.[152] All manner of Protestant societies emerged during the nineteenth century in addition to the Orange Order.[153] Anti-Catholicism reached particular peaks when ardent Protestants felt under threat from what they viewed as 'Papal aggression', particularly following the granting of Roman Catholic emancipation in 1829 and, more especially, the re-establishment of the Roman Catholic Church on the British mainland in 1850, which coincided with the peak of Irish immigration.[154] A 'rich tradition of cheap literature', which viewed Catholicism as immoral, combined with the established press to marginalize this religion.[155]

Anti-Catholicism acted as the ideology for rioters in the 1850s in particular when violence reached its peak. Such working class hostility also found fuel in the everyday tensions which the new arrivals caused in the housing and labour market. Publications such as the *Bulwark* in Scotland, as well as the activities of the Protestant evangelical preacher William Murphy further fuelled the fire.[156] In addition, the periodical press from the 1830s was full of descriptions of the 'dirty' and 'drunken' Irish, confirming middle class prejudices against this immigrant group. Frederick Engels famously wrote of the Irish in essentially racially derogatory terms, focusing especially upon their 'filth', a word which he used several times when describing them.[157] Donald MacRaild has considered such attitudes under the heading of the 'Condition of England' in this early period of industrialization. Those who wrote about the Irish saw them as a race apart.[158]

Social and economic hostility as well as anti-Catholicism declined during the course of the nineteenth century. Integration, a decrease in Irish immigration and an acceptance of the establishment of the Roman Catholic Church in Britain meant that anti-Catholic prejudice generally declined,[159] although it remained potent in Liverpool and Glasgow. But racial anti-Irish sentiment survived and developed. The Irish became caught up in the development of 'scientific' racism during the second half of the nineteenth century, viewed as primitive and distinct from Anglo-Saxons. L. P. Curtis wrote especially of the development of the simian image of the dangerous Irishman, which he argued took place against the background of the Fenian threat and the popularization of Darwin's theories of evolution. The Irish also became outsiders as concepts of the superiority of the Anglo-Saxon race evolved during the second half of the nineteenth century. Such images particularly aimed at the Victorian middle classes, popularized especially in the pages of *Punch* and would not have influenced the working classes to any great extent.[160]

During the course of the twentieth century the Irish have received less negative attention. Part of the explanation lies in the decline of immigration after the middle of the nineteenth century, which helped integration to occur. However, this would not hold true for the post-war period. In reality, the Irish have faded into the background, as Jews, Germans and then 'coloured' people attracted most attention from racists. This does not mean that hostility towards the Irish and their Catholicism has disappeared as witnessed by the perpetuation of sectarianism in Scotland, but also by its survival in twentieth-century Wales.[161] At the same time the culture of the Irish joke, focusing upon the apparent lack of intelligence of Irish people, which became particularly widespread by the 1970s, suggests at least an undercurrent of anti-Irish prejudice in the post-war period.[162] The Irish joke became especially popular during IRA campaigns on the British mainland, which as Hickman and Walter have demonstrated, played a large role in causing anti-Irish hostility.[163]

Jews also became relatively invisible in the post-war period against the background of integration and Commonwealth immigration. However, from the late Victorian period until the 1950s, antisemitism became and remained endemic in British society.[164] Like anti-Catholicism, it could draw upon centuries, and, in this case, perhaps even millennia, of negative stereotypes and images, based especially upon the concept of the Jew as Christ killer and money lender.[165] In the six decades or so from *c*.1880, a series of circumstances came together to marginalize Jews in Britain, above all the immigration of the late Victorian and Edwardian years, the rise of European racism and fascism, which had adherents in Britain, and the First World War. Antisemitism, like anti-Irish hostility, had a series of strands to it.

The Jewish association with money remained important in nineteenth-century literature represented most classically in Charles Dickens' Fagin and Walter Scott's Isaac. As Edgar Rosenberg wrote, 'Good or bad, rich Jew or poor, tyrant or slave, money was almost bound to be at the root of his problem'.[166] On the other hand Nadia Valman has more recently written about the complexity of images of 'the Jewess' in nineteenth-century English literature who 'was spiritual, cultured, patriotic, emotional and modern'.[167] Nevertheless, the connection of Jewish males with money remained and also led to charges of corruption from both the left and the right of the political spectrum. For instance, during the Boer War a pamphlet signed

GROSS IGNORANCE OF HEBREW.

FIGURE 15 An extreme anti-Semitic caricature from *Punch*, 1864

by 83 executive officers of trade unions claimed that 'The capitalists who brought up or hire the press in South Africa and in England to clamour for war are largely Jews and foreigners'.[168] Meanwhile, the liberal journalist J. A. Hobson claimed that the economic resources of the Transvaal had fallen 'into the hands of a small group of international financiers, chiefly German in origin and Jewish in race', for whom Britain fought the South African War.[169] During the Edwardian period rich Jews also came under attack from the right because of their alleged financial corruption especially during the 'Marconi Scandal' when Jewish Cabinet ministers became accused of insider trading, particularly by Hillaire Belloc and G. K. Chesterton, who also created literary stereotypes of rich corrupt Jews.[170]

Hostility towards the Jewish immigrant, especially in the lead up to the Aliens Act of 1905, but also during the 1930s, used similar themes and imagery to the campaigns against other immigrant groups in recent British history. The animosity focused upon their alien nature, their threat to jobs and housing, their unsanitary habits and the apparently large numbers involved, who would threaten British values. Between about 1880 and 1905 public discourse encompassing the newspaper and periodical press as well as government investigations became saturated with the threat of the Jewish alien. While the campaign of the 1930s may not have become so intense, newspapers such as the *Daily Express* and the *Daily Mail* also feared numbers and the threat to jobs, backed up by middle class professional organizations, in view of the social status of many of the immigrants.[171]

Jews also became racialized from the 1870s. As Colin Holmes has demonstrated, Joseph Banister put forward some of the most vicious stereotypes, especially in his 1901 publication *England under the Jews*, using phrases such as 'semitic sewage' and describing poor Jews as disease carriers.[172] Holmes, along with Gisela C. Lebzelter, has also demonstrated the persistence of such discourse into the inter-war years, especially amongst individuals such as Henry Hamilton Beamish and Arnold Leese, the latter of whom saw 'only three possible ways to end the Jewish menace' consisting of 'extermination', 'assimilation' or 'compulsory segregation'.[173]

Perhaps the most vicious trait of antisemitism focused upon Jews as traitors, with no allegiance to Britain, working for themselves, for a foreign power or a foreign ideology. Arnold White, who preached every variety of antisemitism, wrote of 'a Jewish imperium inside the English Empire', which could either 'be destroyed' or assimilated.[174] In the years leading up to the First World War, as well as during the conflict, Jews and Germans became synonymous for some antisemites, especially Leopold Maxse, who believed German Jews in Britain worked for the 'Fatherland'. J. H. Clarke's 1917 book *England Under the Heel of the Jew* put forward similar ideas.[175] After the First World War, Jews also became associated with the threat of Communism and the Soviet Union. The publication of an English translation of the *Protocols of the Elders of Zion* in February 1920 perhaps symbolized the peak of conspiratorial antisemitism as it claimed that 'a Jewish conspiracy was planning to take over the world'.[176]

As Tony Kushner has demonstrated, antisemitic ideas survived into the Second World War[177] and beyond. In 1947 the concept of Jews as traitors led to riots against them following the hanging of two Jewish sergeants in Palestine by Jewish forces.[178] Similarly, David Cesarani demonstrated that antisemitism determined immigration policy towards survivors of the

Holocaust after 1945.[179] Other strands of hostility towards Jews remained beyond the 1950s connected with Israel, the cruelty of Schechita, as well as alleged corrupt business practices. While the extreme right has focused upon Black and Asian migrants, some of the most violent groups, such as Combat 18, remain fiercely antisemitic. Partly because of the move of Jews up the social scale, which has made them less visible, and partly because of the greater visibility of ethnic minorities from the Commonwealth, the all embracing culture of antisemitism, which made Jews the main victims of racial hostility from c.1880–c.1950, has subsided.[180]

Xenophobia in the period from the middle of the nineteenth century until the middle of the twentieth century, did not simply focus upon Jews, but brought in other groups. Lucio Sponza has demonstrated how Italians became victims of social hostility revolving particularly around issues of noise, child abuse and lack of cleanliness during the Victorian period. During the Second World War this group attracted accusations of treachery, even though some people of Italian origin fought with British forces.[181]

Germans faced similar accusations, although, during the Victorian period, they, like the Italians,[182] also attracted positive attention, in this case because of their similar racial origins and because of their traditions of learning. But an undercurrent of social hostility also existed during the nineteenth century. Germans have a special place in the history of British xenophobia as representatives of the most threatening wartime enemy. This stereotype began to surface during the late Victorian and Edwardian period as spy fever, which labelled all Germans as agents of the Fatherland. Spy fever reached a peak during early stages of the Great War. As the conflict progressed and no British victory occurred, it developed into a conspiracy theory, which asserted that Britain could not win the war because Germans controlled the country. The peak of Germanophobic hatred arrived following the sinking of the passenger liner *Lusitania* in May 1915 which resulted in press headlines such as 'No Compromise with a Race of Savages' and 'The Branded Race. Why Are Any Germans Left Outside Gaols in Britain', while the editor of *John Bull*, Horatio Bottomley, declared that he would like to 'exterminate every German-born man (God forgive the term!) in Britain – and to deport every German-born woman and child'. While Bottomley's first wish may not have come true, his second did to a substantial extent. Although Germanophobia declined during the inter-war years, it combined with antisemitism in the decision to introduce internment in 1940. In the post-war period, Germanophobic stereotypes have survived, surfacing especially during England and Germany football matches, although they have not tended to focus upon Germans in Britain.[183]

For most of the period since the end of the Second World War racism has concentrated upon Black and Asian migrants and has regurgitated stereotypes directed against previous waves of immigrants. Like antisemitism and anti-Catholicism, animosity towards people from beyond Europe has deep roots. One of these roots lies in slavery, which had dehumanized Black people in the early modern period so that they had become 'consigned to the level of non-human property'.[184] While emancipation may have changed their image, negative stereotypes remained potent against Black, South Asian and Chinese people. Two background factors perpetuated these negative views. The first of these consisted of the 'imperial encounter' of middle and upper class white literate Britons with the peoples of Africa and Asia who did not have the same cultural or religious norms or the same level of economic development. Events such as the Indian Mutiny and the Jamaican revolt of 1865 meant fear played a role in the images of non-Europeans, which survived well into the twentieth century. Victorians disliked the physical appearance of Black skin and the nakedness of Africans. They also viewed Blacks as lazy, superstitious and sexually promiscuous.[185] Negative attitudes towards Indians focused upon religion, the treatment of women, the caste system, and the Indian temperament, although inter-ethnic marriages also became a feature of life in India, despite the taboos against them.[186] While images of the mysterious Orient circulated in Victorian Britain, by the beginning of the twentieth century the Japanese and, more especially, the Chinese, became feared as powers which could threaten British global dominance. This image became especially widespread following the publication of Sax Rohmer's *The Mystery of Dr Fu-Manchu* in 1913.[187]

Nineteenth- and early twentieth-century attitudes towards non-Europeans also developed against the background of the rise of pseudo scientific racism. While it had its origins before the Victorian period,[188] the influence of the imperial encounter, combined with the application of Darwin's theories of evolution to humanity led to the development of concepts of racial hierarchies in which white men tended to find themselves at the top and those with darker skins towards the bottom. Such racial thinking, which developed throughout the European continent, counted a series of British writers amongst its adherents, most notably Robert Knox (who focused on issues such as racial mixing and brain sizes) together with James Hunt and John Crawford.[189]

The complexity of negative views towards people from beyond Europe which had developed during the course of the nineteenth century influenced attitudes towards the small numbers who found themselves in Britain. During the mid-Victorian period, much attention focused upon their religions, especially from Joseph Salter, who aimed at converting 'Asiatics' to Christianity, particularly in London's docklands. Negative attention also focused upon relationships with white women.[190]

Similarly, the small Black population in Victorian Britain experienced hostility because of the racial ideas which had emerged. Like Asians, they also faced negative stereotyping because of their alien religions. Nevertheless, most commentators upon Africans and West Indians in Britain before the First World War also point to positive images as a reading of Mayhew would indicate.[191] It seems tempting to put this relative tolerance down to the presence of small numbers of Blacks in Victorian Britain, as hostility towards this immigrant group only reached a peak at the end of the First World War when returning white sailors wanted their jobs back. This served as a major cause of the 1919 riots, and received backing from local newspapers, who focused both upon job displacement and interracial relationships.[192] Fear of miscegenation developed further during the inter-war years, as demonstrated by Paul Rich,[193] who has also argued that doctrines of racial segregation influenced by the example of the American South and South Africa, had begun to gain hold in Britain and would influence reactions towards the arrival of Black people after 1945.[194]

A small group who received negative attention in the late Victorian and Edwardian years consisted of the Chinese. Linked to the racial stereotyping which had begun to circulate about the threat of China and its expanding population, hostile attention from trade unionists had begun to develop against the use of a small number of 'cheap' Chinese labourers. This issue not only caused violence, it also resulted in increased attention being devoted to the small Chinese communities from newspapers and periodicals which focused especially upon miscegenation and 'opium dens'.[195]

Chinese people have received relatively little attention in the post-war period in comparison with Black and South Asian migrants. These two groups have collectively faced the type of stereotyping, which European migrants endured before 1945. At the same time fear of the effects of immigration, has also combined with the racial ideas which emerged during the nineteenth century. Lorna Chessum analysed press reactions to the arrival of West Indians in Leicester in the lead up to the passage of the Commonwealth Immigrants Act of 1962. She has demonstrated how imperial images of Black people working in Britain combined with a desire to stop further immigration resulting in suggestions that Britain should introduce a colour bar based on the South African model.[196] Robert Miles and Annie Phizacklea have pointed to racialization of immigration on a national level in the same period while Miles has also shown how the press used the 1958 Nottingham and Notting Hill Riots to justify the introduction of immigration legislation.[197]

Since the early 1960s media discourse on race and immigration from the Commonwealth has focused upon a series of themes.[198] These include the prevention of further immigration, initially of Black people, then Asians, and, more recently, refugees. Something of a peak of such reporting occurred during the Ugandan Asian 'crisis' of 1972.[199] More recently, since the middle of the 1990s, the press has constantly called for the shrinking of the right of asylum.[200] The media has also focused upon the 'problems' caused by ethnic minorities settled in Britain, which, like the hostility towards previous European groups, emphasizes the threat to the 'British way of life'. Key themes have included criminality, especially amongst Black males, viewed as violent and associated especially with mugging and rioting, particularly during the 1980s.[201] At the same time hostility to difference, including language and appearance, became especially apparent when, in 1983, Ray Honeyford, a Bradford Headmaster, criticized multiracial education in favour of integration.[202] A series of writers linked this development to the emergence of a racist discourse in the Thatcher government originating in the early post-war years.[203]

By the beginning of the twenty-first century, especially after 11 September, Muslims, together with 'asylum seekers', had become the main focus of negative media attention in Britain. The marginalization of Muslims had begun to develop with the Honeyford affair and had gained strength from the end of the 1980s when critics throughout the political spectrum criticized those who burnt copies of the *Satanic Verses*. Scholars of Islamophobia have traced its roots back to negative historical Orientalist images.[204] Contemporary prejudice in Britain has emerged against the background of international events, especially the wars in Iraq and the rise of Islamic terrorism.[205] However, much of the hostility has concentrated upon the apparent inability of Muslims to integrate. Central points in this discourse have included separate education, different attitudes towards relationships and marriage, including the objections of Muslim parents to daughters marrying out, and the importance of religion in the lives of Muslims. In this 'discursive construction' separatist Islamic political parties also receive negative attention.[206]

As Nasar Meer and Tahseen Noorani have demonstrated in their comparison of Islamophobia in contemporary Britain with antisemitism a century ago,[207] clear continuities exist in the history of xenophobic and racist images. It seems tempting to suggest that while the identity of the main outsiders changes the charges levelled against them do not. This fear of alien cultures has represented a key component of hostility to immigrants and ethnic minorities so that an increase in immigrants from any one area causes hostility to rise towards them. Historically rooted religious, xenophobic and racial images also play a role, while international politics can shoot a particular minority to prominence at any particular moment.

Negative stereotyping and racial ideology act as a background to more concrete manifestations of racism and xenophobia. These include the emergence of radical right-wing groups, which have remained ever present in twentieth-century Britain. No extremist group has ever gained power, unlike in some parts of continental Europe in the inter-war years. Similarly, a first past the post electoral system has not allowed an extreme right anti-immigration party such as the Front National in France to become a major player in the political system. In fact, radical right-wing groupings have only secured a handful of seats in either local or national politics since the end of the nineteenth century. But despite their limited support, the major political parties have not ignored them as the fear of losing seats to extremist groups has meant that the larger parties have adopted their anti-immigration stance and rhetoric. From the groups which emerged in the East End at the end of the nineteenth century until the present day British National Party (BNP), extremists have had as their primary concern, following the dominant xenophobic discourse, which they sometimes influence, a restriction, or reversal of immigration of the particular group entering Britain in the largest numbers. However, at other times, again mirroring the dominant racist discourse, they have concentrated upon the most threatening group such as the Germans during the First World War.[208]

The Orange Order may serve as one starting point in the history of the extreme right in Britain, but it differs from some of the later groupings because it was not as overtly political and counted the Protestant Irish as its main supporters.[209] The late nineteenth-century East End groups which emerged to oppose Jewish immigration serve as an alternative starting point to the series of parties which have objected to immigration. The first of these consisted of the Society for the Suppression of Destitute Aliens founded in 1886 and partly financed by Arnold White, but it had little impact. There then followed the Association for Preventing the Immigration of Destitute Aliens, which actually counted members of both Houses of Parliament in its ranks, but did not attract ordinary East Enders and also folded. The most significant anti-Jewish immigrant grouping before the First World War consisted of the British Brothers' League, established in 1901 under the leadership of Major William Evans-Gordon, Conservative MP for Stepney. It claimed to count 45,000 members and also organized meetings in Leicester, Kettering and Bedford. It succeeded in its aim of restricting

Jewish immigration from Eastern Europe and played some role, as an East End based pressure group with parliamentary support, in the introduction of the 1905 Aliens Act.[210]

During the First World War the radical right turned its attention to Germans in Britain. The major organizations included the British Empire Union, which may have counted 10,000 members by 1918 and aimed at 'the Extirpation – Root and Branch and Seed – of German Control and Influence from the British Empire'. Smaller pressure groups included the Anti-German League, the League of Londoners and the Britain for the British Movement. The Vigilantes and the National Party actually counted MPs and peddled a right-wing agenda in which Germanophobia formed just one element. These groups thrived in the nationalist atmosphere of the First World War and its immediate aftermath in which the mistreatment of ethnic minorities became government policy.[211]

With the rise of continental fascism a series of antisemitic pressure groups and parties surfaced in inter-war Britain. None of the British manifestations of this ideology came close to seizing power, in view of the long-term democratic traditions of Britain and the opposition which they faced from state forces.[212] Some remained pressure groups or minor political parties such as the early post-war Britons under the leadership of Henry Hamilton Beamish, who called for the extermination or expulsion of British Jews, as did the Imperial Fascist League under the leadership of Arnold Leese.[213] Such parties differed from the German National Socialists not in terms of ideology, but because they did not get into power.

The British Union of Fascists, founded by former Conservative, Labour and New Party MP Sir Oswald Mosley in 1932 became a full blown political party modelled on its continental counterparts with a paramilitary grouping, a corporatist ideology and a strong strand of antisemitism by the middle of the 1930s evident in both its newspaper, the *Blackshirt*, and its attacks on East End Jews. It may have counted a peak membership of 50,000 people but had little influence outside East London. Even here, it failed to have even one councillor elected. Nevertheless, it poisoned the political atmosphere in Britain, especially for East End Jews, and also caused the introduction of the Public Order Act in 1936 to control its activities on the streets. The BUF also received support from the *Daily Mail* until it became associated with violence from 1934. It had passed its peak by the outbreak of war in 1939 and would disappear when its leaders faced internment from 1940.[214]

However, Mosley underwent something of a reincarnation in the post-war period with the formation of the Union Movement in 1948, which, although initially antisemitic and East End based, became anti-Black and campaigned in areas with West Indian settlers during the 1950s including Brixton and Notting Hill, where its activities played a role in whipping up the local white population to participate in rioting in 1958. It had no concrete electoral success and had disappeared by the 1970s.[215]

The increasing focus of the extreme right upon settlers from beyond Europe became clear with the formation of the Birmingham Immigration Control Association in October 1960. This organized protest meetings, distributed leaflets, drew up petitions and wrote to the local press. Its members included Conservative councillors. Mainstream parties used its threat to pursue anti-immigration policies.[216] Miles and Phizacklea have written of a 'crucial interdependence between this association' and some Midlands MPs who 'could cite the association as evidence of "grassroots" opinion, while the association could attempt to realise its aim through political pressure on MPs'.[217] At the 1964 general election Peter Griffiths was elected Tory MP for Smethwick when some of his supporters openly used the slogan: 'If you want a nigger neighbour vote Labour'. This episode played a significant role in changing the Labour Party's attitude from one of opposing the Commonwealth Immigrants Act of 1962, to one that would accept immigration control as legitimate.[218] Racism in the Conservative Party reached a peak at the end of the 1960s when Enoch Powell spoke out against Commonwealth immigration especially in his so called 'rivers of blood' speech, the consequences of what he viewed as unrestricted immigration.[219]

Despite the introduction of new controls during the course of the 1960s and 1970s and the expulsion of Powell from the shadow cabinet, he had helped to give legitimacy[220] to a new extremist force in the form of the National Front. This group primarily focused upon Black and Asian immigrants, although it opposed what it saw as Jewish control and power. It claimed to have 13,000 members by the end of the 1970s, although the true figure probably lay closer to around 5,000. Its highest levels of electoral support occurred in wards with high immigration or areas which neighboured such locations in places such as Leicester, Hackney and Walthamstow. Nevertheless, like all of its predecessors after 1919, it had no concrete electoral success, even at a local council level.[221] It was the party of white racists protesting against immigration and the Labour Party. Its support declined after Margaret Thatcher came to power, having 're-established the Conservatives as the anti-immigration party'[222] following her statement on Granada Televison's *World in Action* programme on 30 January 1978 in which she declared sympathy with those who 'felt rather afraid that this country might be rather swamped by people with a different

FIGURE 16 A line of police officers walks alongside a National Front demonstration in London. Over 100,000 pro-fascist demonstrators from the National Front demonstrated in the streets of London to voice their frustration with the economic situation, blaming an influx of immigrants from southern Europe. London , September 1974. Image © Selwyn Tait/CORBIS SYGMA

culture'.[223] The rise of Thatcher did not, however, eliminate Britain's violent overtly Nazi underground in the form of Combat 18, which did not participate in the political process.[224]

Nevertheless, in 1993 something of a shockwave went through British politics, when, for the first time in over 70 years, a member of an overtly extreme right-wing group won a council seat on the Isle of Dogs in East London for the British National Party. In many senses this proved a false dawn, at least in the short run, but during the twenty-first century, the BNP has won council seats in a variety of locations including Dagenham, Burnley, Barking and Stoke on Trent, which can be seen as either 'white-flight' areas or, in the case of Stoke on Trent, a location with relatively little immigration. Despite its claim to respectability, it is essentially an anti-immigration party, emerging out of the racist National Front. The high profile of its leader, Nick Griffin, partly explains the level of its success, as does its campaigning on the ground in areas where it feels it can do well. At the same time, it made its breakthrough at a time of rising phobia of asylum seekers and Muslims, representing itself as the voice of the white working class. While the Conservative and Labour Parties may keep this group at a distance, its limited electoral success played some role in the anti-immigration rhetoric of both of these parties, especially the Conservatives, in the 2001 and 2005 general elections. The more electoral breakthroughs it makes, the more legitimate it appears, although it remains a long way from the success of similar parties in continental Europe.[225] The success at the 2009 European election may have represented a more significant breakthrough. The 943,598 votes the BNP gained, which meant the election of two MEPs (including Nick Griffin), was not far behind the Labour Party, which only obtained 2,381,760 votes.[226]

What consequences have racist attitudes had upon everyday relations between majorities and minorities in Britain? Two of the most obvious indications of racism in Britain consist of the labour and housing markets. In the short run at least, ethnic minorities tend to find themselves working in jobs at the bottom of the social scale, as British society designates such employment as suitable for them. They also, again initially at least, live in some of the worst available accommodation.[227] The most concrete manifestation of racism consists of violence, which has remained ever present in British society.

However, discrimination also manifests itself in numerous other ways, as studies of relations between the ethnic majority and Germans, Jews and West Indians illustrate. The level of Germanophobia in Britain during the First World War meant that hostility towards Germans emerged in all manner of ways. In 1914 representatives of fifty golf clubs met at the Golfers' Club in Whitehall Court to pass a resolution by a majority of 49 to 1 expelling German members. Stock exchanges and chambers of commerce throughout the country, including those in London, took similar action. German waiters also faced the sack, while, following the sinking of the *Lusitania* in May 1915, anti-German strikes occurred in firms which still employed Germans. Those Germans at the top end of society found that they lost many of their English friends as witch hunts of those with any German connections developed, spreading as far as the Royal Family, which changed its name from Saxe-Coburg to Windsor in 1917.[228]

Several scholars have examined social antisemitism in Britain from the end of the nineteenth century. Bernard Gainer demonstrated the all-pervasive hostility towards East End Jews upon their first settlement. Costermongers, for instance, faced animosity because of their perceived competition. Natives focused upon the sanitary habits, housing conditions, different appearance and food of the newcomers, all of which caused comment and hostility at the local level, partly because they differed from the norms of longer settled East Enders.[229] Colin Holmes also demonstrated antisemitism towards middle class Jews before the First World War illustrating how the 'race' of the historian Lewis Namier prevented him from obtaining a fellowship at All Souls College Oxford in 1911.[230]

During the inter-war years and into the Second World War Jews continued to experience social animosity facing exclusion from tennis clubs, golf clubs and motoring organizations, as well as continuing to face discrimination in employment, which, before the passage of race relations legislation could manifest itself in adverts which specifically excluded Jews.[231] Using Mass Observation surveys and diaries, Tony Kushner has demonstrated the range of antisemitic feeling in Britain during this period. A questionnaire from 1939 revealed responses varying from 'against antisemitism', 'mixed', 'slightly antisemitic' to 'definitely antisemitic'.[232] Kushner examined the diary of the vehemently antisemitic 51-year-old Mrs Grant writing during and immediately after the Second World War who could comment, upon learning of the existence of Nazi death camps in 1942 that 'the greedy Jews have brought it on themselves'.[233] Although this may represent the most extreme of antisemitic views, Jews continued to endure hostility during the war. Jewish children who faced evacuation, for instance, moved into areas with little experience of immigrants where some actually faced questions about whether they possessed horns. Some men's clubs continued to exclude Jewish members, while both public schools and golf clubs operated a *numerus clausus*.[234]

This sort of everyday antisemitism continued after the Second World War, albeit on a reduced scale. Public schools continued to operate restrictions upon Jewish children, while some Jews still found it difficult to gain membership in gentlemen's clubs.[235] 'Snobbish uppercrust antisemitism remained a pervasive irritant. In winebars, restaurants, common rooms, and city and country clubs, snide remarks and knowing looks communicated distaste for Jewish drive, separatism and success'.[236] Jews in Britain also came under attack from Palestinians, while the extreme right has desecrated Jewish headstones and graveyards.[237]

Although scholars of the Irish in Britain have written much about the inter-ethnic violence which characterized their lives during the nineteenth century, they have paid less attention to other aspects of everyday interaction. Donald MacRaild has written of workplace tensions, suggesting that Irish, Scots and English found it difficult to mix and would fight.[238] Several authorities have carried out research upon the everyday lives of the Irish since 1945. They have revealed employment and housing discrimination, especially in Scotland which has meant that the Irish endure greater health problems than society as a whole.[239] Most significantly, the survey carried out by Hickman and Walter on anti-Irish racism revealed the whole gamut of prejudice especially during times of heightened IRA activity, above all in the 1970s. This has included hostility from neighbours and the regular telling of Irish 'jokes' in their presence.[240]

While one aspect of everyday interethnic interaction of Black people (males in particular) consists of the high incidence of relationships with the opposite sex, the history of Black life in Britain has also consisted of racism, especially in terms of employment and educational prospects.[241] When dealing with the everyday of lives of Black people, we therefore need to bear in mind the range of positive and negative responses which have greeted them. At their most extreme, they have manifested themselves in violence and murder, partly because of resentment towards interracial relationships, especially in 1919 and 1958.[242] Behind these outbreaks of violence lies a whole range of other negative responses.

Although intermarriage helps to explain the disappearance of the Black slave community of the early nineteenth century, hostility towards this practice existed.[243] For much of the nineteenth century, when the numbers of Black people remained small, they faced a variety of reactions from the majority white population including hostility and fascination.[244] Animosity increased at the beginning of the twentieth century when a small growth in the number of Black workers occurred. One West Indian employed in Tilbury docks faced a strike, leading him to resign.[245] Such hostility would peak in the 1919 riots, as white soldiers and sailors returning from active service demanded their jobs back.[246]

Everyday animosity continued in the decades which followed. This manifested itself, for instance, in the dock areas where many Black people lived, backed up by the Coloured Seamen's Order passed in 1925.[247] Colin Holmes pointed to the existence of a colour bar during the inter-war years. For instance, 'by the 1930s the British Boxing Board of Control had decided no coloured man could box for a British title'. More ironically, the Black American actor Paul Robeson 'could play Othello' and 'crowds might pay to see Robeson on the stage' but 'the Savoy Grill could still refuse him admission to a party given in his honour'.[248]

This colour bar survived into the Second World War despite the arrival of hundreds of thousands of American and imperial troops. A survey carried out by the Society of Friends revealed that of 172 landladies they questioned 'there were only 40 who were prepared to accept a coloured visitor as a paying guest'.[249] This reflected discrimination in hotels and places of public entertainment, which affected all Black soldiers in Britain. The animosity toward American Blacks partly came from the presence of a Jim Crow Army, as White Americans would attack their Black counterparts if they strayed into areas where they socialized. Nevertheless, many British people reacted positively towards Black Americans, revealed most clearly in the fact that some women had relationships with them and would eventually marry them, although this caused official consternation.[250]

The West Indian immigrants who arrived in Britain from the late 1940s found themselves facing a range of negative reactions from the ethnic majority population. Michael Banton's study of attitudes towards Black and Asian people asserted that there 'is no apartheid, but neither is there complete acceptance'. Banton stressed the importance of social status, asserting that an Asian doctor did command respect.[251] Nevertheless, West Indians certainly encountered discrimination as stressed by Anthony Richmond.[252] Apart from the obvious area of the workplace and housing,[253] West Indians also experienced racism in social situations. George Powe, who settled in Nottingham, found himself excluded from three different pubs which essentially operated a colour bar.[254] Other organizations behaved in a similar manner including restaurants and even churches.[255] Surveys from the 1960s and 1970s continued to reveal the level of discrimination, which existed, especially amongst householders, employers, employees and landladies, which explains the passage of race relations legislation in an attempt to prevent racism in housing and employment.[256] As late as February 1964 over 100 lorry drivers went on strike in East London in protest at the recruitment of a Black person.[257] Nevertheless, we again need to beware of painting a picture of a blanket of racism. Anthony Richmond's study of race relations in Bristol during the 1960s demonstrated that while some white people felt hostility towards immigrants, especially when it came to issues such as welfare, a variety of personal factors determined individual levels of animosity.[258] Similarly, Daniel Lawrence, in his study of Nottingham published in 1974, suggested that only a small minority of white people in that city deserved the description of prejudiced. Again, he stressed housing and employment as the main areas of conflict.[259] The continued social deprivation experienced by many people of African Caribbean origin points to the survival of prejudice in Britain. Those who have written on minorities in the countryside have stressed the still widespread nature of hostility outside urban areas.[260] Similarly, social surveys have continued to demonstrate the prevalence of prejudiced attitudes amongst the population as a whole.[261]

Benjamin Bowling has described how racist violence became a public issue in the final few decades of the twentieth century. Not only do the police now record the number of racial attacks, legislation came into force in 1998 against 'racially aggravated offences'. Bowling points out that the number of 'recorded incidents' by police forces increased from 1,329 in

1984 to 12,199 by 1996. During the same period the number of police forces compiling such statistics grew from 15 to 43, which may not account for the whole increase, but public awareness and political pressure would further explain increased recording.[262]

The fact that police forces now record racial attacks does not mean that their occurrence has reached an all time high. In fact, since the early 1960s, one form of violent racism, the anti-immigrant riot, has disappeared. For many Irish males in Victorian Britain, fighting formed part of their everyday lives against the background of poverty, anti-Catholicism and hostility towards Irish nationalism. While the Irish were often victims, northern towns with large Irish populations experienced bouts of regular inter-ethnic conflict with native working class males often acting with Irish Protestants. Some incidents had particularly local factors which set them off such as the Stockport riot of 1852. The anti-Catholic speeches of the travelling Protestant preacher William Murphy also caused outbreaks of communal disorder during the course of the 1860s in cities throughout the Midlands and north of England including Wolverhampton, Birmingham and smaller locations. One of the last major anti-Irish riots occurred in 1882 when 160 houses faced destruction in Tredegar against the background of a local economic downturn and the Fenian murder of the Chief Secretary of Ireland in Dublin. However, communal violence continued in Glasgow and Liverpool after this time. At the same time Irish people faced attack in Birmingham in 1974 after the IRA pub bombs in that city, although they did not encounter the thousands of people who participated in many nineteenth-century incidents.[263]

In the decades leading up to the First World War the main victims of racist attacks consisted of Jews and the much smaller Chinese community. It seems likely that everyday violence of the type which has affected post-war Commonwealth immigrants occurred in areas such as the East End of London or the Leylands area of Leeds where immigrants settled, but relatively little information about it has emerged.[264] Two of the worst incidents of racist violence in Edwardian Britain occurred in South Wales. The Chinese became victims in Cardiff in July 1911, while Jews faced similar treatment in locations throughout South Wales in the following months. The background factors to these events included deep rooted animosity towards Jews and Chinese people and industrial unrest, which sucked these minorities in as scapegoats either as strike breakers in the case of the Chinese or as relatively wealthy in the case of some Jews.[265] Jews also faced attack in East London and Leeds during 1917 because some of their gentile neighbours believed that they did not carry out their fair share of fighting in the British armed forces, even though the reverse was true.[266]

The two most serious incidents of racist violence in modern Britain occurred during and just after the First World War when Germans and then Black people became victims. The few small scale isolated attacks which occurred against Germans in Britain during the Boer War[267] provided a foretaste of the events which would follow. While a few quite serious incidents occurred in the autumn of 1914, the week following the sinking of the *Lusitania* in May 1915 resulted in the most widespread riots in modern British history, when virtually every German owned shop in the country came under attack in actions involving thousands of people in many cases. These events took place against the background of Germanophobic hysteria and the riots represented one aspect of the ethnic cleansing which took place during the conflict.[268] In 1919 there followed attacks upon the Black communities of Britain which, while not as widespread as the anti-German riots, affected nine different urban locations. They took place against the background of the demobilization of white soldiers who believed that Black people had taken their jobs and women, while the background of killing during the Great War and underlying images of Black people also played a role.[269]

No full scale anti-immigrant riots appear to have taken place during the inter-war years. But with the rise of the British Union of Fascists antisemitic violence became part of the everyday lives of Jews in the East End of London during the course of the 1930s. By this time the increasingly established Jewish community fought back, symbolized in the Battle of Cable Street in 1936.[270] The Italian declaration of war on Britain in June 1940 did lead to riots, which, although not on the scale of those which affected Germans in the First World War, took place on a national level.[271]

While violence may have become a fact of life for many Black and Asian migrants in post-war Britain, the sort of rioting which affected the Irish, Germans and Black people before 1920 did not occur again. Some rioting has broken out, most notably in Nottingham and Notting Hill in 1958[272] and Middlesbrough in 1961.[273] More recently some small scale disorder has occurred against refugees seeking asylum.[274]

Although mass rioting against immigrants may have declined since the 1950s, numerous official and unofficial surveys have pointed to the fact that minorities regularly come under attack, symbolized in the murder of Stephen Lawrence in 1993. By 2004 police forces in Britain recorded 52,694 'racist incidents' varying from murders, of which 25 occurred between 1991 and 2005,[275] to verbal abuse and graffiti. While such incidents may represent the most obvious manifestations of racism, it seems unlikely that ethnic minorities endure more hostility today than they did at any time over the last two centuries, as the state simply did not record racist incidents against the Irish, for instance. The scale of incidents today may also reflect the higher percentage of ethnic minorities in British society.

Racist Britain

The fact that racist attacks occur at all indicates a deeper malaise in society, the pinnacle of racism. Although the decline of racist riots since the 1950s suggests a move away from an early stage of race relations, the attacks upon Germans in 1915 took place decades after the German community in Britain had established itself. But racist riots give way to other types of 'racial incidents' suggesting that racism has remained endemic in British state and society over the past two centuries.

Numerous indicators point to the existence of institutional xenophobia and racism, whether in the form of immigration and nationality laws, school curricula or policing. Similarly, the housing and employment situation of migrants and their offspring also suggest that racism remains potent. While racist parties have never gained power in Britain, mainstream groupings have not ignored their message because of the fear of losing small numbers of votes to them. Inter-ethnic interaction also points to the fact that many British people over the past two centuries have held prejudices and have sometimes attacked ethnic minorities. Underlying racial activism depends upon negative images: while the nationality or origin of the victims may change, the stereotypes remain similar.

Does Britain remain constantly racist or do peaks and troughs occur? To suggest constancy in any historical development seems to negate the purpose of examining any phenomenon over time. At no time over the past two hundred years has Britain remained free from racism and xenophobia, whether official or unofficial. Perhaps in the middle of the nineteenth century with the absence of immigration controls this may appear the case. But Roger Swift suggested biased policing against the Irish in the Victorian period, while anti-Irish riots were a feature of the nineteenth-century urban landscape. Popular hostility has also remained potent throughout the last two centuries manifested most clearly in violence, which virtually all migrants groups have experienced.

Some recent writing has suggested that Britain has entered a new era of racist intolerance, especially towards asylum seekers and Muslim populations. Some of the draconian legislation passed in recent years might support such assertions, comparable with the introduction of internment in the two World Wars, when Britain felt under threat from enemy attack. However, only during the First World War did Britain pursue the type of policies towards minorities which continental regimes implemented when it ethnically cleansed its German population.

While racism and xenophobia remain present throughout the last two centuries, they have reached peaks, notably during the two World Wars and, more recently, during the 'War on terror'. At the same time, new influxes of immigration lead to outbursts of hostility so that the press has regurgitated previously used images to try to stop new waves ranging from Eastern European and German Jews, and migrants from the Commonwealth, to refugees from Eastern Europe and Africa.

The experience of individual groups tends to change over time. Anti-semitism, while it may not have disappeared, has certainly declined in potency since the campaign for the Aliens Act of 1905 and the efforts of the BUF in the 1930s. The same applies to anti-Irish feeling. Yet on two occasions during the era of the First World War the racists succeeded in their aims of expelling the German and Black populations of Britain. Much research on post-war migrants from the Commonwealth stresses the continued survival of hostility towards them, although the introduction of race relations legislation has made some difference.

While official and unofficial racism remains a characteristic of British history over the past two hundred years, this only points to one side of autochthonous reactions to migrant communities. On the other hand, not only has integration taken place, indicated most clearly by intermarriage, but the country has also become increasingly multicultural whether measured in terms of official incorporation of ethnic minorities or through the transformation of Britain through immigration.

Notes and references

1 Kenneth Little, *Negroes in Britain* (London, 1948); Sheila Patterson, *Dark Strangers: A Sociological Study of the Absorption of a Recent West Indian Migrant Group in Brixton, South London* (London, 1963); Michael Banton, *The Coloured Quarter: Negro Immigrants in a British City* (London, 1955).

2 Anthony H. Richmond, *Migration and Race Relations in an English City: A Study in Bristol* (London, 1973).

3 Michael Banton, *Race Relations* (London, 1967); John Rex, *Race Relations in Sociological Theory* (London, 1970); E. J. B. Rose, et al., *Colour and Citizenship: A Report on British Race Relations* (Oxford, 1969).

4 The volumes of Robert Miles include: *Racism and Migrant Labour: A Critical Text* (London, 1982); and *Racism* (1989). The most important volume by John

Solomos is *Race and Racism in Modern Britain* (Basingstoke, 1993), which has gone through several editions and builds upon his *Black Youth, Racism and the State: The Politics of Ideology and Policy* (Cambridge, 1988).

5   See, for instance, Tariq Modood, *Multicultural Politics: Racism, Ethnicity and Muslims in Britain* (Edinburgh, 2005).

6   Little, *Negroes in Britain*.

7   Banton, *Coloured Quarter*.

8   Patterson, *Dark Strangers*.

9   John Rex and Robert Moore, *Race, Community and Conflict* (Oxford, 1967).

10   Richmond, *Migration and Race Relations*.

11   Daniel Lawrence, *Black Migrants, White Natives: A Study of Race Relations in Nottingham* (Cambridge, 1974).

12   Stephen Small, *Racialised Barriers: The Black Experience in the United States and England during the 1980s* (London, 1994).

13   Stephen Castles and Godula Kosack, *Immigrant Workers and Class Structure in Western Europe* (London, 1973); Stephen Castles, et al., eds, *Here for Good: Western Europe's New Ethnic Minorities* (London, 1984).

14   Stephen Castles and Mark J. Miller, *The Age of Migration: International Population Movements in the Modern World*, 3rd edn (Basingstoke, 2003).

15   Colin Holmes, *Anti-Semitism in British Society, 1876–1939* (London, 1979).

16   Most importantly: Tony Kushner, *The Persistence of Prejudice: Anti-Semitism in British Society during the Second World War* (Manchester, 1989); and Panikos Panayi, *The Enemy in Our Midst: Germans in Britain during the First World War* (Oxford, 1991).

17   Colin Holmes: *John Bull's Island: Immigration and British Society, 1871–1971* (Basingstoke, 1988); *A Tolerant Country? Immigrants, Refugees and Minorities in Britain* (London, 1991).

18   See Chapter 1.

19   Bernard Gainer, *The Alien Invasion: The Origins of the Aliens Act of 1905* (London, 1972).

20   Lloyd P. Gartner, *The Jewish Immigrant in England, 1870–1914* (London, 1960).

21   John A. Garrard, *The English and Immigration, 1880–1910* (London, 1971).

22   Gisela C. Lebzelter, *Political Antisemitism in England, 1918–1939* (New York, 1978).

23   John Denvir, *The Irish in Britain* (London, 1892); J. E. Handley, *The Irish in Scotland, 1798–1945* (Cork, 1943); and J. E. Handley, *The Irish in Modern Scotland* (Cork, 1947).

24   Walter L. Arnstein, 'The Murphy Riots: A Victorian Dilemna', *Victorian Studies*, vol. 19 (1975), pp. 51–71; *idem, Protestant Versus Catholic in Mid-Victorian Britain*

(London, 1982); Sheridan Gilley, 'The Garibaldi Riots of 1862', *Historical Journal*, vol. 16 (1973), pp. 697–732; *idem*, 'English Attitudes towards the Irish', in Colin Holmes, ed., *Immigrants and Minorities in British Society* (London, 1978), pp. 81–110; Tom Gallagher, *The Uneasy Peace: Religious Tension in Modern Glasgow, 1819–1940* (Manchester, 1987); Frank Neal, *Sectarian Violence: The Liverpool Experience, 1819–1914* (Manchester, 1988).

25   James Walvin, *Black and White: The Negro and English Society, 1555–1945* (London, 1973).

26   Peter Fryer, *Staying Power: The History of Black People in Britain* (London, 1984).

27   Christine Bolt, *Victorian Attitudes Towards Race* (London, 1971); Douglas Lorimer, *Colour Class and the Victorians: English Attitudes towards the Negro in the Mid-Nineteenth Century* (Leicester, 1978).

28   For the First World War see: Panayi, *Enemy*; J. C. Bird, *Control of Enemy Alien Civilians in Great Britain, 1914–1918* (London, 1986). The studies on the Second World War include: Peter and Leni Gillman, *'Collar the Lot': How Britain Interned and Expelled Its Wartime Refugees* (London, 1980); Miriam Kochan, *Britain's Internees in the Second World War* (London, 1983); and Ronald A. Stent, *Bespattered Page? The Internment of His Majesty's 'Most Loyal Enemy Aliens'* (London, 1980). Much of the work is summarized in David Cesarani and Tony Kushner, eds, *The Internment of Aliens in Twentieth Century Britain* (London, 1993).

29   For Italians see Lucio Sponza: *Italian Immigrants in Nineteenth Century Britain* (Leicester, 1988); 'The British Government and the Internment of Italians', in Cesarani and Kushner, ibid., pp. 125–44; and 'The Anti-Italian Riots, June 1940', in Panikos Panayi, ed., *Racial Violence in Britain in the Nineteenth and Twentieth Centuries* (London, 1996), pp. 131–49. See also Terri Colpi, 'The Impact of the Second World War on the British Italian Community', in Cesarani and Kushner, ibid., pp. 167–87.

30   Summarized in the contributions to Panayi, ibid.

31   Andreas Fahrmeier, *Citizens and Aliens: Foreigners and the Law in Britain and the German States, 1789–1870* (Oxford, 2000); Kathleen Paul, *Whitewashing Britain: Race and Citizenship in the Postwar Era* (Ithaca, NY, 1997); Ian R. G. Spencer, *British Immigration Policy: The Making of Multi-Racial Britain* (London, 1997).

32   See two books edited by Tony Kushner and Kenneth Lunn, *The Politics of Marginality: Race, the Radical Right and Minorities in Twentieth Century Britain* (London, 1990); and *Traditions of Intolerance* (Manchester: 1989). See also Kenneth Lunn, ed., *Hosts, Immigrants and Minorities: Historical Responses to Newcomers in British Society* (Folkestone, 1980); and Panikos Panayi, *Immigration, Ethnicity and Racism in Britain, 1815–1945* (Manchester, 1994).

33   Robert Winder, *Bloody Foreigners: The Story of Immigration to Britain* (London, 2004).

34 Tony Kushner and Katherine Knox, *Refugees in an Age of Genocide: Global, National and Local Perspectives During the Twentieth Century* (London, 1999); Tony Kushner, *We Europeans? Mass-Observation, 'Race' and British Identity in the Twentieth Century* (Aldershot, 2004).

35 Tony Kushner, *Remembering Refugees: Then and Now* (Manchester, 2006).

36 Holmes, *Tolerant Country?*, p. 110.

37 Solomos, *Race and Racism*; Robert Miles, *Racism After 'Race Relations'* (London, 1993); Zig Layton-Henry, *The Politics of Immigration* (Oxford, 1992), pp. 44–99.

38 See, for instance, Fryer, *Staying Power*; Bolt, *Victorian Attitudes Towards Race*; Lorimer, *Colour Class and the Victorians*.

39 Holmes, *Antisemitism*; George Mosse, *Toward the Final Solution: A History of European Racism* (New York, 1978), pp. 66–76.

40 Panayi, *Racial Violence*; Panayi, *Immigration, Ethnicity and Racism*.

41 See the classic Detlev J. K. Peukert, *Inside Nazi Germany: Conformity, Opposition and Racism in Everyday Life* (London, 1993). For a local case study see Panikos Panayi, 'Victims, Perpetrators and Bystanders in a German Town: The Jews of Osnabrück Before, During and After the Third Reich', *European History Quarterly*, vol. 33 (2003), pp. 451–92.

42 Lord Scarman, *The Scarman Report: The Brixton Disorders, 10–12 April 1981* (Harmondsworth, 1982).

43 Brian Cathcart, *The Case of Stephen Lawrence* (London, 1999); Sir William MacPherson, *The Stephen Lawrence Inquiry* (London, 1999).

44 See below.

45 Panayi, *Racial Violence*.

46 Thomas W. Perry, *Public Opinion, Propaganda and Politics in Eighteenth Century England: A Study of the Jew Bill of 1753* (Cambridge, MA, 1962).

47 See below.

48 See, for instance, John Stevenson, *Popular Disturbances in England, 1700–1870* (London, 1979); and Roland Quinault and John Stevenson, eds, *Popular Protest and Public Order: Six Studies in British History* (London, 1975).

49 Macpherson, *Stephen Lawrence Inquiry*, p. 321. See also Stuart Hall, 'From Scarman to Stephen Lawrence', *History Workshop Journal*, Issue 58 (1999), pp. 187–97.

50 Scarman, *Scarman Report*, pp. 79–119.

51 Paul Ward, *Britishness Since 1870* (London, 2004), p. 140.

52 Robert Colls, *Identity of England* (Oxford, 2002).

53 Paul Gilroy, *There Ain't No Black in the Union Jack* (London, 1987), pp. 72–113.

54 See Chapter 6.

55 Panayi, *Enemy in Our Midst*.

56 Cate Haste, *Keep the Home Fires Burning* (London, 1977); Gary S. Messinger, *British Propaganda and the State in the First World War* (Manchester, 1992).

57 Panayi, *Enemy in Our Midst*, pp. 153–83.

58 James Chapman, *The British at War: Cinema, State and Propaganda 1939–45* (London, 1998); Ian McLaine, *Ministry of Morale: Home Front Morale and the Ministry of Information in World War II* (London, 1979).

59 See below.

60 Mike Cole, ' "Brutal and Stinking": and "Difficult to Handle": The Historical and Contemporary Manifestations of Racialisation, Institutional Racism, and Schooling in Britain', *Race, Ethnicity and Education*, vol. 7 (2004), pp. 40–2; Jim English, 'Empire Day in Britain, 1904–1958', *Historical Journal*, vol. 49 (2006), pp. 247–76.

61 Hazel V. Carby, 'Schooling in Babylon', in Centre for Contemporary Cultural Studies, ed., *The Empire Strikes Back: Race and Racism in Contemporary Britain* (London, 1982), pp. 184–5.

62 Lorna Chessum, ' "Sit Down, You Haven't Reached that Stage Yet": African Caribbean Children in Leicester Schools, 1960–74', *History of Education*, vol. 26 (1997), pp. 412–15; Catherine Jones, *Immigration and Social Policy in Britain* (London, 1977), pp. 216–17; Bernard Coard, *How the West Indian Child is Made Educationally Subnormal in the British School System: The Scandal of the Black Child in Schools in Britain* (London, 1971), p. 13.

63 Coard, ibid., pp. 13–14.

64 Ethnic Communities Oral History Project, *The Motherland Calls: African Caribbean Experiences* (London, 1992), pp. 21–2.

65 David Gillborn, *Racism and Antiracism in Schools* (Buckingham, 2000), p. 101.

66 Coard, *West Indian Child*, pp. 18–22.

67 Chessum, ' "Sit Down" ', pp. 415–18.

68 Cole, ' "Brutal and Stinking" ', pp. 44–6; Modood, *Multicultural Politics*, p. 202; Small, *Racialised Barriers*, pp. 104–5; Tony Sewell, *Black Masculinities and Schooling: How Black Boys Survive Modern Schooling* (Stoke-on-Trent, 1997).

69 See Chapter 6.

70 Tony Kushner and Kenneth Lunn, 'Preface', in Kushner and Lunn, *Politics of Marginality*.

71 *The National Curriculum for England and Wales* (London, 1999).

72 Gillborn, *Racism and Antiracism*, p. 135.

73 See Chapter 3.

74 Jill Pellew, 'The Home Office and the Aliens Act, 1905', *Historical Journal*, vol. 32 (1989), p. 373; Vaughan Bevan, *The Development of British Immigration Law* (London, 1986), pp. 67–72.

75 Andreas Fahrmeier, *Citizens and Aliens: Foreigners and the Law in Britain and the German States, 1789–1870* (Oxford, 2000), pp. 43–52.

76 Rogers Brubaker, *Citizenship and Nationhood in France and Germany* (Cambridge, MA, 1992).

77 Panayi, *Enemy in Our Midst*, pp. 61–6; Bird, *Control of Enemy Alien Civilians*, pp. 235–62.

78 See Chapter 2.

79 Paul, *Whitewashing Britain*, p. 98.

80 Layton-Henry, *Politics of Immigration*, pp. 192–3.

81 Danièle Joly, *Haven or Hell? Asylum Policies and Refugees in Europe* (London, 1996), pp. 17–43.

82 Valerie Marett, *Immigrants Settling in the City* (Leicester, 1989), pp. 64–82; Robin Cohen, *Frontiers of Identity: The British and the Others* (Harlow, 1994), pp. 112–14; Kushner and Knox, *Refugees*, pp. 345–6; Derek McGhee, *Intolerant Britain: Hate, Citizenship and Difference* (Maidenhead, 2005), pp. 78–87; Arun Kundani, *The End of Tolerance: Racism in the 21st Century* (London, 2007), pp. 72–89; Rosemary Sales, 'The Deserving and the Undeserving? Refugees, Asylum Seekers and Welfare in Britain', *Critical Social Policy*, vol. 22 (2002), pp. 456–78.

83 Bernard Porter, *The Refugee Question in Mid-Victorian Politics* (Cambridge, 1979).

84 David Feldman, 'Migrants, Immigrants and Welfare from the Old Poor Law to the Welfare State', *Transactions of the Royal Historical Society*, sixth series, vol. 13 (2003), pp. 79–104.

85 Kushner and Knox, *Refugees*.

86 http://www.ukba.homeoffice.gov.uk/brtishcitizenship/applying/, Home Office, UK Border Agency, 'How I apply for British Citizenship?'

87 See James Hampshire, *Citizenship and Belonging: Immigration and the Politics of Demographic Governance in Post-war Britain* (Basingstoke, 2005).

88 Pellew, 'Home Office', p. 373.

89 Colin Holmes, 'The German Gypsy Question in Britain, 1904–1906', in Lunn, *Hosts, Immigrants and Minorities*, pp. 134–59.

90 Panayi, *Enemy*, p. 97.

91 See below.

92 Andrew Bell-Fialkoff, *Ethnic Cleansing* (Basingstoke, 1996).

93 Jacqueline Jenkinson, 'The 1919 Riots', in Panayi, *Racial Violence*, pp. 92–111.

94 Kushner and Knox, *Refugees*, pp. 62–3.

95 Tony Kushner and David Cesarani, 'Alien Internment in Britain during the Twentieth Century: An Introduction', in Cesarani and Kushner, *Internment of*

Aliens, pp. 1–11; Wendy Ugolini and Gavin Schaffer, 'Victims or Enemies? Italians, Refugee Jews and the Reworking of Internment Narratives in Post-war Britain', in M. Riera and Gavin Schaffer, eds, *The Lasting War: Society and Identity in Britain, France and Germany after 1945* (Basingstoke, 2008), pp. 207–25.

96 Repatriation in connection with internment receives attention in a series of publications including: Cesarani and Kushner, *Internment of Aliens*; Richard Dove, ed., *'Totally un-English?' Britain's Internment of 'Enemy Aliens' in Two World Wars* (Amsterdam, 2005), pp. 17–26; Gillman and Gillman, *'Collar the Lot'*; François Lafitte, *The Internment of Aliens* (London, 1988); and Kochan, *Britain's Internees*.

97 Robert Moore and Tina Wallace, *Slamming the Door: The Administration of Immigration Control* (London, 1975), pp. 57–106.

98 Joint Council for the Welfare of Immigrants, *Target Caribbean: The Rise in Visitor Refusals from the Caribbean* (London, 1990).

99 Cohen, *Frontiers*, pp. 126–7.

100 Bill Jordan and Franck Düvell, *Irregular Migration: The Dilemmas of Transnational Mobility* (Cheltenham, 2002), pp. 172–97.

101 Max Travers, *The British Immigration Courts: A Study of Law and Politics* (Bristol, 1999).

102 For individual cases see, for example, Jeremy Seabrook, *The Refuge and the Fortress: Britain and the Flight from Tyranny* (Basingstoke, 2009), pp. 203–25.

103 Roger Swift, 'Crime and the Irish in Nineteenth Century Britain', in Roger Swift and Sheridan Gilley, *The Irish in Britain, 1815–1939* (London, 1989), pp. 163–82.

104 Bernard Porter, *The Origins of the Vigilant State: The London Metropolitan Police Special Branch Before the First World War* (London, 1987), pp. 50–67.

105 Sponza, *Italian Immigrants*, p. 241.

106 J. J. Tobias, 'Police Immigrant Relations in England: 1880–1910', *New Community*, vol. 3 (1974), pp. 213–14.

107 *Daily Telegraph*, 11 February 1909.

108 Panayi, *Enemy*, pp. 223–58.

109 Jenkinson, '1919 Riots', pp. 98–102.

110 D. S. Lewis, *Illusions of Grandeur: Mosley, Fascism and British Society, 1931–81* (Manchester, 1987), p. 166; Richard Thurlow, 'Blaming the Blackshirts: The Authorities and the Anti-Jewish Disturbances of the 1930s', in Panayi, *Racial Violence*, p. 120.

111 Fryer, *Staying Power*, pp. 367–71; Anthony H. Richmond, *Colour Prejudice in Britain: A Study of West Indian Workers in Liverpool, 1941–51* (London, 1954), pp. 102–3.

112 Edward Pilkington, *Beyond the Mother Country: West Indians and the Notting Hill White Riots* (London, 1988), pp. 147–8.

113 Paul Gilroy, 'Police and Thieves', in Centre for Contemporary Cultural Studies, *Empire Strikes Back*, pp. 143–82.

114 Gilroy, ibid., p. 143; Solomos, *Race and Racism*, pp. 120–47; Michael Rowe, *The Racialization of Disorder in Twentieth Century Britain* (Aldershot, 1998), pp. 135–61; Joanna Rollo, 'The Special Patrol Group', in Peter Hain, Martin Kettle, Duncan Campbell and Joanna Rollo, eds, *Policing the Police*, vol. 2 (London, 1980), pp. 153–208; Scarman, *Scarman Report*; Stuart Hall, Chas Critcher, Tony Jefferson, John Clarke and Brian Roberts, *Policing the Crisis: Mugging, the State and Law and Order* (Basingstoke, 1978).

115 Quoted in Panikos Panayi, ed., *The Impact of Immigration: A Documentary History of the Effects and Experiences of Immigrants and Refugees in Britain Since 1945* (Manchester, 1999), p. 132.

116 Paul Gordon, *White Law: Racism in the Police, Courts and Prisons* (London, 1983), pp. 44–5.

117 Institute of Race Relations, *Deadly Silence: Black Deaths in Custody* (London, 1991), pp. 11–12.

118 Mary Hickman and Bronwen Walter, *Discrimination and the Irish Community in Britain* (London, 1997).

119 Catherine Scorer and Patricia Hewitt, *The Prevention of Terrorism Act: The Case for Repeal* (London, 1981).

120 Ronan Bennet, *Double Jeopardy: The Retrial of the Guildford Four* (London, 1993); Louis Bloom-Cooper, *The Birmingham Six and Other Cases: Victims of Circumstance* (London, 1997).

121 Jo Goodey, 'The Criminalization of British Asian Youth: Research from Bradford and Sheffield', *Journal of Youth Studies*, vol. 4 (2001), pp. 429–50.

122 Modood, *Multicultural Politics*, pp. 113–30; Kundani, *End of Tolerance*, pp. 169–70.

123 Bethnal Green and Stepney Trades Council, *Blood on the Streets* (London, 1978), pp. 7–9.

124 Benjamin Bowling, *Violent Racism: Victimization, Policing and Social Context*, Revised Edition (Oxford, 1999), pp. 235–6.

125 Cathcart, *Case of Stephen Lawrence*.

126 Gilroy, 'Police and Thieves', p. 159.

127 Central Office of Information, Ethnic Minorities (London, 1997), pp. 78–80.

128 Ellis Cashmore, 'The Experiences of Ethnic Minority Police Officers in Britain: Under-Recruitment and Racial Profiling in a Performance Culture', *Ethnic and Racial Studies*, vol. 24 (2001), p. 647.

129   Hickman and Walter, *Discrimination and the Irish Community*, p. 182.

130   Quoted in Gordon, *White Law*, p. 71.

131   Cashmore, 'Experiences of Ethnic Minority Police Officers', pp. 649–50.

132   National Association of Probation Officers and the Association of Black Probation Officers, *Race, Discrimination and the Criminal Justice System* (London, 1996), p. 2.

133   Gordon, *White Law*, pp. 85–116; Roger Hood, *Race and Sentencing: A Study in the Crown Court* (Oxford, 1992).

134   Panayi, *Enemy*, pp. 285–7; Cesarani and Kushner, *Internment of Aliens*.

135   Gillman and Gillman, 'Collar the Lot'; Kochan, *Britain's Internees*; Stent, *A Bespattered Page?*; Cesarani and Kushner, *Internment of Aliens*; Dove, 'Totally un-English?'; Lafitte, *Internment of Aliens*; Connery Chappell, *Island of Barbed Wire: Internment on the Isle of Man in The Second World War* (London, 1986).

136   Panayi, *Enemy*, pp. 70–149; Bird, *Control of Enemy Alien Civilians*; Stella Yarrow, 'The Impact of Hostility on Germans in Britain, 1914–1918', in Kushner and Lunn, *Politics of Marginality*, pp. 97–112; Stefan Manz, *Migranten und Internierte: Deutsche in Glasgow, 1864–1918* (Stuttgart, 2003), pp. 262–95.

137   See, for instance, Ruth Gay, *Safe Among the Germans: Liberated Jews After World War II* (London, 2002).

138   James J. and Patience P. Barnes, 'London's German Community in the Early 1930s', in Panikos Panayi, ed., *Germans in Britain since 1500* (London, 1996), pp. 131–46.

139   Graham A. Smith, *When Jim Crow Met John Bull: Black American Soldiers in World War II Britain* (London, 1987); David Reynolds, 'The Churchill Government and the Black American Troops in Britain During World War II', *Transactions of the Royal Historical Society*, Fifth series, vol. 35 (1984), pp. 113–33; Neil A. Wynn, ' "Race War": Black American GIs and West Indians in Britain during the Second World War', *Immigrants and Minorities*, vol. 24 (2006), pp. 324–46; Christopher Thorne, 'Britain and the Black GIs: Racial Issues and Anglo-American Relations in 1942', *New Community*, vol. 3 (1974), pp. 262–71.

140   Panikos Panayi, 'Dominant Societies and Minorities in the Two World Wars', in Panikos Panayi, ed., *Minorities in Wartime: National and Racial Groupings in Europe, North America and Australia during the Two World Wars* (Oxford, 1993), pp. 3–23.

141   Lorimer, *Colour Class and the Victorians*; Elazar Balkan, *The Retreat of Scientific Racism: Changing Concepts of Race In Britain and the United States between the World Wars* (Cambridge, 1992).

142   Gilroy, *There Ain't No Black*, pp. 43–71; Anne Marie Smith, *New Right Discourse on Race and Sexuality* (Cambridge, 1994).

143   See, for instance: Paul Hartmann and Charles Husband, *Racism and the Mass Media* (London, 1974); and Bryan Cheyette, *Constructions of 'the Jew' in English Literature and Society* (Cambridge, 1993).

144 Teun A. van Dijk, *Racism and the Press* (London, 1991).

145 John E. Richardson, *(Mis)Representing Islam: The Racism and Rhetoric of British Broadsheet Newspapers* (Amsterdam, 2004); Elizabeth Poole, *Reporting Islam: Media Representations of British Muslims* (London, 2002).

146 Kushner, *Remembering Refugees*, pp. 102–3, 192–3.

147 R. F. Foster, 'Paddy and Mr Punch', *Journal of Newspaper and Periodical History*, vol. 7 (1991), pp. 33–47.

148 Panayi, *Enemy*.

149 Linda Colley, *Britons: Forging the Nation, 1707–1837* (London, 1994), pp. 10–58.

150 George Rudé, 'The Gordon Riots: A Study of the Rioters and Their Victims', *Transactions of the Royal Historical Society*, Fifth series, vol. 6 (1956), pp. 93–114.

151 E. R. Norman, *Anti-Catholicism in Victorian England* (London, 1968), p. 16.

152 John Wolfe, *The Protestant Crusade in Great Britain, 1829–1860* (Oxford, 1991), p. 2.

153 Listed in ibid., pp. 318–19.

154 Arnstein, *Protestant Versus Catholic*, pp. 3–7.

155 Donald M. MacRaild, *Irish Migrants in Modern Britain, 1750–1922* (Basingstoke, 1999), pp. 169–94.

156 Arnstein, 'Murphy Riots'; Frank Neal, 'English-Irish Conflict in the North West of England: Economic, Racism, Anti-Catholicism or Xenophobia', *North West Labour History*, vol. 16 (1991–2), pp. 14–25; Bernard Aspinwall, 'Popery in Scotland: Image and Reality', *Records of the Scottish Church History Society*, vol. 22 (1986), pp. 235–57.

157 Frederick Engels, *The Condition of the Working-Class in London* (originally 1845; Moscow, 1973), pp. 129–33.

158 MacRaild, *Irish Migrants*, pp. 156–60.

159 Arnstein, *Protestant Versus Catholic*, p. 215; Norman, *Anti-Catholicism*, p. 20.

160 See two volumes by L. P. Curtis: *Anglo-Saxons and Celts* (New York, 1968); and *Apes and Angels: The Irishman in Victorian Caricature* (Newton Abbot, 1971). See also Foster, 'Paddy and Mr Punch'.

161 Enda Delaney, *The Irish in Post-war Britain* (Oxford, 2007), pp. 133–4. See also Chapter 4.

162 Hickman and Walter, *Discrimination and the Irish Community*, pp. 191–4; Christie Davis, 'The Irish Joke as a Social Phenomenon', in John Durant and Jonathan Miller, eds, *Laughing Matters: A Serious Look at Humour* (London, 1988), pp. 44–65.

163 Hickman and Walter, ibid., pp. 201–12.

164 Holmes, *Anti-Semitism*.

165 Edgar Rosenberg, *From Shylock to Svengali: Jewish Stereotypes in English Fiction* (Stanford, 1960).

166 Ibid., p. 262.

167 Nadia Valman, *The Jewess in Nineteenth Century British Culture* (Cambridge, 2007), p. 209.

168 John S. Galbraith, 'The Pamphlet Campaign in the Boer War', *Journal of Modern History*, vol. 24 (1952), pp. 120–1.

169 Colin Holmes, 'J. A. Hobson and the Jews', in Holmes, *Immigrants and Minorities*, pp. 125–57.

170 Holmes, *Antisemitism*, pp. 70–7; Cheyette, *Constructions*, pp. 150–205.

171 The campaign for the Aliens Act of 1905 is covered especially well by: Gainer, *Alien Invasion;* Gartner, *Jewish Immigrant in England*; and Garrard, *English and Immigration*. For the 1930s see, for instance: Andrew Sharf, *The British Press and the Jews under Nazi Rule* (Oxford, 1964), pp. 173–4; Paul Weindling, 'The Contribution of Central European Jews to Medical Science and Practice in Britain, the 1930s to the 1950s', in W. E. Mosse, et al., eds, *Second Chance: Two Centuries of German-Speaking Jews in the United Kingdom* (Tübingen, 1991), pp. 243–54.

172 Holmes, *Antisemitism*, pp. 36–48.

173 Ibid., p. 168; Lebzelter, *Political Antisemitism.*

174 Arnold White, *The Modern Jew* (London, 1899), p. xii.

175 Holmes, *Antisemitism*, pp. 122–40; Panayi, *Enemy*, pp. 30–2, 164–4, 175–6.

176 Holmes, ibid., pp. 141–74; Lebzelter, *Political Antisemitism*, pp. 13–28; Sharman Kadish, ' "Bolche, Bolshie and the Jewish Bogey": The Russian Revolution and Press Antisemitism', *Patterns of Prejudice*, vol. 22 (1988), pp. 24–39; Keith M. Wilson, '*The Protocols of Zion* and the *Morning Post*', *Patterns of Prejudice*, vol. 19, (1985), pp. 5–14.

177 Kushner, *Persistence of Prejudice*, pp. 78–105.

178 Tony Kushner, 'Antisemitism and Austerity: The August 1947 Riots in Britain', in Panayi, *Racial Violence*, pp. 150–70.

179 David Cesarani, *Justice Delayed: How Britain Became a Refuge for Nazi War Criminals* (London, 1992), pp. 77–80.

180 W. D. Rubinstein, *A History of the Jews in the English Speaking World: Great Britain* (Basingstoke, 1996), pp. 381–9; Todd M. Endelman, *The Jews of Britain, 1656–2000* (London, 2002), pp. 243–7; Brian Klug, 'Ritual Murmur: The Undercurrent of Protest Against Religious Slaughter of Animals in Britain in the 1980s', *Patterns of Prejudice*, vol. 23 (1991), pp. 16–28; Nigel Copsey, *Contemporary British Fascism: The British National Party and the Quest for Legitimacy* (Basingstoke, 2004), pp. 87–93.

181 Lucio Sponza, 'Italian Immigrants in Britain: Perceptions and Self-Perceptions', in Kathy Burrell and Panikos Panayi, eds, *Histories and Memories: Migrants and their History in Britain* (London, 2006), pp. 57–74; Wendy Ugolini, 'Communal Myths and Silenced Memories: The Unremembered Experience of Italians in Scotland During The Second World War' (University of Edinburgh Ph.D. thesis, 2006).

182 Sponza, *Italian Immigrants*, pp. 119–33.

183 Panikos Panayi, *German Immigrants in Britain during the Nineteenth Century, 1815–1914* (Oxford, 1995), pp. 201–51; Panayi, *Enemy*, pp. 153–83, 232–4; John Ramsden, *Don't Mention the War: The British and the Germans Since 1890* (London, 2006); Ruth Wittlinger, 'Perceptions of Germany and the Germans in Post-war Britain', *Journal of Multilingual and Multicultural Development*, vol. 25 (2004), pp. 453–65.

184 Walvin, *Black and White*, p. 11.

185 Lorimer, *Colour, Class and the Victorians*, pp. 69–91, 178–200; Bolt, *Victorian Attitudes to Race*, pp. 131–47; Barbara Bush, *Imperialism, Race and Resistance: Africa and Britain* (London, 1999).

186 Bolt, ibid., pp. 168–210; Frances M. Mannsaker, 'The Dog that Didn't Bark: The Subject Races at the Turn of the Century', in David Dabydeen, ed., *The Black Presence in English Literature* (Manchester, 1985), pp. 114–19; Durba Ghosh, *Sex and the Family in Colonial India: The Making of Empire* (Cambridge, 2006).

187 Urmilla Seshagiri, 'Modernity's (Yellow) Perils: Dr Fu-Manchu and English Race Paranoia', *Cultural Critique*, vol. 62 (2006), pp. 162–94; Toshio Yokoyama, *Japan in the Victorian Mind* (London, 1987); Colin Holmes and A. H. Ion, 'Bushidō and the Samurai: Images in British Public Opinion, 1894–1914', *Modern Asian Studies*, vol. 14 (1980), pp. 309–329.

188 See, for instance, Reginald Horsman, 'Origins of Racial Anglo-Saxonism in Great Britain before 1850', *Journal of the History of Ideas*, vol. 37 (1976), pp. 387–410.

189 The development of pseudo-scientific racism in Britain during the nineteenth century can be traced in the following works: Ronald Rainger, 'Race, Politics and Science: The Anthropological Society of London in the 1860s', *Victorian Studies*, vol. 22 (1978), pp. 51–70; Michael Banton, *Racial Theories*, 2nd edn (Cambridge, 1998), pp. 1–116; Michael Biddis, *Images of Race* (Leicester, 1979); and Mosse, *Towards the Final Solution*, pp. 66–76.

190 Joseph Salter, *The Asiatic in England: Sketches of Sixteen Years Work Among Orientals* (London, 1873); Rosina Visram, *Asians in Britain: 400 Years of History* (London, 2002), pp. 67–8; Michael H. Fisher, *Counterflows to Colonialism: Indian Travellers and Settlers in Britain, 1600–1857* (Delhi, 2004), pp. 383–92.

191 Lorimer, *Colour, Class and the Victorians*, pp. 21–44; George F. Rehin, 'Blackface Street Minstrels in Victorian London and its Resorts: Popular Culture and its

Racial Connotations as Revealed in Polite Opinion', *Journal of Popular Culture*, vol. 15 (1981), pp. 19–38.

192 Jenkinson, '1919 Riots', pp. 108–10; Fryer, *Staying Power*, pp. 306–13.

193 Paul B. Rich, *Race and Empire in British Politics*, 2nd edn (Cambridge, 1990), pp. 120–44.

194 Paul B. Rich, 'Doctrines of Racial Segregation in Britain: 1900–1945', *New Community*, vol. 12 (1984–5), pp. 75–88.

195 Seshagiri, 'Modernity's (Yellow) Perils'; J. P. May, 'The Chinese in Britain', in Holmes, *Immigrants and Minorities*, pp. 111–25; P. J. Waller, 'The Chinese', *History Today*, vol. 35 (September 1985), pp. 8–15; Marek Kohn, *Dope Girls: The Birth of the British Drug Underground* (London, 1992), pp. 57–66; Joanne M. Cayford, 'In Search of "John Chinaman": Press Representations of the Chinese in Cardiff, 1906–1911', *Llafur*, vol. 5, no. 4 (1991), pp. 37–50; Michael Diamond, *Lesser Breeds: Racial Attitudes in Popular British Culture, 1890–1940* (London, 2006), pp. 11–60.

196 Lorna Chessum, 'Race and Immigration in the Local Leicester Press, 1945–62', *Immigrants and Minorities*, vol. 17 (1998), pp. 36–56.

197 Robert Miles and Annie Phizacklea, *White Man's Country: Racism in British Politics* (London, 1984), pp. 20–44; Robert Miles, 'The Riots of 1958: The Ideological Construction of Race Relations as a Political Force in Britain', *Immigrants and Minorities*, vol. 3 (1984), pp. 252–75.

198 See, for instance, Van Dijk, *Racism and the Press*; Hartmann and Husband, *Racism and the Mass Media*, pp. 127–31.

199 Marett, *Immigrants Settling in the City*, pp. 51–3.

200 Kushner, *Remembering Refugees*, pp. 181–212.

201 Gilroy, *There Ain't No Black*, pp. 72–113.

202 Barry Troyna, 'Reporting Racism: The "British Way of Life" Observed', in Charles Husband, ed., *'Race' in Britain: Continuity and Change* (London, 1987), pp. 286–8; Ray Honeyford, *The Commission for Racial Equality: British Bureaucracy and the Multicultural Society* (London, 1998).

203 See, for instance, Paul B. Rich, 'Conservative Ideology and Race in Modern British Politics', in Zig Layton-Henry and Paul B. Rich, eds, *Race, Government and Politics in Britain* (Basingstoke, 1986), pp. 45–72; Andy R. Brown, *Political Languages of Race and the Politics of Exclusion* (Aldershot, 1999).

204 Richardson, *(Mis)Representing Islam*, pp. 5–19; Poole, *Reporting Islam*, pp. 28–32.

205 Richardson, ibid., pp. 155–90; Kundani, *End of Tolerance*, pp. 90–105; David Miller, 'Propaganda and the "Terror Threat" in the UK', in Elizabeth Poole and John E. Richardson, eds, *Muslims and the News Media* (London, 2006), pp. 45–52.

206 Poole, *Reporting Islam*, pp. 101–87.

207 Nasar Meer and Tahseen Noorani, 'A Sociological Comparison of Antisemitism and anti-Muslim Sentiment in Britain', *Sociological Review*, vol. 56 (2008), pp. 195–219.

208 Studies which look at the extreme right in Britain over a long period include: Richard Thurlow, *Fascism in Britain* (Oxford, 1987); and Christopher T. Husbands, 'East End Racism, 1900–1980: Geographical Continuities in Vigilantist and Extreme Right-wing Political Behaviour', *London Journal*, vol. 8 (1982), pp. 3–26.

209 See Chapter 4.

210 Husbands, ibid., pp. 7–12; Gainer, *Alien Invasion*, pp. 60–4, 67–73; Holmes, *Antisemitism*, pp. 89–97.

211 Panayi, *Enemy*, pp. 212–15; W. D. Rubinstein, 'Henry Page Croft and the National Party, 1917–22', *Journal of Contemporary History*, vol. 9 (1974), pp. 129–48; G. R. Searle, *Corruption in British Politics, 1895–1930* (Oxford, 1987), pp. 255–68.

212 Mike Cronin, ed., *The Failure of British Fascism: The Far Right and the Fight for Political Recognition* (Basingstoke, 1996); Richard Thurlow, 'The Failure of British Fascism', in Andrew Thorpe, ed., *The Failure of Political Extremism in Inter-war Britain* (Exeter, 1989), pp. 67–84.

213 Holmes, *Antisemitism*, pp. 141–74; Lebzelter, *Political Antisemitism*, pp. 49–85; Thurlow, *Fascism in Britain*, pp. 62–91.

214 There is now a large literature on the history and memory of the BUF including: Robert Benewick, *The Fascist Movement in Britain* (London, 1972); Colin Cross *The Fascists in Britain* (London, 1961); Tony Kushner and Nadia Valman, eds, *Remembering Cable Street: Fascism and Anti-Fascism in British Society* (London, 2000); Kenneth Lunn and Richard Thurlow, eds, *British Fascism: Essays on the Radical Right in Inter-war Britain* (London, 1980); Martin Pugh, *Hurrah for the Blackshirts!: Fascists and Fascism in Britain Between the Wars* (London, 2005); W. F. Mandle, *Antisemitism and the British Union of Fascists* (London, 1968); Lewis, *Illusions of Grandeur*; Thomas P. Linehan, *British Fascism, 1918–1939: Parties, Ideology and Culture* (Manchester, 2000).

215 Husbands, 'East End Racism', pp. 14–15; Thurlow, *Fascism in Britain*, pp. 243–7.

216 Paul Foot, *Immigration and Race in British Politics* (Harmondsworth, 1965), pp. 195–215.

217 Miles and Phizacklea, *White Man's Country*, pp. 38–9.

218 Holmes, *Tolerant Country*, pp. 56–7; Nicholas Deakin, ed., *Colour and the British Electorate: Six Case Studies* (London, 1965); Brown, *Political Languages*.

219 Layton-Henry, *Politics of Immigration*, pp. 79–83; Nicholas Hillman, 'A Chorus of "Execration"? Enoch Powell's "Rivers of Blood" Forty Years On', *Patterns of Prejudice*, vol. 42 (2008), pp. 83–104.

220   Anthony M. Messina, *Race and Party Competition in Britain* (Oxford, 1989), pp. 104–9.

221   Stan Taylor, *The National Front in English Politics* (London, 1982); Christopher T. Husbands, *Racial Exclusionism and the City: The Urban Support of the National Front* (London, 1983); Michael Billig, *Fascists: A Social Psychological Profile of the National Front* (London, 1978).

222   Layton-Henry, *Politics of Immigration*, p. 184.

223   Quoted in ibid.

224   Gerry Gable, 'Britain's Nazi Underground', in Luciano Cheles, Ronnie Ferguson and Michalina Vaughan, eds, *The Far Right in Western and Eastern Europe*, 2nd edn (London, 1995), pp. 258–271.

225   Copsey, *Contemporary British Fascism*; Matthew J. Goodwin, 'The Extreme Right in Britain: Still an "Ugly Duckling" but for How Long?', *Political Quarterly*, vol. 78 (2007), pp. 241–50.

226   http://news.bbc.co.uk/1/shared/bsp/hi/elections/euro/09/html/ukregion_999999.stm

227   See Chapter 3.

228   Panayi, *Enemy*, pp. 184–222.

229   Gainer, *Alien Invasion*, pp. 36–52.

230   Holmes, *Anti-Semitism*, p. 110.

231   Ibid., pp. 203–19.

232   Kushner, *We Europeans?*, p. 109.

233   Ibid., p. 172.

234   Kushner, *Persistence of Prejudice*, pp. 48–105.

235   Rubinstein, *History of the Jews*, p. 385.

236   Endelman, *Jews of Britain*, p. 245.

237   Rubinstein, *History of the Jews*, p. 385.

238   MacRaild, *Irish Migrants*, pp. 165–9.

239   Patricia Wells and Rory Williams, 'Sectarianism at Work: Accounts of Employment Discrimination Against Irish Catholics in Scotland', *Ethnic and Racial Studies*, vol. 26 (2003), pp. 632–62; Martin Mac an Ghaill, 'The Irish in Britain: The Invisibility of Ethnicity and Anti-Irish Racism', *Journal of Ethnic and Migration Studies*, vol. 26 (2000), p. 143.

240   Hickman and Walter, *Discrimination and the Irish Community*, pp. 180–221.

241   See Chapter 3.

242   See below.

243   Fryer, *Staying Power*, pp. 234–6.

244   Walvin, *Black and White*, pp. 189–99.

245   Ibid., p. 203.

246   See below.

247   Little, *Negroes in Britain*, pp. 55–107.

248   Holmes, *John Bull's Island*, p. 153.

249   Harold Moody, *The Colour Bar* (London, 1944), p. 3.

250   John Flint, 'Scandal at the Bristol Hotel: Some Thoughts on Racial Discrimination in Britain and West Africa and its Relationship to the Planning of Decolonization, 1939–47', *Journal of Imperial and Commonwealth History*, vol. 12 (1983), pp. 77–9; Smith, *When Jim Crow Met John Bull*.

251   Michael Banton, *White and Coloured: The Behaviour of British People Towards Coloured Immigrants* (London, 1959), pp. 120, 181.

252   Anthony H. Richmond, *The Colour Problem* (Harmondsworth, 1965), pp. 248–56.

253   See Chapter 3.

254   Pilkington, *Beyond the Mother Country*, p. 45.

255   See the documents quoted in Panayi, *Impact of Immigration*, pp. 131–3.

256   Clifford S. Hill, *How Colour Prejudiced is Britain?* (London, 1971); W. W. Daniel, *Racial Discrimination in England* (Harmondsworth, 1968).

257   Dilip Hiro, *Black British White British* (London, 1971), p. 245.

258   Richmond, *Migration and Race Relations*, pp. 211–38.

259   Lawrence, *Black Migrants, White Natives*.

260   See contributions to Neil Chakraborti and Jon Garland, eds, *Rural Racism* (Cullompton, 2004).

261   See, for instance, Richard Skellington, *'Race' in Britain Today*, 2nd edn (London, 1996), pp. 232–4.

262   Bill Dixon and David Gadd, 'Getting the Message?: "New" Labour and the Criminalization of "Hate"', *Criminology and Criminal Justice*, vol. 6 (2001), pp. 309–28; P. Iganski, 'Why Make "Hate" a Crime?', *Critical Social Policy*, vol. 19 (1999), pp. 386–95; Bowling, *Violent Racism*, p. 6.

263   Alan O'Day, 'Varieties of Anti-Irish Behaviour in Britain, 1846–1922', in Panayi, *Racial Violence*, pp. 26–43; Arnstein, 'Murphy Riots'; Gilley, 'Garibaldi Riots'; Gallagher, *Uneasy Peace*; Neal, *Sectarian Violence*; Pauline Millward, 'The Stockport Riots of 1852: A Study of Anti-Catholic and Anti-Irish Sentiment', in Roger Swift and Sheridan Gilley, eds, *The Irish in the Victorian City* (London, 1985), pp. 207–24; Roger Swift, ' "Another Stafford Street Row": Law, Order and the Irish Presence in Mid-Victorian Wolverhampton', *Midland History*, vol. 9 (1984), pp. 87–108; Jon Parry, 'The Tredegar Anti-Irish Riots of 1882', *Llafur*, vol. 3 (1983), pp. 20–3; John Bohstedt, 'More than One Working Class:

Protestant-Catholic Riots in Edwardian Liverpool', in John Belchem, ed., *Popular Politics, Riot and Labour: Essays in Liverpool History, 1790–1940* (Liverpool, 1992), pp. 173–216; Paul O'Leary, 'Anti-Irish Riots in Wales, 1826–1882', *Llafur*, vol. 5 (1991), pp. 27–36; Panayi, *Impact of Immigration*, pp. 146–8.

264   Panikos Panayi, 'Anti-Immigrant Riots in Nineteenth and Twentieth Century Britain', in Panayi, *Racial Violence*, p. 10.

265   Geoffrey Alderman, 'The Anti-Jewish Riots of August 1911 in South Wales', *Welsh History Review*, vol. 6 (1972), pp. 190–200; Colin Holmes, 'The Tredegar Riots of 1911: Anti-Jewish Disturbances in South Wales', *Welsh History Review*, vol. 11 (1982), pp. 214–25; May, 'Chinese in Britain'; Waller, 'Chinese'.

266   Holmes, *Antisemitism*, pp. 128–37.

267   Panayi, *German Immigrants*, pp. 235–6.

268   Panayi, *Enemy*, pp. 223–58; Nicoletta F. Gullace, 'Friends, Aliens and Enemies: Fictive Communities and the Lusitania Riots of 1915', *Journal of Social History*, vol. 39 (2005), pp. 345–67.

269   Jenkinson, '1919 Riots'.

270   See, for instance, Kushner and Valman, *Remembering Cable Street*; Mandle, *Antisemitism and the British Union of Fascists*; Lewis, *Illusions of Grandeur*, pp. 89–143; Holmes, *Antisemitism*, pp. 191–202.

271   Sponza, 'Anti-Italian Riots'.

272   Pilkington, *Beyond the Mother Country*.

273   Panikos Panayi, 'Middlesbrough 1961: A British Race Riot of the 1960s?', *Social History*, vol. 16 (1991), pp. 139–53.

274   Ralph Grillo, ' "Saltdean Can't Cope": Protests Against Asylum Seekers in an English Seaside Suburb', *Ethnic and Racial Studies*, vol. 28 (2005), pp. 235–60.

275   Diane Frost, 'The "Enemy Within"? Asylum, Racial Violence and "Race Hate" in Britain Today', *21st Century Society*, vol. 2 (2007), pp. 227–48.

CHAPTER 6

The evolution of multiculturalism

Multicultural definitions

By the end of the 1980s a new phrase had emerged to describe the relationship between the ethnic majority and ethnic minorities in Britain, especially those originating in South Asia and the Caribbean. Multiculturalism (or multiracialism or multi-ethnicity) had increasingly come to replace the concept of race relations. Implicit within this new terminology lay the idea that the migrants of the early post-war years had escaped from a life of endemic discrimination. In the new order, equality, at least of opportunity, had arrived between Blacks, Asians and Whites. At the same time, Britain had moved away from the monoculture which had characterized the early post-war years of austerity especially in areas such as food, popular culture and sport, to a richer and more varied society influenced by migrants and their descendants. People from ethnic minorities could now celebrate their own backgrounds in a situation in which diversity became the norm.

This rather simplistic summary of the evolution of multiculturalism, perpetuated in media and official circles, has a series of flaws. In the first place, it lacks historical context. The volume written by Mike and Trevor Phillips entitled *Windrush* and carrying the subtitle of *The Irresistible Rise of Multi-Racial Britain* illustrates this point. The Phillips brothers write about the growth of the West Indian community in Britain, beginning with the arrival of the *Empire Windrush* in Tilbury in 1948. For them, the previous history of immigration of other groups to Britain seems unimportant.[1] Similarly, although Yasmin Alibhai-Brown and Bikhu Parekh recognize that immigration occurred into Britain before 1945, they do not go back into the nineteenth century or before, either because of their own ethnicities and experiences, as Asians settling in Britain in the second half of the twentieth century, or because they are not historians. When they do venture into the past, they tend to focus upon the history of Black and Asian migration to Britain. Alibhai-Brown appreciates that the ethnically White population does have diversity including 'Irish, Italian, Polish, Spanish, Jewish, English, Scots, Welsh and many other groups', but does not investigate this. Her chapter in *Who Do We Think We Are?* entitled 'Long in the Root', tackles the history of Black people in Britain, despite the tiny numbers involved in comparison with the hundreds of thousands of Jews and millions of Irish who made their way to Britain before 1945.[2] Similarly, Parekh's report on the *The Future of Multi-Ethnic Britain* asks us to rethink the national story, but this does not involve tracing the history of immigration to Britain before 1945, although the report does recognize that the multi-ethnic nature of the country involves recognition of a variety of white groups, including Irish and Jewish people.[3] Meanwhile, those scholars who have worked on the history of the structural foundations of multiculturalism, in the form of nationality laws and the passage of race relations legislation, have also focused upon the period after the Second World War. Thus we can point to the example of Adrian Favell who, however, takes a highly critical view of the concept of multi-culturalism.[4] Randell Hansen, who sets out to trace the development of multicultural Britain, also focuses upon the post-war period.[5]

This focus upon the years since 1945 ignores the mass migration which occurred to Britain before then. Most writers on multiculturalism have limited historical background and do not relate it to revolutionary develop-ments either in the scale of migration or in the introduction of legislation before 1945. This lack of historical grounding ignores continuities. The scale of migration may have increased after 1945 but it occurred on a significant level before the Second World War, which means that ethnic and cultural diversity in Britain has a long history. Migrant enclaves and the importation and celebration of new religions, for instance, remain similar before and after 1945. At the same time, migrants also had an influence upon British culture from the nineteenth century whether measured in terms of food, music or business. While the scale of migration after 1945 means that this impact may have become greater, it builds upon patterns well established in the Victorian period. Furthermore, the institutional origins of multi-culturalism do not begin with the passage of the 1948 British Nationality Act as asserted by Hansen,[6] or with the Race Relations legislation of the 1960s and 1970s, which scholars such as Harry Goulbourne have stressed.[7] Andreas Fahrmeier demonstrated the inclusive nature of British nationality law before the First World War from the point of view of its use of *jus solis* and its incorporation of imperial citizens.[8] Without wishing to become an advocate of the Whig interpretation of history,[9] we might suggest that the origins of multicultural Britain begin not in 1948 or some time during the 1960s, but, instead, with the Catholic Relief Act of 1829, which granted Roman Catholics equal rights to Protestants, a step more revolutionary than any of the legislation passed since 1945. This process continued with Jewish emancipation during the Victorian period, which, in view of the history of antisemitism and its consequences in previous British history, also represents dramatic progress. Thus, we need to place the changes which have occurred after 1945 within the institutional and structural developments which took place during the nineteenth century. Unlike Germany, Great Britain did not have a *Sonderweg*, whereby it took the peculiar path of fascism.[10] Instead, while it may have experienced periods of intolerance such as the First World War and the 'War against terror', the rights of minorities have improved significantly and gradually since the beginning of the nineteenth century through a series of stages from the granting of equal rights and citizenship to an attempt to outlaw racial discrimination.

However, before we hurtle at high speed towards the acceptance of the idea of Britain evolving gradually, steadily and surely into a multicultural paradise, we need to press the brakes fairly firmly and remember the realities of racism in everyday life throughout the last two hundred years. Philip Cohen wrote about the 'multicultural illusion' in which the 'dominant and subordinate . . . somehow swap places and learn how the other half lives, while leaving the structures of power intact'.[11] More recently, Graham Huggan has written about 'virtual multiculturalism'. He examined the Stephen Lawrence case which 'effectively made nonsense of the reconciliatory rhetoric of multiculturalism, appearing to confirm the inequality of Britain's minority citizens before the law'.[12] Despite the stream of legislation which has tried to address the problem of ethnic and racial inequalities from the Catholic Relief Act of 1829 to the Human Rights Act of 1998, ethnic minorities usually remain marginalized in political and economic terms, at least in the short term. Writers such as Parekh and Alibhai-Brown stress the ethnic inequalities which exist in post-imperial multicultural Britain, while trying to point to the reality of demographic and cultural change since the end of Empire.[13] While Black sportsmen may have helped to transform the nature of British sport and while Bangladeshi immigrants have changed eating patterns,[14] this does not alter the fact that the majority of African-Caribbeans and Bangladeshis remain relatively underprivileged decades after the arrival of the pioneer members of these communities. This public face of ethnic minorities compared with the reality of the rest of their communities also represents part of the multicultural illusion. Economic and political success may come over a longer period of time, as the example of the late Victorian and Edwardian Jewish influx would suggest. A hundred years later their descendants have achieved cultural, economic and political power. It seems likely that by the middle of the twenty-first century the descendants of many of the original imperial and commonwealth immigrants entering in the decades following the Second World War will become central in British life. In fact, Commonwealth immigrants immediately had the potential for political power, especially when contrasted with people from other European states, because of nationality laws. They could automatically participate in elections because they possessed British nationality. At the same time, the principle of *jus solis* has meant that, even if the first generation has not possessed voting rights, the second generation has. Furthermore, the Irish could always vote both before and after 1921. In the British constituency based electoral system, ethnic minorities can control seats in which they find themselves concentrated from the late nineteenth-century Irish to contemporary South Asians.

However, this may lead to further problems connected with multi-culturalism: it creates and perpetuates difference. This assertion appears to become particularly salient when dealing with state sponsored multi-culturalism such as support for community histories or public events such as carnivals. The emergence of Black History Month in recent years creates a multicultural space in which minorities have their day but might not interact with the mainstream.[15] Varun Uberoi argues that multiculturalism prevents social unity because each group pursues its own individual interest at the expense of the greater national good. He suggests that the way forward lies in a British multicultural identity.[16] Adrian Favell has suggested that the emergence of multicultural Britain based on the interests of imperial migrants has made the country less responsive to refugees and new economic migrants from Europe.[17] These assertions return to the argument that multiculturalism has not eliminated racism not only towards Blacks and Asians but also Eastern Europeans and refugees from beyond Europe. Uberoi and Favell object to state sponsored multiculturalism. However, taking a historical perspective on Britain over the last two hundred years, we realize that change takes place over time. We can again return to the educated and integrated Jewish community of the late twentieth century, which differs completely from its ghettoized Victorian and Edwardian incarnation. Furthermore, members of ethnic communities do not remain fixed, but have a series of identities.[18]

Britain has therefore not moved from tyranny in the early nineteenth century or racism in the middle of the twentieth to become a multicultural paradise by the beginning of the twenty-first. The multicultural illusion which suggests that this has happened needs serious challenging. At the same, however, community initiatives supported by the state do not mean that all members of a particular ethnic group remain unchanging any more than they have done at any other stage over the past two hundred years.

While racism has characterized Britain since the early nineteenth century, discrimination and persecution have formed just one aspect of minority experiences. We can measure the evolution of multicultural Britain in three ways. First, the passage of legislation, from the Catholic Relief Act of 1829, through the emancipation of the Jews in the Victorian period, to the Race Relations Acts of the 1960s and 1970s. The nature of British nationality incorporating people from the Empire and operating upon the principle of *jus solis* has played a major role in the evolution of multiculturalism. Second, we also need to consider the positive ways in which native Britons have interacted with immigrants and refugees. The most obvious example consists of the high incidence of interethnic relationships and marriages, even though these have often led to tensions from those who disapprove of them. Interethnic friendships also represent normality, especially in the inner city. Furthermore, while most immigrant and refugee groups have faced a chorus of disapproval from the press in particular, they have also received assistance from both the state and individual support groups, particularly in the case of refugees. Finally, we also need to consider the impact of immigration both before and after 1945. While the changes which have occurred since the Second World War seem indisputable, whether measured in terms of sport, dress, popular culture or food, migrants also had a significant impact from the Victorian period.

The legal basis of multiculturalism

At the beginning of the nineteenth century civil and political rights remained restricted to men of landed property. The democratization of Britain over the following century involved not simply the granting of the vote to the working classes and to women, but also the emancipation of the two longstanding ethnic minorities in the form of Roman Catholics and Jews.[19] Developments in Britain need contextualization against the European background inspired by the Enlightenment and the French Revolution which meant that, from the end of the eighteenth century, the rights of Jews in particular became a especially important aspect of the spread of liberal ideas.[20]

At the start of the nineteenth century the main minority in Britain consisted of Roman Catholics, deprived of civil rights, and facing persecution
since the Reformation. While they made up a minority of the mainland before
1801, they formed sixth sevenths of the population of Ireland following
the 1801 Act of Union.[21] Emancipation meant 'release not only from legal
restrictions on their political participation and liturgical activities but also, to
a large extent, from unofficial social discrimination'.[22] Some improvement
had taken place in the position of Roman Catholics as a result of legislation
passed in 1778 and 1791. The former allowed them to inherit property,
while the latter meant that they could legally practise their religion. But
they remained second class citizens and could not, for instance, hold high
office or become members of Parliament. In addition, they could not build
churches with spires and priests faced prosecution if caught wearing their
religious clothing in public.[23]

The movement towards the Act of 1829 received an impetus following
the repeal of the Test and Corporation Acts, culminating in legislation
passed in 1828, which essentially gave equal rights to Protestant dissenters.[24]
The literature on Catholic Emancipation points to the importance of a
campaign for equal rights through the establishment of a series of pressure
groups, beginning with the Catholic Committee in 1778, followed by the
Cisalpine Club, and the Board of British Catholics in 1808. The most effective
group consisted of the Catholic Association, launched in 1823 by two
Irish barristers, Richard Lalor Sheil and Daniel O'Connell, the latter of
whom became its leader and figurehead.[25] 'It was one of the first, and one
of the most successful, extra-parliamentary pressure groups in the modern
sense'.[26] The organization had a large membership because of its low sub-
scription fee and by the end of the 1820s had become focused upon Catholic
Emancipation, a measure so dramatic in British politics of the time, that
it became the central issue in Parliament in 1828–9, leading to much Tory
opposition, which would continue into the 1830s and 1840s.[27] The most
important clause of the 1829 Catholic Relief Act allowed Roman Catholics
to sit in Parliament, but it did not grant full emancipation. Catholics could
still not hold posts in schools or Universities controlled by the established
Church while priests could not wear their clothes outside their places of
worship. Full emancipation and equality would not arrive until the end of
the nineteenth century.[28]

Roman Catholic Emancipation set the pattern for subsequent groups
in Britain to obtain equality. In many ways the 1829 measure represented
the most significant passed in favour of a minority group over the past two
hundred years. It signalled the possibility that religious and ethnic minorities

could campaign and successfully obtain equal rights and sit in Parliament as well as participating in mainstream political processes through voting, setting a pattern to improve the position of future groups. As Fergus O'Ferrall has written, 'Catholic Emancipation inaugurated the liberal democratic era.'[29]

Consequently, during the course of the nineteenth century the Irish in Britain not only established their own political groupings supporting nationalist causes,[30] they also became involved in mainstream politics, a clear indication of integration. Rachel O'Higgins asserted that 'It was undeniably in the Chartist Movement that the Irish made their most important contribution to the growth of political radicalism amongst the working classes in nineteenth-century Britain'. Although she partly concentrates upon activity in Ireland, she also points to 'the participation of considerable numbers of Irishmen in the English movement, both among the leaders and the rank and file'.[31] While her assertions have faced challenges and caused controversy,[32] Dorothy Thompson agreed that 'there was a very considerable Irish presence in the Chartist Movement',[33] partly because it unified the disenfranchised and dispossessed English and Irish working classes, whose moment of particular unity arrived in 1848.[34] It then appears that they went their own separate ways as evidenced by the rise of sectarian violence and anti-Irish attacks during the mid-Victorian period following the Famine migration. By the end of the nineteenth century, as the franchise extended, the Irish could influence elections in Britain in the areas in which they concentrated, such as Glasgow. Many voted for Irish Nationalist candidates, but others began to turn their attention towards Liberals and the Independent Labour Party.[35] In fact, the loyalty of some Irish voters for the Liberals, who traditionally supported Home Rule, may actually have slowed the progress of the emerging Labour Party in areas with high Irish concentrations.[36] In the inter-war years support for the Labour party amongst the Irish community demonstrated an increase, as Steven Fielding has shown, but disputes over issues such as birth control, education and the Spanish Civil War, all of which concerned the clergy and those under their influence, made the relationship between Labour and the Irish quite fractious.[37] Only after the Second World War does the pattern of the Irish voting for Labour appear to have become established.[38]

The emancipation of the Irish in Britain and their subsequent incorporation into British electoral politics sets something of a pattern followed by subsequent groups. Some unusual features characterize this minority including the fact that its members often opted for the support of the Irish Nationalist cause rather than British parties. At the same time, their emancipation also occurs before universal suffrage.

The gaining of full civil rights by Jews became fairly inevitable after Roman Catholics had achieved such goals. In fact, Daniel O'Connell became a supporter of Jewish emancipation.[39] While the situation for Jews may need contextualization in the British picture, it also follows developments throughout Europe. Wealthy members of the established community experienced emancipation during the Victorian period, while the newcomers of the later nineteenth century and, more especially, their offspring, moved into mainstream British politics at a quicker pace than the Irish. From Disraeli onwards converted Jews in particular have also played a role in government in Britain.

At the beginning of the nineteenth century Jews in Britain, like most of the rest of the population, had limited rights. 'In 1828 they were still excluded from Crown office, from corporations, from parliament, and from most of the professions, the entrance to which bristled with religious tests'. Although there seemed some doubt as to whether they could legally own land, many did.[40] Equality developed gradually, inspired not only by the achievement of Catholic Emancipation and the other measures passed during the 'Age of Reform', but also by the emergence in the Jewish community 'of a group of leaders of English birth and ancestry', who had become economically successful. Inspired by events around them[41] they launched the Jewish Association for the Removal of Civil and Religious Disabilities.[42] Some of the most prominent figures in Anglo-Jewry at this time, including Moses Montefiore and Lionel de Rothschild, played a role in the move towards Jewish equality. As in the case of Roman Catholics, those who strived to obtain equal rights for Jews also faced an opposition campaign which counted a range of supporters including William Cobbett and Thomas Arnold.[43] Also resembling the development of Roman Catholic equality, the process took place over a long time period. Jews gained a series of privileges from the 1830s before obtaining the right to vote and sit in parliament. In fact, between the 1830s and the 1850s there were 'no less than fourteen attempts to remove parliamentary disabilities'.[44] Before finally reaching the promised land of political equality, a series of measures chipped away at the restrictions faced by Jews including the right to sit at the Bar and to own land from 1833. In addition, Jews increasingly began to take up seats in local corporations during the course of the 1840s and 1850s following the passage of the Jewish Municipal Relief Act in July 1845. Furthermore, they could also matriculate at Oxford and Cambridge from the 1850s.[45] Established Anglo-Jewry achieved political equality in 1858 when Lionel de Rothschild, having previously been elected to the Commons for the City of London in 1847 and 1857, could finally take up his seat following the passage of the

Jews Relief Act. Two years later the Jews Act Amendment allowed entry into the Lords.[46]

The emancipation of Anglo-Jewry, achieved through the efforts of an established and confident community, had a profound influence upon its subsequent history and its role in the British political process. Individuals of Jewish birth would probably play a role more significant than in probably any other European state over the next 150 years. Benjamin Disraeli had served as something of a pioneer in this process. Whatever the extent of antisemitism in late Victorian and Edwardian Britain, the fact that a person born a Jew could become Prime Minister in 1874 seems remarkable and perhaps points as much as any other development in the nineteenth century to the inclusive nature of the British state.[47] In fact, Disraeli might be viewed as the tip of an iceberg, because, as Geoffrey Alderman has pointed out, Jews became over-represented in both national and local politics in contrast to their percentage of the population as a whole. Thus the number of MPs increased from 3 in 1859 to 16 in December 1910, by which time they made up 2.4 per cent of the House of Commons. Unlike the Irish, they sat for the mainstream parties, initially for the Liberals, but then increasingly for the Conservatives.[48] In view of the concentration of the Jewish community in London, its members played a particularly important role in local politics there. In 1910 while Jews formed a fraction of one per cent of the London County Council area, they provided over ten per cent of councillors.[49]

By this time the nature of Anglo-Jewry and its relationship to politics witnessed new developments because of the influx from Eastern Europe. While some of the newcomers found themselves attracted to international causes such as socialism, anarchism[50] and Zionism,[51] others became integrated into the mainstream political processes, developing associations with local working men's clubs in the East End of London.[52] Despite the limited suffrage, Jews constituted as much as forty per cent of the electorate in Whitechapel, which voted for people of their own ethnicity. Thus the MP after 1900, Stuart Samuel, succeeded his uncle, Samuel Montagu, who had held the seat from 1885.[53]

By the beginning of the twentieth century, as many members of established Anglo-Jewry had made it into Edward VII's court,[54] some, following the example of Disraeli, held cabinet posts, a situation which has continued until today. As early as 1871 Sir George Jessel became Solicitor-General while Henry de Worms became Under-Secretary of State for the Colonies in 1888.[55] Herbert Samuel held the position of postmaster-general just before the outbreak of the First World War, while Sir Rufus Isaacs became attorney general, although both faced antisemitic hostility.[56] The same applied to those Jews who held cabinet posts in the immediate aftermath of the First World War including Lord Reading, the Viceroy of India, Sir Alfred Mond, Minister of Health and Edwin Montagu, Secretary of State for India.[57]

Jews continued to become cabinet ministers into the inter-war years including, perhaps most famously, Herbert Samuel, who became Liberal leader and Home Secretary during the 1930s, having previously held the latter position during the First World War.[58] When the Second War broke out Leslie Hore-Belisha had become Secretary of State for War, although the fact that he lost this position in 1940 appears to have had at least some connection with his ethnicity.[59] As a result of the 1935 general election sixteen Jewish MPs sat in Parliament.[60]

Since 1945 the Eastern European Jewish community has increasingly entered Parliament and the Cabinet. Interestingly, allegiances have changed. While half of the sixteen Jewish MPs elected in 1935 stood for the Conservatives, 26 of the 28 in the 1945 Parliament represented the Labour Party, reflecting the move of Jews of Eastern European origin into Labour circles during the inter-war years. But as Eastern European Jewish social mobility occurred after 1945, political preferences shifted. Most symbolically, Margaret Thatcher stood for a constituency with a large Jewish electorate. The number of Jewish MPs reached a peak of 46 in the 1974–9 Parliament, making up a remarkable 7.2 per cent of the House of Commons. At the same time there were 14 Jewish Cabinet ministers between 1945 and 1995, reaching a peak of importance under Thatcher when Nigel Lawson, Leon Brittan, Michael Howard and Malcolm Rifkind held the senior positions of Chancellor of the Exchequer, Home Secretary and Foreign Secretary.[61] Similarly, Jews have also held Cabinet positions under New Labour including the Miliband brothers and Peter Mandelson.

The success of the Jewish community in British politics would have meant nothing to the Black and Asian migrants who entered Britain after 1945. Nevertheless, the same legislative and citizenship basis which had led to Jewish emancipation and political success would also facilitate entry of members of the new communities to Parliament, even if this appears a slow and painful process. Before the breakthrough at the 1987 election when four Black and Asian MPs took their seats in Parliament, a series of measures came into operation which set the groundwork for this development.

Randell Hansen has stressed the importance of the 1948 British Nationality Act, pointing to 'its exceptional liberality and expansiveness between 1948 and 1962 (when some 800,000,000 individuals enjoyed the right to enter the UK)'.[62] Hansen, in common with those scholars who stress the racialization of immigration and nationality laws, accepts that this liberality did not last. At the same time, the new communities found themselves faced with racial prejudice in all aspects of their lives,[63] which increasingly became a political issue by the 1960s, leading to the passage of legislation in an attempt to prevent discrimination.

An important measure came in 1965 in the form of the Race Relations Act. Although attempts at such legislation had occurred from the 1950s and failed,[64] the 1965 Act came at a time when the Labour government had already abandoned its opposition to immigration control feeling particularly threatened following the result of the Smethwick election. Almost simultaneously with the 1965 Act came the White Paper on Immigration which limited the number of entry vouchers issued under the 1962 Commonwealth Immigrants Act. However, the Paper also suggested ways in which immigrants already residing in Britain could have their living and employment conditions improved, especially through the actions of local authorities and trade unions.[65] The Race Relations Act went through Parliament against this background in 1965. It outlawed discrimination in public places and incitement to racial hatred verbally or in writing, but did nothing about the core areas of prejudice in housing and employment. The Act also established the Race Relations Board for the purpose of enforcing the legislation.[66] Harry Goulbourne has regarded it as 'significant because it was a political recognition that racism was an undesirable aspect of British life, and demonstrated a willingness to use the law in the fight against racial discrimination'.[67]

But the weaknesses of the 1965 Act and the findings of further reports which revealed the continued existence of racial discrimination in Britain meant that there followed the 1968 Race Relations Act which extended the provision of the 1965 legislation to cover the obvious areas of housing and employment. It also established the Community Relations Commission for the purpose of creating harmonious community relations and of advising and assisting local voluntary community relations councils with this objective.[68]

The next and most important piece of legislation came under a Labour administration in 1976 in the form of another Race Relations Act.[69] The establishment of the Commission for Racial Equality (CRE) represents its major achievement, taking over the functions of both the Race Relations Board and the Community Relations Commission. In addition, the new legislation strengthened the provisions of the previous measures, introducing the concept of indirect discrimination, which was, however, not very clearly defined.[70] The CRE lasted until 2007 when it became incorporated into the Commission for Equality and Human Rights rooted in the Human

Rights Act of 1998 and protecting individuals against all types of discrimination and prejudice.[71]

Meanwhile, the Stephen Lawrence Inquiry also revealed and created the concept of institutional racism in Britain, through its examination of police forces in the country, when it published its report in 1999. The establishment of the Inquiry revealed the Blair government's commitment to multiculturalism. Police forces up and down Britain held up their hands to declare that they had practised institutional racism.[72] The passage of legislation to outlaw racial 'hatred' may also represent a step forward, although academic and other critics have questioned the effectiveness of such measures.[73]

As well as the measures passed by central government, local councils in Britain have also made attempts to lessen racial prejudice and promote integration. The legislation of the 1960s and 1970s provided for the establishment of local Community Relations Councils, which, after 1976, became Racial Equality Councils, of which 91 existed in 1991. In that year they received £4.5 million, from both the CRE and local councils, to employ racial equality officers. During the 1980s certain inner city local authorities began to introduce measures to deal with racial inequality, especially within London, in the form of the Greater London Council, Lambeth, Brent, Hackney and Haringey. The policies pursued included antiracist education within schools, the granting of local authority contracts to firms which pursued an equal opportunities policy in hiring labour, and the use of anti-racist training to make individuals aware of their own potential prejudice as well as to bring attention to the existing legislation against discrimination. Future developments would occur in the 1990s and beyond as Racial Equality Councils emerged. Local government also increasingly focused upon issues such as racial violence.[74]

Although it had a different aim in mind, the post-war introduction of equality legislation would appear to mirror the emancipation of the nineteenth century in the sense that it aimed to alleviate the disadvantages faced by Black and Asian ethnic minorities. Interestingly, unlike the nineteenth-century measures, the main motivation for those passed during the 1960s and 1970s came from equality conscious Labour governments rather than the campaigning of members of ethnic minorities. The Race Relations Acts appear to have failed in view of the economic position in which most members of ethnic minorities find themselves in relation to the population as a whole.[75] Part of the problem for many post-war migrants, as in the case of the Victorian Irish community, lies in their social status. While they may have equality of opportunity, the environment in which they find themselves means that, even if racism disappeared, they would still find it difficult to have the same social and economic status as most members of the ethnic majority because they face the barriers of both race and class.

Like their Jewish predecessors, the migrants of the post-war period have, however, gradually made their way into the mainstream political processes in both central and, more obviously, local government. The basis of equality here again goes back to the 1948 British Nationality Act and the principle of *jus solis*. Just as Jews have influenced voting in particular locations, so, in the same way, have post-war immigrant groups. However, research into the voting rates of ethnic minorities has revealed that they participate in the electoral process to a lesser extent than the rest of the population.

Black and Asian representation in British politics did not begin in the post-war period, as three Indians had gained seats in the House of Commons from the end of the nineteenth century representing the Liberal, Conservative and Communist Parties. The three individuals consisted of Dadabhai Naoroji, who held Finsbury Central for the Liberals from 1892–5, Mancherjee Bhownaggree who held the seat of Bethnal Green North East for the Conservatives from 1895–1905 and Shapurji Saklatvala who sat in Battersea as the sole representative of the Communist Party of Great Britain from 1922–9. Although they faced hostility because of their colour, their election to Parliament seems remarkable at a time when only a few thousand Indians lived in Britain.[76]

With significant concentrations of working class immigrants in the inner city Labour has represented the natural party for post-war migrant groups. By 1991 a total of 78 parliamentary constituencies counted more than 15 per cent Black and Asian people, including 25 with over 30 per cent. Between October 1974 and May 1997 about 80 per cent of such voters opted for the Labour Party.[77] Nevertheless, participation rates remained relatively low, as did membership of the mainstream parties and political activism in general, especially in the early days of migration, when voter registration amongst Black people in particular had not taken off. By the 1980s, registration and voting rates measured by opinion polls had grown to resemble the level of white neighbours in the inner city, if not the country as a whole.[78]

Rather like the allegiance of the early generations of the Jewish communities to Labour, the post-war Commonwealth ethnic minorities have also displayed a similar level of support for this party. A poll from 1987 suggested that 67 per cent of Asians and 86 per cent of African Caribbean voted for Labour in the general election of that year.[79] Zig Layton-Henry speculated that 'as members of the ethnic minority communities become more prosperous and move out into suburban areas, there would be some

FIGURE 17 Paul Boateng leaves Downing Street after being appointed Britain's Chief Secretary to the Treasury, 29 May 2002. Boateng is the first ever Black cabinet minister in the British government. Image © Reuters/CORBIS

attrition in support' for Labour.[80] Nevertheless, according to polls from 1996 and 1997, admittedly at a time of a landslide Labour victory, support for the Labour Party remained remarkably strong, standing at 70 per cent amongst Asians and 86 per cent for Black people.[81] The problem for the Conservatives lies not only in the class instincts of ethnic minority voters, but also the racist rhetoric of the Party.[82]

The electoral success of Black and Asian candidates in recent decades has therefore tended to occur in connection with the Labour Party on both the local and national level. Part of the reason for this development lies in the pressure which emerged during the course of the 1980s when Black Sections developed in the Labour Party demanding the selection of Black and brown candidates for inner city seats with ethnic minority concentrations.[83] Shamit Saggar and Andrew Geddes viewed this as a 'positive racialization' of British politics because it gave members of ethnic minorities the opportunity to enter the political process.[84] In 1987 the breakthrough took place when four Black and Asian MPs entered Parliament representing constituencies with significant percentages of Black and Asian ethnic minority communities in the form of Diane Abbot in Hackney, Paul Boateng in Brent, Bernie Grant in Tottenham and Keith Vaz in Leicester East. By 1997 a total of 44 ethnic minority candidates stood for all three parties, but while 9 out of 14 of those standing for Labour secured victories, all of the 11 Conservatives and 19 Liberal Democrats failed even though many stood in seats with minority concentrations, suggesting that political allegiances based on class outweighed those based on ethnicity. Following the 2005 general election, 15 Black and Asian MPs were elected, 13 of them for the Labour Party. Despite the increasing numbers of MPs from post-war migrant backgrounds, they still remain under-represented in Parliament and it seems inconceivable, at this stage, that they will reach the kind of over-representation achieved by Jews, especially by 1974. A reflection of the Black and Asian communities in Britain would mean 45 MPs from these backgrounds.[85] Interestingly, however, and again mirroring the Jewish picture both before and after 1945,[86] all political parties have created peers from Black and Asian ethnic minorities, with the total reaching 18 by 2000.[87]

In addition, ethnic minorities have also done especially well in local elections in areas with concentrations of their own group. During the 1980s Black and Asian Mayors began to find themselves elected including, most famously, representing the Labour Party, Bernie Grant in Haringey, Merle Amory in Brent and Linda Bellos in Lambeth. Conservative Asian Mayors found themselves returned in Maidenhead and Leamington Spa (areas without a large concentration of ethnic minorities), while two Greek Cypriots, Andreas Mikkides and Demetris Demetriou, had held the same position in Haringey by the early 1990s.[88] By 1996 there may also have been as many as 600 Asian and African Caribbean local councillors out of a national figure of 25,000, meaning just 3 per cent of the total, which actually declined to 2.5 per cent by 2001, partly due to a fall in Labour Party support. But the number of Black or Asian councillors roughly matches, and sometimes exceeds, the percentage of the populations from which they emerge in cities such as Birmingham, Blackburn, Leicester and Luton.[89] Once again, the relationship between ethnic minorities and the Labour Party proved important for the breakthrough into local politics although ethnic minorities have also begun to sit for other groups. For instance, following local elections in Leicester in 2003 the loss of the Labour Party majority meant that the number of ethnic minority councillors declined from 14 (all Labour) to 10, but the new figures included five Liberal Democrats.[90]

Multiculturalism in Britain has manifested itself in state structures and their responsiveness to the incorporation of minorities over the past two centuries. This begins with the nineteenth century emancipation of both

Roman Catholics and Jews and progresses through to the Race Relations Acts. In all of these cases liberal democratic Britain, emerging during the course of the nineteenth century and firmly in place by the 1960s, responded to the presence of minorities who faced discrimination. In the case of the Irish and post-war ethnic minorities, the legislation which came into operation did not solve their marginalization (although it went some way towards alleviating it) because of their social status. On the other hand, the upwardly mobile Jews of both the nineteenth and twentieth centuries made the most of the emancipation. Nationality legislation, especially the principle of *jus solis* granting equal rights to the second generation, as well as equal status to imperial citizens until the 1960s, have also proved central in bringing different groups of minorities into the body politic. While some members of ethnic minorities have set up transnational political organizations,[91] the overwhelming majority have become incorporated into mainstream parties whether Liberal, Conservative or Labour as either voters or active political players on the local or national level. Although over-representation has characterized Jewish participation in Parliament, under-representation currently affects Black and Asian minorities, although this could change through subsequent generations. While the British state has therefore played a large role in excluding and persecuting migrants from the body politic, emancipation, race relations and nationality legislation, partly acting in response to pressure from minorities, has assisted in helping the political integration of those who have entered the country over the last two centuries.

Support for migrants and refugees

Both historians and social scientists, following the race relations paradigm, have tended to focus their attention on the existence of racism, especially as practised by the state, but also on an everyday basis. Exceptions exist as demonstrated by the early pioneer sociologists of the 1950s who attempted to look at all aspects of the relationship between Black migrants and white natives.[92] While countless publications exist on the history of xenophobia in Britain, little has appeared of a serious nature dealing with positive attitudes towards migrants. The clearest indication of such welcoming responses consists of the level of inter-ethnic relations and marriages, which have taken place at a high level since the Victorian period.[93] Yet much of the research on such relationships has concentrated on the hostility which they have caused.[94] In addition, historians and social scientists have devoted little attention to inter-ethnic friendship, even if it represents part of everyday reality in modern Britain.

FIGURE 18 Girls enjoying themselves on the playground of Melcombe Primary School, a formerly failing inner-city school, which has been transformed by the work of a new head and dedicated senior management. Many of the students come from backgrounds which could present educational challenges, such as refugee status, non native English speaking homes and children in temporary accommodation. Staff successfully address these issues and the school has become a government 'beacon' school. 15 November 2003, London. Image © Gideon Mendel/Corbis

Here we can focus upon the positive reaction which migrants and, more especially, refugees, have attracted over the last two centuries. While Tony Kushner has spent much of his career demonstrating the existence of hostility towards refugees in twentieth-century Britain,[95] he has also recognized the positive responses which some newcomers have drawn especially when they have had a symbolic role to play in the fight against external enemies, such as the Belgians during the First World War.[96] Some groups, such as the Society of Friends, have always supported outsiders, even the most hated group in modern Britain, the Germans during the First World War.[97]

Despite the focus of historians and social scientists upon hostility towards migrants and refugees, some less scholarly accounts concentrated upon the positive responses which they received. A classic volume of this nature consists of Francesa M. Wilson's *They Came as Strangers*, which asserted that while the 'British in general do not love foreigners . . . it is impressive to reveal . . . how passionately they defended the right of asylum'.[98] During the nineteenth century, liberal refugees received support from a variety of groups, often because they represented symbols of freedom against continental oppression.

Bernard Porter has stressed the role of the state in presenting this image during the mid Victorian period, although he has also demonstrated how this came under threat when concern arose over the activities and numbers of refugees in the late 1840s and early 1850s. Porter quoted an editorial from *The Times* of 19 January 1858, which declared that: 'Every civilized people on the face of this earth must be fully aware that this country is the asylum of nations, and that it would defend the asylum to the last drop of its blood'.[99] Similarly, Colin Holmes cited Peter Kropotkin, the Russian anarchist, who spent a spell in Britain at the end of the nineteenth century and described the Union Jack as 'the flag under which so many refugees, Russian, Italian, French, Hungarian and of all nations, have found asylum.'[100]

For most of the Victorian years, therefore, refugees received positive reactions from sections of British society, a fact which they realized. Despite the hostility which poor Italian immigrants faced, early nineteenth-century British high society responded positively to the arrival of 'well-heeled, educated and often learned'[101] Italian exiles escaping the straitjacket imposed on nationalism and liberalism by the Congress of Vienna. This stream of refugees lasted from the 1820s until the 1850s. Their symbolic position as victims of Continental oppression, together with their class status and an admiration for Italian language and culture in this period guaranteed their incorporation, especially into Whig high society.[102] Similarly, German exiles also received a positive response when they arrived in England, as evidenced by the example of the middle class Gottfried Kinkel.[103] Furthermore, the Hungarian revolutionary leader Lajos Kossuth found himself feted as an opponent of Habsburg tyranny in both public meetings and in the press. Wilson described him as 'the greatest hero in Victorian England' until 'the still more glamorous Garibaldi' replaced him.[104]

Those mid nineteenth-century exiles who held extreme left wing political views received less positive attention than middle class nationalists and liberals.[105] At the same time, when the numbers of Jewish refugees reached tens of thousands rather than thousands or hundreds at the end of the nineteenth century, antisemitism began to rise. Nevertheless, Bill and Hilary Rubinstein have demonstrated the existence of philosemitism in the English speaking world, while Todd Endelman has focused upon the ease with which Jews could enter mainstream society. The Rubinsteins argued that positive attitudes towards Jews, mainly those living abroad, found motivation from a series of sources including liberalism, Christianity, support for Zionism and even conservatism.[106] They demonstrated how this philosemitism surfaced during a series of crises for Jewry when antisemitism outside Britain became violent. These included the Russian pogroms in the late nineteenth and early twentieth centuries, the Dreyfus affair and the Holocaust. Thus, during the 1881 pogroms in Russia 'there was considerable outrage amongst gentiles', which manifested itself in articles in *The Times* and 'a great meeting to protest at the suffering of Russian Jewry', which occurred at Mansion House in January 1882 and led to the foundation of the Mansion House Fund. While this movement involved the cream of British society, trade unionists and workers would also pass resolutions against antisemitism in Russia in the decades leading up to the First World War.[107] As well as focusing upon reactions towards violent antisemitism abroad, the Rubinsteins also demonstrated support amongst elites in particular for Jews in Britain.[108] Their study inevitably leads to the portrayal of a generally positive picture towards Anglo-Jewry in the same way in which Colin Holmes painted a generally negative one.[109] In contrast, Todd Endelman's study of radical assimilation proves more complex. Although he accepts the existence of positive feeling towards the Jews in Britain between 1656 and 1945, he argues that 'The toleration that made possible the successful integration of English Jews was hostile to the notion of cultural diversity. Circles and institutions quite willing to tolerate Jews as intimate associates were not willing to endorse the perpetuation of a separate Jewish culture or to see any values in the customs or beliefs of the Jewish religion'.[110]

The era of the Holocaust proves the most controversial in analysing the existence of philosemitism in Britain. Louise London has taken one of the most uncompromising positions, arguing that 'prejudice against Jews was considered unacceptable if it formed part of a social or political programme', which meant that 'moderate indulgence in social anti-Jewish prejudice was so widespread as to be unremarkable'.[111] Thus we would expect from both the perspective of London and the Rubinsteins that British public opinion would abhor the actions of the Nazis.[112] Bill Rubinstein created considerable controversy by stretching his argument to suggest that the western liberal democracies could have done nothing further to help the Jews of Europe during the Second World War, despite their positive attitudes towards them.[113] In between the arguments of Rubinstein and London, and while accepting the existence of strong antisemitic prejudice during the inter-war years, which helped to determine policy towards the number of Jews allowed to enter Britain, positive feeling did exist beyond the condemnation of the acts of the Nazis. In the first place, while policy towards the immigration of Jews remained restrictive for most of the 1930s, it eased following *Kristallnacht*, which meant that Britain took a relatively large number of refugees from the Third Reich.[114] At the same time a series of organizations emerged to campaign on behalf of the immigration to Britain, as well to help those who arrived to integrate. Although established Anglo-Jewry played a large role in such efforts, gentiles also assisted. The most significant bodies included the Central British Fund for German Jewry, established in 1933. A series of other groups also emerged, aiming at assisting individual groups such as academics in the form of the Academic Assistance Council.[115] Jewish refugee children received the most positive attention. They fled after Kristallnacht in November 1938 leaving their parents behind, most of whom would never see them again. Tony Kushner has questioned the popular memory which has viewed this action in a purely positive manner.[116] In his volume on refugees in Britain written with Katherine Knox, Kushner also demonstrated mixed views towards Jewish refugees in the Southampton area throughout the inter-war years.[117] Nevertheless, mass observation reports and diaries reveal genuine sympathy for Jews, even if this sometimes remained somewhat ambiguous.[118]

Any balanced account of philosemitism needs to contrast it with antisemitism and consider the progress which Jews made in British society during the nineteenth and twentieth centuries. While positive attitudes towards Jews certainly existed, especially if they faced persecution at the hands of intolerant continental regimes, it always competed with a powerful strain of antisemitism, which manifested itself especially in social prejudice. Yet because it did not become politically powerful enough, it could not prevent Jewish economic and social success.

As well as positive attitudes towards Jews, other refugee groups also found themselves welcomed by at least a section of British society. In the decades leading up the 1917 Russian Revolution exiles fleeing Tsarist oppression were welcomed by both liberals and socialists, leading to the formation of a variety of groups to work and help with the newcomers including the Society of Friends of Russian Freedom. Some of the exiles would move into and influence socialism in Britain, while others continued their own activities, hoping to return home.[119]

The group which has experienced the most universal approval from both British state and society over the last two hundred years has consisted of the quarter of a million Belgians who fled the German invasion of their country in the autumn of 1914. The attitudes towards Belgians contrasted dramatically with the treatment of Germans during the Great War because, while the latter symbolized the enemy, the former reflected the cause for which Britain fought.[120] While the Germans in Britain faced press vilification, rioting, internment and confiscation of their property, the Belgians, in contrast, represented the fight against the Hun, which meant that, especially in the early stages after their arrival, they received much support from the state, charities and individuals. Initially, the London Borough of Clerkenwell offered assistance, but by September 1914 the Local Government Board established camps to house the refugees. The Board worked together with a private charity called the War Refugees Committee. By February 1916 a total of 69 Belgian relief charities existed. The exiles found support in their search for housing, food, clothing and employment. They worked in armaments factories, helping the British war effort, which also assisted their cause.[121] Individual Britons went out of their way to help Belgians including a Davies family from Llandinam who assisted artists and musicians in Wales.[122] Peter Cahalan has written that 'Charitable work was a form of symbolic enlistment for thousands of citizens too old or of the wrong sex to be able to fight'.[123] The transience of the refugees, the situation of full employment and their symbolic position as victims of the German enemy assured their positive status.[124]

The intervention of the state to help Belgians sets something of a precedent for subsequent resettlement and assistance to refugee groups. In addition, the efforts of individuals and charities to assist refugees would continue, despite the hostility which many of them would face from the press, as Kushner and Knox have demonstrated.[125] At the same time Joanna Herbert has shown that, while much animosity may have existed towards the arrival of Ugandan Asians in Leicester, individual white natives in the city interacted with them in a positive manner symbolized by the exchange of foods.[126]

Similarly, organizations have also evolved to work with immigrants and refugees or to protect them in the fight against racism and intolerance. During the Second World War, for instance, the National Council for Civil Liberties made efforts on behalf of interned aliens. As Liberty, this body continues to have the protection of the rights of ethnic minorities, especially refugees and those persecuted by anti-terrorism legislation, as one of its remits.[127] In the post-war years specific groups have evolved to fight against racism. An early manifestation consisted of the Campaign Against Racial Discrimination, which surfaced between 1964 and 1968 as a sort of British civil rights movement inspired by events in the USA. Its historian believes that it had limited success due to infighting and tensions between the different ethnic groups which drove the organization forward meaning that it did not play the sort of role in influencing government policy as the American civil rights movement did.[128] In the 1970s there followed the Anti-Nazi League which especially aimed its efforts at fighting the National Front on the streets. It also became something of a cultural movement which incorporated elements of Black and Asian popular culture.[129] It played a role in the emergence of the Rock Against Racism movement, which held its first concerts in 1978 and continues to flourish.[130] Furthermore, the Academic Assistance Council, established to help Jewish refugees during the 1930s has developed into the Council for Assisting Refugee Academics.[131] Similarly, the Anti-Racist Alliance makes efforts to tackle racism through a range of activities.[132]

While migrants and refugees faced widespread racism amongst sections of British society, a corresponding strand of tolerance and welcome has run side by side. It tends not to make itself heard to the same extent as hostility because racism has found so much support in the main vehicle of public opinion in the form of the press. Nevertheless, migrants and refugees have found a welcome amongst sections of the British population. The effects of these positive attitudes seem difficult to measure. They appear to have failed to counter the more widespread manifestations of racism except on occasions such as the First World War when Belgian refugees became symbols of fairness at a time, however, when Germans in Britain had virtually come to symbolize evil. Positive attitudes towards Belgians eased the situation of this minority. In contrast, the Campaign Against Racial Discrimination and the Anti-Nazi League may have had less of an impact on the evolution of multicultural Britain during the course of the 1960s and 1970s. If opinion on the ground helped in recent developments, it came from the efforts of the ethnic minorities themselves participating in the political process allowed by nationality laws.

The impact of immigration

The economic and cultural impact of immigration represents perhaps the most visible aspect of the existence of a multicultural society. This seems most apparent in the post-war period when migrants from the New Commonwealth appear to have transformed aspects of British society and popular culture such as eating out, popular music or sport. However, the developments which occurred after 1945 have clear reflections before the Second World War.

An examination of the importance of migration upon Britain can follow two possible paradigms. The impact of newcomers represents one of these. This manifests itself most obviously in the significance of immigrants for the British economy over the past two hundred years, whether as manual workers or as entrepreneurs. Similarly, migrants have also proved important in other areas of British life such as high and popular culture and the army. Examining the impact of immigration requires either measuring the numbers of people involved in a particular activity or attempting to assess the importance of individuals to a particular field. Economists and economic historians have tried, for instance, to assess the role of the Irish in nineteenth-century industrialization[133] and the importance of migrants for the contemporary economy.[134] On the other hand such an approach involves subjective judgements attempting to measure the impact of individuals upon particular fields, such as Sir Charles Hallé on the evolution of classical music in nineteenth-century Manchester.

An alternative approach involves the use of the concept of transfer, especially in the broad area of high and popular culture. Migrants carry with them their own cultural heritage which, in the process of migrating and settling, is transformed,[135] but also inevitably influences the culture of the receiving society. This transfer approach means a move away from a purely demographic perspective to a concentration on manifold interactions that have taken place between majority and minority culture. Just as migrants have evolved into Britons so, in the same way, migrants have transformed Britain. In the same way in which newcomers and their offspring develop hybrid identities, so in the same way, do ethnic minorities change the identity of Britain, most visibly in areas such as food and sport. Many of the dishes which Britons now take for granted as their own, above all fish and chips, actually evolved as a result of immigration. Curry developed because of the influx of immigrants from Bangladesh who served up to Britons what some of them had previously eaten in India. It seems more difficult to measure cultural transfer in areas such as sport, as it would prove controversial to speak of a Black way of playing football or even cricket. On the other hand, the evolution of a Victorian and Edwardian British classical music tradition has roots in Germany in view of the role of individuals such as Felix Mendelssohn, Frederick Delius and Gustav Holst. Similarly, in the post-war period Indian dress has played a role in female clothing.

An examination of individual migrant groups and their interaction with the majority community helps to illustrate the way in which migrants have impacted upon aspects of British life and also demonstrates cultural transfer in operation. One of the areas in which the Irish have had the most profound influence consisted of the reintroduction and revitalization of Roman Catholicism from the elite post-Reformation belief to a mass religion.[136] However, in view of the focus of much of the historiography of the Irish on the social and economic condition of this minority in the mid-Victorian period, it seems difficult to measure the influence of this group other than as a mass labour force which has played a role in the British economy since the Victorian period. The Irish have also proved important in the armed forces over the past two hundred years. For instance, 159,000 Irishmen served in

English regiments between 1793 and 1815. In 1871 a total of 4.38 per cent of Irishmen of 14–54 years of age had joined the British army whereas the figure for Englishmen stood at 2.09 per cent. The former usually consisted of poor Roman Catholics. During the Boer War the Irish formed their own brigade which included former Fenians. Such facts point to Ireland as part of the British state until 1921. Irish regiments also came into existence in London and Liverpool from 1859, while the Tyneside Irish raised their own battalion during the First World War.[137]

Germans in nineteenth-century Britain would appear to have had an influence on at least three areas of British life in the form of business, music and the restaurant trade.[138] While a significant working class migration of Germans took place from the end of the eighteenth century, many of those making their way to Britain consisted of entrepreneurs, who would help to establish some of the largest companies in Britain. Some of these had Jewish backgrounds. The work of Stanley Chapman illustrated the importance of Germans in a variety of areas. In 1850 there were 97 German 'merchant houses' in Manchester, 38 in Bradford, 6 in Leeds, 7 in Nottingham and 12 in Birmingham. Chapman has argued that these firms supplied credit and 'valuable reserves of entrepreneurial experience'.[139] Of merchant banking houses with a capital of more than £1 million before 1914, Chapman iden-tified four founded by first generation immigrants,[140] including Schroeders, Kleinworts and Rothschilds.[141] Germans also became important in the development of the textile industry in Scotland and the north of England during the course of the nineteenth century.[142] Stefan Manz has looked at the example of Otto Ernst Philippi, who moved from sales manager in the Paisley thread making firm of J & P Coats to managing director, arguing, in a reflection of Chapman's earlier work on merchant bankers, that the transfer of management methods from Germany to Britain at the end of the nineteenth century helped in this success.[143] Meanwhile, Ludwig Mond and the Swiss John Brunner established a chemical concern at the end of the nineteenth century, which would later emerge into Imperial Chemical Industries.[144] Taking the cultural transfer approach, Stefan Manz has also pointed to the development of the Tennents brewery in Glasgow, established and staffed by Germans in the decades before the First World War. The beer produced by this firm reached a market beyond the tiny German community in Glasgow and the still small one within Great Britain to emerge into one of the largest breweries in the country.[145]

Germany also sent a wide range of musicians to Britain during the course of the nineteenth century, continuing a trend which had become well estab-lished during the course of the eighteenth.[146] One of the most prominent groups throughout the Victorian period consisted of German brass bands who marched up and down the country, although they appear to have had little influence upon British brass music.[147] On the other hand, Germans in Britain certainly played a role in the development of 'serious' music as they helped to staff many of the major orchestras which would emerge during the course of the nineteenth century, particularly the Hallé, which not only had Charles Hallé as it founder and first conductor, but also employed Hans Richter in this position from 1899. At the same time, German music teachers also resided in Britain during the Victorian period.[148] One of the most famous of British composers, Frederick Delius, born in Bradford in 1863 to middle class German parents, also studied in his country of origin as well as in other parts of Europe.[149]

Germans, together with other European migrants, played a central role in the evolution of catering in Britain before the First World War. They found themselves employed in a variety of roles. In the first place, they introduced new products into the country. Ice cream arrived in Britain as a result of the activities of Italian migrants so that by the 1870s 'ice cream street vendors had become a common feature in London – and they were virtually to a man, Italian'.[150] They would continue to play a role in the selling of ice cream throughout the twentieth century, but the evolution of this product for domestic consumption also had a Jewish influence, as blocks cut up with a knife, largely occurred under the influence of the originally Jewish firm of Lyons.[151] Jewish migrants appear to have played a significant role in the sale of fish and chips, at least in London, before the Second World War, while Italians became important in this trade in South Wales and Scotland in the same period. After 1945 a variety of newcomers sold fish and chips, above all Greek Cypriots. Just as significantly fish and chips may actually have evolved as a result of a marriage of Jewish fried fish traditions combined with chips, which appear to have developed in France. These two products probably came together somewhere in London during the Victorian period illustrating cultural transfer.[152]

Ice cream and fish and chips provide an example of a niche product. On a much broader scale, migrants became central in the development of the restaurant trade as a whole after 1850, from top to bottom, from owners and managers through to cooks and waiters. This process coincided with the spread of French gastronomy.[153] Migrants established two of the most famous dining houses in Britain before 1914. First, the Café Royal in Regent Street, originally opened by Daniel de Nicols, a French wine merchant, who moved to England in 1862. Similarly, the Swiss born César Ritz founded the hotel which bears his name in 1906. The Lyons group, meanwhile, established a range of catering outlets appealing to a wide range of classes. At the top, the Trocadero restaurant opened in Piccadilly in 1896. Simultaneously, the firm also opened teashops, which would develop into a national chain appealing to members of the lower middle classes in particular. In 1909 the first corner house came into existence and would develop into another chain in the inter-war years.[154]

Foreign chefs also became important during the nineteenth century including the French born Alexis Soyer and August Escoffier together with Charles Elmé Francatelli, born in 1805 in London to Italian parents. Collectively, they wrote some of the most widely used and celebrated cookbooks in Victorian and Edwardian Britain.[155] These three form the celebrity tip of an iceberg of foreign chefs staffing establishments throughout Britain before 1945, originating especially in France, Switzerland, Germany and Italy.[156]

Foreigners also found employment as managers of hotels and restaurants, many of whom had made their way up from waiters. Germans proved especially important. Using the 1901 census we can estimate a total of 8,634 foreign waiters in England and Wales of whom 3,039 consisted of Germans. In 1911 about ten per cent of waiters and waitresses in restaurant work in London were German and by this time they worked in cities throughout the country.[157] Twenty-three years later *The New Survey of London Life and Labour* estimated that 122,000 people found employment in the hotel and catering trade in the capital,[158] although, in the intervening period, most Germans had faced the sack during the intolerance of the First World War. Other Europeans would take their place, while Germans returned in the inter-war years. The Second World War meant further dismissals, especially of Italians.

Before 1945 Britons therefore often found themselves eating in establishments staffed by foreigners. In view of the ubiquity of migrants in catering it may have proved difficult to eat in restaurants which did not employ Europeans, especially in central London. In fact, the development of eating out has close links with European immigration. Something of transfer of cooking and waiting skills occurred, although this caused resentment from some Britons who complained about the lack of opportunities open to them, which surfaced in the Germanophobic atmosphere of the late Edwardian period and the First World War, leading to the evolution of organizations such as the Loyal British Waiters Society. As well as eating food served or prepared by Europeans, Britons also consumed products introduced or concocted by migrants, especially in the case of ice cream and, perhaps, fish and chips. At this stage foreign food had not really emerged as a concept except in the form of French *haute cuisine*. Although the first Italian, Chinese and Indian restaurants did begin to emerge,[159] foreign food took off as a concept after 1945 with the arrival of new migrant groups and the development of marketing along ethnic and national lines.[160]

Jews have had an enormous impact upon the evolution of modern Britain. Some of the historiography has stressed this fact, particularly a whole series of volumes which have focused upon the achievements of the middle class exiles from Nazi Germany.[161] Such an approach tends to ignore the larger undifferentiated mass of working class people who arrived from the Russian Pale of Settlement at the end of the nineteenth century. Nevertheless, as contemporary observers stressed, often in a negative manner, the Victorian and Edwardian settlers also had an immediate impact, transforming the urban environment, especially in the East End of London. In 1903, Walter Besant wrote: 'Go up and down the streets of East London – over the shop fronts you will see everywhere German and Jewish names . . . Walk along the Whitechapel Road on a Sunday morning; there you will see most of the hundred thousand, there you will see the peaceful invaders who have occupied a large part of East London'.[162] More recently, Anne Kershen has stressed the transformative impact of Jews, as well as Huguenots and Bangladeshis upon the urban environment in her study of immigration into Spitalfields.[163]

However, much of the research upon the impact of Jewish immigration has tended to focus upon the middle class refugees from Nazism. Many of these newcomers certainly had to overcome adversity in terms of initial poverty and hostility from some sections of British society, which led to Second World War internment in some cases. Nevertheless, as a highly educated group, they possessed skills which would subsequently ease their move into middle class British society. The volume edited by Werner Mosse has listed numerous fields in which the refugees from Nazism, together with their German Jewish predecessors from the nineteenth century, made an impact. While they may count small minorities of people in some pro-fessions, they have had a more profound impact on others. Thus, they have had a limited impact upon British politics, even though significant numbers of German Jews may have made it to Parliament.[164] On the other hand, their role in the evolution of British high culture seems more signifi-cant, certainly in the eyes of Daniel Snowman, who has not only focused upon the émigrés themselves, but also their children.[165] Refugees, some of whom arrived as children, also made contributions to academia. Historians such as Edgar Feuchtwanger, Helmut Koenigsberger, Francis Carsten and Sidney Pollard escaped the Nazis,[166] while other refugees played a role in physics and medicine, for instance.[167] Similarly, their impact on British industry after the Second World War has also received attention.[168]

Despite their arrival before the Second World War, Snowman has stressed that refugees from Nazism made their influence felt after 1945[169] and therefore link with immigrants from the Commonwealth to play a transformative role in development of Britain. Those Jews who have helped to develop British economy, culture and society have not simply consisted of exiles from the Nazis but also the descendants of earlier Jewish waves. Bill Rubinstein has listed a variety of fields and the Jewish individuals who have impacted upon them. He pointed to 47 Fellows of the Royal Society and 23 of the British Academy in 1994. He also listed nine British Jews who won Nobel prizes. Prominent writers have included Harold Pinter, Arnold Wesker, Tom Stoppard and Anita Brookner. Rubinstein also mentioned prominent Jews in the development of popular culture including Frankie Vaughan, Helen Shapiro, Warren Mitchell, Mike and Bernie Winters and Marc Bolan,[170] to whom we could add others since Rubinstein compiled his list in the 1990s. The impact of Jews upon post-war British society clearly links in with the social mobility of those who arrived before 1945, as well as the skills which those from Nazi Germany possessed.

Just as Jews transformed many inner city areas before the First World War, the post-war arrivals have become part of the landscape of British cities since the 1950s, initially West Indians, but increasingly, from the 1970s, South Asians.[171] As a result of continuities of immigration into the East End of London, its character has altered from Jewish to Bangladeshi so that Spitalfields has changed from Little Jerusalem to Banglatown.[172] As well as transforming the nature of some decaying inner city areas Asian migrants in particular have also helped to rejuvenate them. This has happened in Rusholme in Manchester and Belgrave in Leicester. While restaurants have played a large role in the former, the latter has become one of the most important South Asian shopping centres in Europe.[173] The multicultural nature of London, meanwhile, depends upon the patchwork of different ethnic neighbourhoods which emerged during the post-war period.[174]

The post-war economy has also become dependent upon immigration. The arrival of Europeans in the 1940s set the pattern. Migrants from the New Commonwealth and South Asia in particular moved into a variety of economic sectors, beyond factories, so that they now count significant numbers of both small and wealthy businessmen. More recently, migration from the European Union has helped to fill labour shortages.[175]

Dramatic change has occurred in religious practice following patterns established in the Victorian and Edwardian years. Migrants from Ireland and Eastern Europe respectively helped to transform Catholicism and Judaism into mass religions before the First World War. Since 1945 South Asians have introduced new beliefs on a large scale for the first time, especially Islam, but also Hinduism and Sikhism.[176]

Migrants have played a central role in transforming the eating habits of British people since 1945. This becomes particularly apparent with consumption outside the home, continuing the patterns established before 1945. This may seem most obvious in the development of restaurants which market ethnic foods but migrants have also, as in the period before 1945, run and staffed establishments which do not sell overtly foreign produce. Continental waiters and cooks, especially from western Europe, continued to play a central role in the London catering trade in the early post-war period. Many of the most exclusive hotels and restaurants continued to depend upon foreign staff, especially at the top end so that, for instance, the Ritz did not appoint its first chef from the British Isles until the 1980s. More recently, Eastern Europeans, especially from Poland, have moved into catering[177] in the way that Germans, Italian and French people had done before 1945.

In the earlier post-war decades Italians and Greek Cypriots opened establishments which sold fairly traditional British products. The former proved particularly important in the rise of the coffee bar and the sandwich bar. About 2,000 of the former existed by 1960 including 200 in the West End of London. Their number would subsequently decline because they provided small profit margins which meant that some owners turned to cafes and trattorias. The invention of the espresso machine in 1946 had helped the initial emergence of the coffee bar.[178]

Greek Cypriots who moved into the restaurant business often did so shortly after arriving in Britain, suggesting a high propensity for risk taking, but also reflecting a desire for self-sufficiency rooted in the fact that land and home ownership amongst the predominantly agrarian population of Cyprus had become the norm from as early as the sixteenth century.[179] Thus by the 1960s Greek Cypriots owned a variety of establishments both in London and in the provinces. For instance, Cypriot owned restaurants in Leicester in 1963 included the Continental, the Flamingo, the Gourmet and the Steak House. Both Greek and Turkish Cypriots took up Wimpy franchises, when this originally American product began to enter Britain during the 1960s and 1970s, although we can also see a Jewish element to this in the sense that Wimpy formed part of the Lyons chain. This product again illustrates the complexity of national and ethnic origins involved in the evolution of individual food products in Britain.[180]

The most obvious way in which migrants have impacted upon food in Britain since 1945 lies in the evolution of restaurants which sell overtly foreign food. While eating 'ethnic cuisine' may appear 'the easiest and most pleasant way to cross ethnic boundaries' and may demonstrate 'the ultimate reconciliation between a diversity we cherish and a common humanity we must recognize if we are to live amicably together',[181] this seems a simplification of reality. A group of ethnically English friends who eat in a curry house and do not have friends from other communities do not cross boundaries. As Anneke van Otterloo has asked, 'When autochthonous and allochthonous peoples enjoy each others' cuisine, do they come closer together or do the distance and inequalities remain just as they were?',[182] a point also stressed by Elizabeth Buettner.[183] One could argue that class and ethnic boundaries remain as migrants work in a service industry primarily for the benefit of the ethnic majority. It proves difficult to view the provision of food offered by ethnic minorities in restaurants as anything other than a product, as a business transaction, which means that migrants construct meals which would appeal to the wider population, rather than serving the foods which they eat at home. Many of these restaurants operate upon limited profit margins. They do not offer an automatic entry into prosperity, as business failure remains a constant threat.[184]

The fact that they serve new products points to a process of cultural transfer evidenced by both 'Indian' and Chinese food. Curry originates in the British control of India. Those British people who lived and worked in the Raj from the eighteenth century liked the products which Indians ate. These dishes were, however, overwhelmingly vegetarian, but Britons wished to continue eating meat, leading to the development of a new Anglo-Indian cuisine. This involved a process of culinary mapping which constructed, for the first time, an Indian cuisine, through British eyes.[185] Although a handful of Indian restaurants serving curry emerged in Britain before 1945, they tended to have a short life span. Only after the Second World War did the Indian restaurant take off, so that, by the beginning of the twenty-first century, the number of such establishments reached around 9,000. From the 1950s and, more especially, the 1960s and beyond, Bangladeshis, many of whom had served as cooks in the British merchant navy, owned 'Indian' restaurants, which precisely sold the type of food which British people had eaten in the Raj and which appeared in cookbooks on curry from the nineteenth century. In this culinary sense, the Empire came home, in the form of Anglo-Indian curry served by Bangladeshis to the whole of the British population, rather than simply those who had lived in the Raj. From the 1960s new developments in the Indian restaurant menu emerged in the form of Tandoori, followed by Balti during the 1980s. Most recently, predominantly South Indian vegetarian serving establishments have emerged, although Bangladeshis continue to run the vast majority of establishments.[186]

Chinese food also took off in Britain after 1945. Once again, the handful of restaurants, which had developed before the Second World War, mushroomed from the 1950s so that over 10,000 would exist by the beginning of the twenty-first century. Chinese food differs from Indian in the sense that it has little connection with the British Empire. Instead, the dishes served in Chinese restaurants and takeaways in Britain replicate food in similar establishments throughout the west, but not in China. Indeed, Kenneth Lo wrote of Chinese food in the West and Chinese food in the East, so that the foods eaten in the homeland remain quite different from those served throughout the world. A standardized western menu had emerged by the early twentieth century, rather like the curry dishes which had become popular amongst Britons. While Indian food did not spread beyond Britain until quite recently, Chinese dishes had become an international phenomenon by the First World War. Unlike curry in Britain, where the connection between migration and the restaurant business remains indirect, in the sense that most Bangladeshis and other South Asians have not moved to Britain specifically to work in the restaurant trade, much migration from Hong Kong occurred specifically to staff Chinese restaurants and takeaways.[187]

FIGURE 19 Chefs at work in Chinese restaurant *c.* 1990–1999, Chinatown, London. Image © Inge Yspeert/CORBIS

Migrants from South Asia and Hong Kong have caused a revolution in the eating patterns of the British, who, since the 1950s, have moved away from the meat and two veg' culture which represented the majority of midday and evening meals.[188] Once Britons started eating in Indian, Chinese, Italian and other exotic restaurants, they developed a taste for such products and wished to consume them at home. While some Britons went to the extent of cooking such dishes from scratch, as ingredients increasingly became available after the end of rationing in the second half of the 1950s, multinationals and supermarkets really spread foreign foods to the home and, in that sense, domesticated them from the 1980s as they began to produce ready meals, which simply needed heating up for twenty minutes.[189]

Post-war immigration has therefore transformed the nature of food in Britain. During the 1950s, the vast majority of Britons ate fried breakfast in the morning followed by meat and two veg at midday and in the evening,[190] which included dishes such as 'pies, roasts and nursery puddings'. By the end of the twentieth century the 'national cuisine' included 'the rice noodle dishes of Southeast Asia or the delicious food of the Mediterranean', as well as curry and Chinese food.[191]

Immigrants have also helped to transform other aspects of British life, to which we can briefly refer. For instance, taking a global perspective, Parminder Bhachu and Nirmal Puwar have examined the impact of dress from South Asia. The latter has written that 'Multicultural capitalism – capitalism based on the production and consumption of cultural diversity and the marketing of packaged versions of the "exotic" – is at the cutting edge of globalized economic markets'.[192] In such a situation, clothing designers can incorporate the norms of non European, including South Asian, cultures and bring them to western women as important as Cherie Booth or Princess Diana. By 2000 companies such as Oasis, Karen Millen and Diesel had incorporated elements of South Asian dress into their high street collections. By this time 'fashion boutiques, malls, clubs and stalls sparkled with pashmina scarves, or at least with what passed as pashmina scarves, mendhies, bindhies, nose studs, sequinned and embroidered shoes, sandals, handbags, jeans, tops and skirts', so that the exotic, had become part of the mainstream.[193] In a similar way in which curry had moved from the Bangladeshi restaurant into the home via the English high street, so female dress had undergone the same transformation. Parminder Bhachu traced the history of the salwar kamiz from the dress which she and her mother wore rather nervously as Punjabis in Britain during the 1960s and 1970s to an item which royalty and the prime minister's wife sported by the 1990s. Bhachu examines the role of South Asian women designers and factory workers in Britain in the transformation of both this item of clothing and others with South Asian origins.[194]

A brief examination of the impact of Black people on popular music reveals a history dating back to the nineteenth century. During the Victorian and Edwardian period Black music manifested itself most obviously in 'minstrelsy', which would survive in Britain into the second half of the twentieth century in the form of the BBC *Black and White Minstrel Show*. Michael Pickering has also examined whether jazz represents a legacy of such performance, although jazz in Britain is primarily performed by white people.[195] Paul Oliver, on the other hand, has demonstrated the different ways in which Black music had impacted upon Britain by the end of the 1980s whether in the form of 'African bands and solo musicians' or visiting musicians from the USA. As with South Asian inspired fashion, new musical movements emerged in Britain from the 1960s involving cultural exchange between West Indian migrants in Britain, Black musicians still in the West Indies and the USA and white British musicians leading to the development of ska, soul, disco, funk, reggae and hip hop. Again, as in the case of food and dress, such music increasingly moved into the mainstream as record labels emerged to market it, while the large mainstream labels also increasingly became interested in these forms.[196] By the 1990s Black Britons increasingly entered the mainstream, epitomized not only in the composition of groups such as the Spice Girls but also in the chart topping success of artists such as Leona Lewis.

Black people have increasingly become visible in a positive light on British television and film. Certainly in the early post-war decades, they tended to fill racist stereotypes, from which they have still not completely escaped. Before 1945 Paul Robeson found himself cast as an African wearing a leopard skin in the 1935 film adaptation of *Sanders of the River*, reflecting the marginalized parts he often took.[197] The stereotyping continued after 1945 especially in the early decades of Caribbean immigration whether in drama, documentary or comedy, a situation which has not yet disappeared.[198] Nevertheless, partly as a result of the decline of overt racism and partly because Black and Asian people have moved behind the camera and into production roles, significant change has occurred in recent years. We can see this by using the example of the actor Rudolph Walker, who first made his name in the overtly racist situation comedy *Love Thy Neighbour* in the early 1970s. His career would suffer a downturn later in that decade but would begin to take off again after he played Othello at the Young Vic Theatre in 1984. Most significantly, he began to take on 'non-racial' roles (in which his colour did not represent the central issue) by the 1990s in programmes such *The Thin Blue Line* and *Eastenders*.[199] Just as significantly, Black and Asian newsreaders also began to become increasingly common on British television by the 1990s both on local and national TV including, in the latter, Wesley Kerr, George Alagiah, Zeinab Badawi, Moira Stewart, Krishnan Guru-Murthy and, above all, Sir Trevor McDonald, who became the voice of ITN news. Like white newsreaders who dispense with any regional or working class identity by adopting Queen's English, the Black and Asian newsreaders mirrored their white counterparts apart from their skin colour.[200] The fact that Black and Asian faces have become a feature of television newsrooms represents significant progress, reflecting the entry of some African-Caribbeans, Africans and Asians into the elites of British society.

Migrants and their descendants have also increasingly moved into the centre of British literature in the post-war period. In addition to those of Jewish origin, leading writers have also increasingly originated from South Asia, the Caribbean and beyond. Sukhdev Sandhu has traced the predecessors of the post-war generation back to Ignatius Sancho and Olaudah Equiano in the eighteenth century.[201] Some recent British writers and poets, above all Linton Kwesi Johnson, write primarily about their own personal experiences as well as the Black experience in Britain.[202] Similarly, Hanif Kureishi, Zadie Smith, Monica Ali and Andrea Levy have also focused upon multicultural Britain. Salman Rushdie has become one of the most famous writers in the world, even discounting *The Satanic Verses*, although, once again, his prose is influenced by own personal experiences as a migrant.[203] The centrality of writers with origins from outside Europe has given rise to the concept of multicultural fiction,[204] even though, by the beginning of the twenty-first century, writers such as Zadie Smith had brought stories of multicultural London to the mainstream. Yasmin Hussain has recently focused specifically upon South Asian women when tackling the emergence of a culture in the diaspora. She has examined not only writers but also film makers such as Gurinder Chadha whose work includes *Bhaji on the Beach* and *Bend it Like Beckham*.[205]

In addition to food the other area in which migrants have perhaps become most visible consists of sport, where, by the 1980s, they had moved into the competitive mainstream in, for instance, football, athletics and boxing. Much writing has focused upon sport as an avenue for social mobility for Black youth. But Ernest Cashmore has written that sport for Black boys 'profits from failure: the failure of Black kids to integrate more satisfactorily, gain qualifications more readily, find careers more easily'.[206] A footballer such as Ian Wright came to view football as an escape from social

deprivation.[207] Teachers and the education system as
directed Black pupils towards sport from the 1970s.[208]

An examination of football will help to illustrate t
experience of ethnic minorities in sport, especially sinc
the first Black footballer may date back to the 1880s,[209] a s
in numbers did not occur until the 1970s and 1980s, a:
population in Britain originating in the West Indian i_.g.ation of the
1950s, increased. By 1997 15 per cent of professional footballers were Black,
including 33 per cent in the premier league, meaning an increase of 35 per
cent since the 1985 season.[210] Nevertheless, the road to this level of success
by 1997, by which time Black players had become a permanent fixture
in the England national team, had been littered by a variety of racist
obstacles. One of the most obvious of these, which became particularly
prominent as Black players began to increase during the 1970s and 1980s,
consisted of abuse. Les Back, Tim Crabbe and John Solomos have even
gone as far as to draw up a typology of seven forms of racist abuse amongst
fans. These have included straightforward racial insults such as 'you Black
bastard' to more subtle forms of racism expressed through humour.[211] By
the 1990s direct racism became increasingly difficult to articulate as clubs
tried to clear up their act, threatening bans to anyone who used racist
abuse. Such developments partly resulted from government pressure, as
well as from the Let's Kick Racism out of Football campaign.[212] While
Black players may have become ubiquitous in English football, Asians, on
the other hand, have not, despite the fact that they participate in football
on a local level in Asian football leagues. The almost complete absence of
Asian footballers comes from a combination of a resistance of the Asian
community to sport as a profession, combined with continuing racism from
the football establishment itself, beginning at the grassroots level.[213] While
Black and foreign players have increasingly made their presence felt on
the pitch, perhaps the most obvious area of exclusion of ethnic minorities
and migrants from football lies in the stands, as the supporters of many
teams are comprised entirely of members of the ethnic majority. This is probably to be expected in cities with low percentages of Black and Asian people
such as Newcastle or Sunderland, but not in other big cities. Nevertheless,
some teams from multicultural areas such as Arsenal and Manchester City
have always had supporters from ethnic minorities.[214] A precedent for this
development lies in the early twentieth-century development of support
for London clubs amongst the Jewish community. They turned their attention not simply towards Tottenham but also Arsenal and West Ham, even
though, in popular discourse, Spurs has become the Jewish team.[215] The

ost significant recent development in the multiculturalization of football in Britain consists of the influx of foreign players, especially those from the European Union, but also others from beyond. These newcomers have turned the Premier League into one of the most cosmopolitan areas in British life so that by 2008 331 Premier League players from 66 different countries made up 60 per cent of the total.[216]

Britain as a multicultural state and society

Most commentators upon multicultural Britain offer critiques which highlight problems since the 1980s. These focus especially upon the fact that many members of ethnic minorities tend to remain at the bottom of the social and economic ladder despite the opportunities which a multicultural society offers. At the same time, political and social scientists have begun to question the benefits of multiculturalism and have especially focused upon the fact that it entrenches particular ethnic interests and may exclude emerging migrant groups.

Clearly, Britain does not constitute a multicultural paradise and never will do. Nevertheless, over the past two centuries, this nation state and its society has, at the same time as practising overt racism, also incorporated and become enriched by migrant groups. The democratic structures of Britain as a liberal democracy have played a central role in the progress of migration. The milestone of Roman Catholic Emancipation, which heralded the period under discussion here, found itself repeated over the next two hundred years as governments responded to the demands of a series of ethnic minorities. Just as importantly, *jus solis* as the determining factor in nationality law in Britain has played a central role in the incorporation of the descendants of migrants.

At the same time sections of British society have also displayed a positive attitude towards ethnic minorities. Inter-racial friendships, sexual unions and exogamy have represented reality on the streets and in the homes of Britain since the Victorian period. Similarly, while numerous individuals and organizations have displayed their hostility towards foreigners, especially in the short term, groups have also evolved to ease the settlement process of migrants.

Ethnic minorities have also helped to transform Britain. In the first place, they have introduced new religions and languages into the country. They have had a profound impact on aspects of British life. This seems most obvious in the area of eating out since the late Victorian period and, more recently, sport, especially football. Because of the centrality of migrants in the evolution of catering it seems impossible to imagine the history of eating outside the home in any other way. Similarly, it seems difficult to conceive the recent history of football without incorporating the sons of West Indian and African migrants or the influx of players from Europe and beyond. The paradigm of cultural transfer facilitates an understanding of how migrants have helped in the transformation of Britain. This becomes most obvious in the way in which foods have emerged as a result of the migration process.

While racism may have remained alive and well in the development of recent British history, so has multiculturalism. The structures and nature of liberal democracy have facilitated this process. Although changes in British life may appear more obvious since the 1960s, the processes by which migration played a role in the evolution of the country had already become manifest before the Victorian period.

Notes and references

1   Mike Phillips and Trevor Phillips, *Windrush: The Irresistible Rise of Multi-Racial Britain* (London, 1998).

2   Yasmin Alibhai-Brown, *Who Do We Think We Are? Imagining the New Britain* (London, 2000), pp. x, 44–70.

3   Bikhu Parekh, et al., *The Future of Multi-Ethnic Britain* (London, 2000).

4   Adrian Favell, *Philosophies of Integration: Immigrants and the Idea of Citizenship in France and Britain*, 2nd edn (Basingstoke, 2001).

5   Randall Hansen, *Citizenship and Immigration in Post-war Britain: The Institutional Origins of a Multicultural Nation* (Oxford, 2000).

6   Ibid., p. 35.

7   Harry Goulbourne, *Race Relations in Britain Since 1945* (Basingstoke, 1998), pp. 100–22.

8   Andreas Fahrmeier, *Citizens and Aliens: Foreigners and the Law in Britain and the German States, 1789–1870* (Oxford, 2000).

9   Herbert Butterfield, *The Whig Interpretation of History* (London, 1965).

10 See David Blackbourn and Geoff Eley, *The Peculiarities of German History: Bourgeois Society and the Politics of Nineteenth Century Germany* (Oxford, 1984), pp. 1–35.

11 Philip Cohen, 'The Perversions of Inheritance: Studies in the Making of Multi-Racist Britain', in Philip Cohen and Harwant S. Baines, eds, *Multi-Racist Britain* (London, 1988), pp. 12–13.

12 Graham Huggan, 'Virtual Multiculturalism: The Case of Contemporary Britain', *European Studies*, vol. 16 (2001), p. 72.

13 Alibai-Brown, *Who Do We Think We Are?*; Parekh, *Future of Multi-Ethnic Britain*.

14 See below.

15 See the contributions of Tony Kushner and Kevin Myers to Kathy Burrell and Panikos Panayi, eds, *Histories and Memories: Migrants and their History in Britain* (London, 2006).

16 Varun Uberoi, 'Social Unity in Britain', *Journal of Ethnic and Migration Studies*, vol. 33 (2007), pp. 141–57.

17 Adrian Favell, 'Multi-Ethnic Britain: An Exception in Europe', *Patterns of Prejudice*, vol. 35 (2001), pp. 35–57.

18 See Chapters 3 and 4.

19 Classic accounts of the emergence of liberal Britain include Asa Briggs, *The Age of Improvement, 1783–1867* (London, 1959). More recent volumes include W. D. Rubinstein, *Britain's Century: A Political and Social History, 1815–1905* (London, 1998).

20 Rainer Liedtke and Stephan Wendehorst, eds, *The Emancipation of Catholics, Jews and Protestants: Minorities and the Nation State in Nineteenth Century Europe* (Manchester, 1999).

21 Wendy Hinde, *Catholic Emancipation: A Shake to Men's Minds* (Oxford, 1992), pp. 6, 10.

22 Ian Machin, 'British Catholics', in Liedtke and Wendehorst, *Emancipation*, p. 11.

23 Ibid., p. 15; Donald M. MacRaild, *Irish Migrants in Modern Britain, 1750–1922* (Basingstoke, 1999), p. 79.

24 Machin, 'British Catholics', pp. 15–16.

25 Hinde, *Catholic Emancipation*, pp. 9, 13.

26 Rubinstein, *Britain's Century*, p. 23.

27 Hinde, *Catholic Emancipation*; Gilbert A. Cahill, 'Irish Catholicism and English Toryism', *Review of Politics*, vol. 19 (1957), pp. 62–76.

28 Machin, 'British Catholics', pp. 13–23.

29 Fergus O'Ferrall, *Catholic Emancipation: Daniel O'Connell and the Birth of Irish Democracy* (Dublin, 1985), p. 273.

30 See Chapter 4.

31 Rachel O'Higgins, 'The Irish Influence in the Chartist Movement', *Past and Present*, no. 20 (1961), pp. 83, 89.

32 Graham Davis, *The Irish in Britain* (Dublin, 1991), pp. 159–90.

33 Dorothy Thompson, 'Ireland and the Irish in English Radicalism before 1850', in James Epstein and Dorothy Thompson, eds, *The Chartist Experience: Studies in Working-Class Radicalism and Culture, 1830–1960* (London, 1982), p. 12.

34 MacRaild, *Irish Migrants*, pp. 136–8.

35 John McCaffrey, 'The Irish Vote in Glasgow in the Later Nineteenth Century: A Preliminary Survey', *Innes Review*, vol. 21 (1970), pp. 30–6; Ian Wood, 'Irish Immigrants and Scottish Radicalism', in Ian McDougall, ed., *Essays in Scottish Labour History* (Edinburgh, 1979), pp. 65–89.

36 Alan O'Day, 'The Political Behaviour of the Irish in Great Britain in the Later Nineteenth and Early Twentieth Centuries', in John Belchem and Klaus Tenfelde, eds, *Irish and Polish Migration in Comparative Perspective* (Essen, 2003), p. 91.

37 Steven Fielding, *Class and Ethnicity: Irish Catholics in England, 1880–1939* (Buckingham, 1993), pp. 118–26.

38 Enda Delaney, *The Irish in Post-war Britain* (Oxford, 2007), pp. 191–4.

39 Israel Finestein, *Jewish Society in Victorian England: Collected Essays* (London, 1993).

40 U. R. Q. Henriques, 'The Jewish Emancipation Controversy in Nineteenth Century Britain', *Past and Present*, no. 40 (1968), p. 126.

41 V. D. Lipman, 'The Age of Emancipation, 1815–1880', in Lipman, ed., *Three Centuries of Anglo-Jewish History* (London, 1961), p. 77.

42 Finestein, *Short History of Anglo-Jewry*, p. 81.

43 M. C. N. Salbstein, *The Emancipation of the Jews in Britain: The Question of the Admission of the Jews to Parliament* (London, 1982), pp. 57–8, 67–8, 75.

44 Ibid., p. 57.

45 Lipman, 'Age of Emancipation', pp. 79–81; Geoffrey Alderman, *Modern British Jewry* (Oxford, 1992), p. 53; Henriques, 'Jewish Emancipation Controversy', pp. 129–30; Todd M. Endelman, *The Jews of Britain, 1656–2000* (London, 2002), p. 98.

46 Salbstein, *Emancipation*, p. 241; Finestein, *Short History of Anglo-Jewry*, pp. 87–8; Alderman, ibid., p. 63.

47 See Todd M. Endelman and Tony Kushner, eds, *Disraeli's Jewishness* (London, 2002).

48 Geoffrey Alderman, *The Jewish Community in British Politics* (Oxford, 1983), p. 174.

49 Geoffrey Alderman, *London Jewry and London Politics, 1889–1986* (London, 1989), p. 30.

50 William J. Fishman, *East End Jewish Radicals, 1875–1914* (London, 1975).

51 See Chapter 4.

52 Harold Pollins, 'East End Jewish Working Men's Clubs Affiliated to the Working Men's Clubs and Institute Union', in Aubrey Newman, ed., *The Jewish East End* (London, 1982), pp. 173–91.

53 Kenneth Lunn, 'Parliamentary Politics and the "Jewish Vote" in Whitechapel, 1906–1914', in ibid., pp. 255–65.

54 Cecil Roth, 'The Court Jews of Edwardian England', *Jewish Social Studies*, vol. 5 (1943), pp. 355–66.

55 Todd M. Endelman, *Radical Assimilation in English Jewish History, 1656–1945* (Bloomington and Indianapolis, 1990), pp. 74–5.

56 Holmes, *Anti-Semitism in British Society, 1876–1939* (London, 1979), p. 70.

57 W. D. Rubinstein, *A History of the Jews in the English Speaking World: Great Britain* (Basingstoke, 1996), p. 206.

58 Bernard Wasserstein, *Herbert Samuel: A Political Life* (Oxford, 1992).

59 Tony Kushner, *The Persistence of Prejudice: Anti-Semitism in British Society during the Second World War* (Manchester, 1989), pp. 3–4.

60 Alderman, *Jewish Community in British Politics*, p. 174.

61 Alderman, ibid., pp. 174–5; Rubinstein, *History of the Jews*, pp. 392–403; Endelman, *Jews of Britain*, pp. 241–2.

62 Hansen, *Citizenship and Immigration*, p. v.

63 See Chapter 5.

64 Bob Hepple, *Race, Jobs and the Law in Britain*, 2nd edn (Harmondsworth, 1970), pp. 156–9.

65 Sheila Patterson, *Immigration and Race Relations in Britain, 1960–1967* (London, 1969), pp. 42–4; Roy Hattersley, 'Immigration', in C. Cook and D. McKie, eds, *The Decline of Disillusionment: British Politics in the 1960s* (London, 1972), pp. 182–9.

66 Patterson, ibid., pp. 87–91; E. J. B. Rose, et al., *Colour and Citizenship: A Report on British Race Relations* (Oxford, 1969), pp. 519–21; Hepple, *Race, Jobs and the Law*, pp. 162–71.

67 Goulbourne, *Race Relations*, p. 101.

68 Zig Layton-Henry, *The Politics of Immigration* (Oxford, 1992), pp. 46–56; S. Abbot, ed., *The Prevention of Racial Discrimination* (London, 1971).

69 Anthony Lester, 'The Politics of the Race Relations Act 1976', in Muhammad Anwar, Patrick Roach and Ranjit Sondhi, eds, *From Legislation to Integration? Race Relations in Britain* (London, 2000), pp. 32–7.

70 Geoffrey Bindman, 'Law Enforcement or Lack of It', in ibid., pp. 40–57; Goulbourne, *Race Relations*, pp. 100–14.

71 See: the special issue of the *Political Quarterly*, vol. 79, no. 1 (2008); and Linda Dickens, 'The Road is Long: Thirty Years of Equality in Britain', *British Journal of Industrial Relations*, vol. 45 (2007), pp. 463–94.

72 Brian Cathcart, *The Case of Stephen Lawrence* (London, 1999); Sir William MacPherson, *The Stephen Lawrence Inquiry* (London, 1999).

73 Bill Dixon and David Gadd, 'Getting the Message?: "New" Labour and the Criminalization of "Hate" ', *Criminology and Criminal Justice*, vol. 6 (2001), pp. 309–28; P. Iganski, 'Why Make "Hate" a Crime?', *Critical Social Policy*, vol. 19 (1999), pp. 386–95.

74 Martin MacEwan, *Tackling Racism in Europe: An Examination of Anti-Discrimination Law in Practice* (Oxford, 1995), p. 165; Wendy Ball and John Solomos, eds, *Race and Local Politics* (Basingstoke, 1990). See also: Richard Jenkins and John Solomos, eds, *Racism and Equal Opportunity Policies in the 1980s* (Cambridge, 1993); and Alrick X. Cambridge and Stephen Feuchtwang, *Antiracist Strategies* (Aldershot, 1990). I am grateful to Alison Duffy for pointing me to these two references. For antiracism in schools see, for example: Sally Tomlinson, *Home and School in Multicultural Britain* (Batsford, 1984); Jagdish Gundara, Crispin Jones and Keith Kimberley, eds, *Racism, Education and Diversity* (London, 1896); Louise Cohen and Lawrence Mansion, *Multicultural Classrooms* (London, 1985); David Gillborn, *Racism and Antiracism in Schools* (Buckingham, 2000); Frank Reeves, *Race Equality in Local Communities: A Guide to its Promotion* (Birmingham, 2007); and Michael Banton, *Promoting Racial Harmony* (Cambridge, 1985), pp. 99–120.

75 Muhamad Anwar, 'The Impact of Legislation on British Race Relations', in Anwar, Roach and Sondhi, *From Legislation to Integration*, pp. 58–77.

76 Rosina Visram, *Asians in Britain: 400 Years of History* (London, 2002), pp. 126–49, 304–19. For more background on wealthier Indians in Britain see Shompa Lahiri, *Indians in Britain: Anglo-Indian Encounters, Race and Indentity, 1880–1930* (London, 2000); and A. Martin Wainwright, *'The Better Class' of Indians: Social Rank, Imperial Identity, and South Asians in Britain, 1858–1914* (Manchester, 2008).

77 Parekh, *Future of Multi-Ethnic Britain*, p. 230.

78 Zig Layton-Henry, 'The Electoral Participation of Black and Asian Britons: Integration or Alienation', *Parliamentary Affairs*, vol. 38 (1985), pp. 307–18; Martin Fitzgerald, *Political Parties and Black People: Participation, Representation and Exploitation* (London, 1984), pp. 70–86.

79 Layton-Henry, *Politics of Immigration*, p. 112.

80 Ibid., p. 113.

81 Shamit Saggar, 'A Late, Though Not Lost, Opportunity: Ethnic Minority Electors, Party Strategy and the Conservative Party', *Political Quarterly*, vol. 69 (1998), p. 156.

82 Ibid., pp. 148–59.

83 K. Shukra, 'Black Sections in the Labour Party', in Harry Goulbourne, ed., *Black Politics in Britain* (Aldershot, 1990), pp. 165–89.

84 Shamit Saggar and Andrew Geddes, 'Negative and Positive Racialisation: Re-Examining Ethnic Minority Political Representation in the UK', *Journal of Ethnic and Migration Studies*, vol. 26 (2000), pp. 25–44.

85 *Independent*, 7 September 2006.

86 Rubinstein, *History of the Jews*, pp. 262, 403.

87 Parekh, *Future of Multi-Ethnic Britain*, p. 232.

88 Goulbourne, *Race Relations*, p. 64; Layton-Henry, *Politics of Immigration*, p. 105; Panikos Panayi, *The Impact of Immigration: A Documentary History of the Effects and Experiences of Immigrants and Refugees in Britain Since 1945* (Manchester, 1999), p. 119.

89 Romain Garbaye, *Getting into Local Power: The Politics of Ethnic Minorities in British and French Cities* (Oxford, 2005), pp. 7–8.

90 Ibid., pp. 116–41; Gurharpal Singh, 'Multiculturalism in Contemporary Brtiain: Reflections on the "Leicester Model" ', in John Rex and Gurharpal Singh, eds, *Governance in Multicultural Societies* (Aldershot, 2004), pp. 65–8.

91 See Chapter 4.

92 See Chapter 5 and below.

93 See Chapter 3.

94 See Chapter 5.

95 See especially Tony Kushner, *Remembering Refugees: Then and Now* (Manchester, 2006).

96 Tony Kushner and Katherine Knox, *Refugees in an Age of Genocide: Global, National and Local Perspectives During the Twentieth Century* (London, 1999).

97 Panikos Panayi, *The Enemy in Our Midst: Germans in Britain during the First World War* (Oxford, 1991), pp. 266–73.

98 Francesa M. Wilson, *They Came as Strangers: The Story of Refugees to Great Britain* (London, 1959), p. xv.

99 Bernard Porter, *The Refugee Question in Mid-Victorian Politics* (Cambridge, 1979).

100 Colin Holmes, 'Immigrants, Refugees and Revolutionaries', in John Slatter, ed., *From the Other Shore: Russian Political Emigrants in Britain, 1880–1917* (London, 1984), p. 7.

101 Lucio Sponza, *Italian Immigrants in Nineteenth Century Britain* (Leicester, 1988), p. 129.

102 Ibid., pp. 129–33; Margaret C. Wicks, *The Italian Exiles in London, 1816–1848* (New York, 1968).

103 Rosemary Ashton, *Little Germany: Exile and Asylum in Victorian England* (Oxford, 1986), p. 155. See also Sabine Freitag, ed., *Exiles from European Revolutions: Refugees in Mid-Victorian England* (Oxford, 2003).

104 Wilson, *They Came As Strangers*, p. 133; Tibor Frank, 'Lajos Kossuth and the Hungarian Exiles in London', in Freitag, ibid., p. 129.

105 Panikos Panayi, *German Immigrants in Britain during the Nineteenth Century, 1815–1914* (Oxford, 1995), p. 229.

106 William D. and Hilary L. Rubinstein, *Philosemitism and Support in the English-Speaking World For Jews, 1840–1939* (Basingstoke, 1999), pp. 111–88.

107 Ibid., pp. 39–58.

108 Ibid., pp. 111–78.

109 Holmes, *Anti-Semitism*.

110 Endelman, *Radical Assimilation*, p. 209.

111 Louise London, *Whitehall and the Jews, 1933–1948: British Immigration Policy and the Holocaust* (Cambridge, 2000), p. 276.

112 Rubinstein, *Philosemitism*, pp. 83–102.

113 William D. Rubinstein, *The Myth of Rescue: Why the Democracies Could Not Have Saved More Jews from the Nazis* (London, 1997).

114 A. J. Sherman, *Britain and the Refugees from the Third Reich* (London, 1973), p. 267.

115 Norman Bentwich, *They Found Refuge: An Account of British Jewry's Work for the Victims of Nazi Oppression* (London, 1956); Jeremy Seabrook, *The Refuge and the Fortress: Britain and the Flight from Tyranny* (Basingstoke, 2009), pp. 17–75.

116 Kushner, *Remembering Refugees*, pp. 141–80.

117 Kushner and Knox, *Refugees in an Age of Genocide*, pp. 145–54.

118 Tony Kushner, *We Europeans? Mass-Observation, 'Race' and British Identity in the Twentieth Century* (Aldershot, 2004), pp. 189–218.

119 See: Barry Hollingsworth, 'The Society of Friends of Russian Freedon: English Liberals and Russian Socialists, 1890–1917', *Oxford Slavonic Papers*, vol. 3 (1970), pp. 45–64; and contributions to Slatter, *From the Other Shore*.

120 Kushner and Knox, *Refugees in an Age of Genocide*, pp. 47–8.

121 Peter Cahalan, *Belgian Refugee Relief in England during the Great War* (New York, 1982); Lady Lugard, 'The Work of the War Refugees' Committee', *Journal of the Royal Society of Arts*, vol. 43 (1915), pp. 429–40.

122 M. Vincentelli, 'The Davies Family and Belgian Refugee Artists and Musicians in Wales', *National Library of Wales Journal*, vol. 22 (1981), pp. 226–33.

123 Cahalan, *Belgian Refugee Relief*, p. 505.

124 Ibid., p. 508.

125 Kushner and Knox, *Refugees in an Age of Genocide*.

126 Joanna Herbert, 'Migration, Memory and Metaphor: Life Stories of South Asians in Leicester', in Burrell and Panayi, *Histories and Memories*, pp. 145–6.

127   Mark Lilly, *The National Council for Civil Liberties: The First Fifty Years* (London, 1984), pp. 48–56; http://www.liberty-human-rights-.org.uk/

128   Benjamin W. Heineman Jr., *The Politics of the Powerless: A Study of the Campaign Against Racial Discrimination* (London, 1972).

129   Dave Renton, *When We Touched the Sky: The Anti-Nazi League, 1977–1988* (Cheltenham, 2006); Paul Gilroy, *There Ain't No Black in the Union Jack* (London, 1987), pp. 131–5; Panayi, *Impact of Immigration*, pp. 184–6.

130   John Street, Seth Hague and Heather Savigny, 'Playing to the Crowd: The Role of Music and Musicians in Political Participation', *British Journal of Politics and International Relations*, vol. 10 (2008), pp. 269–85.

131   Seabrook, *Refuge.*

132   http://www.antiracistalliance.org.uk

133   Jeffrey Williamson, 'The Impact of the Irish on British Labour Markets during the Industrial Revolution', in Roger Swift and Sheridan Gilley, eds, *The Irish in Britain, 1815–1939* (London, 1989), pp. 134–62.

134   Christian Dustmann and Francesca Fabbri, 'Immigrants in the British Labour Force', *Fiscal Studies*, vol. 26 (2005), pp. 423–70.

135   See Chapter 4.

136   See Chapter 4.

137   Peter Karsten, 'Irish Soldiers in the British Army, 1792–1922: Suborned or Subordinate', *Journal of Social History*, vol. 17 (1983), pp. 31–64; Walter McGrath, 'The Boer Irish Brigade', *Irish Sword*, vol. 5 (1961), pp. 59–60; Michael McDonagh, 'The London Irish', *Irish Soldier*, 1 October 1918; R. G. Harris and H. R. G. Wilson, *The Irish Regiments, 1683–1999* (Staplehurst, 1999).

138   A recent article has also pointed to their influence on the development of mountaineering in the form of Jonathan Westaway, 'The German Community in Manchester, Middle Class Culture and the Development of Mountaneering in Britain', *English Historical Review*, vol. 124 (2009), pp. 571–604.

139   Stanley D. Chapman, 'The International Houses: The Continental Contribution in British Commerce, 1800–1860', *Journal of European Economic History*, vol. 19 (1977), pp. 19, 44–8.

140   Stanley D. Chapman, 'Aristocracy and Meritocracy in Merchant Banking', *British Journal of Sociology*, vol. 37 (1986), pp. 181–4.

141   Stanley D. Chapman, *The Rise of Merchant Banking* (London, 1984); Stefanie Diaper, 'Sir Alexander Drake Kleinwort', in *Dictionary of Business Biography* (London, 1985), pp. 605–6; Richard Roberts, *Schroders: Merchants and Bankers* (London, 1992), pp. 1–151; Niall Ferguson, *The House of Rothschild*, 2 Volumes (London, 2000).

142   See, for instance, A. R. Rollin, 'The Jewish Contribution to the British Textile Industry: "Builders of Bradford" ', *Transactions of the Jewish Historical Society of*

England, vol. 17 (1951); and Harold Pollins, *Economic History of the Jews in England* (London, 1982), pp. 94–6.

143 Stefan Manz, 'Management Transfer in the Textile Industry: The Example of Otto Ernst Philippi at J & P Coats, 1872–1917', in Stefan Manz, Margrit Schulte Beerbühl and John R. Davis, eds, *Migration and Transfer from Germany to Britain, 1660–1914* (Munich, 2007), pp. 161–73.

144 W. J. Reader, *Imperial Chemical Industries*, Vol. 1 (London, 1970), pp. 47–56.

145 Stefan Manz, *Migranten und Internierte: Deutsche in Glasgow, 1864–1918* (Stuttgart, 2003), pp. 133–48.

146 F. Anne M. R. Jarvis, 'German Musicians in London, *c*.1750–1850', in Manz, Beerbühl and Davis, *Migration and Transfer*, pp. 37–47; Herma Fiedler, 'German Musicians in England and their Influence to the End of the Eighteenth Century', *German Life and Letters*, vol. 6 (1939).

147 Panayi, *German Immigrants*, pp. 126–8; Roy Newsome, *Brass Roots: A Hundred Years of Brass Bands and their Music* (Aldershot, 1998).

148 Panayi, ibid., pp. 128–30; Reginald Nettel, *The Orchestra in England: A Social History* (London, 1946).

149 See, especially, Christopher Palmer, *Delius: Portrait of a Cosmopolitan* (London, 1976).

150 Lucio Sponza, 'Italian "Penny Ice-Men" in Victorian London', in Anne J. Kershen, ed., *Food in the Migrant Experience* (Aldershot, 2002), pp. 17–41.

151 Basil Crowhurst, *A History of the British Ice Cream Industry* (Westerham, 2000).

152 http://flan.utsa.edu/conviviumartium/Tebben.html, Maryann Tebben, ' "French" Fries: France's Culinary Identity Since from Brillat-Savarin to Barthes', *Convivium Artium: Food Representation in Literature, Film, and the Arts*, Spring 2006; Panikos Panayi, *Spicing Up Britain: The Multicultural History of British Food*, (London, 2008), pp. 16–18, 78–9, 161–2; Gerald Priestland, *Frying Tonight: The Saga of Fish and Chips* (London, 1972), p. 20; John K. Walton, *Fish and Chips and the British Working Classes, 1870–1940* (Leicester, 1992), pp. 21–6.

153 Priscilla Parkhurst Ferguson, *Accounting for Taste: The Triumph of French Cuisine* (London, 2004).

154 Panayi, *Spicing*, pp. 79–80; Peter Bird, *The First Food Empire: A History of J. Lyons & Co.* (Chichester, 2000), pp. 2–24.

155 Anne Currah, *Chef to Queen Victoria: The Recipes of Charles Elmé Francatelli* (London, 1973); Ruth Brandon, *The People's Chef: Alexis Soyer, A Life in Seven Courses* (Chichester, 2005); Ruth Cowen, *Relish: The Extraordinary Life of Alexis Soyer, Victorian Celebrity Chef* (London, 2006); Kenneth James, *Escoffier: King of Chefs* (London, 2002).

156 Panayi, *Spicing*, pp. 81–3.

157 Panayi, *German Immigrants*, p. 125.

158 Sir Hubert Llewellyn Smith, ed., *The New Survey of London Life and Labour*, vol. 8, *London Industries*, III (London, 1934), pp. 203, 220.

159 Panayi, *Spicing*, pp. 90–3.

160 See below.

161 W. E. Mosse, et al., eds, *Second Chance: Two Centuries of German-Speaking Jews in the United Kingdom* (Tübingen, 1991); Gerhard Hirschfeld, ed., *Exile in Great Britain: Refugees from Hitler's Germany* (Leamington Spa, 1984); Daniel Snowman, *The Hitler Emigres: The Cultural Impact on Britain of Refugees from Nazism* (London, 2003); Marian Malet and Anthony Grenville, eds, *Changing Countries: The Experience and Achievement of German-Speaking Exiles from Hitler in Britain, 1933 to Today* (London, 2002); Peter Alter, ed., *Out of the Third Reich: Refugee Historians in Post-war Britain* (London, 1998); J. M. Ritchie, *German Exiles: British Perspectives* (New York, 1997).

162 Walter Besant, *East London* (London, 1903), p. 191.

163 Anne J. Kershen, *Strangers, Aliens and Asians: Huguenots, Jews and Bangladeshis in Spitalfields, 1660–2000* (London, 2005).

164 See Rudolf Muhs, 'Jews of German Background in British Politics', in Mosse, *Second Chance*, pp. 177–4.

165 Snowman, *Hitler Emigres*, pp. 352–75.

166 Alter, *Out of the Third Reich*.

167 See the contributions of Paul Hoch and Paul Weindling to Mosse, *Second Chance*.

168 Herbert Loebl, 'Refugee Industries in the Special Areas of Britain', in Hirschfeld, *Second Chance*, pp. 219–50.

169 Snowman, *Hitler Emigres*, p. 352.

170 Rubinstein, *History of the Jews*, pp. 403–5.

171 See Chapter 3.

172 See Kershen, *Strangers*.

173 Panayi, *Impact*, pp. 92–3; Panikos Panayi, 'The Spicing Up of English Provincial Life: The History of Curry in Leicester', in Kershen, *Food in the Migrant Experience*, pp. 68–9.

174 Panikos Panayi, 'Cosmopolis: London's Ethnic Minorities', in Andrew Gibson and Joe Kerr, eds, *London from Punk to Blair* (London, 2003), pp. 67–71.

175 Chapter 2 and 3.

176 See Chapter 4.

177 Panayi, *Spicing*, pp. 155–6.

178 Ibid., p. 157.

179 Floya Anthias, *Ethnicity, Class, Gender and Migration: Greek Cypriots in Britain* (Aldershot, 1992), p. 58.

180 Panayi, *Spicing*, pp. 157–61; Digby Anderson, *The English at Table* (London, 2006), pp. 13–14.

181 Pierre L. van den Berghe, 'Ethnic Cuisine: Culture in Nature', *Ethnic and Racial Studies*, vol. 7 (1984), p. 396.

182 Anneke H. Van Otterloo, 'Foreign Immigrants and the Dutch at Table, 1945–1985: Bridging or Widening the Gap?', *Netherlands Journal of Sociology*, vol. 23 (1987), p. 139.

183 Elizabeth Buettner, ' "Going for an Indian": South Asian Restaurants and the Limits of Multiculturalism in Britain', *Journal of Modern History*, vol. 80 (2008), pp. 865–91.

184 Monder Ram, Tahir Abbas, Balihar Sanghera, Guy Hillin, ' "Currying Favour with the Locals": Balti Owners and Business Enclaves', *International Journal of Entrepreneurial Behaviour and Research*, vol. 6 (2000); Monder Ram, Tahir Abbas, Balihar Sanghera, Gerald Barlow and Trevor Jones, ' "Apprentice Entrepreneurs"? Ethnic Minority Workers in the Independent Restaurant Sector', *Work, Employment and Society*, vol. 15 (2001), pp. 353–72.

185 Lizzie Collingham, *Curry: A Biography* (London, 2005); David Burton, *The Raj at Table: A Culinary History of the British in India* (London, 1993).

186 Panayi, *Spicing*, pp. 172–5.

187 Ibid., pp. 169–72; J. A. G. Roberts, *China to Chinatown: Chinese Food in the West* (London, 2002); Kenneth Lo, *Chinese Food* (Newton Abbot, 1972).

188 Geoffrey C. Warren, ed., *The Foods We Eat* (London, 1958).

189 Panayi, *Spicing*, pp. 196–209.

190 Warren, *The Foods We Eat*.

191 Rose Prince, *The New English Kitchen: Changing the Way You Shop, Cook and Eat* (London, 2005), pp. vii–ix.

192 Nirmal Purwar, 'Multicultural Fashion: Stirrings of Another Sense of Aesthetics and Memory', *Feminist Review*, vol. 71 (2002), p. 64.

193 Ibid., p. 67.

194 Parminder Bhachu, *Dangerous Designs: Asian Women Fashion the Diaspora Economies* (London, 2004).

195 George F. Rehin, 'Blackface Street Minstrels in Victorian London and its Resorts: Popular Culture and Its Racial Connotations As Revealed in Polite Opinion', *Journal of Popular Culture*, vol. 15 (1981), pp. 19–38; Michael Pickering, *Blackface Minstrelsy in Britain* (Aldershot, 2008); Catherine Parsonage, *The Evolution of Jazz in Britain, 1880–1935* (Aldershot, 2005); Jeffrey Green, *Black Edwardians: Black People in Britain, 1901–1914* (London, 1998), pp. 80–114.

196 Paul Oliver, ed., *Black Music in Britain: Essays on the Afro-Asian Contribution to Popular Music* (Buckingham, 1990); Paul Gilroy, *The Black Atlantic: Modernity*

and *Double Consciousness* (London, 1993), pp. 72–110; Michael de Konigh and Marc Griffiths, *Tighten Up:The History of Reggae in the UK* (London, 2003).

197   Stephen Bourne, *Black in the British Frame: The Black Experience in British Film and Television* (London, 2001), pp. 10–31.

198   See, for instance, Sarita Malik, *Representing Black Britain: Black and Asian Images on Television* (London, 2002).

199   Jim Pines, *Black and White in Colour: Black People in British Television Since 1936* (London, 1992), pp. 76–84.

200   Malik, *Representing Black Britain*, pp. 80–1.

201   Sukhdev Sandhu, *London Calling: How Black and Asian Writers Imagined a City* (London, 2003), pp. 19–58.

202   Linton Kwesi Johnson, *Mi Revalueshanary Fren: Selected Poems* (London, 2002).

203   *Guardian,* 25 July 2006; Stephen Morton, *Salman Rushdie: Fictions of Postcolonial Modernity* (Basingstoke, 2008); Andrew Teverson, *Salman Rushdie* (Manchester, 2007).

204   A. Robert Lee, ed., *Other Britain, Other British: Contemporary Multicultural Fiction* (London, 1995).

205   Yasmin Hussain, *Writing Diaspora: South Asian Women, Culture and Ethnicity* (Aldershot, 2005).

206   Ernest Cashmore, *Black Sportmen* (London, 1982), p. 207.

207   Ian Wright, *Mr Wright: The Explosive Autobiography of Ian Wright* (London, 1996).

208   Cashmore, *Black Britain*, pp. 98–110.

209   Phil Vasili, *Colouring Over the White Line: The History of Black Footballers in Britain* (London, 2000), pp. 17–60.

210   Ibid., p. 190.

211   Les Back, Tim Crabbe and John Solomos, *The Changing Face of Football: Racism, Identity and Multiculture in the English Game* (Oxford, 2001), pp. 107–17.

212   Ibid., pp. 186–218.

213   Ibid., pp. 177–9; Vasili, *Colouring*, pp. 155–78; Daniel Burdsey, 'Obstacle Race? "Race", Racism and the Recruitment of British Asian Professional Footballers', *Patterns of Prejudice*, vol. 38 (2004), pp. 279–99.

214   Back, Crabbe and Solomos, ibid., pp. 85–95; Christos Kassimeris, *European Football in Black and White: Tackling Racism in Football* (Plymouth, 2008), p. 89.

215   John Efron, 'When Is a Yid Not a Jew? The Strange Case of Supporter Identity at Tottenham Hotspur', in Michael Brenner and Gideon Reuvni, eds, *Emancipation Through Muscles: Jews and Sports in Europe* (London, 2006), pp. 235–56.

216   Pierre Lanfranchi and Matthew Taylor, *Moving with the Ball: The Migration of Professional Footballers* (Oxford, 2001); http://news.bbc.co.uk/1/hi/uk_politics/7225110.stm, 'Limit Foreign Footballers say MPs', 3 February 2008.

CHAPTER 7

Conclusions, contradictions and continuities

Since the beginning of the nineteenth century Britain has witnessed a series of migratory streams, which have helped the country to constantly transform and reinvent itself. The mainstream historians who have tended to ignore the 9 million or so people who have moved into the country since *c.*1800 have therefore closed their eyes to an important aspect of the country's history, especially those working on the years since the end of the Second World War.

Migrants and their offspring have helped the development of Britain in a variety of ways. While controversy exists about the economic impact of Irish newcomers during the Victorian period, there seems more unanimity about the economic importance of those people who moved to the country after 1945. At the same time, while it seems difficult to conceive the nature of post-war Britain without the large scale immigration which occurred after 1945, the changes which affected food, music, dress and sport have nineteenth-century precedents, especially the first two of these.

Migration to Britain over the past two centuries presents us with a series of continuities, as well as contradictions and breaks. The approach of this particular volume, summarizing the research on the history of migration and ethnicity, allows a long term perspective, unlike much of the social science and historical literature, which takes a short term approach often by focusing upon a particular minority over a few decades. Clearly exceptions exist to this rule, as long term perspectives have appeared by historians on, for instance, Black, Asian, Irish and Jewish people.[1] While many of the long term studies of the Jews have examined social mobility and change over time,[2] the volumes on Black people and the Irish in particular, have often focused upon poverty and prejudice.[3] Nevertheless, the long term approach allows an examination of transformations which have taken place over the past two centuries. We can deal with these changes by focusing upon migration as a whole and by discussing individual groups. Such an analysis helps to reveal the contradictions apparent in British immigration history over the past two hundred years.

Migration versus control

For much of the nineteenth century Britain pursued an open door policy towards immigration. The passage of the Aliens Act of 1905 brought an end to this laissez-faire approach. It has served as a template for the subsequent passage of other measures to control immigration. These, like the 1905 Act which aimed to keep out Eastern European Jews, have always focused upon particular migrant groups, whether Germans in the First World War, Commonwealth immigrants in the 1960s and 1970s, or refugees from the 1980s. Yet, despite these measures, around nine million people have made their way to Britain over the past two centuries. The obvious explanation for this contradiction lies in the fact that the state aims to control the nature and origins of migration. When a particular migrant community becomes too visible to the press, whether in the form of Jews in the late Victorian period, West Indians in the 1950s or refugees from the 1980s, it campaigns for the passage of legislation to control the influx of a particular group. Consequently, the migration history of Britain over the past two centuries essentially consists of a series of waves. These often peak during periods of economic growth and consequent labour demand such as the immediate post-war period and the early twenty-first century. Yet, as soon as a particular group becomes too visible, it faces restrictions, sometimes in connection with an economic downturn. British governments since the 1905 Aliens Act have therefore had two basic motivating factors which have determined the level of migration which has occurred in the form of the needs of the British economy and the hostility of public opinion driven by the xenophobic press.

This animosity and the measures passed have not, however, prevented or even lessened overall migration over the past two centuries. Indeed, it has probably reached its highest peak during the New Labour government before the 2008 economic crash in a situation in which migration had become more controlled than ever. The obvious explanation for this peak lies in the loophole of the European Union, which allows free movement of labour, although an analysis of census statistics demonstrates that some of the largest communities originate outside Europe and include refugees, illegal immigrants and skilled workers.[4]

Immigration laws have not, therefore, lessened immigration as a whole, although, as they follow the demands of the press, they have racialized it so that the particular group which faces the most hostility finds itself excluded. For much of the early twentieth century this group consisted of Jews, as antisemitism represented the most consistent strand of British xenophobia between *c.*1880 and 1950. After the Second World War, despite the early arrival of migrants from the New Commonwealth facilitated by the 1948 British Nationality Act, Black and Asian people found themselves excluded by the 1970s. More recently, asylum seekers have become the new threat.

This racialization thesis put forward by scholars such as John Solomos and Robert Miles also means that the British state can have its cake and eat it because some groups remain immune allowing migration to continue. While the Irish represented the main racial threat for most of the Victorian period, they did not have restrictions placed upon them at any time between 1837 and 1902 or, indeed, since that time, even when Ireland gained its independence in 1922. Similarly, despite the tight and wide ranging immigration controls which now exist against movement from all over the world, the British state has an obvious labour reserve in the form of the citizens of the poorer states of the European Union.

Over the past two centuries immigration has represented a constant in Britain's history caused by a series of factors in the lands of origins of newcomers, the needs of the economy and the implementation of controls, as well as individual choice, often determined by the existence of networks. The areas of origin of migration have certainly changed over the past two centuries. On the one hand, they appear to have become increasingly international spreading from Ireland in the Victorian period, to incorporate other parts of Europe by the twentieth century. Since the Second World War, and especially in its immediate aftermath, a dramatic transformation occurred as people arrived in hundreds of thousands for the first time from outside Europe. Census statistics reveal the cosmopolitan nature of the British, and especially London, population at the start of the twenty-first century. Yet they also reveal the fact that Europeans continue to outnumber people from beyond the continent. Similarly, the Irish have remained the largest migrant group (even if they have increasingly not seen themselves as such in recent decades) for most of the past two centuries.

Migration represents a constant but it has certainly experienced peaks and troughs according to the dictates of the British economy and British immigration controls, as well as international factors. The early nineteenth century resulted in relatively little movement to Britain until the Irish potato famine in the middle of the 1840s, which resulted in a significant peak. People trickled into the country from Europe and beyond until the 1880s, when a new peak occurred from the Russian Pale of Settlement. The early decades of the twentieth century also witnessed relatively small scale immigration with the exception of the short-lived Belgian refugees and the temporary European exiles during the First and Second World Wars respectively. The only other significant exception consisted of those who fled the Nazis. All of these developments illustrate the birth of refugee crises as a result of nationalism and fascism. Migration took off on a different scale after 1945 due to a wide range of factors rooted in the international strength of the British economy and imperial connections. Peaks may have occurred, such as under the New Labour government, while something of a trough arrived in the 1980s and early 1990s. Nevertheless, migration has characterized and helped to shape Britain since 1945 in a manner perhaps not seen since the Anglo-Saxon, Viking and Norman invasions.

Poverty versus social mobility

Much academic writing on migration, together with contemporary social surveys, points to the underprivileged status of migrants in modern Britain whether Irish, Jewish, West Indian or South Asian. The vast majority of serious writing upon newly arrived immigrants from the Famine Irish through the Jewish migrants of the late Victorian period to the post-war Common- wealth migrants abounds with descriptions and statistics of underprivileged newcomers. Indeed, poverty and the immigrant have become almost syn- onymous. The picture of the Victorian Irish or the late nineteenth-century Jewish migrants in the East of London (constructed by both contemporary commentators, often using racist language, and historians, deploying social and economic history methodology) remains one characterized by deprivation. Similarly, social scientists working on Commonwealth migration such as John Rex, John Solomos, Stephen Castles and Robert Miles, have painted a picture in which racism and poverty kept Black and Asian people in 'the ghetto'. It therefore seems indisputable that the four groups considered here in the form of the Irish and Eastern European Jews of the Victorian and Edwardian periods and the Black and Asian communities of the post-war period remain at the bottom of the economic and social scale. The reality remains difficult to challenge. Contemporary descriptions, social surveys and the work of academics have confirmed this image.

Nevertheless, the connection between poverty and the immigrant needs qualification. Throughout the last two centuries Britain has attracted not only poor migrants searching for any work they can find, but also those with skills or money pulled by the greater opportunities available in one of the world's most advanced economies. The development of the idea of people moving as a result of networks confirms this fact. While this approach often focuses upon connections based upon kinship or geographical origins, networks also operate upon an occupational basis. The German migration to Britain during the nineteenth century helps to illustrate this process. While some Germans may have found themselves working at the bottom of the social scale in manual labour residing in Victorian slums, the research upon this community has demonstrated that much of the migration occurred because of occupational networks, whether bakers, waiters, musicians or entrepreneurs.[5] Similarly, while the refugees from Nazism may have desperately fled to escape persecution and therefore initially found themselves in straitened circumstances, they eventually re-established their middle class position in the post-war decades. At the same time, while most post-war migration may have consisted of people moving towards a vast economy which gave most of them positions at the bottom of the occupational ladder, this also remains an over simplification. Professionals have certainly

FIGURE 20 Immigrants driving buses for a living, 1 January 1967. Photo by Terrence Spencer//Time Life Pictures/Getty Images

moved to Britain, epitomized by Indian doctors,[6] but also, by the end of the twentieth century in particular, the movement of the very rich. At the same time, while membership of the European Union facilitated the migration of hundreds of thousands of Poles to work in employment shunned by much of British society from 2004, free movement of labour within Europe has also resulted in the arrival of professionals from throughout the continent in Britain.[7]

The connection between migration and poverty also ignores inter-generational social mobility as suggested by Leo Lucassen. His examination of the descendants of post-war West Indian migrants demonstrates that they have witnessed some social mobility,[8] although he accepts that relative poverty still characterizes Black lives in Britain. Similarly, social surveys also tend to confirm the underprivileged position of the descendants of Bangladeshi and Pakistani migrants. It may be too early to come to firm conclusions about the social mobility of South Asian immigrants, just four decades after they began to establish themselves. However, figures upon educational attainment demonstrate greater success than the ethnic majority.

Long established communities provide greater ammunition about generational change and challenge the notion of the poor immigrant. Unfortunately, the historiography of the Irish does not allow us to prove this. The majority of the literature on this community focuses on the decades of mass Irish immigration and poverty from c.1840–c.1880. M. A. G. Ó Tuathaigh has challenged this research,[9] but his integration paradigm has rarely been utilized. The only scholars who have followed this path include Steven Fielding who implies that the Irish in Manchester mirrored the norms of the working classes as a whole, while maintaining their Roman Catholicism.[10] Paul O'Leary, meanwhile, who took his study of the Irish in Wales to 1922, also asserted that the migrants of the nineteenth century had integrated by the start of the twentieth using measures such as the decline of anti-Irish feeling and the use of the Welsh language.[11] On the other hand, the experience of the German community in the First World War warns us against the inevitability of social mobility and integration because the xenophobia of that conflict resulted in the ethnic cleansing of a community which appeared to have become increasingly integrated by the Edwardian period.[12]

The community which provides the best example of social mobility consists of Jews. Their historiography helps us. On the one hand numerous studies focus upon the poverty of the newly arrived exiles from the Pale of Settlement who found themselves in the East End of London at the start of the twentieth century. But this represents just one paradigm. Writers on

Jews in Britain are not stuck in a time warp like many historians of the Irish. In fact, a whole series of scholars have taken the long term perspective, which usually encompasses the entire history of Jewish settlement in Britain since the readmission under Cromwell. Such an approach, which allows an examination covering hundreds of years, demonstrates fairly conclusively the social mobility of different waves of Jews, whether focusing upon the Eastern European arrivals of the late nineteenth century or those who came from the continent earlier. In less than a century those who moved from the Russian Pale of Settlement progressed from the bottom of British society to the top as all manner of indicators have suggested.

However, just because Jews moved up the social and economic ladder, this does not automatically mean that other groups will follow the same path. It probably remains too early to come to firm conclusions about most post-war groups. At the same time some social and economic indicators suggest that the descendants of Pakistani, Bangladeshi and West Indian migrants have experienced limited social mobility. On the other hand, it seems difficult to accept that those sections of the Irish who moved into Victorian Britain have not moved upward, although in the absence of concrete research on this subject, it proves difficult to come to any firm conclusions. Perhaps this group simply integrated and assimilated into the surrounding working classes, rather than, like the Jews, moving through the British social system in the space of a century.

No single paradigm therefore exists to cover the social and economic situation of all migrant communities in Britain over the last two centuries, perhaps inevitably in view of the millions of people under consideration here. However, we can come to the following conclusions. There seems no reason to reject the dominant paradigm in both historical and social science research which views migrants as a predominantly working class group, who tend to find themselves towards the bottom of the social and economic scale in Britain. However, we need to qualify this in two main ways. First, a minority of migrants who have moved to Britain have consisted of the wealthy and the highly skilled, often welcomed with open arms. Second, change takes place through generations. Viewing any ethnic group as trapped in a permanent cycle of poverty ignores the reality which a historical approach allows.

Ethnicity, identity and Britishness

The long term approach also helps with an analysis of migrant identities. When newcomers first settle in Britain, they have a strong desire to hold on more closely to the norms of their homeland, whether these revolve around religion, language or politics. Consequently, the first generation attempts to recreate aspects of their homeland in their new surroundings. This situation changes through their descendants who become increasingly incorporated into British norms. While the first generation might appear the most foreign, their descendants usually become increasingly British so that, eventually, the original aspects of their identity may disappear.

Once again, a classic example of this paradigm consists of the Jewish newcomers who arrived from Eastern Europe in the late Victorian and Edwardian period. They brought with them their own religion, their own language and their own food. Contemporary accounts about them from both mainstream society and established Anglo-Jewry focused upon the level of their difference from the rest of the British population, whether Jewish or gentile. But just as the Eastern European newcomers moved up the social scale they also witnessed a similar development of their identities. By the end of the twentieth century, as a result of exogamy and increasing secularization, the Jewish community of Britain had decreased from its immediate post War peak of around half a million to about half that size. Jews had also moved into the centre of British identity construction as the lists of those involved in the entertainment industry would indicate. However, in this move from Eastern European Jewish to British during the course of a century, we should not forget the fact that a large percentage of the descendants of those who moved from the Pale of Settlement have retained their Jewishness while also moving towards British norms. In fact, the very existence of Judaism in Britain arises from the fact that a significant percentage of the descendants of those who entered Britain with this religion have retained the belief of their forefathers.

The same applies to the arrival of the Irish community in Britain, especially the millions who migrated during the Victorian period and the post-war decades. Before the influx of the middle of the nineteenth century, Roman Catholicism largely remained the elite religion of those who had managed to retain their beliefs following the Reformation. While Irish immigration during the eighteenth century had laid the roots for developments in Victorian Britain, the influx after the famine reintroduced Catholicism on a mass scale for the first time since the sixteenth century. The fact that it survived into the twentieth century also indicates that at least some of the descendants of those Irish people who moved to Britain in the Victorian years retained this aspect of their identity, bolstered by the new Irish immigration after 1945.[13] In the case of Glasgow in particular, partly as a result of the level of hostility which the Irish community and their descendants have faced, this Irishness has manifested itself in other ways, such as supporting the Irish football team of Celtic.[14]

Mass migration helps the development of organized ethnicity. But early pioneers often find it difficult to reconstruct aspects of their homeland in their new environment. While South Asians may have developed into one of the most sophisticated ethnic groups in recent British history, this process only took off from the 1970s, when numbers significantly increased. The early pioneers simply lacked the numbers to create a market for the food and clothes of their homeland, which meant that they quickly adapted to the norms of the British. In the case of Sikhs this meant sacrificing meat eating and traditional dress.

Only the growth of the South Asian communities from the 1970s allowed the development of a solid South Asian ethnicity with the opening of places of worship and the evolution of political groups. The birth of Islam, Sikhism and Hinduism in post-war Britain mirrors the renaissance of the Roman Catholic religion during the nineteenth century. Similarly, the German and Irish political groupings of the Victorian years find reflection in the Zionist parties of the late nineteenth and early twentieth centuries and homeland political organizations of the decades after 1945.

Continuities exist in the development of organized ethnicity. The extent to which individuals participate in religion and politics seems more difficult to ascertain. Some political groupings, such as those for German exiles in mid-Victorian Britain, whatever their persuasion, remained minority interests. The same applies to Zionism. On the other hand, Irish Nationalists in Liverpool obtained enough support to return MPs. Religion proves most difficult to measure in terms of participation. On the one hand, the opening of Roman Catholic churches in the nineteenth century, or mosques and Hindu and Sikh temples in the post-war period, suggest devout flocks continuing to practise the religion of their homelands. However, those studies which have tried to break down religious attendance have usually found a patchy picture in which small proportions of particular groups regularly practise their faith. Studies of Anglo-Jewry have demonstrated that religious attendance declines over time and generations.

In fact, the work of Endelman, Alderman and Rubinstein is partly a history of the Anglicization of the Jewish community in the generations which follow the first migrants, whether the focus lies upon those arriving in the seventeenth, eighteenth, nineteenth, or twentieth centuries. The attempt to construct ethnic organizations by elites always remains a contradictory and complex process because the new environment plays a large role in their nature, whether they consist of synagogues and mosques initially functioning in terraced houses, or political groupings. The Islamic extremism which has evolved in contemporary Britain has little to do with the Pakistani homeland as left by male emigrants during the 1960s and more to do with discontented inner city youth resentful of their social and economic position, blighted by racism which they have seen reflected in their perception of an anti-Islamic British foreign policy. Almost upon first arrival hybrid identities emerge influenced by both the land of origin and the land of settlement. The experience of the descendants of Jewish and Irish immigrants suggests a move towards Britishness in which, in many cases, the original religious and national identity disappears. It seems too early to assert whether this will become the fate of the communities which have emerged from non-European migration since 1945. The history of both Roman Catholic and Jewish immigrants also points to the fact that these religions thrive, or at least survive, centuries after migration occurs, particularly if more fervent newcomers arrive. As recent research increasingly demonstrates, identities only fully expose themselves to understanding if examined upon an individual basis. While at the one extreme, some people may live a devout Muslim or Jewish religious life, at the other, especially over generations, many accept secular Britishness.

Racism or multiculturalism?

Perhaps the most obvious contradiction in the history of immigration to Britain since c.1800 consists of the one between racism and multiculturalism. While both social scientists and historians have devoted much attention to the history of racism in Britain, they have only recently begun to focus upon multiculturalism, usually in a critical fashion. In reality, over the last two centuries Britain has somehow emerged as a state in which racism remains endemic yet in which migrants and, more especially, their descendants, have often witnessed significant economic and social mobility.

Most studies of first generation migrants, whether the mid-Victorian Irish, late Victorian Jewry or post-war African-Caribbeans, Bangladeshis and Pakistanis have pointed to the fact that they remain heavily focused at the bottom of the economic and social ladder. At the same time, social scientists have also shown how the second and subsequent generations of post-war migrants remain trapped in a cycle of poverty, crime and deprivation in the inner city. Those scholars such as Steven Fielding who have gone beyond the end of the nineteenth century in their study of the Irish in Britain have also suggested that members of this community experienced limited social mobility.

Meanwhile, studies of the British state have revealed clear evidence of racist practices. Researchers who have focused upon immigration laws and immigration policy from the end of the nineteenth century cannot come to other any other conclusion. Similarly, studies of policing and the judiciary in recent decades, have revealed the racist nature of the former in particular. Historians have demonstrated that in times of war the British state takes virtually any measures which it deems necessary to protect national security against the 'enemy within'. During the Second World War this resulted in the internment and deportation of thousands of Jews and Italians. More recently, the 'war on terror' has meant the surveillance and arrest of anyone believed to have the remotest connection to any Islamic groups regarded as beyond the pale. Nevertheless, the most intolerant period in British history occurred during the First World War, when state and society ethnically cleansed its German population through a policy of internment followed by deportation and property confiscation.

In liberal democratic Britain public opinion has worked hand in hand and often forced racist policies upon governments, seen especially in the way in which immigration legislation has emerged against the backdrop of public hostility towards succeeding groups of immigrants. This unofficial animosity towards immigrants and ethnic minorities manifests itself in three main ways. First, through the existence of a significant, influential and substantial section of the press which, since the arrival of Jewish immigrants from eastern Europe at the end of the nineteenth century, has displayed its displeasure at each migrant influx viewed as threatening to 'the British way of life' and undermining the living and working conditions of Britons as well as threatening sexual norms. In addition, a whole series of racist political groupings have emerged in Britain since the Edwardian period from the British Brothers League through the British Union of Fascists and the National Front to, most recently, the British National Party. Only the last of these appears to have had any political impact by securing a few dozen local council seats and two members of the European Parliament, which, in the context of developments in continental Europe, seems small. However, in post-war British political history in which every vote counts for the Labour and Conservative party machines, such groupings have had an impact following the Smethwick election of 1964 when the Immigration Control Association created an atmosphere in which ignoring the extreme right could mean electoral defeat, at least on the local level. Overtly racist groups therefore have power beyond their apparent limited support. Meanwhile, unofficial animosity has also manifested itself in violence against ethnic minorities, which has tended, like press animosity, to move from one main focus group to another, from the Irish in the mid nineteenth century, to Jews, Germans and then post-war newcomers from the Empire and Commonwealth. While rioting remained normal in the century or so after 1850, this form of violent animosity has disappeared since the early 1960s, although attacks upon individuals have remained.

Racism and xenophobia from both the state and the public have greeted all migrant groups which have moved to Britain over the last two hundred years. The patterns have remained similar and we can argue that while the main victim group has changed, the nature of the animosity has remained similar throughout. Some periods certainly resulted in more intense persecution, especially the two World Wars, and we clearly need to accept the difference in the hostility towards different groups.

The continuity lies in the persistence of prejudice. The contradiction demonstrates itself in the fact that the racism which has greeted migrants somehow runs together with an acceptance of difference, which has recently attracted the label of multiculturalism. While social scientists have pointed to the simplicity of the multicultural message, there seems no doubt that ethnic minorities in Britain have also found welcome in a variety of ways. As we have seen liberal democratic Britain has incorporated outsiders into the body politic since the Catholic Relief Act of 1829. At the same time, hand in hand with hostility towards newcomers runs a strand of humanitarianism, focusing especially upon refugees. Similarly, we cannot ignore the impact which ethnic minorities have made upon a variety of aspects of the 'British way of life' both before and, especially, after 1945. Furthermore, the process of social mobility, while uneven between different groups and while it may take several generations, also suggests a welcoming and multicultural aspect of Britain. Because of the contradictions which can emerge in a liberal democratic parliamentary democracy, modern Britain has displayed both welcoming and hostile attitudes towards migrants and their descendants over the past two centuries. Perhaps the phrase that best sums up the recent history of British attitudes towards ethnic minorities consists of multicultural racism, the ultimate contradiction, but one which points to the complexities of migrant life in Britain over the past two centuries.

Notes and references

1 See Chapter 1.

2 See especially: Geoffrey Alderman, *Modern British Jewry* (Oxford, 1992); Todd M. Endelman, *The Jews of Britain, 1656–2000* (London, 2002); W. D. Rubinstein, *A History of the Jews in the English Speaking World: Great Britain* (Basingstoke, 1996).

3 For the Irish see: Roger Swift and Sheridan Gilley, eds: *The Irish in the Victorian City* (London, 1985); *The Irish in Britain, 1815–1939* (London, 1989); and *The Irish in Victorian Britain: The Local Dimension* (Dublin, 1999). For Black people see, for instance, Peter Fryer, *Staying Power: The History of Black People in Britain* (London, 1984).

4 A good account of recent immigration is Will Somerville, *Immigration Under New Labour* (Bristol, 2007).

5 Panikos Panayi, *German Immigrants in Britain during the Nineteenth Century, 1815–1914* (Oxford, 1995); Stefan Manz, *Migranten und Internierte: Deutsche in Glasgow, 1864–1918* (Stuttgart, 2003); Stefan Manz, Margrit Schulte Beerbühl and John R. Davis, eds, *Migration and Transfer from Germany to Britain, 1660–1914* (Munich, 2007); Ulrike Kirchberger, *Aspekte deutsch-britischer Expansion: Die Überseeinteressen der deutschen Migranten in Großbritannien in der Mitte des 19. Jahrhunderts* (Stuttgart, 1999).

6 Paramjit S. Gill, Robert Arnott and John Stewart, 'Doctors from the Indian Subcontinent in UK General Practice', *Lancet*, vol. 362 (2003), p. 1335.

7 Adrian Favell, *Eurostars and Eurocities: Free Movement and Mobility in an Integrating Europe* (Oxford, 2008).

8 Leo Lucassen, *The Immigrant Threat: The Integration of Old and New Migrants in Western Europe since 1850* (Urbana and Chicago, 2005), pp. 113–44.

9 M. A. G. Ó Tuathaigh, 'The Irish in Nineteenth Century Britain: Problems of Integration', *Transactions of the Royal Historical Society*, vol. 31 (1981).

10 Steven Fielding, *Class and Ethnicity: Irish Catholics in England, 1880–1939* (Buckingham, 1993).

11 Paul O'Leary, *Immigration and Integration: The Irish in Wales, 1789–1922* (Cardiff, 2000), pp. 302–8.

12 Panikos Panayi, *The Enemy in Our Midst: Germans in Britain during the First World War* (Oxford, 1991).

13 Michael P. Hornsby-Smith, *Roman-Catholics in England: Studies in Social Structure since the Second World War* (Cambridge, 1987), pp. 20–6.

14 Joseph M. Bradley, 'Marginal Voices: Football and Identity in a Contested Space', in Kathy Burrell and Panikos Panayi, eds, *Histories and Memories: Migrants and their History in Britain* (London, 2006), pp. 234–52.

Bibliography

Books and pamphlets

Abbot, S., ed., *The Prevention of Racial Discrimination* (London, 1971).

Adams, Carole, ed., *Across Seven Seas and Thirteen Rivers: Life Stories of Pioneer Sylhetti Settlers in Britain* (London, 1987).

Adi, Hakim, *West Africans in Britain, 1900–1960: Nationalism, Pan-Africanism and Communism* (London, 1998).

Alderman, Geoffrey, *The History of the Hendon Synagogue* (London, 1978).

—— *The Jewish Community in British Politics* (Oxford, 1983).

—— *London Jewry and London Politics, 1899–1986* (London, 1989).

—— *Modern British Jewry* (Oxford, 1992).

Ali, N., Kalra, V. S. and **Sayyid, S.,** eds, *A Postcolonial People: South Asians in Britain* (London, 2006).

Alibhai-Brown, Yasmin, *Who Do We Think We Are? Imagining the New Britain* (London, 2000).

Allan, Graham and **Crow, Graham,** *Families, Households and Society* (Basingstoke, 2001).

Allandina, Safder and **Edwards, Viv,** eds, *Multilingualism in the British Isles: The Older Tongues and Europe* (London, 1991).

Alter, Peter, ed., *Out of the Third Reich: Refugee Historians in Post-War Britain* (London, 1998).

Anderson, Benedict, *Imagined Communities: Reflections on the Origin and Spread of Nationalism* (London, 1991).

Anderson, Digby, *The English at Table* (London, 2006).

Ansari, Humayun, 'The Infidel Within': Muslims in Britain Since 1800 (London, 2004).

Anthias, Floya, *Ethnicity, Class, Gender and Migration: Greek Cypriots in Britain* (Aldershot, 1992).

Anwar, Muhamad, *British Pakistanis: Demographic, Social and Economic Position* (Coventry, 1996).

—— *The Myth of Return: Pakistanis in Britain* (London, 1979).

—— **Roach, Patrick** and **Sondhi, Ranjit,** eds, *From Legislation to Integration? Race Relations in Britain* (London, 2000).

Arnold, C. J., *Roman Britain to Saxon England* (Bloomington, IN, 1984).

Arnstein, Walter L., *Protestant Versus Catholic in Mid-Victorian Britain* (London, 1982).

Ashton, Rosemary, *Little Germany: Exile and Asylum in Victorian England* (Oxford, 1986).

Atkin, Nicolas, *The Forgotten French: Exiles in the British Isles, 1940–44* (Manchester, 2003).

Back, Les, *New Ethnicities and Urban Culture: Racism and Multiculture in Young Lives* (London, 1996).

—— **Crabbe, Tim** and **Solomos, John,** *The Changing Face of Football: Racism, Identity and Multiculture in the English Game* (Oxford, 2001).

Bade, Klaus J., ed., *Homo Migrans: Wanderungen aus und nach Deutschland: Erfahrungen und Fragen* (Essen, 1994).

—— ed., *Menschen über Grenzen: Grenzen über Menschen: Die Multikulturelle Herausforderung* (Herne, 1995).

—— *Migration in European History* (Oxford, 2003).

—— ed., *Population, Labour and Migration in 19th and 20th Century Germany* (Leamington Spa, 1987).

Baines, Dudley, *Emigration from Europe 1815–1930* (London, 1991).

Baldoli, Claudia, *Exporting Fascism: Italian Fascists and Britain's Italians in the 1930s* (Oxford, 2003).

Balkan, Elazar, *The Retreat of Scientific Racism: Changing Concepts of Race in Britain and the United States between the World Wars* (Cambridge, 1992).

Ball, Wendy and **Solomos, John,** eds, *Race and Local Politics* (Basingstoke, 1990).

Ballard, Roger, ed., *Desh Pradesh: The South Asian Presence in Britain* (London, 1994).

Banton, Michael, *The Coloured Quarter: Negro Immigrants in a British City* (London, 1955).

—— *Promoting Racial Harmony* (Cambridge, 1985).

—— *Race Relations* (London, 1967).

—— *Racial Theories*, 2nd edn (Cambridge, 1998).

—— *White and Coloured: The Behaviour of British People Towards Coloured Immigrants* (London, 1959).

Barnes, James J. and **Patience P.**, *Nazis in Pre-War London, 1930–1939: The Fate and Role of German Party Members and British Sympathisers* (Brighton, 2005).

Baron, Salo W., *The Russian Jew Under Tsars and Soviets* (London, 1964).

Besant, Walter, *East London* (London, 1903).

Beishon, Sharon, Modood, Tariq and **Virdee, Satnam,** *Ethnic Minority Families* (London, 1998).

Belchem, John, ed., *Irish, Catholic and Scouse: The History of the Liverpool-Irish, 1800–1939* (Liverpool, 2007).

—— *Popular Politics, Riot and Labour: Essays in Liverpool History, 1790–1940* (Liverpool, 1992).

—— and **Tenfelde, Klaus,** eds, *Irish and Polish Migration in Comparative Perspective* (Essen, 2003).

Bell-Fialkoff, Andrew, *Ethnic Cleansing* (Basingstoke, 1996).

Benewick, Robert, *The Fascist Movement in Britain* (London, 1972).

Bennet, Ronan, *Double Jeopardy: The Retrial of the Guildford Four* (London, 1993).

Benson, Susan, *Ambiguous Ethnicity: Interracial Families in London* (Cambridge, 1981).

Bentwich, Norman, *They Found Refuge: An Account of British Jewry's Work for the Victims of Nazi Oppression* (London, 1956).

Benyon, John, ed., *Scarman and After: Essays Reflecting on Lord Scarman's Report, the Riots and their Aftermath* (Oxford, 1984).

—— and **Solomos, John,** eds, *The Roots of Urban Unrest* (Oxford, 1987).

Berger, Stefan, Donovan, Mark and **Passmore, Kevin,** eds, *Writing National Histories: Western Europe Since 1800* (London, 1999).

Berghahn, Marion, *Continental Britons: German-Jewish Refugees from Nazi Germany* (Oxford, 1988).

Bermant, Chaim, *Point of Arrival: A Study of London's East End* (London, 1975).

Best, Geoffrey, *Mid-Victorian Britain, 1851–1875* (London, 1971).

Bethnal Green and Stepney Trades Council, *Blood on the Streets* (London, 1978).

Bevan, Vaughan, *The Development of British Immigration Law* (London, 1986).

Bhachu, Parminder, *Dangerous Designs: Asian Women Fashion the Diaspora Economies* (London, 2004).

—— *Twice Migrants: East African Sikh Settlers in Britain* (London, 1985).

Bielenberg, Andy, ed., *The Irish Diaspora* (London, 2000).

Billig, Michael, *Banal Nationalism* (London, 1995).

—— *Fascists: A Social Psychological Profile of the National Front* (London, 1978).

Bird, J. C., *Control of Enemy Alien Civilians in Great Britain, 1914–1918* (London, 1986).

Bird, Peter, *The First Food Empire: A History of J. Lyons & Co.* (Chichester, 2000).

Black, Eugene C., *The Social Politics of Anglo-Jewry, 1880–1920* (Oxford, 1988).

Blackbourn, David and **Eley, Geoff,** *The Peculiarities of German History: Bourgeois Society and the Politics of Nineteenth Century Germany* (Oxford, 1984).

Bloch, Alice, *The Migration and Settlement of Refugees in Britain* (Basingstoke, 2002).

—— and **Levy, Carl,** eds, *Refugees, Citizenship and Social Policy in Europe* (Basingstoke, 1999).

Bloom-Cooper, Louis, *The Birmingham Six and Other Cases: Victims of Circumstance* (London, 1997).

Bolt, Christine, *Victorian Attitudes Towards Race* (London, 1971).

Bourne, Stephen, *Black in the British Frame: The Black Experience in British Film and Television* (London, 2001).

Bowling, Benjamin, *Violent Racism: Victimization, Policing and Social Context,* Revised edn (Oxford, 1999).

Braber, Ben, *Jews in Glasgow 1879–1939: Immigration and Integration* (London, 2007).

Bradley, Joseph M., *Sport, Culture, Politics and Scottish Society: Irish Immigrants and the Gaelic Athletic Association* (Edinburgh, 1998).

Brah, Avtar, *Cartographies of Diaspora: Contesting Identities* (London, 1996).

Brandon, Ruth, *The People's Chef: Alexis Soyer, A Life in Seven Courses* (Chichester, 2005).

Braunthal, Julius, *History of the International, 1864–1914* (London, 1966).

Brenner, Michael and **Reuvni, Gideon,** eds, *Emancipation Through Muscles: Jews and Sports in Europe* (London, 2006).

Brettell, Caroline B. and **Hollifield, James F.,** eds, *Migration Theory: Talking Across Disciplines* (London, 2000).

Briggs, Asa, *The Age of Improvement, 1783–1867* (London, 1959).

Brown, Andy R., *Political Languages of Race and the Politics of Exclusion* (Aldershot, 1999).

Brown, Colin, *Black and White Britain: The Third PSI Survey* (Aldershot, 1984).

Brubaker, Rogers, *Citizenship and Nationhood in France and Germany* (Cambridge, MA, 1992).

Bruce, Steve, *Religion in Modern Britain* (Oxford, 1995).

Buckman, Joseph, *Immigrants and the Class Struggle: The Jewish Immigrant in Leeds, 1880–1914* (Manchester, 1983).

Burn, W. L., *The Age of Equipoise: A Study of the Mid-Victorian Generation* (London, 1964).

Burrell, Kathy, *Moving Lives: Narratives of Nation and Migration among Europeans in Post-War Britain* (Aldershot, 2006).

—— ed., *Polish Migration to the UK in the 'New' Europe After 2004* (Farnham, 2009).

—— and **Panayi, Panikos,** eds, *Histories and Memories: Migrants and their History in Britain* (London, 2006).

Burton, David, *The Raj at Table: A Culinary History of the British in India* (London, 1993).

Bush, Barbara, *Imperialism, Race and Resistance: Africa and Britain* (London, 1999).

Butterfield, Herbert, *The Whig Interpretation of History* (London, 1965).

Byron, Margaret, *Post-War Caribbean Migration to Britain: The Unfinished Cycle* (Aldershot, 1994).

Cahalan, Peter, *Belgian Refugee Relief in England during the Great War* (New York, 1982).

Cambridge, Alrick X. and **Feuchtwang, Stephen,** *Antiracist Strategies* (Aldershot, 1990).

Campbell, A. B., *The Lanarkshire Miners* (Edinburgh, 1979).

Cannadine, David, *Class in Britain* (London, 1998).

Cantle, Ted, *Community Cohesion: A New Framework for Race and Diversity* (Basingstoke, 2005).

Cashmore, Earnest, *Black Sportsmen* (London, 1982).

—— *Rastaman: The Rastafarian Movement in England* (London, 1979).

Castles, Stephen, et al., *Here for Good: Western Europe's New Ethnic Minorities* (London, 1984).

—— and **Kosack, Godula,** *Immigrant Workers and Class Structure into Western Europe* (London, 1973).

—— and **Miller, Mark J.,** *The Age of Migration: International Population Movements in the Modern World*, 3rd edn (Basingstoke, 2003).

Cathcart, Brian, *The Case of Stephen Lawrence* (London, 1999).

Centre for Contemporary Cultural Studies, ed., *The Empire Strikes Back: Race and Racism in Contemporary Britain* (London, 1982).

Cesarani, David, *The Jewish Chronicle and Anglo-Jewry, 1841–1991* (Cambridge, 1994).

—— *Justice Delayed: How Britain Became a Refuge for Nazi War Criminals* (London, 1992).

—— ed., *The Making of Modern Anglo-Jewry* (Oxford, 1990).

—— and **Kushner, Tony,** eds, *The Internment of Aliens in Twentieth Century Britain* (London, 1993).

Chakraborti, Neil and **Garland, Jon,** eds, *Rural Racism* (Cullompton, 2004).

Chamberlain, Mary, *Narratives of Exile and Return* (London, 1997).

Chapman, James, *The British at War: Cinema, State and Propaganda 1939–45* (London, 1998).

Chapman, Stanley D., *The Rise of Merchant Banking* (London, 1984).

Chappell, Connery, *Island of Barbed Wire: Internment on the Isle of Man in World War Two* (London, 1986).

Cheles, Luciano, Ferguson, Ronnie and **Vaughan, Michalina,** eds, *The Far Right in Western and Eastern Europe,* 2nd edn (London, 1995).

Chessum, Lorna, *From Immigrants to Ethnic Minority: Making Black Community in Britain* (Aldershot, 2000).

Cheyette, Bryan, *Constructions of 'the Jew' in English Literature and Society* (Cambridge, 1993).

—— ed., *Contemporary Jewish Writing in Britain and Ireland: An Anthology* (London, 1998).

Clarke, Colin, Peach, Ceri and **Vertovec, Steven,** eds, *South Asians Overseas: Migration and Ethnicity* (Cambridge, 1990).

Clebert, Jean-Paul, *The Gypsies* (London, 1964).

Coard, Bernard, *How the West Indian Child is Made Educationally Subnormal in the British School System: The Scandal of the Black Child in Schools in Britain* (London, 1971).

Cohen, Louise and **Mansion, Lawrence,** *Multicultural Classrooms* (London, 1985).

Cohen, Mark R., *Under Crescent and Cross: The Jews in the Middle Ages* (Princeton, 1994).

Cohen, Philip and **Baines, Harwant S.,** eds, *Multi-Racist Britain* (London, 1988).

Cohen, Robin, *Frontiers of Identity: The British and the Others* (Harlow, 1994).

—— *Global Diasporas: An Introduction* (Abingdon, 1999).

—— *Migration and Its Enemies: Global Capital, Migrant Labour and the Nation State* (Aldershot, 2006).

Cohen, Stuart A., *English Zionists and British Jews: The Communal Politics of Anglo-Jewry, 1895–1920* (Princeton, 1982).

Cole, G. D. H. and **Postgate, Raymond,** *The Common People* (London, 1938).

Coleman, D. A., ed., *Demography of Immigrant and Minority Groups* (London, 1982).

Coleman, David and **Salt, John,** eds, *Ethnicity in the 1991 Census,* vol. 1, *Demographic Characteristics of the Ethnic Minority Population* (London, 1996).

Colley, Linda, *Britons: Forging the Nation, 1707–1837* (London, 1994).

Collingham, Lizzie, *Curry: A Biography* (London, 2005).

Collins, Kenneth E., *Second City Jewry: The Jews of Glasgow in the Age of Enterprise, 1790–1919* (Glasgow, 1990).

Colls, Robert, *Identity of England* (Oxford, 2002).

Colpi, Terri, *The Italian Factor: The Italian Community in Great Britain* (Edinburgh, 1991).

Colvin, Ian, *The Germans in England, 1066–1598* (London, 1915).

Constantinides, Michael, *The Greek Orthodox Church in London* (Oxford, 1933).

Conway, Martin and **Gotovich, José,** eds, *Europe in Exile: European Exile Communities in Britain, 1940–45* (Oxford, 2001).

Conzen, Kathleen Neils, *Immigrant Milwaukee, 1836–1860: Accommodation in a Frontier City* (London, 1976).

Coogan, Tim Pat, *The IRA,* 2nd edn (London, 1994).

Cook, C. and **McKie, D.,** eds, *The Decline of Disillusionment: British Politics in the 1960s* (London, 1972).

Cooper, John, *Pride Versus Prejudice: Jewish Doctors and Lawyers in England, 1890–1990* (Oxford, 2003).

Copsey, Nigel, *Contemporary British Fascism: The British National Party and the Quest for Legitimacy* (Basingstoke, 2004).

Cottrett, B. J., *The Huguenots in England: Immigration and Settlement, c. 1550–1700* (Cambridge, 1992).

Cowen, Ruth, *Relish: The Extraordinary Life of Alexis Soyer, Victorian Celebrity Chef* (London, 2006).

Crafts, Nicholas, Gazeley, Ian and **Newell, Andrew,** eds, *Work and Pay in Twentieth Century Britain* (Oxford, 2007).

Cronin, Mike, ed., *The Failure of British Fascism: The Far Right and the Fight for Political Recognition* (Basingstoke, 1996).

—— *Sport and Nationalism in Ireland: Gaelic Games, Soccer and Irish Identity Since 1884* (Dublin, 1999).

—— and **Adair, Daryl,** *The Wearing the Green: A History of St Patrick's Day* (London, 2002).

Cross, Colin, *The Fascists in Britain* (London, 1961).

Crowhurst, Basil, *A History of the British Ice Cream Industry* (Westerham, 2000).

Cunningham, William, *Alien Immigrants in Britain* (London, 1897).

Currah, Anne, *Chef to Queen Victoria: The Recipes of Charles Elmé Francatelli* (London, 1973).

Curtis, L. P., *Anglo-Saxons and Celts* (New York, 1968).

—— *Apes and Angels: The Irishman in Victorian Caricature* (Newton Abbot, 1971).

Dabydeen, David., ed., *The Black Presence in English Literature* (Manchester, 1985).

Dalglish, Carol, *Refugees from Vietnam* (London, 1989).

Daniel, W. W., *Racial Discrimination in England* (Harmondsworth, 1968).

Davis, Graham, *The Irish in Britain, 1815–1914* (Dublin, 1991).

Davison, R. B., *Black British Immigrants to England* (London, 1966).

Daye, Sharon J., *Middle Class Blacks in Britain: A Racial Fraction of a Class Group or a Class Fraction of a Racial Group* (Basingstoke, 1994).

Deakin, Nicholas, ed., *Colour and the British Electorate: Six Case Studies* (London, 1965).

Debrunner, Hans Werner, *Presence and Prestige: Africans in Europe: A History of Africans in Europe Before 1918* (Basel, 1979).

Delaney, Enda, *Demography, State and Society: Irish Migration to Britain, 1921–1971* (Liverpool, 2000).

—— *The Irish in Post-War Britain* (Oxford, 2007).

Dench, Geoff, *Maltese in London: A Case Study in the Erosion of Ethnic Consciousness* (London, 1975).

—— **Gavron, Kate** and **Young, Michael,** *The New East End: Kinship, Race and Conflict* (London, 2006).

Denvir, John, *The Irish in Britain* (London, 1892).

Desai, Rashmi, *Indian Immigrants in Britain* (London, 1963).

Devine, T. M., ed., *Irish Immigrants and Scottish Cities in the Nineteenth and Twentieth Centuries* (Edinburgh, 1991).

Diamond, Michael, *Lesser Breeds: Racial Attitudes in Popular British Culture, 1890–1940* (London, 2006).

Dictionary of Business Biography (London, 1985).

Din, Ikhlaq, *The New British: The Impact of Culture and Community on Young Pakistanis* (Aldershot, 2006).

Dobson, R. B., *The Jews of Medieval York and the Massacre of March 1190* (York, 1974).

Dorgeel, Heinrich, *Die Deutsche Colonie in London* (London, 1881).

Dove, Richard, ed., *'Totally un-English?' Britain's Internment of 'Enemy Aliens' in Two World Wars* (Amsterdam, 2005).

Dummett, Michael, *On Immigrants and Refugees* (London, 2001).

Durant, John and **Miller, Jonathan,** eds, *Laughing Matters: A Serious Look at Humour* (London, 1988).

Dyos, H. J. and **Wolff, M.,** eds, *The Victorian City: Images and Realities* (London, 1973).

Eade, John, *Placing London: From Imperial Capital to Global City* (Oxford, 2000).

Endelman, Todd M., *The Jews of Britain, 1656–2000* (London, 2002).

—— *The Jews of Georgian England: Tradition and Change in a Liberal Society* (Philadephia, PA, 1979).

—— *Radical Assimilation in English Jewish History, 1656–1945* (Bloomington and Indianapolis, 1990).

—— and **Kushner, Tony,** eds, *Disraeli's Jewishness* (London, 2002).

Engels, Frederick, *The Condition of the Working-Class in England* (originally 1845; Moscow, 1973).

Epstein, James and **Thompson, Dorothy,** eds, *The Chartist Experience: Studies in Working-Class Radicalism and Culture, 1830–1960* (London, 1982).

Erickson, Charlotte, *Leaving England: Essays on British Emigration in the Nineteenth Century* (London, 1994).

Ethnic Communities Oral History Project, *The Motherland Calls: African Caribbean Experiences* (London, 1992).

—— *Asian Voices: Life-Stories from the Indian Sub-Continent* (London, 1993).

—— *Passport to Exile: The Polish Way to London* (London, 1988).

—— *Xeni: Greek Cypriots in London* (London, 1990).

Fahrmeier, Andreas, *Citizens and Aliens: Foreigners and the Law in Britain and the German States, 1789–1870* (Oxford, 2000).

Faucher, Leon M., *Manchester in 1844: Its Present Condition and Future Prospects* (London, 1844).

Favell, Adrian, *Eurostars and Eurocities: Free Movement and Mobility in an Integrating Europe* (Oxford, 2008).

—— *Philosophies of Integration: Immigrants and the Idea of Citizenship in France and Britain,* 2nd edn (Basingstoke, 2001).

Feldman, David, *Englishmen and Jews: Social Relations and Political Culture, 1840–1914* (London, 1994).

Ferguson, Niall, *The House of Rothschild*, 2 Volumes (London, 2000).

Ferguson, Priscilla Parkhurst, *Accounting for Taste: The Triumph of French Cuisine* (London, 2004).

Finestein, Israel, *Jewish Society in Victorian England: Collected Essays* (London, 1993).

Finnegan, Frances, *Poverty and Prejudice: A Study of Irish Immigrants in York, 1840–1875* (Cork, 1982).

Finney, Nissa and **Simpson, Ludi,** *'Sleepwalking to Segregation?': Challenging Myths About Race and Immigration* (Bristol, 2009).

Fisher, Michael H., *Counterflows to Colonialism: Indian Travellers and Settlers in Britain, 1600–1857* (Delhi, 2004).

—— **Lahiri, Shompa** and **Thandi, Shinder,** *A South Asian History of Britain* (Oxford, 2007).

Fishman, William J., *East End Jewish Radicals, 1875–1914* (London, 1975).

Fitzgerald, Martin, *Political Parties and Black People: Participation, Representation and Exploitation* (London, 1984).

Fitzpatrick, David, *Irish Emigration, 1801–1921* (Dublin, 1984).

Foot, Paul, *Immigration and Race in British Politics* (Harmondsworth, 1965).

Forte, Charles, *Forte: The Autobiography of Charles Forte* (London, 1986).

Fortier, Anne Marie, *Migrant Belongings: Memory, Space, Identity* (Oxford, 2000).

Fraser, Angus, *The Gypsies* (Oxford, 1992).

Freitag, Sabine, ed., *Exiles from European Revolutions: Refugees in Mid-Victorian England* (Oxford, 2003).

Frost, Diane, ed., *Ethnic Labour and British Imperial Trade: A History of Ethnic Seafearers in the UK* (London, 1995).

—— *Work and Community Among West African Migrant Workers Since the Nineteenth Century* (Liverpool, 1999).

Fry, Geoffrey K., *The Growth of Government: The Development of Ideas about the Role of the State and the Machinery and Functions of Government in Britain Since 1780* (London, 1979).

Fryer, Peter, *Staying Power: The History of Black People in Britain* (London, 1984).

Fukuyama, Francis, *The End of History and the Last Man* (London, 1992).

Gabaccia, Donna R., *Italy's Many Diasporas* (London, 2000).

Gainer, Bernard, *The Alien Invasion: The Origins of the Aliens Act of 1905* (London, 1972).

Gallagher, Tom, *Edinburgh Divided: John Cormack and No Popery in the 1930s* (Edinburgh, 1987).

—— *The Uneasy Peace: Religious Tension in Modern Glasgow, 1819–1940* (Manchester, 1987).

Garbaye, Roman, *Getting into Local Power: The Politics of Ethnic Minorities in British and French Cities* (Oxford, 2005).

Gardner, Katy, *Age, Narrative and Migration: The Life Course of Bengali Elders in London* (Oxford, 2002).

Garrard, John A., *The English and Immigration, 1880–1910* (London, 1971).

Gartner, Lloyd P., *The Jewish Immigrant in England, 1870–1914* (London, 1960).

Gay, Ruth, *Safe Among the Germans: Liberated Jews After World War II* (London, 2002).

Geiss, Immanuel, *The Pan-African Movement* (London, 1974).

George, Dorothy M., *London Life in the Eighteenth Century* (London, 1979 reprint).

Ghosh, Durba, *Sex and the Family in Colonial India: The Making of Empire* (Cambridge, 2006).

Gibson, Andrew and Kerr, Joe, eds, *London from Punk to Blair* (London, 2003).

Gillborn, David, *Racism and Antiracism in Schools* (Buckingham, 2000).

Gillman, Peter and Leni, *'Collar the Lot': How Britain Interned and Expelled Its Wartime Refugees* (London, 1980).

Gilroy, Paul, *The Black Atlantic: Modernity and Double Consciousness* (London, 1993).

—— *There Ain't No Black in the Union Jack: The Cultural Politics of Race and Nation* (London, 1987).

Glass, D. V., *Population Policies and Movements in Europe* (London, 1940).

Glass, Ruth, *Newcomers: The West Indians in London* (London, 1960).

Glazier, Ira D. and Roza, Luigi De, eds, *Migration Across Time and Nations: Population Mobility in Historical Context* (London, 1986).

Glazier, Nathan and Moynihan, Daniel P., eds, *Ethnicity: Theory and Experience* (Cambridge, MA, 1975).

Glees, Anthony, *Exile Politics during the Second World War: The German Social Democrats in Britain* (Oxford, 1982).

Godley, Andrew, *Jewish Immigrant Entrepreneurship in New York and London, 1880–1914: Enterprise and Culture* (Basingstoke, 2001).

Goffart, Walter, *Barbarian Tides: The Migration Age and the Later Roman Empire* (Philadelphia, PA, 2006).

Goodman, Paul, *Zionism in England, 1899–1949* (London, 1949).

Goose, Nigel and **Luu, Lien Bich,** eds, *Immigrants in Tudor and Early Stuart England* (Brighton, 2005).

Gordon, Paul, *White Law: Racism in the Police, Courts and Prisons* (London, 1983).

Goulbourne, Harry, ed., *Black Politics in Britain* (Aldershot, 1990).

—— *Caribbean Transnational Experiences* (London, 2002).

—— *Ethnicity and Nationalism in Post-Imperial Britain* (Cambridge, 1991).

—— *Race Relations in Britain Since 1945* (Basingstoke, 1998).

Goulding, Brian, *Conquest and Colonization: The Normans in Britain, 1066–1100* (London, 1994).

Graham, David, *Secular or Religious: The Outlook for London's Jews* (London, 2003).

—— **Schmool, Marlena** and **Waterman, Stanley,** *Jews in Britain: A Snapshot from the 2001 Census* (London, 2007).

Graves, Robert, *Goodbye to All That* (Harmondsworth, 1985).

Green, Jeffrey, *Black Edwardians: Black People in Britain, 1901–1914* (London, 1998).

Guindi, Fadwa El, *Veil: Modernity, Privacy and Resistance* (Oxford, 1999).

Gundara, Jagdish S. and **Duffield, Ian,** eds, *Essays on the History of Blacks in Britain* (Aldershot, 1992).

—— **Jones, Crispin** and **Kimberley, Keith,** eds, *Racism, Education and Diversity* (London, 1996).

Gwynn, Robin D., *Huguenot Heritage: The History and Contribution of the Huguenots in Britain* (London, 1988).

Habib, Imtiaz, *Black Lives in the English Archives, 1500–1677: Imprints of the Invisible* (Aldershot, 2008).

Hain, Peter, Kettle, Martin, Campbell, Duncan and **Rollo, Joanna,** eds, *Policing the Police*, Vol. 2 (London, 1980).

Hall, Stuart, Critcher, Chas, Jefferson, Tony, Clarke, John and **Roberts, Brian,** *Policing the Crisis: Mugging, the State and Law and Order* (Basingstoke, 1978).

—— and **du Gay, Paul,** eds, *Questions of Cultural Identity* (London, 1996).

Halliday, Fred, *Arabs in Exile: Yemeni Migrants in Urban Britain* (London, 1992).

Hammond, J. L. and **L. B.,** *The Skilled Labourer, 1760–1832* (London, 1919).

Hampshire, James, *Citizenship and Belonging: Immigration and the Politics of Demographic Governance in Post-war Britain* (Basingstoke, 2005).

Handley, J. E., *The Irish in Modern Scotland* (Cork, 1947).

—— *The Irish in Scotland, 1798–1845* (Cork, 1943).

Handlin, Oscar, *The Uprooted: The Epic Story of the Great Migration that Made the American Peoples,* 2nd edn (Boston, MA, 1973).

Hansen, Randall, *Citizenship and Immigration in Post-War Britain* (Oxford, 2000).

Harris, R. G. and **Wilson, H. R. G.,** *The Irish Regiments, 1683–1999* (Staplehurst, 1999).

Harris, Ruth-Ann, *The Nearest Place That Wasn't Ireland: Early Nineteenth Century Irish Labour Migration* (Ames, IO, 1994).

Harrison, Malcolm, Phillips, Deborah, Chahal, Kusminder, Hunt, Lisa and **Perry, John,** *Housing, 'Race' and Community Cohesion* (Coventry, 2005).

Hartmann, Paul and **Husband, Charles,** *Racism and the Mass Media* (London, 1974).

Haskey, John, Kiernan, Kathleen, Morgan, Patricia and **David, Miriam E.,** *The Fragmenting Family: Does it Matter?* (London, 1998).

Haste, Cate, *Keep the Home Fires Burning* (London, 1977).

Hatton, Timothy J. and **Williamson, Jeffrey G.,** *The Age of Mass Migration: Causes and Economic Impact* (Oxford, 1998).

—— and **Williamson, Jeffrey G.,** eds, *Migration and the International Labour Market* (London, 1994).

Heineman Jr., Benjamin W., *The Politics of the Powerless: A Study of the Campaign Against Racism and Discrimination* (London, 1972).

Heinrick, Hugh, *A Survey of the Irish in England* (London, 1872).

Helweg, Arthur Wesley, *Sikhs in England: The Development of a Migrant Community* (Oxford, 1979).

Hennessy, Peter, *Whitehall* (London, 1990).

Hennings, C. R., *Deutsche in England* (Stuttgart, 1923).

Henriques, Ursula, *The Jews of South Wales: Historical Studies* (Cardiff, 1993).

Hepple, Bob, *Race, Jobs and the Law in Britain,* 2nd edn (Harmondsworth, 1970).

Herberg, Will, *Protestant-Catholic-Jew: An Essay in American Religious Sociology* (Chicago, 1983).

Herbert, Ulrich, *A History of Foreign Labor in Germany, 1880–1980: Seasonal Workers/Forced Laborers/Guest Workers* (Ann Arbor, MI, 1990).

Hewitt, Martin, ed., *An Age of Equipoise? Reassessing Mid-Victorian Britain* (Aldershot, 2000).

Hickman, Mary, *Religion, Class and Identity: The State, the Catholic Church and the Education of the Irish in Britain* (Aldershot, 1994).

—— and **Walter, Bronwen,** *Discrimination and the Irish Community in Britain* (London, 1997).

Higham, Nicholas J., *The Norman Conquest* (Stroud, 1998).

—— *Rome, Britain and the Anglo-Saxons* (London, 1992).

Hill, Clifford S., *How Colour Prejudiced is Britain?* (London, 1971).

Hills, Catherine, *Origins of the English* (London, 2003).

Hinde, Wendy, *Catholic Emancipation: A Shake to Men's Minds* (Oxford, 1992).

Hiro, Dilip, *Black British White British* (London, 1971).

Hirschfeld, Gerhard, ed., *Exile in Great Britain: Refugees from Hitler's Germany* (Leamington Spa, 1984).

Hobsbawm, Eric, *Age of Extremes: A Short History of the Twentieth Century* (London, 1994).

Hoerder, Dirk, *Labor Migration in the Atlantic Economies: The European and North American Working Classes during the Period of Industrialization* (London, 1985).

—— and **Moch, Leslie Page,** eds, *European Migrants: Global and Local Perspectives* (Boston, MA, 1996).

Holmes, Colin, ed., *Anti-Semitism in British Society, 1876–1939* (London, 1979).

—— *Immigrants and Minorities in British Society* (London, 1978).

—— *John Bull's Island: Immigration and British Society, 1871–1971* (Basingstoke, 1988).

—— *A Tolerant Country? Immigrants, Refugees and Minorities in Britain* (London, 1991).

Honeyford, Ray, *The Commission for Racial Equality: British Bureaucracy and the Multicultural Society* (London, 1998).

Horne, John and **Kramer, Alan,** *German Atrocities, 1914: A History of Denial* (London, 2001).

Hornsby-Smith, Michael P., *Roman-Catholics in England: Studies in Social Structure since the Second World War* (Cambridge, 1987).

Hood, Roger, *Race and Sentencing: A Study in the Crown Court* (Oxford, 1992).

Hughes, Colin, *Lime, Lemon and Sarsaparilla: The Italian Community in Wales, 1881–1945* (Bridgend, 1991).

Husband, Charles, ed., *'Race' in Britain: Continuity and Change* (London, 1987).

Husbands, Christopher T., *Racial Exclusionism and the City: The Urban Support of the National Front* (London, 1983).

Hussain, Yasmin, *Writing Diaspora: South Asian Women, Culture and Ethnicity* (Aldershot, 2005).

Huttman, E. D., Blanco, W. E. and **Saltman, S.,** eds, *Urban Housing: Segregation of Minorities in Western Europe and the United States* (London, 1991).

Hyamson, A. M., *The History of the Jews in England* (London, 1908).

Iglicka, Krystyna, *Poland's Post-War Dynamic of Migration* (Aldershot, 2001).

Institute of Race Relations, *Deadly Silence: Black Deaths in Custody* (London, 1991).

Isaac, Julius, *British Post-War Migration* (Cambridge, 1954).

Jackson, J. A., *The Irish in Britain* (London, 1963).

Jackson, Peter, ed., *Race and Racism: Essays in Social Geography* (London, 1987).

Jackson, Robert and **Nesbitt, Eleanor,** *Hindu Children in Britain* (Stoke-on-Trent, 1993).

James, Edward, *Britain in the First Millennium* (London, 2001).

James, Harold, *A German Identity: 1770 to the Present Day* (London, 1994).

James, Kenneth, *Escoffier: King of Chefs* (London, 2002).

James, Simon, *The Atlantic Celts: Ancient People or Modern Invention?* (London, 1999).

James, Winston and **Harris, Clive,** eds, *Inside Babylon: The Caribbean Diaspora in Britain* (London, 1993).

Jarvie, Grant, ed., *Sport, Racism and Ethnicity* (London, 1991).

Jenkins, Richard, and **Solomos, John,** eds, *Racism and Equal Opportunity Policies in the 1980s* (Cambridge, 1993)

Jewish Year Book, 1903–4 (London, 1903).

Johnson, Linton Kwesi, *Mi Revalueshanary Fren: Selected Poems* (London, 2002).

Joint Council for the Welfare of Immigrants, *Target Caribbean: The Rise in Visitor Refusals from the Caribbean* (London, 1990).

Joly, Danièle, *Britannia's Crescent: Making a Place for Muslims in British Society* (Aldershot, 1995).

—— *Haven or Hell? Asylum Policies and Refugees in Europe* (London, 1996).

Jones, Catherine, *Immigration and Social Policy in Britain* (London, 1977).

Jordan, Bill and **Düvell, Franck,** *Irregular Migration: The Dilemmas of Transnational Mobility* (Cheltenham, 2002).

Joshua, Harris, Wallace, Tina and **Booth, Heather,** *To Ride the Storm: The 1980 Bristol 'Riot' and the State* (London, 1983).

Kadish, Sharman, *'A Good Jew and a Good Englishman': The Jewish Lads' and Girls' Brigade, 1895–1995* (London, 1995).

Kassimeris, Christos, *European Football in Black and White: Tackling Racism in Football* (Plymouth, 2008).

Katz, David S., *The Jews in the History of England, 1485–1850* (Oxford, 1994).

Kay, Billy, ed., *Odyssey: Voices from Scotland's Recent Past* (Edinburgh, 1982).

Kay, Diana and **Miles, Robert,** *Refugees or Migrant Workers? European Volunteer Workers in Britain* (London, 1992).

Kershen, Anne J., ed., *Food in the Migrant Experience* (Aldershot, 2002).

—— ed., *Language, Labour and Migration* (Aldershot, 2000)

—— ed., *The Promised Land: The Migrant Experience in a Capital City* (Aldershot, 1997).

—— ed., *A Question of Identity* (Aldershot, 1998).

—— *Strangers, Aliens and Asians: Huguenots, Jews and Bangladeshis in Spitalfields, 1660–2000* (London, 2005).

—— *Uniting the Tailors: Trade Unionism Amongst the Tailors of London and Leeds, 1870–1939* (London, 1995).

Khan, Yasmin, *The Great Partition: The Making of India and Pakistan* (London, 2007).

Killingray, David, ed., *Africans in Britain* (London, 1993).

Kirchberger, Ulrike, *Aspekte deutsch-britischer Expansion: Die Überseeinteressen der deutschen Migranten in Großbritannien in der Mitte des 19. Jahrhunderts* (Stuttgart, 1999).

Kirk, Neville, *Change, Continuity and Class: Labour in British Society, 1850–1920* (Manchester, 1998).

Kirkham, Pat and **Thumin, Janet,** eds, *You Tarzan: Masculinity, Movies and Men* (London, 1993).

Kochan, Miriam, *Britain's Internees in the Second World War* (London, 1983).

Kohn, Marek, *Dope Girls: The Birth of the British Drug Underground* (London, 1992).

Kölnisches Stadtmuseum, ed., *Hanse in Europa: Brücke zwischen den Märkten 12.–17. Jahrhundert* (Cologne, 1973).

Knodel, John E., *The Decline of Fertility in Germany, 1871–1939* (Princeton, 1974).

Konigh, Michael de and **Griffiths, Marc,** *Tighten Up: The History of Reggae in the UK* (London, 2003).

Kosmin, Barry A. and **Levy, Caren,** *The Work and Employment of Suburban Jews: The Socio-Economic Findings of the 1978 Redbridge Jewish Survey* (London, 1981).

Krausz, Ernest, *Leeds Jewry: Its History and Social Structure* (Cambridge, 1964).

Kuepper, William G., Lackey, G. Lynne and **Swinerton, E. Nelson,** *Ugandan Asians in Great Britain: Forced Migration and Social Absorption* (London, 1975).

Kulischer, Eugene, *Europe on the Move: War and Population Changes, 1917–1947* (New York, 1948).

Kundani, Arun, *The End of Tolerance: Racism in the 21st Century* (London, 2007).

Kushner, Tony, ed., *The Jewish Heritage in British History: Englishness and Jewishness* (London, 1992).

—— *The Persistence of Prejudice: Anti-Semitism in British Society during the Second World War* (Manchester, 1989).

—— *Remembering Refugees: Then and Now* (Manchester, 2006).

—— *We Europeans? Mass Observation, 'Race' and British Identity in the Twentieth Century* (Aldershot, 2004).

—— and **Lunn, Kenneth,** eds, *The Politics of Marginality: Race, the Radical Right and Minorities in Twentieth Century Britain* (London, 1990).

—— and **Knox, Katherine,** *Refugees in an Age of Genocide: Global, National and Local Perspectives During the Twentieth Century* (London, 1999).

—— and **Valman, Nadia,** eds, *Remembering Cable Street: Fascism and Anti-Fascism in British Society* (London, 2000).

—— and **Lunn, Kenneth,** eds, *Traditions of Intolerance: Historical Perspectives on Fascism and Race Discourse in Britain* (Manchester, 1989).

Lafitte, François, *The Internment of Aliens* (London, 1988).

Lahiri, Shompa, *Indians in Britain: Anglo-Indian Encounters, Race and Identity, 1880–1930* (London, 2000).

Lane, Thomas, *Victims of Stalin and Hitler: The Exodus of Poles and Balts to Britain* (Basingstoke, 2004).

Lanfranchi, Pierre and **Taylor, Matthew,** *Moving with the Ball: The Migration of Professional Footballers* (Oxford, 2001).

Lattek, Christine, *Revolutionary Refugees: German Socialism in Britain, 1840–1860* (London, 2006).

Lawless, Richard I., *From Ta'izz to Tyneside: An Arab Community in the North-East of England during the Early Twentieth Century* (Exeter, 1995).

Lawrence, Daniel, *Black Migrants, White Natives: A Study of Race Relations in Nottingham* (Cambridge, 1974).

Layton-Henry, Zig *The Politics of Immigration* (Oxford, 1992).

—— and **Rich, Paul B.,** eds, *Race, Government and Politics in Britain* (Basingstoke, 1986).

Lee, A. Robert, ed., *Other Britain, Other British: Contemporary Multicultural Fiction* (London, 1995).

Lees, Lynn Hollen, *Exiles of Erin: Irish Immigrants in Victorian London* (Manchester, 1979).

Legarreta, Dorothy, *The Guernica Generation: Basque Refugee Children of the Spanish Civil War* (Reno, NV, 1984).

Lewis, D. S., *Illusions of Grandeur: Mosley, Fascism and British Society, 1931–81* (Manchester, 1987).

Lewis, Philip, *Islamic Britain: Religion, Politics and Identity among British Muslims* (London, 2002).

Liedtke, Rainer and **Wendehorst, Stephan,** eds, *The Emancipation of Catholics, Jews and Protestants: Minorities and the Nation State in Nineteenth Century Europe* (Manchester, 1999).

Lilly, Mark, *The National Council for Civil Liberties: The First Fifty Years* (London, 1984).

Linehan, Thomas P., *British Fascism, 1918–1939: Parties, Ideology and Culture* (Manchester, 2000).

Lingelbach, W. E., *The Merchant Adventurers of England: Their Laws and Ordinances* (Philadelphia, 1902).

Lipman, V. D., *A History of the Jews in Britain Since 1858* (Leicester, 1990).

—— *A Social History of the Jews in England, 1850–1950* (London, 1954).

—— ed., *Three Centuries of Anglo-Jewish History* (London, 1961).

Little, Kenneth, *Negroes in Britain* (London, 1972).

Littler, Jo and **Naidoo, Roshi,** eds, *The Politics of Heritage: The Legacies of Race* (London, 2005).

Livi-Bacci, Massimo, *A Concise History of World Population,* 2nd edn (Oxford, 1977).

Lloyd, T. H., *Alien Merchants in England in the High Middle Ages* (Brighton, 1982).

Lo, Kenneth, *Chinese Food* (Newton Abbot, 1972).

Loizos, Peter, *The Heart Grown Bitter: A Chronicle of Cypriot War Refugees* (Cambridge, 1981).

London, Louise, *Whitehall and the Jews, 1933–1948: British Immigration Policy and the Holocaust* (Cambridge, 2000).

Lorimer, Douglas, *Colour, Class and the Victorians: English Attitudes towards the Negro in the Mid-Nineteenth Century* (Leicester, 1978).

Lowe, W. J., *The Irish in Mid-Victorian Lancashire: The Shaping of a Working Class Community* (New York, 1989).

Lucassen, Leo, *The Immigrant Threat: The Integration of Old and New Migrants in Western Europe since 1850* (Chicago, 2005).

Luebke, Frederick C., *Bonds of Loyalty: German Americans and World War I* (De Kalb, IL, 1974).

—— *Germans in the New World: Essays in the History of Immigration* (Urbana and Chicago, 1990).

Lunn, Kenneth, ed., *Hosts, Immigrants and Minorities: Historical Responses to Newcomers in British Society* (Folkestone, 1980).

—— and **Thurlow, Richard,** eds, *British Fascism: Essays on the Radical Right in Inter-War Britain* (London, 1980).

Luu, Lien Bich, *Immigrants and the Industries of London, 1500–1700* (Aldershot, 2005).

MacClancy, Jeremy, ed., *Sport, Identity and Ethnicity* (Oxford, 1996).

McCord, Norman, ed., *Essays in Tyneside Labour History* (Newcastle-upon-Tyne, 1977).

McDougall, Ian, ed., *Essays in Scottish Labour History* (Edinburgh, 1979).

McGhee, Derek, *Intolerant Britain: Hate, Citizenship and Difference* (Maidenhead, 2005).

McGladdery, Gary, *The Provisional IRA in England: The Bombing Campaign, 1973–1997* (Dublin, 2006).

MacEwan, Martin, *Tackling Racism in Europe: An Examination of Anti-Discrimination Law in Practice* (Oxford, 1995).

McLaine, Ian, *Ministry of Morale: Home Front Morale and the Ministry of Information in World War II* (London, 1979).

Mac Laughlin, Jim, ed., *Location and Dislocation in Contemporary Irish Society: Emigration and Identities* (Cork, 1997).

MacRaild, Donald M., *Culture, Conflict and Migration: The Irish in Victorian Cumbria* (Liverpool, 1998).

—— *Faith, Fraternity and Fighting: The Orange Order and Irish Migration in Northern England, c.1850–1920* (Liverpool, 2005).

—— ed., *The Great Famine and Beyond: Irish Migrants in Britain in the Nineteenth and Twentieth Centuries* (Dublin, 2000).

—— *Irish Migrants in Modern Britain, 1750–1922* (Basingstoke, 1999).

—— and **Martin, David E.,** *Labour in British Society, 1830–1914* (Basingstoke, 2000).

Malet, Marian and **Grenville, Anthony,** eds, *Changing Countries: The Experience and Achievement of German-Speaking Exiles from Hitler in Britain, 1933 to Today* (London, 2002).

Malik, Sarita, *Representing Black Britain: Black and Asian Images on Television* (London, 2002).

Mandle, W. F., *Antisemitism and the British Union of Fascists* (London, 1968).

Manz, Stefan, *Migranten und Internierte: Deutsche in Glasgow, 1864–1918* (Stuttgart, 2003).

—— **Beerbühl, Margrit Schulte** and **Davis, John R.,** eds, *Migration and Transfer from Germany to Britain, 1660–1914* (Munich, 2007).

Margoliouth, Moses, *The History of the Jews in Great Britain*, 3 Volumes (London, 1851).

Marrett, Valerie, *Immigrants Settling in the City* (Leicester, 1989).

Marrus, Michael, *The Unwanted: European Refugees in the Twentieth Century* (Oxford, 1985).

Martin, John and **Singh, Gurharpal,** *Asian Leicester* (Stroud, 2002).

Mason, David, *Race and Ethnicity in Modern Britain*, 2nd Edn (Oxford, 2000).

Mathias, Peter, *The First Industrial Nation: The Economic Transformation of Britain, 1700–1914* (London, 2001).

Mayall, David, *English Gypsies and State Politics* (Hatfield, 1995).

Mayhew, Henry, *London Labour and the London Poor*, Vol. 1 (originally 1861, London, 1968).

Medaglia, Anthony, *Patriarchal Structures and Ethnicity in the Italian Community in Britain* (Aldershot, 2001).

Merriman, Nick, ed., *The Peopling of London: 15,000 Years of Settlement from Overseas* (London, 1993).

Messina, Anthony M., *Race and Party Competition in Britain* (Oxford, 1989).

Messinger, Gary S., *British Propaganda and the State in the First World War* (Manchester, 1992).

Metcalf, Hilary, Modood, Tariq and **Virdee, Satnam,** *Asian Self-Employment: The Interaction of Culture and Economics in England* (London, 1996).

Miles, Robert, *Racism* (London, 1989).

—— *Racism and Migrant Labour* (London, 1982).

—— *Racism After 'Race Relations'* (London, 1993).

—— and **Phizacklea, Annie,** *White Man's Country: Racism in British Politics* (London, 1984).

Mills, John, *The British Jews* (London, 1863).

Moch, Leslie Page, *Moving Europeans: Migration in Western Europe Since 1650,* 2nd edn (Bloomington and Indiana, 2003).

Modood, Tariq, et al. *Ethnic Minorities in Britain: Diversity and Disadvantage* (London, 1997).

—— *Multicultural Politics: Racism, Ethnicity and Muslims in Britain* (Edinburgh, 2005).

Moody, Harold, *The Colour Bar* (London, 1944).

Moore, R. I., *The Formation of a Persecuting Society: Power and Deviance in Western Europe, 950–1250* (Oxford, 1987).

Moore, Robert and **Wallace, Tina,** *Slamming the Door: The Administration of Immigration Control* (London, 1975).

Morgan, D., *Harvesters and Harvesting, 1840–1900* (London, 1982).

Morton, Stephen, *Salman Rushdie: Fictions of Postcolonial Modernity* (Palgrave, 2008).

Mosse, George, *Toward the Final Solution: A History of European Racism* (New York, 1978).

Mosse, W. E., et al., eds, *Second Chance: Two Centuries of German-Speaking Jews in the United Kingdom* (Tübingen, 1991).

Mundill, Robin R., *England's Jewish Solution: Experiment and Expulsion* (Cambridge, 1998).

Murray, Bill, *The Old Firm: Sectarianism, Sport and Society in Scotland* (Edinburgh, 2000).

Myers, Norma, *Reconstructing the Black Past: Blacks in Britain, 1780–1830* (London, 1996).

Nadel, Stanley, *Little Germany: Ethnicity, Religion and Class in New York City, 1845–80* (Urbana and Chicago, 1990).

National Association of Probation Officers and the Association of Black Probation Officers, *Race, Discrimination and the Criminal Justice System* (London, 1996).

Neal, Frank, *Black '47: Britain and the Irish Famine* (Basingstoke, 1998).

—— *Sectarian Violence: The Liverpool Experience, 1819–1914* (Manchester, 1988).

Nettel, Reginald, *The Orchestra in England: A Social History* (London, 1946).

Newman, Aubrey, ed., *The Jewish East End* (London, 1982).

—— ed., *Provincial Jewry in Victorian England* (London, 1978).

—— *The United Synagogue, 1880–1970* (London, 1977).

Newsinger, John, *Fenians in Mid-Victorian Britain* (London, 1994).

Newsome, Roy, *Brass Roots: A Hundred Years of Brass Bands and their Music* (Aldershot, 1998).

Ng, K. C., *The Chinese in London* (London, 1968).

Nichols, Dylan, *What Are You Doing Here? The Question of Australians in London* (Brighton, 2007).

Niedhardt, Gottfried., ed., *Großbritannien als Gast- und Exilland für Deutsche im 19. und 20. Jahrhundert* (Bochum, 1985).

Nirenberg, David, *Communities of Violence: Persecution of Minorities in the Middle Ages* (Princeton, NJ, 1996).

Nolan, Jay P., *The Immigrant Church: New York's Irish and German Catholics, 1815–1865* (London, 1975).

Norman, E. R., *Anti-Catholicism in Victorian England* (London, 1968).

Oakley, Robin, *Changing Patterns of Distribution of Cypriot Settlement* (Coventry, 1987).

O'Connor, Kevin, *The Irish in Britain* (Dublin, 1974).

O'Day, Alan, *The English Face of Irish Nationalism* (Dublin, 1977).

O'Ferrall, Fergus, *Catholic Emancipation: Daniel O'Connell and the Birth of Irish Democracy* (Dublin, 1985).

O'Leary, Paul, *Immigration and Integration: The Irish in Wales, 1789–1922* (Cardiff, 2000).

—— ed., *Irish Migrants in Modern Wales* (Liverpool, 2004).

Oliver, Paul, *Black Music in Britain: Essays on the Afro-Asian Contribution to Popular Music* (Milton Keynes, 1990).

Oltmer, Jochen, ed., *Migrationsforschung und Interkulturelle Studien: Zehn Jahre IMIS* (Osnabrück, 2002).

Ormond, David, *The Dutch in London: The Influence of an Immigrant Community* (London, 1973).

O'Sullivan, Patrick, ed., *The Irish World Wide: History, Heritage, Identity,* 6 Volumes (Leicester and London, 1992–7).

Palmer, Christopher, *Delius: Portrait of a Cosmopolitan* (London, 1976).

Panayi, Panikos, *The Enemy in Our Midst: Germans in Britain during the First World War* (Oxford, 1991).

—— *German Immigrants in Britain during the Nineteenth Century, 1815–1914* (Oxford, 1995).

—— ed., *Germans in Britain Since 1500* (London, 1996).

—— *Immigration, Ethnicity and Racism in Britain, 1815–1945* (Manchester, 1994).

—— *The Impact of Immigration: A Documentary History of the Effects and Experiences of Immigrants and Refugees in Britain Since 1945* (Manchester, 1999).

—— ed., *Minorities in Wartime: National and Racial Groupings in Europe, North America and Australia during the Two World Wars* (Oxford, 1993).

—— *Outsiders: A History of European Minorities* (London, 1999).

—— ed., *Racial Violence in Britain in the Nineteenth and Twentieth Centuries* (London, 1996).

—— *Spicing Up Britain: The Multicultural History of British Food* (London, 2008).

Parekh, Bikhu, et al., *The Future of Multi-Ethnic Britain* (London, 2000).

Parsonage, Catherine, *The Evolution of Jazz in Britain, 1880–1935* (Aldershot, 2005).

Patterson, Sheila, *Dark Strangers: A Sociological Study of the Absorption of a Recent West Indian Migrant Group in Brixton, South London* (London, 1963).

—— *Immigration and Race Relations in Britain, 1960–1967* (London, 1969).

Paul, Kathleen, *Whitewashing Britain: Race and Citizenship in the Post-war Era* (Ithaca, NY, 1997).

Peach, Ceri, *West Indian Migration to Britain: A Social Geography* (London, 1968).

—— **Robinson, Vaughan** and **Smith, Susan,** eds, *Ethnic Segregation in Cities* (London, 1981).

Perry, Thomas W., *Public Opinion, Propaganda and Politics in Eighteenth Century England: A Study of the Jew Bill of 1753* (Cambridge, MA, 1962).

Peters, Inge-Maren, *Hansekaufleute als Gläubiger der Englischen Krone (1294–1350)* (Cologne, 1978).

Pettegree, Andrew, *Foreign Protestant Communities in Sixteenth Century London* (Oxford, 1986).

Peukert, Detlev J. K., *Inside Nazi Germany: Conformity, Opposition and Racism in Everyday Life* (London, 1993).

Phillips, Mike and **Trevor,** *Windrush: The Irresistible Rise of Multi-Racial Britain* (London, 1998).

Philpott, Stuart B., *West Indian Migration: The Montserrat Case* (London, 1973).

Pickering, Michael, *Blackface Minstrelsy in Britain* (Aldershot, 2008).

Pilkington, Edward, *Beyond the Mother Country: West Indians and the Notting Hill White Riots* (London, 1988).

Pines, Jim, *Black and White in Colour: Black People in British Television Since 1936* (London, 1992).

Pollins, Harold, *Economic History of the Jews in England* (London, 1982).

—— *Hopeful Travellers: Jewish Migrants and Settlers in Nineteenth Century Britain* (London, 1991).

Poole, Elizabeth, *Reporting Islam: Media Representations of British Muslims* (London, 2002).

—— and **Richardson, John E.,** eds, *Muslims and the News Media* (London, 2006).

Porter, Bernard, *The Origins of the Vigilant State: The London Metropolitan Police Special Branch Before the First World War* (London, 1987).

—— *The Refugee Question in Mid-Victorian Politics* (Cambridge, 1979).

Priestland, Gerald, *Frying Tonight: The Saga of Fish and Chips* (London, 1972).

Prince, Rose, *The New English Kitchen: Changing the Way You Shop, Cook and Eat* (London, 2005).

Proudfoot, M. J., *European Refugees, 1939–52* (London, 1957).

Pugh, Martin, *Hurrah for the Blackshirts: Fascists and Fascism in Britain Between the Wars* (London, 2005).

Quinault, Roland and **Stevenson, John,** eds, *Popular Protest and Public Order: Six Studies in British History* (London, 1975).

Quinlivan, Patrick and **Rose, Paul,** *The Fenians in England, 1865–1872* (London, 1982).

Ram, Sodhi, *Indian Immigrants in Great Britain* (New Delhi, 1986).

Ramdin, Ron, *The Making of the Black Working Class in Britain* (Aldershot, 1987).

—— *Reimagining Britain: 500 Years of Black and Asian History* (London, 1999).

Ramsden, John, *Don't Mention the War: The British and the Germans Since 1890* (London, 2006).

Rath, Jan, ed., *Unravelling the Rag Trade: Immigrant Entrepreneurship in Six World Cities* (Oxford, 2002).

Rea, Anthony, *Manchester's Little Italy: Memories of the Italian Colony of Ancoats* (Manchester, 1988).

Reader, W. J., *Imperial Chemical Industries,* Vol. 1 (London, 1970).

Reeves, Frank, *Race Equality in Local Communities: A Guide to its Promotion* (Birmingham, 2007).

Renton, Dave, *When We Touched the Sky: The Anti-Nazi League, 1977–1988* (Cheltenham, 2006).

Rex, John *The Ghetto and the Underclass: Essays on Race and Social Policy* (Aldershot, 1988).

—— *Race Relations in Sociological Theory* (London, 1970).

—— and **Singh, Gurharpal,** eds, *Governance in Multicultural Societies* (Aldershot, 2004).

—— **Joly, Danièle** and **Wilpert, Czarina,** eds, *Immigrant Associations in Europe* (Aldershot, 1987).

—— and **Moore, Robert,** *Race, Community and Conflict* (Oxford, 1967).

Rich, Paul B., *Race and Empire in British Politics* (Cambridge, 1990).

Richards, Julian D., *Viking Age England* (London, 1991).

Richardson, H. G., *The English Jewry under Angevin Kings* (London, 1960).

Richardson, John E., *(Mis)Representing Islam: The Racism and Rhetoric of British Broadsheet Newspapers* (Amsterdam, 2004).

Richmond, Anthony H., *Colour Prejudice in Britain: A Study of West Indian Workers in Liverpool, 1941–51* (London, 1954).

—— *The Colour Problem* (Harmondsworth, 1965).

—— *Migration and Race Relations in an English City: A Study in Bristol* (London, 1973).

Riera, Monica and **Schaffer, Gavin,** eds, *The Lasting War: Society and Identity in Britain, France and Germany after 1945* (Basingstoke, 2008).

Ritchie, J. M., *German Exiles: British Perspectives* (New York, 1997).

Roberts, J. A. G., *China to Chinatown: Chinese Food in the West* (London, 2002).

Roberts, Richard, *Schroders: Merchants and Bankers* (London, 1992).

Robinson, Vaughan, *The International Refugee Crisis: British and Canadian Responses* (London, 1993).

—— ed., *Transients, Settlers and Refugees: Asians in Britain* (Oxford, 1986).

—— **Anderson, Roger** and **Musterd, Sako,** *Spreading the 'Burden'? A Review of Policies to Disperse Asylum Seekers and Refugees* (Bristol, 2003).

Roche, T. W. E., *The Key in the Lock: Immigration Control in England from 1066 to the Present Day* (London, 1969).

Rocker, Rudolf, *The London Years* (London, 1956).

Rose, E. J. B., et al., *Colour and Citizenship: A Report on British Race Relations* (London, 1968).

Rosenberg, Edgar, *From Shylock to Svengali: Jewish Stereotypes in English Fiction* (Stanford, 1960).

Roth, Cecil, *A History of the Jews in England* (Oxford, 1941).

—— *The Rise of Provincial Jewry: The Early History of the Jewish Communities in the English Countryside* (London, 1950).

Rowe, Michael, *The Racialization of Disorder in Twentieth Century Britain* (Aldershot, 1998).

Rubinstein, William D., *Britain's Century: A Political and Social History* (London, 1998).

—— *A History of the Jews in the English Speaking World: Great Britain* (Basingstoke, 1996).

—— *Men of Property: The Very Wealthy in Britain since the Industrial Revolution* (London, 1981).

—— *The Myth of Rescue: Why the Democracies Could Not Have Saved More Jews from the Nazis* (London, 1997).

—— and **Hilary L.,** *Philosemitism and Support in the English-Speaking World for Jews, 1840–1939* (Basingstoke, 1999).

Rudé, George, *The Crowd in History: A Study of Popular Disturbances in France and England* (London, 1985).

Rutherford, Jonathan, ed., *Identity: Community, Culture, Difference* (London, 1990).

Ryan, Louise and **Webster, Wendy,** eds, *Gendering Migration: Masculinity, Femininity and Ethnicity in Post-War Britain* (Ashgate, 2008).

Salbstein, M. C. N., *The Emancipation of the Jews in Britain: The Question of the Admission of the Jews to Parliament* (London, 1982).

Salter, Joseph, *The Asiatic in England: Sketches of Sixteen Years Work Among Orientals* (London, 1873).

—— *The East in the West or Work Among the Asiatics and Africans in Britain* (London, 1896).

Sandhu, Sukhdev, *London Calling: How Black and Asian Writers Imagined a City* (London, 2003).

Sarre, Philip and **Blanden, John,** eds, *An Overcrowded World? Population, Resources and the Environment* (Oxford, 2000).

Sawyer, P. H., *From Roman to Norman England*, 2nd edn (London, 1998).

Schaible, Karl Heinrich, *Geschichte der Deutschen in England* (Strasbourg, 1885).

Schulz, Friedrich, *Die Hanse und England: Von Edwards III bis auf Heinrichs VIII Zeit* (Stuttgart, 1978).

Scobie, Edward, *Black Britannia: A History of Blacks in Britain* (Chicago, 1972).

Scorer, Catherine and **Hewitt, Patricia,** *The Prevention of Terrorism Act: The Case for Repeal* (London, 1981).

Seabrook, Jeremy, *The Refuge and the Fortress: Britain and the Flight from Tyranny* (Basingstoke, 2009).

Searle, G. R., *Corruption in British Politics, 1895–1930* (Oxford, 1987).

—— *A New England? Peace and War, 1886–1918* (Oxford, 2004).

Sewell, Tony, *Black Masculinities and Schooling: How Black Boys Survive Modern Schooling* (Stoke-on-Trent, 1997).

Sharf, Andrew, *The British Press and the Jews under Nazi Rule* (Oxford, 1964).

Shaw, Alison, *Kinship and Continuity: Pakistani Families in Britain* (London, 2000).

Sherman, A. J., *Britain and Refugees from the Third Reich* (London, 1973).

Short, K. R. M., *The Dynamite War: Irish-American Bombers in Victorian Britain* (Dublin, 1979).

Shyllon, Florian, *Black People in Britain, 1555–1833* (London, 1977).

Singh, Gurharpal and **Tatla, Darshan Singh,** *Sikhs in Britain: The Making of a Community* (London, 2006).

Skellington, Richard, *'Race' in Britain Today*, 2nd edn (London, 1996).

Slack, Paul and **Ward, Ryk,** eds, *The Peopling of Britain: The Shaping of a Human Landscape* (Oxford, 2002).

Slatter, John, ed., *From the Other Shore: Russian Political Emigrants in Britain, 1880–1917* (London, 1984).

Small, Stephen, *Racialised Barriers: The Black Experience in the United States and England during the 1980s* (London, 1994).

Smith, Anne Marie, *New Right Discourse on Race and Sexuality* (Cambridge, 1994).

Smith, Gilly, *Nigella Lawson: The Unauthorised Biography* (London, 2005).

Smith, Graham A., *When Jim Crow Met John Bull: Black American Soldiers in World War II Britain* (London, 1987).

Smith, Sir Hubert Llewellyn, ed., *The New Survey of London Life and Labour*, 9 Volumes (London, 1930–5).

Snowman, Daniel, *The Hitler Emigres: The Cultural Impact on Britain of Refugees from Nazism* (London, 2003).

Solomos, John, *Black Youth, Racism and the State: The Politics of Ideology and Policy* (Cambridge, 1988).

—— *Race and Racism in Britain* (Basingstoke, 1993).

Somerville, Will, *Immigration Under New Labour* (Bristol, 2007).

Spellman, Kathy, *Religion and Nation: Iranian Local and Transnational Networks in Britain* (Oxford, 2004).

Spencer, Ian R. G., *British Immigration Policy: The Making of Multi-Racial Britain* (London, 1997).

Sponza, Lucio, *Divided Loyalties: Italians in Britain during the Second World War* (Frankfurt, 2000).

—— *Italian Immigrants in Nineteenth Century Britain* (Leicester, 1988).

Srebrnik, Henry, *London Jews and British Communism* (London, 1995).

Stachura, Peter D., ed., *The Poles in Britain, 1940–2000: From Betrayal to Assimilation* (London, 2004).

Steel, David, *No Entry: The Background and Implications of the Commonwealth Immigrants Act, 1968* (London, 1969).

Steinert, Johannes-Dieter and **Weber-Newth, Inge,** *European Immigrants in Britain* (Munich, 2003).

—— eds, *Labour & Love: Deutsche in Grossbritannien nach dem Zweiten Weltkrieg* (Osnabrück, 2000).

Stent, Ronald A., *Bespattered Page? The Internment of His Majesty's 'Most Loyal Enemy Aliens'* (London, 1980).

Stevenson, John, *Popular Disturbances in England, 1700–1870* (London, 1979).

Stone, Norman and **Glenny, Michael,** *The Other Russia* (London, 1990).

Sudbury, Julia, *'Other Kinds of Dreams': Black Women's Organizations and the Politics of Transformation* (Abingdon, 1998).

Swift, Roger and **Gilley, Sheridan,** eds, *The Irish in Britain, 1815–1939* (London, 1989).

—— eds, *The Irish in the Victorian City* (London, 1985).

—— eds, *The Irish in Victorian Britain: The Local Dimension* (Dublin, 1999).

Sword, Keith with Davies, Noman and **Ciechanowski, Jan,** *The Formation of the Polish Community in Great Britain, 1939–1950* (London, 1989).

Tannahill, J. A., *European Volunteer Workers in Britain* (Manchester, 1958).

Tatla, Darshan S., *The Sikh Diaspora: The Search for Statehood* (London, 1999).

Tawney, R. H., *Religion and the Rise of Capitalism* (London, 1926).

Taylor, Philip M., *The Distant Magnet: European Migration to the USA* (London, 1971).

Taylor, Simon, *A Land of Dreams: A Study of Jewish and Caribbean Migrant Communities in England* (London, 1993).

Taylor, Stan, *The National Front in English Politics* (London, 1982).

Teverson, Andrew, *Salman Rushdie* (Manchester, 2007).

Thompson, E. P., *The Making of the English Working Classes* (London, 1963).

Thorpe, Andrew, ed., *The Failure of Political Extremism in Inter-War Britain* (Exeter, 1989).

Thurlow, Richard, *Fascism in Britain* (Oxford, 1987).

Tinker, Hugh, *The Banyan Tree: Overseas Emigration from India, Pakistan and Bangladesh* (Oxford, 1977).

Tomlinson, Sally, *Home and School in Multicultural Britain* (London, 1984).

Travers, Max, *The British Immigration Courts: A Study of Law and Politics* (Bristol, 1999).

Trebilcock, Clive, *The Industrialization of the Continental Powers, 1780–1914* (London, 1981).

Udelson, Joseph H., *Dreamer of the Ghetto: The Life and Works of Israel Zangwill* (London, 1990).

Valman, Nadia, *The Jewess in Nineteenth Century British Culture* (Cambridge, 2007).

van Dijk, Teun A., *Racism and the Press* (London, 1991).

Vasili, Phil, *Colouring Over the White Line: The History of Black Footballers in Britain* (London, 2000).

Vaughan, W. E., ed., *A New History of Ireland*, vol. 5 (Oxford, 1989).

Vesey-Fitzgerald, Brian, *Gypsies of Britain: An Introduction to their History*, 2nd edn (Newton Abbot, 1973).

Vigne, Randolph and Littleton, Charles, eds, *From Strangers to Citizens: The Integration of Immigrant Communities in Britain, Ireland and Colonial America, 1550–1750* (Brighton, 2001).

Virdee, Pippa, *Coming to Coventry: Stories from the South Asian Pioneers* (Coventry, 2006).

Visram, Rosina, *Asians in Britain: 400 Years of History* (London, 2002).

Wainwright, A. Martin, *'The Better Class' of Indians: Social Rank, Imperial Identity, and South Asians in Britain, 1858–1914* (Manchester, 2008).

Walter, Bronwen, *Outsiders Inside: Whiteness, Place and Irish Women* (London, 2001).

Walton, John K., *Fish and Chips and the British Working Classes, 1870–1940* (Leicester, 1992).

Walvin, James, *Black and White: The Negro and English Society, 1555–1945* (London, 1973).

—— *Black Ivory: Slavery in the British Empire*, 2nd edn (Oxford, 2001).

—— *Passage to Britain: Immigration in British History and Politics* (Harmondsworth, 1984).

Ward, Paul, *Britishness Since 1870* (London, 2004).

Warren, Geoffrey C., ed., *The Foods We Eat* (London, 1958).

Wasserstein, Bernard, *Herbert Samuel: A Political Life* (Oxford, 1992).

—— *Vanishing Diaspora: The Jews of Europe Since 1945* (London, 1996).

Watson, Arnold R., *West Indian Workers in Britain* (London, 1942).

Watson, James L., ed., *Between Two Cultures: Migrants and Minorities in Britain* (Oxford, 1977).

Weber, Max, *The Protestant Ethic and the Spirit of Capitalism* (Originally 1904, London, 1976 edn).

Werbner, Pnina, *Imagined Diasporas among Manchester Muslims* (Oxford, 2002).

—— *The Migration Process: Capital, Gifts and Offerings among British Pakistanis* (Oxford, 1990).

White, Arnold, *The Modern Jew* (London, 1899).

Wicks, Margaret C., *The Italian Exiles in London, 1816–1848* (New York, 1968).

Williams, Bill, *The Making of Manchester Jewry, 1740–1875* (Manchester, 1976).

Williamson, Charlotte, Evans, Neil and **O'Leary, Paul,** eds, *A Tolerant Nation? Exploring Ethnic Diversity in Wales* (Cardiff, 2003).

Wilpert, Czarina, ed., *Entering the Working World: Following the Descendants of Europe's Immigrant Labour Force* (Aldershot, 1988).

Wilson, Amrit, *Finding a Voice: Asian Women in Britain* (London, 1981).

Wilson, Francesca M., *They Came as Strangers: The Story of Refugees to Great Britain* (London, 1959).

Wilson, Trevor, *The Myriad Faces of War: Britain and the Great War, 1914–1918* (Cambridge, 1986).

Winder, Robert, *Bloody Foreigners: The Story of Immigration to Britain* (London, 2004).

Wolfe, John, *The Protestant Crusade in Great Britain, 1829–1860* (Oxford, 1991).

Wong, Maria Lin, *Chinese Liverpudlians: A History of the Chinese Community in Liverpool* (Birkenhead, 1989).

Wrench John, Rea, Andrea and **Ouali, Nouria,** eds, *Migrants, Ethnic Minorites and the Labour Market* (Brighton, 1999).

—— and **Solomos, John,** eds, *Racism and Migration in Western Europe* (Oxford, 1993).

Wright, Ian, *Mr Wright: The Explosive Autobiography of Ian Wright* (London, 1996).

Wyatt, Michael, *The Italian Encounter with Tudor England: A Cultural Politics of Translation* (Cambridge, 2005).

Yokoyama, Toshio, *Japan in the Victorian Mind* (London, 1987).

Zubrzycki, Jerszy, *Polish Immigrants in Britain: A Study of Adjustment* (The Hague, 1956).

Zucchi, John E., *The Little Slaves of the Harp: Italian Child Street Musicians in Nineteenth-Century Paris, London and New York* (London, 1992).

Articles in books and journals

Abbas, Tahir, 'A Theory of Islamic Political Radicalism in Britain: Sociology, Theology and International Political Economy', *Contemporary Islam*, vol. 1 (2007).

Adler, Henrietta, 'Jewish Life and Labour in East London', in Sir Hubert Llewelyn Smith, ed., *New Survey of London Life and Labour*, vol. 6 (London, 1934).

Alderman, Geoffrey, 'The Anti-Jewish Riots of August 1911 in South Wales', *Welsh History Review*, vol. 6 (1972).

—— 'The Political Impact of Zionism in the East End of London Before 1940', *London Journal*, vol. 9 (1983).

Aldrich, Howard E., Carter, John C., Jones, Trevor P. and **McEvoy, David,** 'Business Development and Self-Segregation: Asian Enterprise in Three British Cities', in Ceri Peach, Vaughan Robinson and Susan Smith, eds, *Ethnic Segregation in Cities* (London, 1981).

Amin, Ash, 'Unruly Strangers? The 2001 Urban Riots in Britain', *International Journal of Urban and Regional Research*, vol. 27 (2003).

Anderson, Gregory, 'German Clerks in England, 1870–1914: Another Aspect of the Great Depression Debate', in Kenneth Lunn, ed., *Hosts, Immigrants and Minorities: Historical Responses to Newcomers in British Society* (Folkestone, 1980).

Anwar, Muhamed, 'The Impact of Legislation on British Race Relations', in Muhammad Anwar, Patrick Roach and Ranjit Sondhi, eds, *From Legislation to Integration? Race Relations in Britain* (London, 2000).

Archer, J. W., 'The Steelyard', *Once a Week*, vol. 5 (1861).

Arnstein, Walter L., 'The Murphy Riots: A Victorian Dilemna', *Victorian Studies*, vol. 19 (1975).

Aspinwall, Bernard, 'Popery in Scotland: Image and Reality', *Records of the Scottish Church History Society*, vol. 22 (1986).

Backhouse, Marcel, 'The Strangers at Work in Sandwich', *Immigrants and Minorities*, vol. 10 (1991).

Baines, Dudley, 'Immigration and the Labour Market', in Nicholas Crafts, Ian Gazeley and Andrew Newell, eds, *Work and Pay in Twentieth Century Britain* (Oxford, 2007).

Ballard, Roger, 'Differentiation and Disjunction Among the Sikhs in Britain', in Roger Ballard, ed., *Desh Pradesh: The South Asian Presence in Britain* (London, 1994).

—— and **Ballard, Catherine,** 'The Sikhs: The Development of South Asian Settlements in Britain' in Roger Ballard, ed., *Desh Pradesh: The South Asian Presence in Britain* (London, 1994).

Barber, Sarah, 'Irish Migrant Agricultural Labourers in Nineteenth Century Lincolnshire', *Saothar*, vol. 8 (1982).

Barnes, James J. and **Patience P.,** 'London's German Community in the Early 1930's', in Panikos Panayi, ed., *Germans in Britain Since 1500* (London, 1996).

Belchem, John, 'Class, Creed and Country: The Irish Middle Class in Victorian Liverpool', in Roger Swift and Sheridan Gilley, eds, *The Irish in Victorian Britain: The Local Dimension* (Dublin, 1999).

Benyon, John, 'Interpretations of Civil Disorder' in John Benyon and John Solomos, eds, *The Roots of Urban Unrest* (Oxford, 1987).

Berghaus, Günter, 'The Emigres from Nazi Germany and their Contribution to the British Theatrical Scene', in Werner E. Mosse, et al., eds, *Second Chance: Two Centuries of German-Speaking Jews in the United Kingdom* (Tübingen, 1991).

Berridge, Virginia, 'East End Opium Dens and Narcotic Use in Britain', *London Journal*, vol. 4 (1978).

Bhachu, Parminder, 'Culture, Ethnicity and Class Among Punjabi Sikh Women in 1990s Britain', *New Community*, vol. 17 (1991).

Bindman, Geoffrey, 'Law Enforcement or Lack of It', in Muhammad Anwar, Patrick Roach and Ranjit Sondhi, eds, *From Legislation to Integration? Race Relations in Britain* (London, 2000).

Bloch, Alice, 'Zimbabweans in Britain: Transnational Activities and Capabilities', *Journal of Ethnic and Migration Studies*, vol. 34 (2008).

Bogan, D., 'History of Irish Immigration to England', *Christus Rex*, vol. 12 (1958).

Bohstedt, John, 'More than One Working Class: Protestant-Catholic Riots in Edwardian Liverpool', in John Belchem, ed., *Popular Politics, Riot and Labour: Essays in Liverpool History, 1790–1940* (Liverpool, 1992).

Boyce, Frank, 'Irish Catholicism in Liverpool between the Wars', *Labour History Review*, vol. 57 (1992).

Bradley, Joseph M., 'Integration or Assimilation? Scottish Society, Football and Irish Immigrants', *International Journal of the History of Sport*, vol. 13 (1996).

—— 'Marginal Voices: Football and Identity in a Contested Space', in Kathy Burrell and Panikos Panayi, eds, *Histories and Memories: Migrants and their History in Britain* (London, 2006).

Brettell, Caroline B. and **Hollifield, James F.,** 'Introduction: Migration Theory – Talking Across Disciplines', in Caroline B. Brettell and James F. Hollifield, eds, *Migration Theory: Talking Across Disciplines* (London, 2000).

Brock, Peter, 'Polish Democrats and English Radicals, 1832–1862: A Chapter in the History of Anglo-Polish Relations', *Journal of Modern History*, vol. 25 (1953).

—— 'The Polish Revolutionary Commune in London', *Slavonic and East European Review*, vol. 35 (1956).

Brown, Mark S., 'Religion and Economic Activity in the South Asian Population', *Ethnic and Racial Studies*, vol. 23 (2000).

Burdsey, Daniel, 'Obstacle Race? "Race", Racism and the Recruitment of British Asian Professional Footballers', *Patterns of Prejudice*, vol. 38 (2004).

Burrell, Kathy, 'Homeland Memories and the Polish Community in Leicester', in Peter D. Stachura, ed., *The Poles in Britain 1940–2000: From Betrayal to Assimilation* (London, 2004).

—— 'Introduction: Migration to the UK from Poland: Continuity and Change in East-West Mobility', in Kathy Burrell, ed., *Polish Migration to the UK in the 'New' Europe After 2004* (Farnham, 2009).

—— 'War, Cold War and the New World Order: Political Borders and Polish Migration to Britain', 'History in Focus', Issue 11, http://www.history.ac.uk/ihr/Focus/Migration/articles/burrell.html.

Cahill, Gilbert A., 'Irish Catholicism and English Toryism', *Review of Politics*, vol. 19 (1957).

Carby, Hazel V., 'Schooling in Babylon', in Centre for Contemporary Cultural Studies, ed., *The Empire Strikes Back: Race and Racism in Contemporary Britain* (London, 1982).

Carus-Wilson, Elenora M., 'Die Hanse in England', in Kölnisches Stadtmuseum, ed., *Hanse in Europa: Brücke zwischen den Märkten 12.–17. Jahrhundert* (Cologne, 1973).

Cashmore, Ernest, 'The Experiences of Ethnic Minority Police Officers in Britain: Under-Recruitment and Racial Profiling in a Performance Culture', *Ethnic and Racial Studies*, vol. 24 (2001).

Castles, Stephen, 'Why Migration Policies Fail', *Ethnic and Racial Studies*, vol. 27 (2004).

Cayford, Joanne M., 'In Search of "John Chinaman": Press Representations of the Chinese in Cardiff, 1906–1911', *Llafur*, vol. 5 (1991).

Cesarani, David and **Kushner, Tony,** 'Alien Internment in Britain during the Twentieth Century: An Introduction', in David Cesarani and Tony Kushner, eds, *The Internment of Aliens in Twentieth Century Britain* (London, 1993).

Chance, Judy, 'The Irish in London: An Exploration of Ethnic Boundary Maintenance', in Peter Jackson, ed., *Race and Racism: Essays in Social Geography* (London, 1987).

Chapman, Stanley, 'Aristocracy and Meritocracy in Merchant Banking', *British Journal of Sociology*, vol. 37 (1986).

—— 'The International Houses: The Continental Contribution in British Commerce, 1800–1860', *Journal of European Economic History*, vol. 19 (1977).

—— 'Merchants and Bankers' in Werner E. Mosse, et al., eds, *Second Chance: Two Centuries of German-Speaking Jews in the United Kingdom* (Tübingen, 1991).

Chase, Malcolm, 'The Teeside Irish in the Nineteenth Century', *Labour History Review*, vol. 57 (1992).

Chessum, Lorna, 'Race and Immigration in the Local Leicester Press, 1945–62', *Immigrants and Minorities*, vol. 17 (1998).

—— ' "Sit Down, You Haven't Reached that Stage Yet": African Caribbean Children in Leicester Schools, 1960–74', *History of Education*, vol. 26 (1997).

Chinn, Carl, ' "Sturdy Catholic Emigrants": The Irish in Early Victorian Birmingham', in Roger Swift and Sheridan Gilley, eds, *The Irish in Victorian Britain: The Local Dimension* (Dublin, 1999).

Chitty, C. W., 'Aliens in England in the Sixteenth Century', *Race*, vol. 8 (1966).

Coates, Sue, 'Manchester's German Gentlemen: Immigrant Institutions in a Provincial City, 1840–1920', *Manchester Region History Review*, vol. 5 (1991–2).

Cohen, Philip, 'The Perversions of Inheritance: Studies in the Making of Multi-Racist Britain', in Philip Cohen and Harwant S. Baines, eds, *Multi-Racist Britain* (London, 1988).

Cole, Mike, ' "Brutal and Stinking": and "Difficult to Handle": The Historical and Contemporary Manifestations of Racialisation, Institutional Racism, and Schooling in Britain', *Race, Ethnicity and Education*, vol. 7 (2004).

Coleman, David and **Salt, John,** 'The Ethnic Group Question in the 1991 Census: A New Landmark in British Social Statistics', in David Coleman and John Salt, eds, *Ethnicity in the 1991 Census*, vol. 1, *Demographic Characteristics of the Ethnic Minority Population* (London, 1996).

Collins, Brenda, 'The Origins of Irish Immigration to Scotland in the Nineteenth and Twentieth Centuries', in T. M. Devine, ed., *Irish Immigrants and Scottish Cities in the Nineteenth and Twentieth Centuries* (Edinburgh, 1991).

——— 'Proto-Industrialization and pre-Famine Emigration', *Social History*, vol. 7 (1982).

Collins, E. J. T., 'Migrant Labour in British Agriculture in the Nineteenth Century', *Economic History Review*, vol. 29 (1976).

Colpi, Terri, 'The Impact of the Second World War on the British Italian Community' in David Cesarani and Tony Kushner, eds, *The Internment of Aliens in Twentieth Century Britain* (London, 1993).

Comite, Luigi di, 'Aspects of Italian Emigration, 1881–1915', in Ira D. Glazier and Luigi De Roza, eds, *Migration Across Time and Nations: Population Mobility in Historical Context* (London, 1986).

Conradson, David and **Latham, Alan,** 'Friendship, Networks and Transnationality in a World City: Antipodean Transmigrants in London', *Journal of Ethnic and Migration Studies*, vol. 31 (2005).

Constantinides, Pamela, 'The Greek Cypriots: Factors in the Maintenance of Ethnic Identity', in James L. Watson, ed., *Between Two Cultures: Migrants and Minorities in Britain* (Oxford, 1977).

Conzen, Kathleen Neils, 'Immigrants, Immigrant Neighbourhoods, and Ethnic Identity: Historical Issues', *Journal of American History*, vol. 66 (1979).

Cross, Malcolm, 'Ethnic Minority Youth in a Collapsing Labour Market: The UK Experience', in Czarina Wilpert, ed., *Entering the Working World: Following the Descendants of Europe's Immigrant Labour Force* (Aldershot, 1988).

Dahya, Badr, 'Pakistanis in Britain: Transients or Settlers?', *Race*, vol. 14 (1973).

Dalit Solidarity Network UK, 'No Escape: Caste Discrimination in the UK', 2006, http://www.dalits.nl/pdf/noescape.pdf

Davies, Norman, 'The Poles in Great Britain, 1914–1919', *Slavonic and East European Review*, vol. 50 (1972).

Davis, Christie, 'The Irish Joke as a Social Phenomenon', in John Durant and Jonathan Miller, eds, *Laughing Matters: A Serious Look at Humour* (London, 1988).

Demandt, Alexander, 'Patria Gentium: Das Imperium Romanum als Vielvölkerstaat', in Klaus J. Bade, ed., *Menschen über Grenzen: Grenzen über Menschen: Die Multikulturelle Herausforderung* (Herne, 1995).

Dewey, Michael, 'The Survival of an Irish Culture in Britain', *Irish Historical Studies*, vol. 20 (1982).

Diaper, Stefanie, 'Sir Alexander Drake Kleinwort', in *Dictionary of Business Biography* (London, 1985).

Dickens, Linda, 'The Road is Long: Thirty Years of Equality in Britain', *British Journal of Industrial Relations*, vol. 45 (2007).

Dixon, Bill and **Gadd, David,** 'Getting the Message? "New" Labour and the Criminalization of "Hate"', *Criminology and Criminal Justice*, vol. 6 (2001).

Dustmann, Christian and **Fabbri, Francesca,** 'Immigrants in the British Labour Force', *Fiscal Studies*, vol. 26 (2005).

Eade, John, 'The Search for Wholeness: The Construction of National and Islamic Identities Among British Bangladeshis', in Anne J. Kershen, ed., *A Question of Identity* (Aldershot, 1998).

Edwards, Owen Dudley and **Storey, Patricia J.,** 'The Irish Press in Victorian Britain', in Roger Swift and Sheridan Gilley, eds, *The Irish in the Victorian City* (London, 1985).

Edwards, Paul, 'The Early African Presence in the British Isles' in Jagdish S. Gundara and Ian Duffield, eds, *Essays on the History of Blacks in Britain* (Aldershot, 1992).

Efron, John, 'When Is a Yid not a Jew? The Strange Case of Supporter Identity at Tottenham Hotspur', in Michael Brenner and Gideon Reuvni, eds, *Emancipation Through Muscles: Jews and Sports in Europe* (London, 2006).

Eisenberg, Christiane, '"German Gymnastics" in Britain, or the Failure of Cultural Transfer', in Stefan Manz, Margrit Schulte Beerbühl and John R. Davis, eds, *Migration and Transfer from Germany to Britain, 1660–1914* (Munich, 2007).

Endelman, Todd M., '"Practices of a Low Anthropological Level": A Schechita Controversy of the 1950s', in Anne J. Kershen, ed., *Food in the Migrant Experience* (Aldershot, 2002).

English, Jim, 'Empire Day in Britain, 1904–1958', *Historical Journal*, vol. 49 (2006).

Esser, Raingard, 'Germans in Early Modern Britain', in Panikos Panayi, ed., *Germans in Britain Since 1500* (London, 1996).

Favell, Adrian, 'Multi-Ethnic Britain: An Exception in Europe', *Patterns of Prejudice*, vol. 35 (2001).

Feldman, David, 'Migrants, Immigrants and Welfare from the Old Poor Law to the Welfare State', *Transactions of the Royal Historical Society*, sixth series, vol. 13 (2003).

Fiedler, Herma, 'German Musicians in England and their Influence to the End of the Eighteenth Century', *German Life and Letters*, vol. 6 (1939).

Fitzpatrick, David., ' "A Peculiar Tramping People": The Irish in Britain, 1801–70', in W. E. Vaughan, ed., *A New History of Ireland*, vol. 5 (Oxford, 1989).

Flint, John, 'Scandal at the Bristol Hotel: Some Thoughts on Racial Discrimination in Britain and West Africa and Its Relationship to the Planning of Decolonization, 1939–47', *Journal of Imperial and Commonwealth History*, vol. 12 (1983).

Foster, R. F., 'Paddy and Mr Punch', *Journal of Newspaper and Periodical History*, vol. 7 (1991).

Frank, Tibor, 'Lajos Kossuth and the Hungarian Exiles in London', in Sabine Freitag, ed., *Exiles from European Revolutions: Refugees in Mid-Victorian England* (Oxford, 2003).

Frost, Diane, 'The "Enemy Within"? Asylum, Racial Violence and "Race Hate" in Britain Today', *21st Century Society*, vol. 2 (2007).

Gable, Gerry, 'Britain's Nazi Underground', in Luciano Cheles, Ronnie Ferguson and Michalina Vaughan, eds, *The Far Right in Western and Eastern Europe*, 2nd edn (London, 1995).

Galbraith, John S., 'The Pamphlet Campaign in the Boer War', *Journal of Modern History*, vol. 24 (1952).

Gardner, Katy and **Shukur, Abdus,** ' "I'm Bengali, I'm Asian and I'm Living Here": The Changing Face of British Bengalis', in Roger Ballard, ed., *Desh Pradesh: The South Asian Presence in Britain* (London, 1994).

George, Vic and **Millerson, Geoffrey,** 'The Cypriot Community in London', *Race*, vol. 8 (1967).

Gill, Paramjit S., Arnott, Robert and **Stewart, John,** 'Doctors from the Indian Subcontinent in UK General Practice', *Lancet*, vol. 362 (2003).

Gilley, Sheridan, 'Catholic Faith of the Irish Slums: London, 1840–70', in H. J. Dyos and M. Wolff, eds, *The Victorian City: Images and Realities* (London, 1973).

—— 'English Attitudes towards the Irish', in Colin Holmes, ed., *Immigrants and Minorities in British Society* (London, 1978).

—— 'The Garibaldi Riots of 1862', *Historical Journal*, vol. 16 (1973).

—— 'The Roman Catholic Church and the Nineteenth-Century Irish Diaspora', *Journal of Ecclesiastical History*, vol. 35 (1984).

—— 'The Roman Catholic Mission to the Irish in London, 1840–1860', *Recusant History*, vol. 10 (1969–70).

Gilroy, Paul, 'Police and Thieves', in Centre for Contemporary Cultural Studies, ed., *The Empire Strikes Back: Race and Racism in Contemporary Britain* (London, 1982).

Glazier, Nathan and **Moynihan, Daniel P.,** 'Introduction', in Nathan Glazier and Daniel P. Moynihan, eds, *Ethnicity: Theory and Experience* (Cambridge, MA, 1975).

Goodey, Jo, 'The Criminalization of British Asian Youth: Research from Bradford and Sheffield', *Journal of Youth Studies*, vol. 4 (2001).

Goodwin, Matthew J., 'The Extreme Right in Britain: Still an "Ugly Duckling" but for How Long?', *Political Quarterly*, vol. 78 (2007).

Goose, Nigel, 'The "Dutch" in Colchester', *Immigrants and Minorities* vol. 1 (1982).

Greengrass, Mark, 'Protestant Exiles and their Assimilation in Early Modern England', *Immigrants and Minorities*, vol. 4 (1985).

Griffiths, David J., 'Fragmentation and Consolidation: The Contrasting Cases of Somali and Kurdish Refugees in London', *Journal of Refugee Studies*, vol. 13 (2000).

Grillo, Ralph, ' "Saltdean Can't Cope": Protests Against Asylum Seekers in an English Seaside Suburb', *Ethnic and Racial Studies*, vol. 28 (2005).

Grzbienowski, T., 'The Polish Cause in England a Century Ago', *Slavonic Review*, vol. 11 (1932).

Gullace, Nicoletta F., 'Friends, Aliens and Enemies: Fictive Communities and the Lusitania Riots of 1915', *Journal of Social History*, vol. 39 (2005).

Hall, Ray, 'Stabilizing Population Growth: The European Experience', in Philip Sarre and John Blanden (eds), *An Overcrowded World? Population, Resources and the Environment* (Oxford, 2000).

Hall, Stuart, 'From Scarman to Stephen Lawrence', *History Workshop Journal*, Issue 58 (1999).

Halpern, Brendan, 'Who are the Irish in Britain? Evidence from Large-Scale Surveys', in Andy Bielenberg, ed., *The Irish Diaspora* (London, 2000).

Hamlett, John, Bailey, Adrian R, Alexander, Andrew and **Shaw, Gareth,** 'Ethnicity and Consumption: South Asian Shopping Patterns in Britain, 1947–75', *Journal of Consumer Culture*, vol. 8 (2008).

Haslett, John and **Lowe, W. J.,** 'Household Structure and Overcrowding Among the Lancashire Irish, 1851–1871', *Histoire Social*, vol. 10 (1977).

Hatch, E., 'Belgian Refugees in the United Kingdom', *Quarterly Review*, vol. 446 (1916).

Hattersley, Roy, 'Immigration', in C. Cook and D. McKie, eds, *The Decline of Disillusionment: British Politics in the 1960s* (London, 1972).

Henderson, Jeff and **Khan, Valerie,** 'Race, Class and the Allocation of Public Housing in Britain', *Urban Studies*, vol. 21 (1984).

Henriques, U. R. Q., 'The Jewish Emancipation Controversy in Nineteenth Century Britain', *Past and Present*, vol. 40 (1968).

Henriques, Ursula, 'The Jewish Community of Cardiff, 1813–1914', *Welsh History Review*, vol. 14 (1988).

Herbert, Joanna, 'Migration, Memory and Metaphor: Life Stories of South Asians in Leicester', in Kathy Burrell and Panikos Panayi, eds, *Histories and Memories: Migrants and their History in Britain* (London, 2006).

Herson, John, 'Migration, "Community" or Integration? Irish Families in Victorian Stafford', in Roger Swift and Sheridan Gilley, eds, *The Irish in Victorian Britain: The Local Dimension* (Dublin, 1999).

Hickey, John, 'Irish Settlement in Nineteenth Century Cardiff', in Paul O'Leary, ed., *Irish Migrants in Modern Wales* (Liverpool, 2004).

Hillman, Nicholas, 'A Chorus of "Execration"? Enoch Powell's "Rivers of Blood" Forty Years On', *Patterns of Prejudice*, vol. 42 (2008).

Hollingsworth, Barry, 'The Society of Friends of Russian Freedom: English Liberals and Russian Socialists', *Oxford Slavonic Papers*, vol. 3 (1970).

Holmes, Colin, 'The German Gypsy Question in Britain, 1904–1906', in Kenneth Lunn, ed., *Hosts, Immigrants and Minorities: Historical Responses to Newcomers in British Society* (Folkestone, 1980).

—— 'Immigrants, Refugees and Revolutionaries', in John Slatter, ed., *From the Other Shore: Russian Political Emigrants in Britain, 1880–1917* (London, 1984).

—— 'J. A. Hobson and the Jews', in Colin Holmes, ed., *Immigrants and Minorities in British Society* (London, 1978).

——'The Tredegar Riots of 1911: Anti-Jewish Disturbances in South Wales', *Welsh History Review*, vol. 11 (1982).

—— 'Trotsky and Britain', *Society for the Study of Labour History Bulletin*, vol. 39 (1979).

—— and **Ion, A. H.,** 'Bushidō and the Samurai: Images in British Public Opinion, 1894–1914', *Modern Asian Studies*, vol. 14 (1980).

Holmes, Martin, 'Evil May-Day 1517: The Story of a Riot', *History Today*, vol. 15 (September 1965).

Horsman, Reginald, 'Origins of Racial Anglo-Saxonism in Great Britain before 1850', *Journal of the History of Ideas*, vol. 37 (1976).

Howald, Stefan, 'Everyday Life in Prewar and Wartime Britain', in Marian Malet and Anthony Grenville, eds, *Changing Countries: The Experience and Achievement of German-Speaking Exiles from Hitler in Britain, 1933 to Today* (London, 2002).

Huggan, Graham, 'Virtual Multiculturalism: The Case of Contemporary Britain', *European Studies*, vol. 16 (2001).

Husbands, Christopher T., 'East End Racism, 1900–1980: Geographical Continuities in Vigilantist and Extreme Right-wing Political Behaviour', *London Journal*, vol. 8 (1982).

Hutchinson, John and **O'Day, Alan,** 'The Gaelic Revival in London, 1900–22: Limits of Ethnic Identity', in Roger Swift and Sheridan Gilley, eds, *The Irish in Victorian Britain: The Local Dimension* (Dublin, 1999).

Huttman, E. D., 'Housing Segregation in Western Europe: An Introduction', in E. D. Huttman, W. E. Blanco and S. Saltman, eds, *Urban Housing: Segregation of Minorities in Western Europe and the United States* (London, 1991).

Hutton, Seán, 'The Irish in London', in Nick Merriman, ed., *The Peopling of London: 15,000 Years of Settlement from Overseas* (London, 1993).

Hyams, Paul, 'The Jewish Minority in Medieval England, 1066–1290', *Journal of Jewish Studies*, vol. 25 (1974).

Iganski, P., 'Why Make "Hate" a Crime?', *Critical Social Policy*, vol. 19 (1999).

James, Winston, 'Migration, Racism and Identity Formation: The Caribbean Experience in Britain', in Winston James and Clive Harris, eds, *Inside Babylon: The Caribbean Diaspora in Britain* (London, 1993).

Jarvis, F. Anne M. R., 'German Musicians in London, *c.*1750–1850', in Stefan Manz, Margrit Schulte Beerbühl and John R. Davis, eds, *Migration and Transfer from Germany to Britain, 1660–1914* (Munich, 2007).

Jenkinson, Jacqueline, 'The 1919 Riots', in Panikos Panayi, ed., *Racial Violence in Britain in the Nineteenth and Twentieth Centuries* (London, 1996).

Johnston, Ron, Forrest, James and **Poulsen, Michael,** 'Are there Ethnic Enclaves/Ghettos in English Cities', *Urban Studies*, vol. 39 (2002).

Jones, Trevor, 'South Asian Businesses in Retreat? The Case of the UK', *Journal of Ethnic and Migration Studies*, vol. 29 (2003).

Joseph, C. L., 'The British West Indies Regiment, 1914–1918', *Journal of Caribbean History*, vol. 2 (1971).

Josephides, Sasha, 'Associations Amongst the Greek Cypriot Population in Britain', in John Rex, Danièle Joly and Czarina Wilpert, eds, *Immigrant Associations in Europe* (Aldershot, 1987).

—— 'Principles, Strategies and Anti-Racist Campaigns: The Case of the Indian Workers' Association', in Harry Gouldbourne, ed., *Black Politics in Britain* (Aldershot, 1990).

Kadish, Sharman, ' "Bolche, Bolshie and the Jewish Bogey": The Russian Revolution and Press Antisemitism', *Patterns of Prejudice*, vol. 22 (1988).

Kamphoefner, Walter D., 'At the Crossroads of Economic Development: Background Factors Affecting Emigration from Nineteenth Century Germany', in Ira D. Glazier and Luigi De Roza, eds, *Migration Across Time and Nations: Population Mobility in Historical Context* (London, 1986).

Karsten, P., 'Irish Soldiers in the British Army, 1792–1922: Suborned or Subordinate', *Journal of Social History*, vol. 17 (1983).

Kennedy, David and **Kennedy, Peter,** 'Ambiguity, Complexity and Convergence: The Evolution of Liverpool's Irish Football Clubs', *International Journal of the History of Sport*, vol. 24 (2007).

Kerr, B. M., 'Irish Seasonal Migration to Great Britain, 1800–38', *Irish Historical Studies*, vol. 3 (1942–3).

Kershen, Anne J., 'Mother Tongue as a Bridge to Assimilation?: Yiddish and Sylhetti in East London', in Anne J. Kershen, ed., *Language, Labour and Migration* (Aldershot, 2000).

Kettenecker, Lothar, 'The Germans After 1945', in Panikos Panayi, ed., *Germans in Britain Since 1500* (London, 1996).

Khan, Verity Saifullah, 'The Pakistanis: Mirpuri Villagers at Home and in Bradford', in James L. Watson, ed., *Between Two Cultures: Migrants and Minorities in Britain* (Oxford, 1977).

Kiernan, V. G., 'Britons Old and New', in Colin Holmes, ed., *Immigrants and Minorities in British Society* (London, 1978).

Klug, Brian, 'Ritual Murmur: The Undercurrent of Protest Against Religious Slaughter of Animals in Britain in the 1980s', *Patterns of Prejudice*, vol. 23 (1991).

Kosmin, Barry A., 'Nuptuality and Fertility Patterns of British Jewry, 1850–1980', in D. A. Coleman, ed., *Demography of Immigrant and Minority Groups* (London, 1982).

Krause, Kristine, 'Transnational Therapy Networks Among Ghanaians in London', *Journal of Ethnic and Migration Studies*, vol. 34 (2008).

Kushner, Tony, 'Antisemitism and Austerity: The August 1947 Riots in Britain', in Panikos Panayi, ed., *Racial Violence in Britain in the Nineteenth and Twentieth Centuries* (London, 1996).

—— 'Great Britons: Immigration, History and Memory', in Kathy Burrell and Panikos Panayi, eds, *Histories and Memories: Migrants and their History in Britain* (London, 2006).

—— and **Lunn, Kenneth,** 'Introduction', in Tony Kushner and Kenneth Lunn, eds, *The Politics of Marginality: Race, The Radical Right and Minorities in Twentieth Century Britain* (London, 1990).

Lannes, Xavier, 'International Mobility of Manpower in Western Europe', *International Labour Review*, vol. 73 (1956).

Large, David, 'The Irish in Bristol in 1851: A Census Enumeration', in Roger Swift and Sheridan Gilley, ed., *The Irish in the Victorian City* (London, 1985).

Layton-Henry, Zig, 'The Electoral Participation of Black and Asian Britons: Integration or Alienation', *Parliamentary Affairs*, vol. 38 (1985).

Lester, Anthony, 'The Politics of the Race Relations Act 1976', in Muhammad Anwar, Patrick Roach and Ranjit Sondhi, eds, *From Legislation to Integration? Race Relations in Britain* (London, 2000).

Lewis, Philip, 'Being Muslim and Being British: The Dynamics of Islamic Reconstruction in Britain', in Roger Ballard, ed., *Desh Pradesh: The South Asian Presence in Britain* (London, 1994).

Lipman, V. D., 'The Age of Emancipation, 1815–1880', in V. D. Lipman, ed., *Three Centuries of Anglo-Jewish History* (London, 1961).

—— 'The Origins of Provincial Anglo-Jewry', in Aubrey Newman, ed., *Provincial Jewry in Victorian England* (London, 1978).

—— 'A Survey of Anglo-Jewry in 1851', *Transactions of the Jewish Historical Society of England*, vol. 17 (1951–2).

Livshin, Rosalyn, 'The Acculturation of the Children of Immigrant Jews in Manchester, 1890–1930', in David Cesarani, ed., *The Making of Modern Anglo-Jewry* (Oxford, 1990).

Loebl, Herbert, 'Refugee Industries in the Special Areas of Britain', in Gerhard Hirschfeld, ed., *Exile in Great Britain: Refugees from Hitler's Germany* (Leamington Spa, 1984).

Lugard, Lady, 'The Work of the War Refugees' Committee', *Journal of the Royal Society of Arts*, vol. 43 (1915).

Luk, Wai-ki E., 'Chinese Ethnic Settlements in Britain: Spatial Meanings of an Orderly Distribution', *Journal of Ethnic and Migration Studies*, vol. 34 (2009).

Lunn, Kenneth, 'Parliamentary Politics and the "Jewish Vote" in Whitechapel, 1906–1914', in Aubrey Newman, ed., *The Jewish East End* (London, 1982).

Luu, Lien Bich, 'Alien Communities in Transition', in Nigel Goose and Lien Bich Luu, eds, *Immigrants in Tudor and Early Stuart England* (Brighton, 2005).

—— 'Dutch and their Beer Brewing in England, 1400–1700', in Anne J. Kershen, ed., *Food in the Migrant Experience* (Aldershot, 2002).

Mac an Ghaill, Martin, 'The Irish in Britain: The Invisibility of Ethnicity and Anti-Irish Racism', *Journal of Ethnic and Migration Studies*, vol. 26 (2000).

McCaffrey, John, 'The Irish Vote in Glasgow in the Late Nineteenth Century: A Preliminary Survey', *Innes Review*, vol. 21 (1970).

MacDermott, T. P., 'Irish Workers in Tyneside in the Nineteenth Century', in Norman McCord, ed., *Essays in Tyneside Labour History* (Newcastle-upon-Tyne, 1977).

McDonagh, Michael, 'The London Irish', *Irish Soldier*, 1 October 1918.

MacDonald, Roderick J., 'Dr Harold Arundel Moody and the League of Coloured Peoples, 1931–1947: A Retrospective View', *Race*, vol. 14 (1973).

McGrath, Walter, 'The Boer Irish Brigade', *Irish Sword*, vol. 5 (1961).

McGregor, JoAnn, ' "Joining the BBC (British Bottom Cleaners)": Zimbabwean Migrants and the UK Care Industry', *Journal of Ethnic and Migration Studies*, vol. 33 (2007).

Machin, Ian, 'British Catholics', in Rainder Liedtke and Stephan Wendehorst, eds, *The Emancipation of Catholics, Jews and Protestants: Minorities and the Nation State in Nineteenth Century Europe* (Manchester, 1999).

Mahler, Raphael, 'The Economic Background of Jewish Emigration from Galicia to the United States', *YIVO Annual of Jewish Social Science*, vol. 7 (1952).

Malcolm, Elizabeth, ' "A Most Miserable Looking Object": The Irish in English Asylums, 1850–1901: Migration, Poverty and Prejudice', in John Belchem and Klaus Tenfelde, eds, *Irish and Polish Migration in Comparative Perspective* (Essen, 2003).

Mannsaker, Frances M., 'The Dog that Didn't Bark: The Subject Races at the Turn of the Century', in David Dabydeen, ed., *The Black Presence in English Literature* (Manchester, 1985).

Manz, Stefan, 'Management Transfer in the Textile Industry: The Example of Otto Ernst Philippi at J & P Coats, 1872–1917', in Stefan Manz, Margrit Schulte Beerbühl and John R. Davis, eds, *Migration and Transfer from Germany to Britain, 1660–1914* (Munich, 2007).

Marchlewicz, Krzysztof, 'Continuities and Innovations: Polish Emigration after 1849', in Sabine Freitag, ed., *Exiles from European Revolutions: Refugees in Mid-Victorian England* (Oxford, 2003).

May, J. P., 'The Chinese in Britain', in Colin Holmes, ed., *Immigrants and Minorities in British Society* (London, 1978).

Meer, Nasar, 'Muslim Schools in Britain: Challenging Mobilisations or Logical Developments?', *Asia Pacific Journal of Education,* vol. 27 (2007).

—— 'The Politics of Voluntary and Involuntary Identities: Are Muslims in Britain an Ethnic, Racial or Religious Minority?', *Patterns of Prejudice,* vol. 42 (2008).

—— and **Noorani, Tahseen,** 'A Sociological Comparison of Antisemitism and anti-Muslim Sentiment in Britain', *Sociological Review,* vol. 56 (2008).

Merriman, Nick, 'From Prehistoric Times to the Huguenots', in Nick Merriman, ed., *The Peopling of London: 15,000 Years of Settlement from Overseas* (London, 1993).

Miles, Robert, 'The Riots of 1958: The Ideological Construction of Race Relations as a Political Force in Britain', *Immigrants and Minorities,* vol. 3 (1984).

Miller, David, 'Propaganda and the "Terror Threat" in the UK', in Elizabeth Poole and John E. Richardson, eds, *Muslims and the News Media* (London, 2006).

Millward, Pauline, 'The Stockport Riots of 1852: A Study of Anti-Catholic and Anti-Irish Sentiment', in Roger Swift and Sheridan Gilley, eds, *The Irish in the Victorian City* (London, 1985).

Model, Suzanne and **Fisher, Gene,** 'Unions Between Blacks and Whites: England Compared with the USA', *Ethnic and Racial Studies,* vol. 25 (2002).

Moran, Gerard, 'Nationalists in Exile: The National Brotherhood of St Patrick in Lancashire, 1861–5', in Roger Swift and Sheridan Gilley, eds, *The Irish in Victorian Britain: The Local Dimension* (Dublin, 1999).

Muhs, Rudolf, 'Jews of German Background in British Politics', in Werner E. Mosse, et al., eds, *Second Chance: Two Centuries of German-Speaking Jews in the United Kingdom* (Tübingen, 1991).

Myers, Kevin, 'Historical Practice in the Age of Pluralism: Educating and Celebrating Identities', in Kathy Burrell and Panikos Panayi, eds, *Histories and Memories: Migrants and their History in Britain* (London, 2006).

Neal, Frank, 'A Criminal Profile of the Liverpool Irish', *Transactions of the Historic Society of Lancashire and Chesire,* vol. 140 (1990).

—— 'English-Irish Conflict in the North West of England: Economics, Racism, Anti-Catholicism or Xenophobia', *North West Labour History,* vol. 16 (1991–2).

—— 'Liverpool, the Irish Steamship Companies and the Famine Irish', *Immigrants and Minorities,* vol. 5 (1986).

—— 'South Wales, the Coal Trade and the Irish Famine Refugee Crisis', in Paul O'Leary, ed., *Irish Migrants in Modern Wales* (Liverpool, 2004).

—— 'A Statistical Profile of the Irish Community in Gateshead: The Evidence of the 1851 Census', *Immigrants and Minorities*, vol. 27 (2009).

O'Connell, Bernard, 'Irish Nationalism in Liverpool, 1873–1923', *Eire Ireland*, vol. 10 (1975).

O'Day, Alan, 'The Political Behaviour of the Irish in Great Britain in the Later Nineteenth and Early Twentieth Centuries', in John Belchem and Klaus Tenfelde, eds, *Irish and Polish Migration in Comparative Perspective* (Essen, 2003).

—— 'Varieties of Anti-Irish Behaviour in Britain, 1846–1922', in Panikos Panayi, ed., *Racial Violence in Britain in the Nineteenth and Twentieth Centuries* (London, 1996).

Ó Gráda, Cormac, 'A Note on Nineteenth Century Irish Emigration Statistics', *Population Studies*, vol. 29 (1975).

O'Higgins, Rachel, 'The Irish Influence in the Chartist Movement', *Past and Present*, no. 20 (1961).

O'Leary, Paul, 'Anti-Irish Riots in Wales, 1826–1882', *Llafur*, vol. 5 (1991).

—— 'Skill and Workplace in an Industrial Economy: The Irish in South Wales', in John Belchem and Klaus Tenfelde, eds, *Irish and Polish Migration in Comparative Perspective* (Essen, 2003).

O'Neill, Brendan, 'How Migrants Really Live', *New Statesman*, 4 June 2007.

Ó Tuathaigh, M. A. G., 'The Irish in Nineteenth Century Britain: Problems of Integration', *Transactions of the Royal Historical Society*, vol. 31 (1981).

Panayi, Panikos, 'Anti-German Riots in London During the First World War', *German History*, 7 (1989).

—— 'Anti-Immigrant Riots in Nineteenth and Twentieth Century Britain', in Panikos Panayi, ed., *Racial Violence in Britain in the Nineteenth and Twentieth Centuries* (London, 1996).

—— 'Cosmopolis: London's Ethnic Minorities', in Andrew Gibson and Joe Kerr, eds, *London from Punk to Blair* (London, 2003).

—— 'Dominant Societies and Minorities in the Two World Wars', in Panikos Panayi, ed, *Minorities in Wartime: National and Racial Groupings in Europe, North America and Australia during the Two World Wars* (Oxford, 1993).

—— 'Germans in Eighteenth Century Britain', in Panikos Panayi, ed., *Germans in Britain Since 1500* (London, 1996).

—— 'Immigration and Food in Twentieth-Century Britain: Exchange and Ethnicity', *Journal for the Study of British Cultures*, vol. 13 (2006).

—— 'Middlesbrough 1961: A British Race Riot of the 1960s?', *Social History*, vol. 16 (1991).

—— 'One Last Chance: Masculinity, Ethnicity and the Greek Cypriot Community of London', in Pat Kirkham and Janet Thumin eds, *You Tarzan: Masculinity, Movies and Men* (London, 1993).

—— 'Refugees in Twentieth-Century Britain: A Brief History', in Vaughan Robinson, ed., *The International Refugee Crisis: British and Canadian Responses* (London, 1993).

—— 'Sausages, Waiters and Bakers: German Migrants and Culinary Transfer to Britain', in Stefan Manz, Margrit Schulte Beerbühl and John R. Davis, eds, *Migration and Transfer from Germany to Britain, 1660–1914* (Munich, 2007).

—— 'The Spicing Up of English Provincial Life: The History of Curry in Leicester', in Anne J. Kershen, ed., *Food in the Migrant Experience* (Aldershot, 2002).

—— 'Victims, Perpetrators and Bystanders in a German Town: The Jews of Osnabrück Before, During and After the Third Reich', *European History Quarterly*, vol. 33 (2003).

Papadaki, Evienia and **Roussou, Maria,** 'The Greek Speech Community', in Safder Allandina and Viv Edwards, eds, *Multilingualism in the British Isles: The Older Tongues and Europe* (London, 1991).

Parker-Jenkins, Marie, 'Equal Access to State Funding: The Case of Muslim Schools in Britain', *Race, Ethnicity and Education*, vol. 5 (2002).

Parry, Jon, 'The Tredegar Anti-Irish Riots of 1882', *Llafur*, vol. 3 (1983).

Patterson, Sheila, 'The Poles: An Exile Community in Britain', in James L. Watson, ed., *Between Two Cultures: Migrants and Minorities in Britain* (Oxford, 1977).

Peach, Ceri, 'Does Britain Have Ghettos?', *Transactions of the Institute of British Geographers*, New Series, vol. 21 (1996).

—— 'Empire, Economy, and Immigration: Britain 1850–2000', in Paul Slack and Ryk Ward, eds, *The Peopling of Britain: The Shaping of a Human Landscape* (Oxford, 2002).

—— 'A Geographical Perspective on the 1981 Urban Riots in England', *Ethnic and Racial Studies*, vol. 9 (1986).

—— 'South Asian Migration and Settlement in Great Britain, 1951–2001', *Contemporary South Asia*, vol. 15 (2006).

—— 'Social Geography: New Religions and Ethnosuburbs – Contrasts with Cultural Geography', *Progress in Human Geography*, vol. 26 (2002).

Pellew, Jill, 'The Home Office and the Aliens Act, 1905', *Historical Journal*, vol. 32 (1989).

Phillips, Deborah, 'Black Minority Ethnic Concentration, Segregation and Dispersal in Britain', *Urban Studies*, vol. 35 (1998)

—— 'Moving Towards Integration: The Housing of Asylum Seekers and Refugees in Britain', *Housing Studies*, vol. 21 (2006).

Philpott, Stuart, 'The Montserratians: Migration Dependency and the Maintenance of Island Ties in England', in James L. Watson, ed., *Between Two Cultures: Migrants and Minorities in Britain* (Oxford, 1977).

Pollins, Harold, 'East End Jewish Working Men's Clubs Affiliated to the Working Men's Clubs and Institute Union', in Aubrey Newman, ed., *The Jewish East End* (London, 1982).

Pooley, Colin G., 'The Residential Segregation of Migrant Communities in Mid-Victorian Liverpool', *Transactions of the Institute of British Geographers*, New Series, vol. 2 (1977).

—— 'Segregation or Integration? The Residential Experience of the Irish in Mid-Victorian Britain', in Roger Swift and Sheridan Gilley, eds, *The Irish in Britain, 1815–1939* (London, 1989).

Purwar, Nirmal, 'Multicultural Fashion: Stirrings of Another Sense of Aesthetics and Memory', *Feminist Review*, vol. 71 (2002).

Rainger, Ronald, 'Race, Politics and Science: The Anthropological Society of London in the 1860s', *Victorian Studies*, vol. 22 (1978).

Ram, Monder, Abbas, Tahir, Sanghera, Baliha and **Hillin, Guy,** ' "Currying Favour with the Locals": Balti Owners and Business Enclaves', *International Journal of Entrepreneurial Behaviour and Research*, vol. 6 (2000).

—— **Abbas, Tahir, Sanghera, Baliha, Barlow, Gerald** and **Jones, Trevor,** ' "Apprentice Entrepreneurs"? Ethnic Minority Workers in the Independent Restaurant Sector', *Work, Employment and Society*, vol. 15 (2001).

Ravenstein, E. G., 'The Laws of Migration', *Journal of the Royal Statistical Society*, vols 48 and 52 (1885 and 1888).

Rehin, John F., 'Blackface Street Minstrels in Victorian London and its Resorts: Popular Culture and its Racial Connotations as Revealed in Polite Opinion', *Journal of Popular Culture*, vol. 15 (1981).

Rex, John, 'The Social Segregation of the Immigrant in British Cities', *Political Quarterly*, vol. 39 (1968).

Reynolds, David, 'The Churchill Government and the Black American Troops in Britain During World War II', *Transactions of the Royal Historical Society*, Fifth series, vol. 35 (1984).

Reynolds, Tracey, 'Caribbean Families, Social Capital and Young People's Diasporic Identities', *Ethnic and Racial Studies,* vol. 29 (2006).

Rich, Paul B., 'Conservative Ideology and Race in Modern British Politics', in Zig Layton-Henry and Paul B. Rich, eds, *Race, Government and Politics in Britain* (Basingstoke, 1986).

—— 'Doctrines of Racial Segregation in Britain: 1900–1945, *New Community,* vol. 12 (1984–5).

Richardson, C., 'Irish Settlement in Mid-Nineteenth Century Bradford', *Yorkshire Bulletin of Economic and Social Research,* vol. 20 (1968).

Rogers, Murdoch, 'Glasgow Jewry: The History of the City's Jewish Community', in Billy Kay, ed., *Odyssey: Voices from Scotland's Recent Past* (Edinburgh, 1982).

Rojek, Wojciech, 'The Government of the Republic of Poland in Exile, 1945–92', in Peter D. Stachura, ed., *The Poles in Britain, 1940–2000: From Betrayal to Assimilation* (London, 2004).

Rollin, A. R., 'The Jewish Contribution to the British Textile Industry: "Builders of Bradford" ', *Transactions of the Jewish Historical Society of England,* vol. 17 (1951).

Rollo, Joanna, 'The Special Patrol Group', in Peter Hain, Martin Kettle, Duncan Campbell and Joanna Rollo, eds, *Policing the Police,* vol. 2 (London, 1980).

Rosenblaum, S., 'A Contribution to the Study of the Vital and other Statistics of the Jews in the United Kingdom', *Journal of the Royal Statistical Society,* vol. 68 (1905).

Rössler, Hans, ' "Die Zuckerbäcker waren vornehmlich Hannoveraner": Zur Geschichte der Wanderung aus dem Elbe-Weser-Dreieck in die Britische Zuckerindustrie', *Jahrbuch der Männer vom Morgenstern,* vol. 81 (2003).

Roth, Cecil, 'The Court Jews of Edwardian England', *Jewish Social Studies,* vol. 5 (1943).

Rubinstein, W. D., 'Henry Page Croft and the National Party, 1917–22', *Journal of Contemporary History,* vol. 9 (1974).

Rudé, George, 'The Gordon Riots: A Study of the Rioters and Their Victims', *Transactions of the Royal Historical Society,* Fifth series, vol. 6 (1956).

Ryan, Louise, 'Passing Time: Irish Women Remembering and Re-Telling Stories of Migration to Britain', in Kathy Burrell and Panikos Panayi, eds, *Histories and Memories: Migrants and their History in Britain* (London, 2006).

—— 'Who Do You Think You Are? Irish Nurses Encountering Ethnicity and Constructing Identity in Britain', *Ethnic and Racial Studies*, vol. 30 (2007).

Saggar, Shamit, 'A Late, Though Not Lost, Opportunity: Ethnic Minority Electors, Party Strategy and the Conservative Party', *Political Quarterly*, vol. 69 (1998).

—— and **Geddes, Andrew,** 'Negative and Positive Racialisation: Re-Examining Ethnic Minority Political Representation in the UK', *Journal of Ethnic and Migration Studies*, vol. 26 (2000).

Sales, Rosemary, 'The Deserving and the Undeserving? Refugees, Asylum Seekers and Welfare in Britain', *Critical Social Policy*, vol. 22 (2002).

—— 'Secure Borders, Safe Haven: A Contradiction in Terms?', *Ethnic and Racial Studies*, vol. 28 (2005).

Schapiro, Leonard, 'The Russian Background of the Anglo-American Jewish Immigration', *Transactions of the Jewish Historical Society of England*, vol. 20 (1959–60).

Scouloudi, Irene, 'Alien Immigration in London, 1558–1640', *Proceedings of the Huguenot Society of London*, vol. 16 (1938).

Seed, John, 'Limehouse Blues: Looking for Chinatown in the London Docks, 1900–40', *History Workshop Journal*, Issue 62 (2006).

Seshagiri, Urmilla, 'Modernity's (Yellow) Perils: Dr Fu-Manchu and English Race Paranoia', *Cultural Critique*, vol. 62 (2006).

Shang, Anthony, 'The Chinese in London' in Nick Merriman, ed., *The Peopling of London: 15,000 Years of Settlement from Overseas* (London, 1993).

Sheller, Mimi and **Urry, John,** 'The New Mobilities Paradigm', *Environment and Planning A*, vol. 38 (2006).

Shimoni, Gideon, 'Poale Zion: A Zionist Transplant in Britain 1905–1945', *Studies in Contemporary Jewry*, vol. 2 (1986).

Shukra, K., 'Black Sections in the Labour Party', in Harry Goulbourne, ed., *Black Politics in Britain* (Aldershot, 1990).

Singh, Gurharpal, 'Multiculturalism in Contemporary Britain: Reflections on the "Leicester Model" ', in John Rex and Gurharpal Singh, eds, *Governance in Multicultural Societies* (Aldershot, 2004).

Smith, Elaine R., 'Jewish Responses to Political Antisemitism and Fascism in the East End of London', in Tony Kushner and Kenneth Lunn, eds., *Traditions of Intolerance: Historical Perspectives on Fascism and Race Discourse in Britain* (Manchester, 1989).

Spencer, A. E. C. W., 'Catholics in Britain and Ireland', in D. A. Coleman, ed., *Demography of Immigrant and Minority Groups* (London, 1982).

Sponza, Lucio, 'The Anti-Italian Riots, June 1940', in Panikos Panayi, ed., *Racial Violence in Britain in the Nineteenth and Twentieth Centuries* (London, 1996).

—— 'The British Government and the Internment of Italians', in David Cesarani and Tony Kushner, eds, *The Internment of Aliens in Twentieth Century Britain* (London, 1993).

—— 'Italian Immigrants in Britain: Perceptions and Self-Perceptions', in Kathy Burrell and Panikos Panayi, eds, *Histories and Memories: Migrants and their History in Britain* (London, 2006).

—— 'Italian "Penny Ice-Men" in Victorian London', in Anne J. Kershen, ed., *Food in the Migrant Experience* (Aldershot, 2002).

—— 'Italians in War and Post-War Britain', in Johannes Dieter-Steinert and Inge Weber-Newth, eds, *European Immigrants in Britain* (Munich, 2003).

Stadulis, Elizabeth, 'The Resettlement of Displaced Persons in United Kingdom', *Population Studies*, vol. 5 (1952).

Steinmetz, Susanne, 'The German Churches in London, 1669–1914' in Panikos Panayi, ed., *Germans in Britain Since 1500* (London, 1996).

Stent, Ronald, 'Jewish Refugee Organizations', in Werner E. Mosse, et al., eds, *Second Chance: Two Centuries of German-Speaking Jews in the United Kingdom* (Tübingen, 1991).

Stillwell, John and **Phillips, Deborah,** 'Diversity and Change: Understanding the Ethnic Geographies of Leeds', *Journal of Ethnic and Migration Studies*, vol. 32 (2006).

Strauss, Herbert A., 'Jewish Emigration in the Nazi Period: Some Aspects of Acculturation', in Werner E. Mosse, et al., eds, *Second Chance: Two Centuries of German-Speaking Jews in the United Kingdom* (Tübingen, 1991).

Street, John, Hague, Seth and **Savigny, Heather,** 'Playing to the Crowd: The Role of Music and Musicians in Political Participation', *British Journal of Politics and International Relations*, vol. 10 (2008).

Swift, Roger, ' "Another Stafford Street Row": Law, Order and the Irish Presence in Mid-Victorian Wolverhampton', *Midland History*, vol. 9 (1984).

—— 'Anti-Catholicism and the Irish Disturbances: Public Order in Mid-Victorian Wolverhampton', *Midland History*, vol. 9 (1984).

—— 'Crime and the Irish in Nineteenth Century Britain', in Roger Swift and Sheridan Gilley, *The Irish in Britain, 1815–1939* (London, 1989).

Syamken, Georg, 'Englandfahrer und Merchant Adventurers', *Hamburger-Wirtschafts-Chronik*, vol. 5 (1975).

Sze, Szeming, 'Chinese Students in Great Britain', *Asiatic Review*, vol. 27 (1931).

Tananbaum, Susan L., 'Ironing Out the Ghetto Bend: Sports and the Making of Modern British Jews', *Journal of Sport History*, vol. 31 (2004), pp. 53–75.

Tebben, Maryann, ' "French" Fries: France's Culinary Identity from Brillat-Savarin to Barthes', *Convivium Artium: Food Representation in Literature, Film, and the Arts*, Spring 2006, http://flan.utsa.edu/conviviumartium/Tebben.html

Theodorou, Zena and **Kyriacou, Sav,** 'Cypriots in London', in Nick Merriman, ed., *The Peopling of London: 15,000 Years of Settlement from Overseas* (London, 1993).

Thompson, Dorothy, 'Ireland and the Irish in English Radicalism before 1850', in James Epstein and Dorothy Thompson, eds, *The Chartist Experience: Studies in Working-Class Radicalism and Culture, 1830–1960* (London, 1982).

Thompson, E. P., 'The Moral Economy of the English Crowd in the Eighteenth Century', *Past and Present*, no. 50 (1971).

Thompson, Paul, 'Moving Stories: Oral History and Migration Studies', *Oral History*, vol. 27 (1999).

Thorne, Christopher, 'Britain and the Black GIs: Racial Issues and Anglo-American Relations in 1942', *New Community*, vol. 3 (1974).

Thurlow, Richard, 'Blaming the Blackshirts: The Authorities and the Anti-Jewish Disturbances of the 1930s', in Panikos Panayi, ed., *Racial Violence in Britain in the Nineteenth and Twentieth Centuries* (London, 1996).

—— 'The Failure of British Fascism', in Andrew Thorpe, ed., *The Failure of Political Extremism in Inter-War Britain* (Exeter, 1989).

Tobias, J. J., 'Police Immigrant Relations in England: 1880–1910', *New Community*, vol. 3 (1974).

Tolia-Kelly, Divya P., 'A Journey Through the Material Geographies of Disapora Cultures: Four Modes of Environmental Memory', in Kathy Burrell and Panikos Panayi, eds, *Histories and Memories: Migrants and their History in Britain* (London, 2006).

Townsend, Robert D., 'The Status of Women and Minorities in the History Profession', *Perspectives* (April 2002).

'The Transfer of Irish Workers to Great Britain', *International Labour Review*, vol. 48 (1943).

Treble, J. H., 'Irish Navvies in the North of England, 1830–50', *Transport History*, vol. 6 (1973).

Troyna, Barry, 'Reporting Racism: The "British Way of Life" Observed', in Charles Husband, ed., *'Race' in Britain: Continuity and Change* (London, 1987).

Uberoi, Varun, 'Social Unity in Britain', *Journal of Ethnic and Migration Studies*, vol. 33 (2007).

Ugolini, Wendy, 'Memory, War and the Italians in Edinburgh: The Role of Communal Myth', *National Identities*, vol. 8 (2006).

—— 'Reinforcing Otherness? Edinburgh's Italian Community and the Impact of the Second World War', *Family and Community History*, vol. 1 (1998).

—— and **Schaffer, Gavin,** 'Victims or Enemies? Italians, Refugee Jews and the Reworking of Internment Narratives in Post-War Britain', in M. Riera and Gavin Schaffer, eds, *The Lasting War: Society and Identity in Britain, France and Germany after 1945* (Basingstoke, 2008).

van den Berghe, Pierre L., 'Ethnic Cuisine: Culture in Nature', *Ethnic and Racial Studies*, vol. 7 (1984).

Van Otterloo, Anneke H., 'Foreign Immigrants and the Dutch at Table, 1945–1985: Bridging or Widening the Gap?', *Netherlands Journal of Sociology*, vol. 23 (1987).

Vertovec, Steven, 'Caught in an Ethnic Quandary: Indo-Caribbean Hindus', in Roger Ballard, ed., *Desh Pradesh: The South Asian Presence in Britain* (London, 1994).

—— 'Transnationalism and Identity', *Journal of Ethnic and Migration Studies*, vol. 27 (2001).

Vincentelli, M., 'The Davies Family and Belgian Refugee Artists and Musicians in Wales', *National Library of Wales Journal*, vol. 22 (1981).

Walker, Graham, 'The Orange Order in Scotland Between the Wars', *International Review of Social History*, vol. 37 (1992).

Walker, W. M., 'Irish Immigrants in Scotland: Their Priests, Politics and Parochial Life', *Historical Journal*, vol. 15 (1972).

Waller, P. J., 'The Chinese', *History Today*, vol. 35 (September 1985).

Walter, Bronwen, 'Contemporary Irish Settlement in London: Women's Worlds, Men's Worlds', in Jim Mac Laughlin, ed., *Location and Dislocation in Contemporary Irish Society: Emigration and Identities* (Cork, 1997).

Waterman, Stanley and **Kosmin, Barry,** 'Ethnic Identity, Residential Concentration and Social Welfare: The Jews in London', in Peter Jackson, ed., *Race and Racism: Essays in Social Geography* (London, 1987).

Watson, James L., 'The Chinese: Hong Kong Villagers in the British Catering Trade', in James L. Watson, ed., *Between Two Cultures: Migrants and Minorities in Britain* (Oxford, 1977).

Weber-Newth, Inge, 'Bilateral Relations: British Soldiers and German Women', in Louise Ryan and Wendy Webster, eds, *Gendering Migration: Masculinity, Femininity and Ethnicity in Post-War Britain* (Ashgate, 2008).

Weindling, Paul, 'The Contribution of Central European Jews to Medical Science and Practice in Britain, the 1930s to the 1950s', in W. E. Mosse, et al., eds, *Second Chance: Two Centuries of German-Speaking Jews in the United Kingdom* (Tübingen, 1991).

Wells, Patricia and **Williams, Rory,** 'Sectarianism at Work: Accounts of Employment Discrimination Against Irish Catholics in Scotland', *Ethnic and Racial Studies*, vol. 26 (2003).

Werly, J. M., 'The Irish in Manchester, 1832–49', *Irish Historical Studies*, vol. 17 (1973).

Westaway, Jonathan, 'The German Community in Manchester, Middle Class Culture and the Development of Mountaineering in Britain', *English Historical Review*, vol. 124 (2009).

Wilkin, Andrew, 'Origins and Destinations of the Early Italo-Scots', *Association of Teachers of Italian Journal*, no. 29 (1979).

Williams, Bill, ' "East and West": Class and Community in Manchester Jewry, 1850–1914', in David Cesarani, ed., *The Making of Modern Anglo-Jewry* (Oxford, 1990).

Williams, Chris, ' "Decorous and Creditable": The Irish in Newport', in Paul O'Leary, ed., *Irish Migrants in Modern Wales* (Liverpool, 2004).

Williamson, Jeffrey, 'The Impact of the Irish on British Labour Markets during the Industrial Revolution', in Roger Swift and Sheridan Gilley, eds, *The Irish in Britain, 1815–1939* (London, 1989).

Wilson, Keith M., 'The Protocols of Zion and the *Morning Post*', *Patterns of Prejudice*, vol. 19 (1985).

Wittlinger, Ruth, 'Perceptions of Germany and the Germans in Post-War Britain', *Journal of Multilingual and Multicultural Development*, vol. 25 (2004).

Wood, Ian, 'Irish Immigrants and Scottish Radicalism', in Ian McDougall, ed., *Essays in Scottish Labour History* (Edinburgh, 1979).

Wynn, Neil A., ' "Race War": Black American GIs and West Indians in Britain during the Second World War', *Immigrants and Minorities*, vol. 24 (2006).

Yarrow, Stella, 'The Impact of Hostility on Germans in Britain, 1914–1918', in Tony Kushner and Kenneth Lunn, eds, *The Politics of Marginality: Race, The Radical Right and Minorities in Twentieth Century Britain* (London, 1990).

Zamojski, Jan E., 'The Social History of Polish Exile (1939–1945): The Exile State and the Clandestine State', in Martin Conway and José Gotovich, eds, *Europe in Exile: European Exile Communities in Britain, 1940–45* (Oxford, 2001).

Official Publications and Reports

Census of England and Wales 1931: General Tables (London, 1935).

Census of Scotland 1931: Report of the Fourteenth Census of Scotland, vol. 2 (Edinburgh, 1993).

Central Office of Information, *Ethnic Minorities* (London, 1997).

Home Office, Department of Work and Pensions, H M Revenue and Customs and Department for Communities and Local Government, 'Accession Monitoring Report, May 2004–June 2006'.

MacPherson, Sir William, *The Stephen Lawrence Inquiry* (London, 1999).

The National Curriculum for England and Wales (London, 1999).

Office for National Statistics, *Focus on Ethnicity and Identity* (London, 2005).

Royal Commission on the Conditions of the Poorer Classes in Ireland, Appendix G, *The State of the Irish Poor in Great Britain* (London, 1836).

Scarman, Lord, *The Scarman Report: The Brixton Disorders, 10–12 April 1981* (Harmondsworth, 1982).

Scottish Office Central Research Unit Papers, 'Ethnic Minorities in Scotland', June 1983.

Select Committee on Emigration and Immigration (Foreigners) (London, 1888).

United Nations Department of Economics and Social Affairs, Population Division, 'The World at Six Billion', http://www.un.org/esa/population/publications/sixbillion/sixbillion.htm.

United Nations High Commission for Refugees, *The State of the World's Refugees: In Search of Solutions* (Oxford, 1995).

Newspapers

Daily Telegraph

Guardian

Independent

Jewish Chronicle

Observer

Sunday Telegraph

The Times

Theses

Baxter, Susan Chui Chie, 'A Political Economy of the Ethnic Chinese Catering Industry' (Aston Ph.D Thesis, 1988).

Dee, Dave, ' "Your Religion is Football!" Soccer and the Jewish Community in London, 1900–1960' (De Montfort MA Thesis, 2007).

Dudrah, Rajinder Kurmar, 'British South Asian Identities and the Popular Cultures of British Banghra, Bollywood Film and Zee TV in Birmingham' (Birmingham Ph.D Thesis, 2001).

Jones, M. A., 'The Role of the United Kingdom in the Transatlantic Emigrant Trade, 1815–1875' (Oxford D. Phil thesis, 1955).

Ugolini, Wendy, 'Communal Myths and Silenced Memories: The Unremembered Experience of Italians in Scotland During World War Two' (Edinburgh Ph.D Thesis, 2006).

Websites

Anglo-German Family History Society, http://www.art-science.com/agfhs/events.html

Anti-Racist Alliance, http://www.antiracistalliance.org.uk

BBC, http://www.bbc.co.uk

Black History Month, http://www.black-history-month.co.uk/home.html

CASBAH [Caribbean Studies, Black and Asian History], http://www.casbah.ac.uk

Centre for German and Austrian Exile Studies at the University of London, http://www.sas.ac.uk/igs/HPEXILECENTRE.htm

Centre for Research in Ethnic Relations, University of Warwick, http://www.warwick.ac.uk/CRER/index.html

Dalit Solidarity Network UK, http://www.dalits.nl/pdf/noescape.pdf

Federation of Family History Societies, http://www.ffhs.org.uk

GENUKI, Family History and Genealogy Societies, http://www.genuki.org.uk/Societies/index.html

Highfields Remembered, http://westworld.dmu.ac.uk/fmp/web/highfields/mainmenu.html

History in Focus, http://www.history/ac.uk/ihr/Focus

Home Office, UK Border Agency, http://www.ukba.homeoffice.gov.uk

Huguenot Society of Great Britain, http://www.huguenotsociety.org.uk/

Irish Studies Centre, London Metropolitan University, http://www.londonmet.ac.uk/pg-prospectus-2004/research/centres/isc.cfm

Irish Studies Institute, University of Liverpool, http://www.liv.ac.uk/irish/

Jewish Genealogical Society of Great Britain, http://www.jgsgb.org.uk

Jewish Historical Society of England, http://www.jhse.dircon.co.uk/html/about_us.html

Jewish Museum London, http://www.jewishmuseum.org.uk

Liberty, http://www.liberty-human-rights-.org.uk/

Manchester Jewish Museum, http://www.manchesterjewishmuseum.com

Moving Here, http://www.movinghere.org.uk/default.htm

National Statistics, http://www.statistics.gov.uk

Parkes Centre for Jewish Non-Jewish Relations, University of Southampton, http://www.parkes.soton.ac.uk/

United Nations Department of Economics and Social Affairs, Population Division, http://www.un.org/esa/population

Index